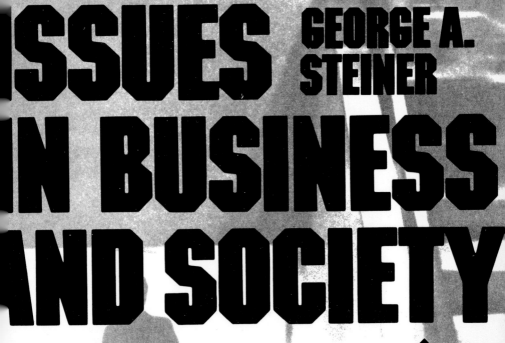

# ISSUES IN BUSINESS AND SOCIETY

## GEORGE A. STEINER

RANDOM HOUSE BOOKS IN MANAGEMENT

# Issues in
# Business
# and
# Society

Consulting Editor

BARRY RICHMAN
University of California
Los Angeles

Other books by George A. Steiner

*Top Management Planning*
*Strategic Factors in Business Success*
*Industrial Project Management* (with William G. Ryan)
*Multinational Corporate Planning* (with Warren M. Cannon)
*Managerial Long-range Planning*
*National Defense and Southern California, 1961–1970*
*Government's Role in Economic Life*
*Wartime Industrial Statistics* (with David Novick)
*Economic Problems of War*
*Economic Problems of National Defense*
*Business and Society*

# Issues in Business and Society

**George A. Steiner**

University of California Los Angeles

Random House  New York

ISBN: 0–394–31233–3

Library of Congress Catalog Card Number: 77–138630

Manufactured in the United States of America by Kingsport Press, Inc., Kingsport, Tennessee

Designed by James McGuire

First Edition

987654

# Preface

In this volume of readings and cases I have chosen materials that can be used to illuminate and provide a provocative basis for deeper classroom discussion of major issues in business and society. Emphasis in selection is on current and potentially important future issues. Whenever it is possible and appropriate, I have selected articles on each side of an issue. Except for a few readings, I have avoided extreme, irresponsible polemics from either the right or the left. It is my view that debate about the issues that arise in the business-society arena is most helpful to students, business, and society when it is as dispassionate, objective, informed, and rational as one can make it.

To facilitate classroom discussion, I have explained at the beginning of each selection the essential reason why it was included. In addition, for all selections I have raised questions that I hope will stimulate analysis and discussion. If questions do not appear at the end of a reading, they will be found in immediately succeeding selections. Sometimes questions are better raised after reading several articles.

I have eliminated footnotes in the readings throughout when permission to do so has been granted. Those who wish to pursue a subject in greater depth can, of course, return to the original article for references.

Although this present compilation can readily be used alone as a readings and case book for an elementary course in business and society or in conjunction with other readings, it also serves to complement my basic text *Business and Society*. The order of presentation and choice of materials are closely interrelated with the chapter outline of and discussion in the basic text. The possible mix is almost limitless in light of the variety of issues in this field and the volume of literature that is available.

The subject matter of both these books, in my judgment, should be part of the intellectual equipment of managers who think of themselves as being enlightened and of the general reader who wants to be informed about deep issues and currents in society. It is my hope, therefore, that both groups will find these books to be of high interest and value.

I acknowledge here and at appropriate points in the book my gratitude to various publishers and authors for permission to use their writings. I express my debt to the Research Program in Competition and Business Policy, Graduate School of Business Administration, University of California at Los Angeles, and its director, Professor J. Fred Weston, for financial aid in the compilation of this material. Mr. Demitrius Gasparis helped me in posing the questions at the end of each article or set of readings. Miss Marcelle Fortier was, as always, extremely helpful in preparing the manuscript, including permission letters, for the publisher.

*Los Angeles*                                                    *George A. Steiner*
*December 1971*

# Contents

# Issues in
# Business
# and
# Society

# Critics of the Past Business System

1

# Critics of business: stonethrowers and gravediggers

## clarence c. walton

**Clarence C. Walton, President of the Catholic University of America, examines in this article the elegant obituaries on the business system that have been an occupational necessity of the intellectual for a long period of time. The "corpse" refuses to die, but Walton asks whether it might die eventually "not because of internal defects but because too few expect it to live or plan for its future."**

The promoters and organizers who forged the world's business systems have, together with their creation, long been targets for acidulous criticism. If an imaginary seismograph were to sweep public opinion over a broad arc of time and space—from ancient Athens or medieval Milan to modern Manhattan—it would quickly detect everywhere rumbles of discontent with the business classes. Long ago in a single act that was both symbol and prophecy for the western world, the Greeks blurred the line between thieves and merchants by making Hermes the god of both. Plato in the Hellenistic and Tertullian in the Roman tradition expressed views that found an echoing chorus among the early Church Fathers who felt with St. John Chrysostom (347–407) that "no Christian ought to be a merchant, and if he should wish to become one, he should be ejected from the Church of God!"

A millennium later, and despite bustling economic ferment and burgeoning town life, St. Thomas Aquinas (1225–1274) could be found not only arguing that "a good society ought but moderately to employ merchants," but adding the practical advice that princes should construct towns only in fertile places to curb an unhealthy influx of, and dependence on, foreign merchants. Throughout the entire period of the early Middle Ages only a handful of Jewish moralists, like Maimonides, took a fairly tolerant view of mercantile and financial pursuits, but even here tight strictures on pricing policies and the accumulation of wealth were enjoined.

With the sundering of Christendom in the sixteenth century and the secularization of Western Europe, it might have been expected that the vestiges of these ancient hostilities would wither and that the businessman's role in society would be more appropriately recognized. In due course intellectual breakthroughs of historic dimensions were recorded when John Calvin propounded a theological apologia for the business *man* and Adam Smith developed an economic defense for the business *system*. In Calvin's formulation the individual faced restraints from a conscience governed by a moral imperative to aid the less fortunate; in Smith's, the symmetry of the market was preserved through the disciplining forces of competition. Personal commitments and impersonal sanctions thus combined to provide the underpinnings of the new ideology, and the brilliant virtuosity of these two star performers was reflected and perpetuated in the New World through the expansion of the Puritan work ethic and the emergence of the laissez-faire state.

## CRITICS CHANGE, CRITICISMS DON'T

But though he had advanced in acceptance and respectability, the businessman was by no means home free. From a new crop of secular moralists (novelists and poets, historians and philosophers), who had dethroned the theologians as influence-wielders over society, came a persistent stream of criticism that differed little from traditional attacks. The businessman's profit motive was held suspect, his competitive instincts were deemed deplorable, the deployment of his growing power was judged reprehensible. In a real sense, Charles Dickens's characterization of Scrooge as a heartless urban businessman who had no time for Yuletide love effectively summed up the animosities felt by the creative communities toward their respective business contemporaries.

And when not a devil, the businessman was a dolt. Thackeray in *Vanity Fair* and Molière in *Le Bourgeois Gentilhomme* had great sport poking fun at the ludicrous behavior of the social-climbing, gauche merchant. To be termed "bourgeois" was the equivalent of today's "hick." If Napoleon's sneer at England as a nation of shopkeepers reflected the soldier's contempt for the businessman, the Prussian military class went even further by barring, at soirées, even the wealthiest burghers from "their" section of the ballroom floor.

The business of demolition continues uninterrupted in the twentieth century. MacHeath and Peachum, two leading figures in Bertolt Brecht's *Three-Penny Opera*, are cunning entrepreneurs who turn all property and even murder into a profit-and-loss calculus. Jean Paul Sartre used an obsessive commitment to business to explain family corruption in *The Condemned of Altona*. To Ignazio Silone the marriage of business and government is a malignant cancer in the social organism. To Friedrich Dürrenmatt the business ideology is articulated by his fictional Alfredo Traps, who acts ruthlessly on the principle that it is "dog eat dog in business, you know—an eye for an eye and a tooth for a tooth. . . . I had to get on. No help for it. Business is business after all!"

## SHELLS OF STEEL, BODIES OF PULP

Perhaps D. H. Lawrence best capsulized this view of the businessman when he described Sir Clifford, a key figure in *Lady Chatterley's Lover*, as "almost a creature, with a hard efficient shell of an exterior and a pulpy interior, one of the amazing crabs and lobsters of the modern industrial and financial world, invertebrates of the crustacean order, with shells of steel like machines and inner bodies of soft pulp."

And on it goes. But why? The stream of abuse and calumny strikes many as an anachronistic preoccupation of the creative. The mature man cries out: peace, have done; has not this same businessman and business system brought America and now Europe within sight of general affluence? But still the stones fly, and the cause is a phenomenon perhaps most ably described by two perceptive Frenchmen. The first, Raymond Aron, declared:

"For most European intellectuals anti-capitalism is much more than a mere economic theory; it is an article of faith. It pervades Catholic and Protestant circles to some extent, as well as anticlerical Socialist circles. For those intellectuals to agree to debate the merits of free enterprise versus nationalized enterprise, the free market versus national planning, in the light of their respective achievements, would be to agree to surrender both the emotional and the philosophical basis of their belief. They will not look at what has happened to capitalism in (America) and thus learn what can be done with it socially. They have shut their eyes and have swallowed wholesale the Marxist argument that the sole cause of man's exploitation of man is private ownership of the means of production.

"This being so, when Americans come along and proclaim that the capitalist system, supported on a base of political democracy, is a truer and nobler heir of humanism than the falsely named 'proletarian' dictatorship founded on the regime of the single party, those Americans do violence to every idea cherished by our anti-capitalist and anti-Stalinist intelligentsia. Nothing is more irritating to an intellectual than to question his basic assumptions; nobody likes to be asked to start thinking all over again from the beginning. Their basic assumption is that capitalism is evil; take that away from them and they are left high and dry."

## A FASCINATION WITH FAILURE

Aron's distinguished colleague, Bertrand de Jouvenel, phrased his observation in a quasi-psychoanalytical vein:

"The world of business is, to the intellectual, one in which the values are wrong, the motivations low, the rewards misaddressed. A convenient gateway into the intellectual's inner courtyard where his judgments are rendered is afforded by his *deficit preference* [italics added]. It has been observed that his sympathies go to institutions which run at a loss—nationalized industry supported by the treasury, colleges dependent upon grants and subsidies, newspapers which never get out of the red."

## ANY RESPITE FROM THE AMERICAN?

Such is at least a plausible explanation of the European intellectual's penchant to deride and despise. What about his country cousin—the American man of intellect? How has he felt and what does he now feel about the business system and its practitioners? One would expect the American's attitudes to be different from those of the European for a variety of reasons, of which the following three are perhaps most significant:

(1) America has been peopled by immigrants imbued with the intoxicating notion of equality and unaffected by the traditional prejudices of the older aristocracies toward business.

(2) American business leaders, unlike European entrepreneurs, developed close rapport with some of the nation's best institutions of higher learning and presumptively, or so it seemed, with the American intellectual classes. The Baltimore Quaker who made a fortune in mercantile and business pursuits, Johns Hopkins, endowed the first exclusively graduate school in this country. Ezra Cornell and Andrew Carnegie in the east and Leland Stanford in the west memorialized themselves through universities bearing their names. Some of the most distinguished of the women's colleges—Vassar, Wellesley, and Smith—owed much of their strength to business interest in their welfare. The buoyancy and sparkle of the emergent *zeitgeist* seemed to have been captured by Williams College President Mark Hopkins, who declared fervently that it was not the contemplative or the quietist but the man of property and action who had done most for public institutions.

(3) The American labor movement, again unlike its European counterparts, early accommodated itself to the business system. No

continental unionist could mount the kind of assault on all brands of socialism that Samuel Gompers was able to muster as head of the American Federation of Labor.

To suggest, however, that labor's adjustment and acceptance of the American business system was relatively painless and well-nigh universal is to overstate the consensus. There was Eugene Debs, who denounced Gompers's brand of voluntarism as a form of bondage for the worker with chains supplied by a capitalist constitution and a business-minded judiciary. More radical and more passionate was Socialist Labor Party Leader Daniel de Leon, a Columbia Law School graduate in 1878 and later lecturer in Columbia College. De Leon pictured the American labor leader as "nothing but a massed battery behind which the capitalist class can encompass what it could not do without him—the work of enslaving and slowly degrading the working class . . ." Lesser luminaries like Vincent St. John and James P. Cannon, avowed Marxists, became associated with the radical Industrial Workers of the World.

Yet the tempest remained in the teapot. The frontier as a "safety valve" may have been one factor inhibiting the growth of radicalism but it was less important than the fact that the country was rich and ready for the able and the willing. In the light of these circumstances it might well have been anticipated that the intellectual transplanting of seedlings from Calvin and Smith would have flourished in thistle-free soil.

## FIVE OF SIX DISAPPROVED

Nothing could be further from the facts. In a society impressed by bulk two comments are worth recording. Surveying the post-Civil War world of American letters, Merle Curti noted that "some sixty novels dealing with the American businessman were written before the end of the nineteenth century, and of these at least fifty were critical of the activities and values of this group."

A century ago there were some who would agree with Freeman Hunt, prominent editor of influential trade publications, that business is both a deep science and a high art. But the outstanding writers of that epoch would not be found in Hunt's camp. In the Gilded Age Mark Twain denounced land promoters and lobbyists who corrupted society in their lust for money. William Dean Howells employed the newer techniques of literary realism to drive home much the same lesson in a novel appropriately called *Hazard of New Fortunes*. Hamlin Garland, who poured forth the anguish of the dispossessed farmer who knew not how to cope with spreading industrialism, observed in the 1922 preface to his *Main Traveled Roads* that "if these stories seem unduly austere, let the reader remember the time in which they were composed. They were true of the farmers of that day and no one can know better than I. For I was there."

## ULTIMATE INDICTMENT

In our own day the two great "trilogists," John Dos Passos and James T. Farrell, have railed at the evils of business. In many respects, Dos Passos is an exemplar. His three-page profile of Charles Steinmetz in *U.S.A.* is a classic. When the European-born Steinmetz arrived in America he felt fortunate to hold down a twelve-dollar-a-week job with Rudolf Eichemeyer. It was this genius who worked out the famous law of hysteresis that, in Dos Passos' picturesque phrasing, "makes possible all the transformers that crouch in little boxes in gable-roofed houses in all the high tension lines all over everywhere. . . . In 1892 when Eichemeyer sold out to the corporation that was to form General Electric, Steinmetz was entered in the contract along with other valuable apparatus. All his life Steinmetz was a piece of valuable apparatus belonging to General Electric . . . until he wore out and died." These last six words were the ice of cold contempt toward a corporate system which transformed even the most gifted of human beings into a piece of disposable property.

And what was true of the individual genius was even true for society at large. In 1919, Dos Passos reminded his readers that ours is a time of "wars and panics on the stock exchange, machine-gun fire and arson, bankruptcies, war and loans, starvation, lice, cholera and typhus, good growing weather for the House of Morgan." *U.S.A.* closes with a description of a young hitchhiker, restless and hungry, sitting at the edge of a road while a silver Douglas plane passes overhead. Dos Passos muses:

"Transcontinental passengers sit pretty, big men with bank accounts, highly-paid jobs, who are saluted by doormen; telephone girls saying good morning to them. . . . The transcontinental passenger thinks contracts, profits, vacation trips, mighty continent between Atlantic and Pacific, power, wires humming dollars . . . ; and in the bumpy air over the desert ranges toward Las Vegas sickens and vomits into the carton container the steak and mushrooms he ate in New York. No matter, silver in the pocket, greenbacks in the wallet, drafts, certified checks, plenty restaurants in L.A."

Again we see the unfolding of the pattern. The American creative artist, no less than the European, opts for the "loser" and scorns the accomplishments of the "winner," however substantial these may be.

Yet the artist is not the most impassioned.  While he hisses and throws stones, he does not prophesy dissolution.  He leaves it to scholars, and particularly to the economist, to compose the obituaries and describe the chiliastic finale.

## THE SCHOLAR BECOMES "ENGAGÉ"

By definition a scholar is one who searches assiduously for facts, relates them causally, theorizes circumspectly, and tests hypotheses meticulously.  If the novelist speaks with compassion, the scholar speaks with detachment; if the former legitimately takes a raw slice of life to make it the whole, the latter must generalize only with extreme caution; if poetic license is willingly accorded to one, it is rigorously denied the other.  Yet in looking at the scholarly community it is worth pondering the implications of the fact that the word "intellectual" itself has recently been taken to mean writers who oppose the "establishment," reject the "system," repudiate "mass culture."  Are the business system and the total society that bad?  Or are many intellectuals that wrong?  One refuses instinctively to be led into the "either-or" pit.  It is instructive consequently to review samplings from some of the social sciences if for no other reason than to be on guard against generalizations offered by others.

Take the historians, for example.  When preoccupation with political history was finally broadened in this century to take into account social and cultural events, the one thing that fascinated historians was the social impact of the Industrial Revolution.  What portrait emerges?  In the works of craftsmen like Ruggiero and the Hammonds, in the studies of popularists like Bertrand Russell, what comes through is the unspeakable horrors of industrialism and the misery it has wrought on mankind—with no thought of its concomitant benefits.  This intellectual selectivity springs from an ideological commitment that, procrustean-like, forces facts and data into a mold of its own liking.

For present purposes one need only note the profound influence exercised by the German historical school on American scholars and the further fact that this group included the most influential students of economic history during the half century preceding the First World War.  In Germany the circle took the name of *Kathedersozialisten*, which meant the "socialist of the chair."  Many of the founders of the American Economic Association—Adams and Clark, Patten and James, Seligman and Ely—had studied in Germany and returned with perspectives that led them easily into rebellion against the American business system.  Professor Ely may be taken as a fair representative.

Holder of a doctorate from Heidelberg, he returned to an America that impressed him as incredibly dirty and poorly run. The manner of producing material goods was examined critically and pronounced faulty while the labor movement itself was declared to be crisis-ridden.

How fair and impartial, how valid and reasoned, were Ely's criticisms? No one dare gainsay the fact that a tremendous upheaval was under way and that the older canons for ordering a humane society were crumbling. But Professor F. A. Hayek has argued that the whole atmosphere in the *Kathedersozialisten* and in the American Institutional School "was such that it would have required an exceptional independence of mind for a young scholar not to succumb to the pressure of academic opinion. No reproach was more feared nor more fatal to academic prospects than that of being an apologist of the capitalist system; and, even if a scholar dared to contradict dominant opinion on a particular point, he would be careful to safeguard himself against such accusations by joining in the general condemnation of the capitalist system. To treat the existing economic order as merely a historical phase and to be able to predict from the laws of historical development the emergence of a better future system became the hallmark of what was then regarded as the truly scientific spirit."

In the indigenous American tradition itself, however, no historian was more important than Charles Beard, whose *Rise of American Civilization* revealed the moral premises in Beard's own thinking. To him the Gilded Age of American business represented a departure from the values of an eighteenth-century enlightenment epitomized by Jefferson. Sweeping into dominance were crass, hard-hitting, and hardheaded businessmen whose sole interest was self-interest. The classic struggle between Hamilton and Jefferson has been of major concern to American historians, with the scholar's vote traditionally cast in favor of the Jeffersonian ideal. It was Jefferson who championed natural rights, who articulated the ideal of equality, who advocated church-state separation, who urged the wide diffusion of property, who denounced monopoly in any form.

## EMERGENCE OF THE "TIRED MAN"

Almost everything Jefferson stood for the American businessman seemingly stood against: broad natural rights turned into narrow property rights, elitism replaced equality, property went to the gifted minority, and monopoly became essential to allow room for necessary "bigness." By cruel irony this eerie businessman-predator became a weary psychotic. The one to note this development, in an extension of the irony, was Charles Beard's gifted wife, historian Mary Beard, who wrote that "some strain on the nervous system has always been brought by the effort to organize activities and to calculate profits and risks. This has ever distinguished the businessman from other types. No other profession, apparently, equals business in its power to wear man out. Certainly there was no such generic term as the Tired Soldier. Politicians lived to a great age. Priests flourished on a meager diet and flagellation. Farmers bore toil and misfortune, growing stronger. All through the eras of epic carnage and herculean labors, explorers and pioneers kept burly and jolly. Only the effort to organize and calculate has brought forth the strange phenomenon, 'The Tired Man.'" Turn, then, either side of the historical coin and the motto is an insistent "caveat": beware of the businessman who is too energetic—beware of the businessman who is too tired.

When it comes to the field of sociology, there is little doubt that the voice most widely heard and the message most vigorously discussed was that of C. Wright Mills, whose *Power Elite* has become part of everyday conversation. Among European sociologists Mills was, in effect, "Mr. American Sociology" and he remains to this day enormously popular among pro-socialists all over the world. Influenced by Veblen, Mills accepted the distinction between industry, which was good because it made products for others, and business, which was bad because it made profits for itself. On this Veblenesque painting was super-imposed Mills' Jefferson-type love for the small entrepreneur and his fear of gigantic organizations. Thus Mills inveighed against a society wherein corporations had become states within states and added:

"The economy of America has been largely incorporated, and within their incorporation the corporate chiefs have captured technological innovation, accumulated the existing great fortunes as well as much lesser, scattered wealth, and capitalized the future. Within the financial boundaries of the corporation, the industrial revolution itself has been concentrated. Corporations command raw materials, and the patents on invention with which to turn them into finished products. They command the most expensive and, therefore, what must be the finest legal minds in the world, to invent and refine their defenses and their strategies. They employ man as producer and they make that which he buys as consumer. They clothe him and feed him and invest his money. They make that with which he fights the wars and they finance the ballyhooed advertisements and the obscurantist bunk of public relations that surround him during the wars and between them. Their private decisions, responsibly made in the interests of the feudal-like world of private property and income, determine the size and shape of the national economy, the level of employment, the purchasing power of the consumer, the prices that are advertised, the investments that are channeled.  Not Wall Street financiers or bankers, but large owners and executives in their self-financing corporations hold the keys of economic power.  Not the politicians of the visible government, but the chief executives who sit in the political directorate, by fact and by proxy, hold the power and the means of defending the privileges of their corporate world."

## THE UNMITIGATED EVIL

Criticisms of Mills have been ample.  Except in a few instances, he failed to specify what the "big" decisions are and what power exists to do what things.  He has been accused by a faculty colleague, the distinguished Paul Lazarsfeld, of purveying charlatanism and not knowledge, and he has been rebuked in *World Affairs* (October 1957) by Talcott Parsons for an "unjustifiably anticapitalist posture."  Yet the popularity of his approach retains singular vigor.  Perhaps its vitality derives from the fact that big business necessarily represents power and power itself is looked upon as unmitigated evil.  This, incidentally, was the tack taken by Robert Brady in a prewar book that attracted considerable critical attention.  Brady argued in *Business as a System of Power* that the emergence of "peak" industry associations (strategic industrial associations which exert political as well as economic power) was the key factor in the rise of both national socialism and fascism, and that British and American societies are destined to follow the same tortured pathways to the same predetermined and agonizing results.  For Brady, it was a worldwide phenomenon.  Representative groupings included, in Germany, the Reichsverband der Deutschen Industrie (RDI), in Italy the General Confederation of Italian Industry, in Japan the Zaibatsu ("money cliques"), in France the Confederation Générale du Patronat Français, and in England the Federation of British Industries.  In the United States the National Association of Manufacturers, supported by the National Industrial Conference Board, was moving us toward a fascist state.  Like Mills, Brady saw these peak associations as states within states with a concept of self-government in business not unlike that of the corporate guild economy in the medieval period—except that while leadership in the guild was widely distributed among individual proprietors, in the modern-day association it was the huge corporate combines that dominated.

It is from economists especially—and often with a special cruelty—that businessmen have received their heaviest critical barrages.  One can find condemnations even among those founding fathers of the classical theory who were presumed to be so hospitable to the businessman:  Adam Smith and David Ricardo.  Did not these gentlemen by implication minimize the role of the businessman when they called labor the source of all value?  And when Smith did talk about businessmen, it was only in terms of castigation for their "mean rapacity, their monopolizing spirit . . . , their sneaking arts. . . ."

Of the American economists none was more impressively devastating in his critique of contemporary business civilization than the nation's adopted son—the magisterial paradox—Joseph Alois Schumpeter (1883–1950).  Austrian-born and emotionally attached to Europe, he fled to Harvard in a mood more of resignation than of enthusiasm. Reared in the Catholic faith, he would up fascinated by Marx.  Scornful of the notion that a scientific work could ever become an instrument for policy (he could not tolerate Keynesian economics), he nonetheless tried as an Austrian finance minister and as a Viennese bank president, albeit unsuccessfully, to be a scientific policy maker.  All his life he won points and lost arguments.

But in that one "big" argument over the future of capitalism, Schumpeter felt serenely confident of victory and vindication.  With extraordinary perception he divined the need to view the business system not simply in terms of capitalism's technical apparatus but rather from the perspective of a capitalist "civilization."  This civilization and all that it embodied was incredibly innovative and productive.  So productive, Schumpeter felt, that average per-capita real income in 1978 would be double the 1928 figure.  "The capitalist achievement," he opined in an untypically homely illustration, "does not consist in providing more silk stockings for queens but in bringing them within the reach of factory girls for steadily decreasing amounts of effort."

In the face of such evident successes how could anything possibly go wrong?  Yet when it came time to ask the critical question, "Can capitalism survive?" Schumpeter answered bluntly, "No!"  The reasons were crystal clear: everything is at work to destroy the businessman's drive for achievement—the evaporation of traditional property rights, the disintegration of the bourgeois family, the toadying of businessmen to government pressures in ways that made the working of private enterprise little different from socialist undertakings, the automatizing and routinizing of innovation itself, the disappearing need for strong will and leadership.  Since the small group of entrepreneurs is becoming smaller, the bourgeois class, which has historically been replenished by infusions of new blood from successful entrepreneurs, will itself vanish from the earth.

And now the syllogism relentlessly drives onward to its somewhat unexpected conclusion.  Since democracy is so much a bourgeois creation, it would not survive the passing of its creator.  Socialism will succeed democracy as surely as night follows day, with the whole process accelerated by the intellectual classes who have become even more hostile to business because they have a vested interest in social unrest. But there is no cause for alarm because democracy itself is simply a technique whereby "individuals acquire the power to decide the means of competitive struggle for the people's vote." Socialism, too, is a technique which readily lends itself to various forms and values: to democracy or oligarchy, to theocracy or atheism, to egalitarianism or aristocracy, to peace or aggression. This mechanistic view of democracy led David McCord Wright to wonder wryly if Schumpeter had ever read the American Constitution. A further point may be made. In Schumpeter's brand of socialism, the economic process is placed under the control of a competent bureaucracy of professionals. Presumably these experts, thus freed from parliamentary processes and their related irrationalities, would behave with the same wisdom, vision, and courage as the old entrepreneurs they had replaced.

### "WRONG DIAGNOSIS, RIGHT PRESCRIPTION"

Any truncated interpretation of Schumpeter admittedly leaves much to be desired. But the thrust of his thinking can be garnered from the valedictory address delivered to the American Economic Association in 1949 just a few days before his death: "I do not intend to prophesy. I merely recognize the facts and point out the tendencies which those facts indicate. . . . Marx was wrong in his diagnosis of the manner in which the capitalist society would break down; he was not wrong in his prediction that it would break down eventually. The stagnationists are wrong in their diagnosis of the reasons why the capitalist process should stagnate; they still may turn out to be right in their prognosis that it will stagnate—with sufficient help from the public sector."

The magnetic attraction of Schumpeter's "grand design" for the present crop of American business critics is hard to determine, but certain of the old master's basic ideas keep recurring. There is, for example, less inclination to accuse the business system of actual failure, as is done by Andrew Shonfield of the Royal Institute of International Studies in London, who notes that the American economy since the war yielded a gain in real income per employed person of little over 2%, has generated an unemployment rate of over 5% from 1951 to 1964, has allowed effective power to slide perceptibly to private corporations on the false assumption that corporations are nothing more than voluntary associations of private individuals, and has lived too long with the faulty logic of both liberal democracy and Keynesian economics. American critics, on the other hand, tend to agree with Schumpeter's basic view that in terms of production and distribution capitalism has been a magnificent success but that the dynamics of a *business civilization* (which is something larger than the economy itself) dictate its demise.

Robert Heilbroner provides an interesting example. A highly sensitive human being, an extraordinarily gifted writer, and a careful craftsman, Heilbroner initially seemed to suggest, in *The Future As History*, that exogenous forces (represented by the developing nations with which we were ill-prepared to cope) would bring radical changes in American society: "Unlike our forefathers who lived very much *in* and *for* history, we ourselves appear to be adrift in an historic void" at the very moment when capitalism is waning in the mature nations of western society and is unpopular among the immature states of the nonwestern world.

Possibly less interested than Schumpeter in ideologies and more preoccupied with "forces" in history, he nevertheless shares the Schumpeterian view that business elites are destined for a subordinate role in future affairs. There is reason to believe that his forthcoming book, previewed in a recent magazine article, may have even more important insights on the domestic scene. Here Heilbroner projects a world where the traditional stimuli of capitalism have lost their zest: profit motives are subordinated to power and prestige; work is a matter of personal choice and not economic necessity; market mechanisms are replaced by planning boards which allocate resources for jobs that are considered essential to society.

## THE WAGES OF PRODIGALITY

Another critic is Professor Kenneth Boulding, who observed that capitalism's successes can be appreciated—as Schumpeter fully did—only if we remember that per capita real income in the Roman Empire of old, or in India and Morocco today, approximates $100, whereas it is nearly $2,500 in the United States. And this will be dwarfed by predicted incomes of $10,000 per capita toward the end of this century. But these successes have been due to a technology that is profoundly suicidal and which cannot last more than a few centuries longer because the fossil fuels on which it is based will be exhausted. Moreover, this crowded space capsule called earth is becoming ever more jammed with human beings. Austere parsimony is required for future survival. Since voluntary or spontaneous action is not adequate to the needs of such a time, it must give way to a degree of planning and controls never dreamed of by industrial and liberal western societies.


## "A COLOSSAL ACCIDENT"

Preoccupation with the ravages wrought by technology also marks the views of Michaél Harrington, who, although not a professional economist, writes frequently on economic questions and of the catastrophic social consequences flowing from a "coldly decadent" business order. Like Schumpeter, Harrington represents an interesting blending of Catholicism and Marxism; like Schumpeter, Harrington sees the revolutionary dynamism of business as producing an unplanned, unexpected, and unbearable strain on the whole social system. Although the system is planned to the very last detail in its most minute parts the total result is a colossal accident.

The Schumpeterian vision of corporations that minimize the virtues of individualism, risk-taking, and bold enterprise, which have invalidated the sacrosanct law of supply and demand, which have provided enough affluence to "buy off" the poor and, with the purchase, the idealism that misery forced on millions—all these things have come to pass. And so, too, must come to pass the final stage of transition into the socialist society foretold by Schumpeter.

In all these analyses the common themes are the necessary decline of the business elites, the erosion of the profit motive, the disappearance of the spirit of adventure, and the inexorable and inevitable advent of centralized planning by professional public servants. Only Harrington seems to qualify the centralizing trend by granting the poor the right to run themselves and their own programs.

It would appear that the critics of business can be divided roughly and perhaps too schematically into a normative and a psychological segment—between those who argue that the business system will disappear because it ought to and those Schumpeterian souls who say that, regardless of virtues, it is doomed.


## DISENCHANTED YOUTH

Whether these critiques have any independent validity or no, their popularity and persuasiveness lends them something of the character of self-fulfilling prophecies. Let me illustrate with an anecdote that may provide a convenient gateway to understanding the larger problems. In a course required of all doctoral candidates in business at the Columbia Business School, the year came to close with lectures by two prominent executives—Frank Nunlist, President of Worthing Corporation, and John Fox, President of United Fruit.  In a dialogue that followed the formal presentation, each guest was asked this same question: "What do you feel is the most important future problem for business?"  Somewhat to the amazement of the startled auditors came identical responses: "You people!"

The businessmen then went on to express the view that the manifest disinterest of able young people in business careers was causing them profound worry.  Their observations simply reinforced the views of David Reisman, author of *The Lonely Crowd*, who told an audience at York University in Canada that his own contacts with students at Chicago, Johns Hopkins, and Harvard convinced him that there exists a tremendous revulsion against business careers among gifted and sensitive young people.  The depreciation of business in books as different as Whyte's *Organization Man* and Packard's *Pyramid Climbers* is creating two illusions:  "One is that business is a field in which one could only have a dull and complacent, if secure and well-paid, life, and this is one of the self-confirming prophecies. . . .  Hardly any Harvard students of quality go to the Business School.  The Harvard undergraduate at the Harvard Business School is a rarity, and he is likely to come from the lower part of the class. . . .  We are creating an image of business leadership which may tend to become self-confirming and which is an injustice to what is possible in the business career—and that is its intellectual possibilities, its adventurous possibilities.  But the converse illusion seems to me no less dangerous, namely, that academic life is not a business, that there are no business or commercial elements in a profession.  When these elements are discovered, then cynicism and disillusion beset those people who thought they had escaped commercialism by entering an academic career."

Shortly before leaving the Carnegie Foundation to become Secretary of the Department of Health, Education, and Welfare, John Gardner voiced a similar concern, albeit in even broader context, saying that in colleges and universities "the best students are carefully schooled to avoid leadership responsibilities. . . .  We are approaching a point at which everyone will want to educate the technical expert who advises the leader, or the intellectual who stands off and criticizes the leader, but no one will want to educate the leader himself."

## TALKING THE SYSTEM TO DEATH

There is a real danger, then, that the business system will die not because of internal defects but because too few expect it to live or plan for its future.  Surely critics of the Schumpeter variety would be surprised and perhaps dismayed if they realized that they were actors and not spectators in the drama of dissolution—if, in other words, their pronouncements were helping to foster an intellectual impoverishment of the business community from which it could not recover. And if their view of the inherent vitality of the business system is correct, how sad would be the consequences for all mankind were the nation's finest human resources to flow into channels inhospitable or even hostile to business.

If prophets are not honored in their own countries, they should at least be heeded. And it would be sheer folly to ignore the premises and the logic of those who thoughtfully survey the business system and pronounce it sick—even to the point of death. A skeptical posture toward any prophecy is, however, not amiss since man's history has borne eloquent witness to the dangers of prediction of wholesale changes. One need only remember the early Thirties, for instance, when exponents of the mature economy argued that the American business society had fully developed, that population growth would stabilize, that science had exploited its most valid principles, that the future meant a state of decreasing capital investment and economic stagnation. The burden of proof, therefore, is on the prophet.

## GOD'S FROZEN PEOPLE

The willingness of the secular prophets of our day to carry that burden of criticizing is as remarkable as their apparent inability to contribute toward the practical solution of society's immediate problems. Shortly before leaving his special White House counseling assignment, Richard Goodwin told a group of foreign students that "nothing is more disheartening than the failure of much of the American intellectual community to evolve answers to the crisis of American public life." Of insights there are many, he said, but rarely are they helpful to those who must direct affairs. The intellectuals themselves have become God's frozen people. Who dares prophesy that the prophets themselves will be warmed by the fires of a socialist state simply because they have been chilled by capitalism? One could argue plausibly that the intellectual's ideological fires have been more dampened than fed by "corporate" behavior—indeed they may have been banked too abruptly—and one could argue further that, as Schumpeter averred, any system—not simply the capitalist order—will be criticized by intellectuals simply because they have the time and capacity to do so.

It makes no sense, however, to pillory intellectuals for not becoming experts in policy formulation and execution. That is not, after all, their main function.  They have erected an impressive edifice of critical assessments and one wonders how these appraisals may themselves be appraised.  Certain facts and developments that have loomed large in the evolution of a business civilization and which continue to characterize it even to this day are often ignored or minimized by the critics.

The issue is not change itself, since change is a constant in our kind of world.  Rather, the question that needs to be asked is this: throughout the coming transformations will the private businessman and the voluntary business association survive?  And if so, will they continue to exercise sufficient power of initiative to retain a crucial, determining role over the allocation of scarce resources in the production of goods and services?  And in the fruitful employment of human beings?  There are grounds for rendering affirmative answers to these questions and for arguing that the critics have so dramatized society's future needs that the ability of the businessman not simply to adjust to change, but to generate change, has been overlooked.

## ACHIEVEMENTS OF AN AWKWARD YOUTH

Amidst all the tumult one must not forget that the "factory capitalism" which replaced Smith's concept of market capitalism is about a century and a half old and that economists only lately have begun to take into account its theoretical meaning.  Corporate capitalism is of even more recent vintage.  In a sense it is still an awkward youth that appeared suddenly and dramatically after the last war.  Yet despite that short time, entrepreneurs and organizers have radically altered the concept of corporate social responsibility, have innovated excitingly with the multinational corporation, have experimented with new organizational theories that may fundamentally alter the old chain-of-command theory in management, have exposed themselves to critical reassessments of their value structures, have broken the old WASP (white, Anglo-Saxon Protestant) barriers to the executive suites, have fostered organizations like the Committee on Economic Development to shatter stereotyped thinking, and have improved the mechanisms of ancillary business communities like the stock exchanges.

These are scarcely signs of a moribund business civilization.  Yet Schumpeter and those who came after him are right on a very fundamental point.  A business civilization must be assessed in terms more commodious than its capacity to change mechanisms.  There exists a definite *esprit* built around certain values.  Among these values, commitment to the vitality of a plural society—with its openness and its resiliency—is no less important than the work ethic or market competition, which are undergoing admittedly substantial change.

## THE ENTREPRENEUR: A POST-SOCIALIST TRIUMPH?

Above all, two aspects of the entrepreneurial story—one societal and the other individual—need to be resurrected and reexamined. The neglected lesson from social history is that only the rich nations accepted Adam Smith's advice to free the businessman from mercantilistic restraints by the state. The poor nations did not! And the reason in both cases is intriguing and relevant: only the relatively wealthy nations can afford to encourage risk taking and risk takers. Whereas a failure in a poor society means catastrophe, in an affluent one it usually means a delay coupled with the ability to start over again. Consequently as societies become richer they can afford to foster—not diminish—the risk-taking functions of their business communities. And as they become peopled with better educated citizens they enlarge the range of possibilities for imaginative new designs, new processes, new ventures. When corporations become slow to innovate, the innovator himself will find alternative possibilities. Indeed one ponders the implications of a society like ours where the government itself contracts out one of its most important activities—*thinking*—to a private corporation like Rand simply because the latter can move organizationally more quickly, prod individuals more directly, and reward them for success more handsomely than government bureaucracies. Note how Russia is moving, with increased affluence, to soften the rigors of centralized control. The conclusion that private enterprise has no future in the developing nations may rest on the curious premise that centralized planning will not pull backward economies up to those levels of wealth where innovation can be encouraged. In such an event, socialism fails the developing society. Where it succeeds, socialism creates a climate within which risk taking becomes more possible because failure is more tolerable. One can argue and, indeed, prophesy, that such entrepreneurial functions will be undertaken by competent bureaucrats within the government; but history makes both the argument and the prophecy suspect. An attractive alternative interpretation, therefore, suggests that innovators will emerge and flourish outside big government or big business.

Even in America, the free-enterprise system is, after all, a *limited* system. It does not, cannot, and should not preempt all economic functions in a given society. The line between private and public initiative is never irrevocably fixed. Our reasoning suggests that as an economy develops there may be more rather than less room for the private businessman, and that this heresy requires a respectful hearing.

In a sense, the requiems chanted over the business "corpse" are analogous to the obituaries read so frequently on our party system, and recall Arthur Schlesinger, Jr.'s comment that "Political observers have always been careless in distinguishing between sleep and death. The reading of funeral rites over a badly beaten party is a favorite diversion of American history; but too often the corpse, like Aaron Burr in Mark Twain's sketch, sits up and talks with the coachman. . . ."

# Chapter 1 Questions

1. Trace some of the major attacks of the past on business.
2. Do you believe that the attacks of so-called intellectuals have always been intellectually honest?  Have the attacks been based, in your judgment, on carefully balanced facts or isolated facts?
3. There is no doubt about the fact that in the past the business system has been guilty of evils.  Yet at the same time the business system has brought huge benefits.  Which outweighs the other?
4. Do you agree that the business system is more likely to die "not because of internal defects but because too few expect it to live or plan for its future"?
5. Are there lessons in Walton's essay that will be helpful in judging current attacks on business?

# Today's "New Left" Attacks on the Business-Society Relationship

**2**

# Rebellion against the "corporate state"

## george a. steiner

During the past half dozen years a new attack against the so-called Corporate State has been developing. A comprehensive articulation of this "New Left" view is contained in *The Greening of America* (New York: Random House, 1970), a best-selling book written by Charles A. Reich, Professor of Law at Yale University. The following résumé, prepared by the editor, tries to catch some of the major themes of Reich's book that relate directly to the business-society nexus. (For another condensed version of *The Greening of America*, see *The New Yorker*, September 26, 1970, pp. 70–111.)

The theme and tone of Reich's book *The Greening of America* is captured in his beginning and ending sentences. He begins with the statement that "America is dealing death, not only to people in other lands, but to its own people" (p. 3). He ends with the observation that the new consciousness that is rising today will result in "a veritable greening of America" (p. 395). Between these remarks Reich deals at length with what is wrong with America (with little or no reference to what is right) and how a new consciousness has miraculously arisen out of the terrible current state of affairs. This new consciousness will revolutionize today's institutions and bring "a new and enduring wholeness and beauty—a renewed relationship of man to himself, to other men, to society, to nature, and to the land" (p. 4).

## WHAT IS WRONG WITH TODAY'S SOCIETY?

What is the nature of today's crisis, which has brought the revolt of its youth and the rise of a new consciousness? First, says Reich, this is a society in which the social fabric is disintegrating. Corruption is widespread, as is hypocrisy. War both exacerbates and reflects these sores. Second, America is a land of great poverty in the midst of plenty. Priorities are distorted, and private power is exercised "without concern for the general good" (p. 7). Third, while technology and production can be beneficial to mankind, they have become uncontrolled instruments that "pulverize everything in their path" (p. 7). Fourth, democracy and liberty have been eroded by the rise of bureaucracy, and dissent has met with repression. Fifth, for most people work has become sheer drudgery, and our society is dominated by crass commercialism. Sixth, modern institutions create anticommunity forces that replace family, friendship, and closeness with competition, hostility, and artificiality.   Seventh, the individual is lost and finds "death in life" (p. 9).

In the face of such devastating forces as these, there seems to be an inability to do anything.   The system is obsolete but yet has unrestrained power to dominate the lives of people.   The only salvation is a change in consciousness.


## CONSCIOUSNESS I

By the word "consciousness" Reich refers to "a total configuration in any given individual, which makes up his whole perception of reality, his whole world view" (p. 14).   It is a person's total system of beliefs, values, attitudes, and way of thinking.   Three major types of consciousness exist today in the United States.   Consciousness I developed in the nineteenth century; Consciousness II arose in the mid-twentieth century; and Consciousness III is found in today's new generation.

Consciousness I stretches back to the very founding of this society. It began with an exhilarating philosophy that free men, facing a vast continent, could achieve a prosperity and well-being (if they worked hard) that was impossible for them to achieve under previous confining social customs and class structures.   This humanistic conception, however, was soon blemished by a concept of materialism.

Materialism emphasizes self-interest and competition, and it fosters suspicion of fellow-men.   Underneath this operational code is a basic view that man is fundamentally bad and that it is natural for him to struggle against his fellow-men.   The name of the game under Consciousness I is to win.   Conflict, struggle for power, and domination are more important than love of fellow-men.

Consciousness I is a philosophy held today by many people who fail to see, says Reich, that there has been a vast change in the American way of life, that this is no longer a world of small towns, small businesses, and the simple virtues.   They still think that material growth is the way to happiness; that if people work hard, they will be successful; and that aggressive self-interest is the touchstone to a better world.

With the great changes that have taken place in this society, Consciousness I has lost touch with reality.   The competitive market economy and technology devastated the environment, produced outrageous slums and mill towns, shattered family ties as men moved from homes into factories, and turned free men into automatons geared to advancing the interests of the productive machine. Non-human values rose in ascendancy, and environmental forces ignored human happiness. The factory system exerted a degrading exploitative control over men's lives. Employees were caught in a web of terrible working conditions and unable to lead self-fulfilling lives.

Toward the end of the nineteenth century, business consolidations resulted in a new power over markets to parallel power over individuals in their working conditions. The result was subjugation of a free people and a free economy. Corporations have come to possess an overwhelming power, the consequences of which Consciousness I does not recognize.

## CONSCIOUSNESS II

Consciousness II came into existence because of the gaping holes in Consciousness I. It has accepted many of the basic tenets of Consciousness I but has added new views to overcome perceived deficiencies in the way in which society operates. For instance, Consciousness II has a pessimistic view of man and sees him as basically aggressive, competitive, and power hungry. The priority of institutions is accepted as is the corollary view that the destiny of the individual is tied more to society than to himself. Individual interests are subordinate to the public interest. The individual in Consciousness II should try to prepare himself to function within the system and adapt to the values and standards set by his chosen occupation and the organizations in which he works. He has no existence outside his career. He has great fear of failure in competing and ends up with an inability to enjoy life apart from his work.

But Consciousness II is dedicated to reform. It believes that evils in the socioeconomic system can be corrected by reform, such as social security, collective bargaining, anti-discrimination laws, and public projects like TVA. It believes that more social responsibility on the part of business, more government action in the economic system, and better administration will resolve the crises confronting this nation. It believes that improved planning, organization, and rational analysis is the path to a better society.

There are many shortcomings in the philosophy of Consciousness II, but fundamentally it is a hoax. It assumes that human satisfaction, the quality life, and the free individual are to be found in material success, power, status, and acceptance in organizational life. These values pass for "reality." Actually, the search for and finding of self is the real reality, which Consciousness II does not make possible.

## THE CORPORATE STATE

At the heart of our problems is the Corporate State, a monolithic combination of government and business that is a mindless, uncontrolled monster, in the face of which the individual is powerless. It is conceptually a single vast corporation with but one value, "the value of technology-organization-efficiency-growth-progress" (p. 90).

There are five main features of this Corporate State. First, the government uses private industry to perform most of its "public" functions, and most of what government does itself turns out to be services for the benefit of the private sector. The result is a degree of integration that gives the impression of a single corporation, a monolithic power that is not controlled by traditional checks and balances and to which men are hopelessly subjected.

Second, activities in the Corporate State are carried out through a bureaucratic organizational hierarchy, an "administrative" state that has replaced the "political" state. Decisions are made by experts rather than through the political process.

Third, the political process operates so badly that voters cannot enforce their wills to solve such problems as pollution, inadequate mass transportation, the arms race, and so on. To make matters worse, stockholders have no power in corporations, and corporations can control their own markets, as described by J. Kenneth Galbraith in *The New Industrial State* (Boston: Houghton Mifflin, 1967).* Tragically, the Corporate State is autonomous.

Fourth, the Corporate State has brought about a new type of property—status wealth. The Corporate State can confer great wealth on individuals (e.g., licenses, franchises, or Ph.D. degrees). The Consciousness II person relates his happiness to his status position in the hierarchy. This sort of thing creates great distortions in society, such as professors who are more interested in their status than in their students or a company more interested in profits than the effects of its polluting the environment. The new property of status creates a new power over individuals.

Fifth, the Corporate State has radically changed the force of law. Basically, law is a codification of values that society wishes to preserve. The Constitution of the United States sets forth basic rights, but under the Corporate State we have two great powers, one under the Constitution and one not. The Constitution, for example, protects freedom of speech. But corporations can fire individuals for speaking their mind. Supreme Court decisions in this and many areas are not reassuring

---

* See Neil H. Jacoby's review of Galbraith's book in Chapter 16.

about the control of corporate power.   Indeed, the application of law has furthered the power of the Corporate State.

Life in the Corporate State is deadening, observes Reich.   Man is separated from his sources of real meaning.   He is a robot, deprived of self-expression and fulfillment.   It is a repressive organization covered with a massive web of restraint and force.   The product is a hollow man—who has a meaningless life and no power to do anything about it.

To make matters worse, the Corporate State is aggressive in controlling the individual.   There is a pervasive "substitution phenomenon" (p. 162) in which substitutes for natural phenomena are generated by the Corporate State.   A man's appreciation for body odors, for instance, is taken away in order to sell him deodorants and perfumes.   The awareness of people is benumbed, and then a substitute is foisted on them.   At Disneyland, for example, people are asked to pay for a substitute Main Street that is only a pretense of reality.   Everywhere the genuine is replaced by the simulated.   We are even subjected to premixed peanut butter and jelly (p. 178)!   What is worse, all this is not developed by the people themselves, but is imposed by the Corporate State.

## CONSCIOUSNESS III

Out of the inhospitable soil of today's Corporate State has arisen Consciousness III with the promise that it will correct these evils by bringing the revolution that is needed.   Consciousness III has arisen from two interacting forces, namely, the great promise of this society and the threats to that promise.

In this opulent society, which has in it many ideals of high value, a new life for each person is possible.   The following illustrates the point:   It is not that surfing is possible, but that surfing as a way of life is possible, if one wants to go that route.   The youth of this society, however, have been betrayed.   They see that the discrepancy between what is and what could be is too wide.   They see, for example, that possibilities of beauty, abundance, freedom, and a "rich" life are threatened by war, race riots, boring jobs, environmental ugliness, and insecurity.

The first commandment of Consciousness III is to "be true to oneself" (p. 225).   III starts with self and asserts that self is the true reality.   This does not mean selfishness.   Rather, it asserts the worth of every human being.   It rejects the competitive philosophy of life, except in such matters as sports.   People are brothers.   A second commandment of III is that people do not judge others.   The idea of excellence and comparative merit, so important in Consciousness II, is not accepted. Each person has his own individuality and is not judged upon common standards. The world is considered to be a community in which men join hands in a circle of affection. A third commandment of III is honesty in dealing with others. This means not to "use" others, not to change oneself for someone else's use, and not to be dishonest in love. III rejects authority and subservient relationships. It does not give commands nor does it follow them. Imposed duties are rejected.

These values, says Reich, inevitably lead to a radical criticism of society. Consciousness III sees things differently. It sees poverty in the midst of plenty, unjust treatment of minorities, the ugly, the artificial, the hypocritical, and the destructive. It "sees through the Establishment verities of our society with corrosive ease" (p. 229).

III is committed to improving society but in a different way than is II. Rather than make himself subservient to the society, III commits himself to reform the society in the fundamental directions already espoused by the society, such as equality, better education, and so on. III assumes a personal responsibility to bring necessary reforms. For example, III becomes deeply involved personally in a ghetto school in a job that offers little or no pay or prestige but that promises to improve conditions.

The clothing of the young expresses a number of themes of Consciousness III. One is freedom from social restraints, and another is freedom from the convention that prescribes one set of clothing for office, another for social life, and another for play. Clothes also express democratic values, since there is no distinction between wealth and status. Music also expresses different themes of III. Music is not a pastime but an inherent part of III's culture. It expresses beauty, tension, excitement, and all the other many facets of the interrelationship of youth to its environment.

III looks at goals to achieve status, money, power, or recognition not only as being wrong, but as being unreal. III people do not look toward careers in the conventional way of II. When a II person meets the head of a large corporation, he notices status, but a III person is unaware of titles and reputations of people he meets.

Consciousness III is very concerned with community, with the relationships among people who feel the same things, see the same things, and want to experience the same things. Such sharing of experience does not mean loss of individuality but rather the increasing of satisfactions.

One of the devastating impacts of the Corporate State is the impairment of consciousness or the dulling of man's awareness of his self, of other people, and of his environment. Consciousness III seeks to rectify this by making a man aware, by enhancing his ability to savor new experiences, and by giving him new life. III, therefore, seeks to shake off the false consciousness of society.

Consciousness III is highly suspicious of logic, reason, and rational analysis. III may not know the facts, but he will know the truth that appears to be hidden from others. III can easily see what is phony in politics, what is ugly in architecture, "whereas an older person has to go through years of education to make himself equally aware" (p. 261).

Consciousness III man is not violent, is nonaggressive, and is absorbed in how to lead a better life. He wants to be left alone to pursue the life-style he has chosen, not what fits into someone else's scheme of values or existing institutions. The freedom to choose life-styles is at the core of the new awakening. People must be freed from the machine and at liberty to determine their own values. III does not reject technology but realizes that III could survive only on the foundation of current technology. It insists, however, that only Consciousness III will assure the survival of man in this age of technology.

## THE METHOD OF REVOLUTION

How will Consciousness III bring a revolution? The answer is that the Corporate State is founded upon consciousness. Change the consciousness and the Corporate State will change. Those who have discovered III must educate those who have not. People will be amenable to accepting the philosophy of III as their eyes are opened to the defects of the Corporate State and the possibilities for enriching their lives when basic values are changed.

When Consciousness III sweeps across the nation, the Corporate State as it now exists will disappear. Neither the state nor the economic machine, however, will be obliterated. Rather, they will be controlled by the new values of Consciousness III. This is the revolution of consciousness. Public opinion is not enough to bring the desired result. Rather, it will come about only by a massive change of individual ways of life. Each person must change his consciousness. There are many ways in which an individual can influence the Corporate State once he accepts Consciousness III. He can become a different, and not a passive, consumer. He can seek to bring change from the position of his own job. He may help to educate others. There are other ways, but the method is to change the system from within rather than to try to change it by outside assault. The method is for people to start to live their own lives without waiting for changes in structure, institutions, or ideologies. As each life is changed and as the movement spreads, the revolution will create a new, beautiful society.

Consciousness III is workable and realistic, concludes Reich. It does not seek to destroy anything that is essential to our life. There is no suggestion that work or excellence be abolished, only that irrationality and involuntary servitude be eliminated. It is not proposed that law, organization, or government be abolished, only that they serve rational and human ends. A Consciousness III man is not indifferent, dilatory, or incompetent. He does not reject technology but only the domination of technique. He "is practical in the most profound sense, because the historic time for man's transcendence over the machine has come" (p. 356).

# The real greening of america

## max ways

**Max Ways, member of the Board of Editors of *Fortune* magazine, raises a few major questions of perspective about Reich's views.**

Serious public discussion is shifting from the perennial concerns of politics and economics to another area. Encompassing government, business, and all other institutions of our day is the complex of beliefs, values, standards, aspirations, habits, emotional patterns, and artistic expressions that is called a culture. The American culture is now undergoing a transformation that will engage public attention for decades ahead.

The U.S. culture as it will be in the year 2000 is not preordained. It is being shaped now by business patterns and Broadway plays, by family life, by the words exchanged in classrooms, street demonstrations, newspapers, and songs. Another shaping influence is the way we appraise change. In the last few years professional and amateur observers have intensified discussion of what's going on in the U.S. culture—and why.

Into this discussion obtrudes the word revolution and the attitudes that go with it. In current usage revolution refers not merely to the magnitude of a change; it stresses the opposition and conflict between what is emerging and what it replaces. Proclamations abound that the existing society is totally evil in all its institutions, which must be exterminated root and branch. As might be expected, this assault produces its mirror image: a counterrevolutionary reaction. Since one side wants to sweep away everything that existed before the mid-Sixties, their opposites, also accepting the premise that a revolution impends, deplore all novelty, including those great changes in the culture that are flowing logically and vigorously from the very institutions (e.g., the business system, the democratic system, and the major religions) which the self-styled conservatives think they are defending.

If this obsession with the concept of revolution tightens its hold on the most articulate segments of this society, we will have little chance of distinguishing intelligently and sensitively between one cultural development and another. Distracted by generalized conflict, we will

---

Max Ways, Member, Board of Editors, *Fortune* magazine, "The Real Greening of America," *Fortune*, Vol. LXXXII, November 1970, pp. 63–65. Reprinted by permission.

botch the emergence of what could be a glorious new phase in the unfolding of American civilization.


## A NEW BUZZ WORD HAS ARRIVED

One revolutionary proclamation attracting a lot of attention these days
is *The Greening of America*, by Charles A. Reich, a forty-two-year-old
professor at the Yale Law School. . . . Professor Reich's is perhaps
the best-written of the many all-out attacks upon the American system
as it exists. [He sees] "The Corporate State" . . . as a monolithic,
antihuman merger of government, business, and all the other main
institutions of society.

It would be easy to stimulate the adrenalin of many *Fortune* readers
by summarizing and deriding what Reich has to say about the corporate state, a term that seems destined to become one of those buzz
words, like "the Establishment," that obscure our understanding of
what's going on. More interesting and less divisive is the second part
of Reich's essay, dealing with some main characteristics of the emerging culture. He calls this section "The New Consciousness." His description of the "new consciousness" itself is both eloquent and essentially valid. But his account of its origin is distorted by his insistence
on its "revolutionary" character. For reasons very different from
Reich's premises, business leadership has a special need to recognize
and understand "the new consciousness."

. . .

Let all those in the *Fortune* audience who are in favor of Consciousness III . . . say aye. Those opposed say no. It can be confidently
presumed that the ayes have it—overwhelmingly. And for a reason
that destroys Reich's account of the origin and the revolutionary destiny of Consciousness III: this new cultural phase has evolved naturally—and to some extent even intentionally—out of the preceding
phases of American development. To its immediate parent, the "organizational society," Consciousness III owes not only its technological-
material base but also its strengthened vision of freedom, individuality,
compassion, and cooperation.

If it's a wise parent, business leadership will embrace the essential
Consciousness III. Reich and the other devotees of the revolutionary
myth fear that this embrace will, in fact, occur. They call it being "co-
opted." So obsessed are they with their format of historical movement through the clash of opposites, that they refuse to recognize the
abundant evidence that *all through the twentieth century—and emphatically in the last twenty years—the main institutions of American*

*society have been moving very rapidly in the direction of the values and*
*patterns of Consciousness III.*

In those twenty years material production *did* open the doors of serious aesthetic, intellectual, and spiritual pursuits to millions of men and women formerly bound by a dreary round of material necessity. When organizations became more dependent on individual knowledge they *did* tend to lose their rigid, impersonal machine-like structure. Arbitrary authority *did* decline, making way for persuasion and initiative. Law *did* become more flexible and compassionate. Welfare for the needy at home and foreign aid abroad *did* become massive, if clumsy, evidence that this society was not gripped by a dog-eat-dog philosophy of scarcity.

That a new generation should ask "What next?" is thoroughly expectable and consistent with what had gone before. Within the next fifty years the U.S. can indeed become a country where most people will enjoy the goods they buy with their pay. Already, in this "organizational society" there are perhaps a million or more people, including most professors and most managers, whose chief "consumer good" is their enjoyment of their own work. This is a secret we have unwisely kept from the young (and in most cases from ourselves) because the "lag" in consciousness bids us pretend that we are toiling in misery for "a living."

## THE INTELLECTUAL REAR GUARD

The "lag" also helps to explain other aspects of the present scene, including Professor Reich. When a society is moving slowly its intellectual class will naturally form a kind of avant-garde. But where the actual conditions of life change rapidly, as they began to do in the nineteenth century, intellectuals fall behind, caught in the intractabilities of language and ideas. Many American intellectuals are still so trapped in the values and patterns of the preindustrial society (Consciousness I) that they have refused to believe that individuality and voluntary cooperation have flowered within large organizations. When freedom increased, these intellectuals saw slavery. When power became more widely spread, they said it was concentrating. When higher standards of social morality appeared, they diagnosed hypocrisy. These intellectuals, rather than the leaders of "the corporate state," have been manipulating the present American consciousness.

Naturally, laggards who have not caught up with Consciousness II will insist that Consciousness III should slay its true parent. Naturally, we are presented with such distortions as Reich's "corporate state," which is a mixture of cooled-down Marx and warmed-up Galbraith. Read Reich's description of a monolithic government-business tyranny and judge whether it corresponds to the reality of today's U.S. system. But don't get so enraged by "the corporate state" that you become trapped in Reich's scenario. His plot requires that the leaders of the "organizational society" accept his picture of them and set their faces against all that is best in the emergent American culture. If that happens, many of the young who have been told that their aspirations can be pursued only *against* the system will see a confirmation.

There is, indeed, a chance for a "greening of America," a new growth of the spirit. The nation has been pregnant with it for years. What can abort or deform it is acceptance of the manipulators' myth that the present must be trampled upon before the future can be born.

# The illusion of consciousness III

robert eisner

**Robert Eisner, Professor of Economics, Northwestern University, strikes at a few of the fundamental weaknesses of Reich's Consciousness III concepts in the following article.**

"Consciousness III," according to Yale law professor Charles A. Reich, "is deeply suspicious of logic, rationality, analysis, and principles." If you have arrived at Consciousness III, you will like this book.

Reich constructs three categories of "consciousness," or "whole perception of reality," on which the progress and survival of society depend. Consciousness I is the free-enterprise "traditional outlook of the American farmer, small businessman, and worker who is trying to get ahead. . . . II represents the values of an organizational society. . . . III is the new generation." Our current "corporate state" (a phrase borrowed from John Kenneth Galbraith's much more finely etched *New Industrial State*) is somehow trapped between the anachronistic Consciousness I and the conformist Consciousness II. We thus have "depersonalization" and "repression," and are threatened with the destruction of "all meaning and all life."

It strikes me that Consciousness I, II, and III represent about the extent of Reich's use of numbers; *The Greening of America* is stronger on purple prose than on quantitative analysis. One could immediately smell success in this opus (excerpted in *The New Yorker* and widely commented on prior to publication), not because it is intellectually rigorous but because it is just the opposite. Like *Easy Rider*, it is easy on the mind and carries a rich appeal to the senses. Consciousness II will gain masochistic pleasure from reading a rundown of its sins, and both Consciousness II and III will derive delight and titillation from Reich's description of the new life-style.

But the problems Reich takes as his departure points are terrifyingly real. We do have poverty in the midst of plenty. We do have a heritage of exploitation of our black minority. We do have violence in our schools, which both literally and spiritually destroys children, and violence in our cities. We do choke in our own smoke and destroy our own land, even while our youth are being forced to destroy another land in a dirty war we seem to lack the collective ability to stop. Above

Robert Eisner, Review of *The Greening of America* by Charles A. Reich, *Saturday Review*, December 5, 1970, pp. 24–26. Copyright 1970 Saturday Review, Inc.

all, we are frustrated in our quest for individuality in a world of inter-dependence. We are challenged on the meaning and value of freedom of choice when the values that determine our choices are themselves determined by forces that seem to be out of our control. All these are serious, weighty issues, and failure to resolve them may lead to the destruction of our society—although that is a possibility to which a cautious social scientist might not wish to assign a high probability. But Reich's discussion of these issues and what to do about them employs none of the professional tools of any social science.

Reich makes short shrift of Consciousness I. It "was appropriate to the nineteenth-century society of small towns, face-to-face relationships, and individual economic enterprise. . . . its reality centered on the truth of individual effort." It cherishes a nostalgic belief that that government is best which governs least, and one may presume it still contributes much to the mass support of the Republican Party, if not to its power structure.

Despite our lingering faith in the virtue of individual effort, self-discipline, and even competition, most readers of this review—along with the reviewer—are likely to be found in the admittedly diverse general area of Reich's Consciousness II, which includes "businessmen (new type), liberal intellectuals, the educated professionals and technicians, middle-class suburbanites, labor union leaders, Gene McCarthy supporters, blue-collar workers with newly purchased homes, old-line leftists, and members of the Communist Party, U.S.A. Classic examples of Consciousness II are the Kennedys and the editorial page of *The New York Times*." The one characteristic we Consciousness II types all share, according to Reich, "is the insistence on being competent and knowledgeable."

We may be carried along by some of Reich's criticisms of life under the corporate state, of the pressure for conformity, the toadying, the cant, the materialism, the conscienceless tie-in with the military and war. His jibes at advertising may be welcome. Suggestions that much work is routine and repetitive and boring will be received with sympathy. But what does it mean to say that man now lives a "robot life"? How seriously can we treat assertions that "the state has undertaken to define, within rather strict limits, the life-style of its citizens with respect to sex life, culture, and consciousness, and political thought and activity. . . . Sex life shall consist of a monogamous marriage. . . . Cultural life shall include anything produced and prescribed by the machine. . . . Political life shall be limited to loyalty to the Corporate State. . . ."?

Perhaps we should excuse the rhetoric. There are certainly elements of truth, if not of novelty, in those statements. Reich is objecting, however, not to specific evils but to the whole system, and he claims that elimination of the evils calls for rebelling against the system's regimentation and rejecting its life-style at every turn.

In the schools we have a mindless violence to the spirit, which must be ended. Youth must no longer be "prolonged by studying, so that young, energetic, and restless bodies are confined to chairs in lecture halls and libraries, memorizing facts, writing papers and cramming for exams. . . ." There must be no slavish devotion to a career, to a job where one does what the boss or the organization expects. One must be free to work or not as one pleases, to surf, or ski, or ride a motorcycle, or live in a commune, to enjoy sex when one wishes and with whom one wishes however one wishes. And one must be allowed mind-expanding, sense-accentuating drugs.

This is the life-style of Consciousness III. Its freedom, its sensuousness, its power are all expressed, according to Reich, in the clothes and music of youth. The faded jeans, worn over and over until every body crease shows, bring out individuality, since different bodies have different shapes and creases. They also permit freedom: If one decides to stop work and go for a motorcycle ride one is prepared; the same blue jeans can serve all purposes. And the new music "expresses the whole range of the new generation's experiences and feelings." In its richness and variety and loudness, in its profanity and irreverence, and in its shared enjoyment by performers and audiences who are jointly and mutually stoned by drugs, it somehow exemplifies all that is natural, free, sensuous and alive—as "when Janis Joplin, a white girl, sang 'Ball and Chain' to a pulsing communal audience of middle-class young white people."

It is striking how pot and psychedelic drugs recur as a vital element of Consciousness III, bracketed with other things one might think could stand by themselves. Thus Reich writes: "If a Consciousness II person, old or young, is asked whether he wants to see a far-out film, try a new drug, or spend a week living in a nature-food commune, he feels uncomfortable and refuses. . . ." Reactions to such varied propositions would probably be quite different. But perhaps the essential unity in Reich's schema is that somehow everything depends on the rejection of reason, the systematic thought-processes that man has slowly and painfully acquired in his rise from the apes. "It might take a Consciousness II person twenty years of reading radical literature to 'know' that law is a tool of oppression: the young drug user just plain 'knows' it." One might expect that the drug user knows because he is "oppressed," but Reich insists that "All of the various efforts of the new generation to increase awareness [including the use of drugs] combine to produce a remarkable phenomenon: the Consciousness III person, no matter how young and inexperienced he may be, seems to possess an extraordinary 'new knowledge.'" The author ascribes this to "the repeal of pretense and absurdity." I wonder.

On the political level, Reich's attitude comprises a jumble of insights and suicidal impulses. He perceives the psychic injury suffered by blue-collar workers, which has made them prey to the George Wallaces of the land, but it is not clear that he comprehends the economic realities of their lives, both good and bad. He warns of the folly of guerrilla tactics that serve not to convert but to harden reaction and prejudice. But he finds that "Burning draft cards is an effective and pointed commentary on the war."

Yet Reich rejects "both the liberal and the SDS theories of how to bring about change in America." Even a successful liberal effort at mass organizing, politics and law "would end as the New Deal ended, with reforms that proved illusory," while radical "believers in class struggle would engage in a hopeless head-on fight against a machine that could work for them instead. . . ." The solution, according to Reich, is a "revolution by consciousness." The spontaneity, the lack of discipline, the anarchy of Consciousness III youth can and will be spread through the entire population. As we all refuse to buy what we are told to buy, to work when and at what we are told to work, the whole corporate state with its acquisitiveness and repression will just wither away. It is that simple.

In elementary economics courses we sometimes take as our text the fallacy of composition: the incorrect deduction that what is true for individual parts is also true for the whole. It is all very well for the young sons and daughters of affluence to cop out of the competitive race. If they do it briefly, they can return to their places in the establishment, as distrustful blacks and hostile white hard-hats are aware. And even if they do it longer they will have sacrificed only themselves. But what if Reich's Consciousness III were to sweep the nation? What if everyone worked as he pleased and when he pleased? Who would make the blue jeans and the motorcycles and the sleeping bags and the electric guitars and the pills?

Reich may think he has an easy answer. We are, he says, producing too much now anyway. Free from the tyranny of the corporate state and its advertising, we could produce only to satisfy "real need." We would all "put great effort into any work that is worthwhile." And so Reich slips over the central issues of our society, and of any society. What are real needs? What work is worthwhile? What should be the mechanism for deciding, for choosing? The thoughtful members of Reich's Consciousness I have an answer, that in its ideal form has a logical consistency and a record of achievement, which, with all its imperfections, cannot properly be dismissed out of hand. A world of individual freedom, subject to the rules of competitive markets, can in many situations give us most of what we want and what we as individuals think we "really need." A kind of social optimum with desirable efficiency can indeed result if how much we can get depends in large part on how hard we work, on how we choose to allocate our time and effort.

If Reich better understood the meaning of a market economy he might better reconcile the contradictions and confusions in his mind between the "depersonalization" he identifies with the corporate state and the striving for freedom and equality. For, whatever the existing inequality before the law, the impersonality of markets can be equalizing and liberating. Business is business and a dollar is a dollar, as blacks have learned from successful bus boycotts and from their ability to buy what they wanted when they had the money, and as some victims of McCarthyism learned in the Fifties when they found that government blacklists did not prevent them from selling their talents to less political and more profit-minded employers.

Reich is apparently anxious to appear Marxist, but he has stood Marx on his head. Marx never called for "a community bound together by moral-esthetic standards such as prevailed before the Industrial Revolution." Rather, he paid eloquent tribute to capitalism's development of the "colossal productive forces" that had slumbered in the lap of social labor." The utopia of plenty for all would follow upon the highest achievement of social labor and a scientifically based and guided technology, not upon the destruction of social labor and the abandonment of social rules and reason. And it would come by tackling not the superstructure of life-style but the organization and control of the means of production.

The author does reveal a certain inner logic to the "youth rebellion" which may have escaped those of us who are not part of it. And it would be easy to acquiesce in many of Reich's strictures against contemporary society. In the pleasant glow of communal joints—or in the light of old-fashioned drinks around the fireplace—we might excuse or pass over much of his rhetoric. Most of us, like Reich, loved Holden Caulfield, and take heart and sustenance from the vigor and freedom and searching of his successors almost a generation later. There is much in the world to question, much to change, much to construct. But there is illusion and an invitation to tragedy, hard to excuse in a mature adult, in Reich's counsel, that the answer is to be found by imitating Holden—or Janis Joplin.

# The fuzzing
of america

## samuel mc cracken

Samuel McCracken, Assistant Professor of Literature and Humanities at Reed College, is highly critical of Charles Reich's *The Greening of America*.

The fellowship of authors enrolls any number whose influence has been as profound as their silliness: the names of Mrs. Stowe, Gobineau, and Norman Angell come readily to mind. To this honorable company must now, I suspect, be added the name of Charles A. Reich, Professor of Law at Yale University, pop-culture hero, and author of *The Greening of America: How the Youth Revolution is Trying to Make America Livable*. Despite a title well calculated to compete in what must be an increasingly satiated ecological marketplace, Reich deals only tangentially with considerations of environment. His main thesis, expounded with a dogged repetitiousness which the linear mind finds wracking is, briefly:

> *The New Industrial State is dreadful, and its subjects exist at three distinct levels of consciousness: I, which reads the American Legion Magazine, II (Commentary) and III (Rolling Stone, if it reads). Consciousness III, as near to moral perfection as a consciousness can get, is going to make the revolution, not through political action, but through a process of conversion or infection.*

This argument lies jellied in an aspic compounded of about equal parts of vulgarized Marx, uncritical admiration for just about every behavioral fad of the times, and nerveless intellectual irresponsibility stiffened by a compulsive inconsistency which must be experienced to be believed, the whole dish sauced with a prose style sometimes more appropriate to the sort of ad Kent cigarettes have lately been beaming at the Now Generation.

All of which may suggest that what follows can do no more than flog a freaked-out horse; but Reich's academic credentials, the extraordinary play he and his book have been getting (a great deal of *New York Times* ink, virtually a whole recent issue of the *New Yorker*) and his increasing status as thaumaturge to a generation, all conspire to make it likely that he will be influential.

Were it otherwise, I could stint myself at this point, and forego any

Samuel McCracken, "The Fuzzing of America," *Change*, 8 (January–February 1971), 60–64.

consideration of the work's relevance to higher education.  For Consciousness III, as limned by Reich, clearly neither wants nor needs higher education.  It may, possibly, want to read the new book Reich has recently promised, setting forth a program of action, and which will doubtless serve as a platform now that 18-year-olds have the national vote.  But of the sort of sterile "knowledge" the academy can offer, there will be no need, and knowledgeable academics will lay in a supply of bell-bottoms and T-shirts before the paychecks stop.

Intellectually *The Greening of America* resembles nothing so much as your typical educationist tractate: a stock of truism accepted these fifty years or more (in the present case, an analysis of the frontier mind with its robber-baron consequents, and of liberalism and its trust in reason and institutional safeguard), spiced with trivia categorized into apotheosis (here, such notions as the Substitution Phenomenon—when one thing is substituted for another, you call it the Substitution Phenomenon).  While Reich's account of Consciousness III, purporting as it does to describe the recent phenomena, is perforce less unoriginal, even here his catalog of symptoms (not his celebration thereof) will hardly be news to anyone who has taught in college these past few years.

The most striking quality of the book is a pervading inconsistence interpretable either as a symptom of intellectual confusion on the order of Alfred Rosenberg's *The Myth of the Twentieth Century*, or as the tactic of a clever lawyer defending a generation before a jury with a very short memory.

The Reichian conception of nature and the natural suggests the first interpretation: it very nearly defies formulation.  While it does too much justice to read the words as simplified and vulgarized Wordsworthism, that is pretty clearly the tune.  When Reich says that III clothes itself in green, brown and blue because those are nature's colors, the narrow-minded may claim that the spectrum is as much a part of nature as grass, dirt and sky, the rainbow, like these elements, being discoverable in Central Park (Nature's *pied-à-terre* when she leaves New Haven Green for a weekend), and that those willing to include gems, flowers and fish as part of God's grandeur may well find nature's palette more extended than III's.  But this is to respond to the words; the tune sings out that natural colors are the ones one finds lying about *in situ*, artificial ones those distributed by the obscene intervention of man and his technology.

Then there is peanut butter.  (By his constant references to peanut butter, Reich suggests that he considers it central to the present crisis.)  The peanut butter of nature is unhomogenized, and appears to be extracted from the earth's breast by some inhuman and nontechnological means.  Artificial peanut butter is homogenized peanut butter, the cruelest imposition of the Corporate State upon the young save pre-mixed peanut-butter-and-jelly.

Wood is natural; plastic and metal are artificial, also sterile. Plastic and metal, as is well known, do not naturally exist on earth at all, were first discovered by spectographic analysis of Alpha Centauri B, and have been produced on earth since 1914 by the smelting of meteorites. If the Youth Revolution integrates this notion with a decent ecological respect for trees, and then tries to design a chair, it is likely to be known as the Standing Generation.

The pattern is not very original: whatever one likes—on other grounds—and one may plausibly call natural, one calls natural; whatever one dislikes—on other grounds—and one may plausibly call artificial, one calls artificial. Whatever exists, one may plausibly call natural; whatever man makes, artificial. The paradigm accommodates with similar results such pairs as living and sterile, free and repressive, *und so weiter*.

Beyond the mushiness of Reich's definition lies a more elemental, grander confusion, pregnant with an entirely distressing concept of man. Implicit in any pejorative use of the term *artificial* (meaning that which is generally man-made, as opposed to the merely ersatz, say margarine as artificial butter), is the acceptance of man as a creature alienated from nature, not by some institutional defect, but simply by his existence as man. Nor is this notion, of man the sole vilificator of otherwise pleasing prospects, entirely original. And it requires its holders to have rather stricter standards for man than for nature, blaming him for the bomb, excusing her of such peccadilloes as anthrax and the typhoon. Reich is hardly the first person to accommodate these contradictory attitudes within one personality; but his hidden—perhaps unperceived—assumption of human nature requires a view of it bizarrely incompatible with his own celebration of that nature.

Like a recent free-school innovator whose seat was to be in the wilds of British Columbia, because "learning is impossible in an artificial, man-centered environment," Reich is a humanist at odds with humanity. Here on a larger scale terms of art replace reason: whatever human behavior one approves, is human; whatever one disapproves, in-human. It is a dangerous habit of thought: we will never exorcise the demon within by assuming it to be without. The surest way to avoid confronting the enemy is to mistake his location.

There are many inconsistencies perhaps attributable to Reich's desire to make a case for his subjects. I can do no more than select from beauties stretching out to the edges of the galaxy. His ordering of the relations among II, III and technology is perhaps most striking.

The Reichian view of nature, like so much of the present commune movement, is a sort of qualified call to primitivism. The answering of the call is charged with contradictions quite sufficient to blow it to atoms. For Reich cheerily ignores the profoundly parasitic quality of III's way of life. Now, while much of III currently exists on the labor of II, there is no compelling theoretical reason why this should be so. Surely, some portion of III could ignore all of II's technology and scratch out a subsistence life as bronze-age farmers. But there is pretty clearly a limit to the proportion of the present population of this land which even *it* could support at bronze-age levels of efficiency, which would proscribe such sophistications as tractors, requiring the existence of an elaborate technology, and the technicians to operate it. Again, if III suffers an inflamed appendix and wishes to avoid peritonitis—an end having nothing but naturalness in its favor—he may well wish for surgery. But anything resembling modern medicine requires not only the theoretical existence of a technology, but a supply of type I or II rationalists who wish to be doctors, and who may well wish to lead type I or II lives.

If III's very existence—unless he will settle for the lifespan current in the fifteenth century—requires that he preserve a support corps of I and II people on which to batten, his very culture is technologically even more parasitic. For his music exists at an amplitude obtainable only by means electronic or possibly chemical (but recent experimentation suggests that the problems inherent in modulating dynamite have yet to be overcome). I will refrain from estimating the relative naturalness of Segovia's guitar as opposed to III's electric-cum-fuzzbox model, but certain it is that if III is to have his 200-watt amplifier, II will have to build it for him.

The relationship among III, II and technology is no less hazy when we come to clothes. III's fondness for jeans and T-shirts shows it has learned to live with mass production, while II neurotically sees values in hand tailoring. I will leave it to the reader to work out which attitude is the more natural.

And finally, the production of Professor Reich's preferred consciousness expander, LSD, including the making of the requisite centrifuge, is not likely to become a cottage industry. (It might be said that quite the nastiest thing in *The Greening of America* is Reich's unqualified endorsement of LSD. He apparently has never seen anyone in the throes of a bad trip. It is reading such passages in Reich that tempts one to cry out, Charlie! The whole world is watching!)

The rejection of technology must then be for III a partial one. And only a small and favored minority can exercise such an option. The semiprimitivism Reich exalts is possible for III only because I and II are around to operate the part of the technology on which III can groove. Nice work if III can get it, but hardly a program for revolution.

The Reichian esthetic is as inconsistent.  For Reich, the principal motif of Corporate State esthetic is neon, considered as at all times irremediably ugly; but Dayglo—neon in a bottle—is one of the zippy adornments of Ken Kesey's bus.  Loud noise is insufferable when produced by a 747 (it is, of course) but delightful coming out of a rock band.  Here, as everywhere, technology is intrinsically evil when used by II, merely a proof of superiority when used by III.

The cosmic inconsistency, however, involves Reich's view of reality. He seems pretty clear that reality exists only in consciousness, surely a view with respectable antecedents.  But one wonders what Bishop Berkeley would have made of Reich's notion that the consciousness— hence reality—can be chemically restored (marijuana) or expanded (LSD).  The view seems in sharp variance with Reich's iterated rejection of technological substitutions.  It is hard to see why a convinced naturist like Reich strains at the gnat of ersatz peanut butter while swallowing the camel of an ersatz reality, especially since in this case the camel contains the gnat.  He shares this problem with III in general (it is never clear, by the way, whether he thinks of himself as II, III, or perhaps a sort of universal-donor IV), considering the ease with which III harmonizes his ecological concerns and partisanship of organically grown food with his pollution of his own bloodstream with synthesized LSD.  But then III doesn't write books about it.

While it is tempting to assign such fuzziness to mere cynical advocacy, that is an unlikely motivation to ascribe to a philosopher of the law.  At the heart of all this intellectual confusion lies an explicit rejection of the primacy of reason, after which, of course, anything goes. While sometimes the assault on rationality appears to derive simply from a bad case of the sophomore sillies, as when III's distrust of reason is justified by its having seen some bad examples of reason used to justify the Vietnam war (just as its having seen faulty addition must lead it to mistrust mathematics), Reich's most explicit defection from rationality is a good deal worse than silly.  When Nelson Rockefeller said that he had been "heartened" by his reception in Latin America, III

"knew" that he had in fact been practically run out of each country and survived only by virtue of forceful repression of protest by each regime.  III does not "know" the facts, but [he] still "knows" the truth that seems hidden from others. . . . One of the ways to describe this "new knowledge" is to say that it is capable of ignoring categories.  We are all limited in our thinking by artificially drawn lines; we cannot get beyond the idea that a university is "private property" or that prose is different from poetry.  When the category-barriers are removed, "new" relationships are seen. But the "new knowledge" is more than this; it is as if everything, from political affairs to esthetics, were seen with new eyes; the young people of Consciousness ĮII see effortlessly what is phony or dishonest in politics, or what is ugly and meretricious in architecture and city planning, whereas an older person has to go through years of education to make himself equally aware.  It might take a Consciousness II person twenty years of reading radical literature to "know" that law is a tool of oppression; the young drug user just plain "knows" it.  Nothing is more difficult for an older person to believe in than this "new knowledge," but it is such a striking phenomenon, extending even to longhaired California teen-agers hitch-hiking their way to the beach, whose experience with political thinking or newspaper reading is limited, that it must be taken seriously.

This preposterous nonsense is typical of what passes for thought in the book.  In the first anecdote, the simple truth that ignorant prejudice is occasionally correct is inflated into the notion of "new knowledge."  The supporting examples say merely that III's biases (how often arrived at with the help of Reich and others like him?) are also Reich's.  Doubtless, Reich and his subjects "know" that the sort of analysis to which I have been subjecting his argument is irrelevant to the higher truth, their "knowledge" that my discussion is meretricious and phony.  The sad truth is that much of the book is supportable only by some such notion of invincible ignorance directed by a pipeline to the Infinite.  It used to be (paraphrasing Brutus Jones) that when you reasoned like Reich, they questioned your professional qualifications; now, they publish you in the *New Yorker* and at Random House.  Reich's apparent unwillingness to talk to II about III in any mutually acceptable frame of reference puts him in the position of the cancer quack who refuses to have his nostrum tested by Food and Drug.  You doubt whether such an author really wants to talk to you.

While the author's flight from reason explains the defects of the book I have been discussing, it does more.  It allows Reich effortlessly to be extraordinarily silly, and finally to effortlessly be caught up in a malicious snobbery which is the least pleasant aspect of the book.  Of the silliness, I will cite three examples:

Bell bottoms have to be worn to be understood.  They express the body, as jeans do, but they say much more.  They give the ankles a special freedom as if to invite dancing right on the street.  They bring back dance into our sober lives.  A touch football game, if the players are wearing bell bottoms, is like a folk dance or a ballet.  Bell bottoms, on girls or boys, are happy and comic.  No one can take himself entirely seriously in bell bottoms.  Imagine a Consciousness II university professor, or even a college athlete, in bell bottoms, and all his pretensions become funny; he has to laugh at himself.

When, in the fall of 1969, the courtyard of the Yale Law School, that Gothic citadel of the elite, became for a few weeks the site of a commune, with tents, sleeping bags, and outdoor cooking, who could any longer doubt that the clearing wind was blowing?

What have we all lost?  What aspects of the human experience are either missing altogether from our lives or present only in feeble imitation of their real quality?  Let us take our list off the yellow pad where it was jotted down one fine morning in early summer.

[What is lost is a very long list, voracious of space if not time.  I cite the entries themselves in more compact form, omitting the glosses Reich supplies for a few of the entries. . . .]

Adventure, travel, sex, nature, physical activity, clothes, morality, bravery, worship, magic and mystery, awe, wonder, reverence, fear, dread, awareness of death, spontaneity, romance, dance, play, ceremony and ritual, performing for others, creativity, imagination, mind-expanding drugs, music as a part of daily life, multimedia experiences, alternations of time, seasons, growth, learning, change, harmony, inner life, responding to own needs, own special excellence, wholeness, sensuality, new feelings, expanded consciousness, new environments, creating an environment, conflict, disorder, suffering, pain, challenge, transcendence, myth making and telling, literature, art, theatre, films, bare feet, aesthetic enjoyment of food, new ways of thinking, nonrational thoughts [surely not!], new ideas, ability to listen to others, people: perceiving them nonverbally, seeing the uniqueness of each one, creativity in relationships, exchanging experiences, exchanging feelings, being vulnerable with them, friendship, affection, community, solidarity, brotherhood, liberation [oh, wow!] [SMcC].

A hostile critic who is a confirmed parodist is quite unable to come up with an additional entry for that list, the presence of which would be clearly mocking.  Putty?  Dental Floss?  The Eschaton?  Double-Entry Bookkeeping?  The Black Death?  Peanut Butter?  If all items on the list really *are* missing from Reich's existence, then one can but express one's heartfelt sympathy and trust that he found the writing of his book therapeutic.

As to the silliness, further anatomy would only spoil the delicate natural beauty; but of the assumptions behind that list of losses, and behind Reich's view elsewhere of Consciousness I and II, something needs to be said.  In his opinion all enjoyments but his enjoyments are an imposition of the Corporate State.  Secretaries take up skiing not because they really like it, even though they may *think* they like it, but because the State wants them to.  If they really wanted to enjoy themselves, they would take up snowshoeing.  He provides an effective picture of a civilized young couple and their entertaining habits, then tells us that the conversation at their dinner parties is sterile.  They can't be enjoying themselves.  This unwillingness to imagine that anyone can have fun except by joining Reich, by donning bell bottoms and smoking dope, the explicit charge that such qualities and entities as affection, friendship, art, literature, films and new ideas are either missing entirely or present in feeble imitations in the lives of everyone but himself and his epigones, betrays in its smug assertion of superiority a bigotry of the order one normally associates with nineteenth-century America, that is, with Consciousness I. If Reich really feels so desperate a need to believe himself in a small class possessing the sole key to truth and joy, that's his problem. But one ought to pity a man whose experience and interpretation has led him to believe that just about everyone else is neurotic and sterile. It is very nearly pathetic that he would preface his book with the epigraph, "Come on people now/Smile on your brother/Everybody get together/Try to love one another right now."

It is, I suppose, reasonably clear that I think the book is nine-tenths sheer fudge. And yet, there is that fudgeless tenth, which if not exactly sheer genius, does talk about reality. For Reich is not a pure fantasist: as anyone who has been around college campuses the past seven years can testify, something has been happening to the youthful intellect, something of critical importance to higher education.

The symptoms are familiar enough: the growing and uncritical admiration for and acceptance of the esoteric and the occult, indications of breakdown in critical abilities, explicit rejections of rationality in politics. The I-Ching becomes a best-seller; colleges admit witchcraft and astrology to the para-curriculum (a recent Esalen Institute brochure suggests the degree to which any nonsense is now called a *science*); if interest in Zen wanes, there is the rise of Transcendental Meditation and the lunacies of the Hare Krishna cult. (Chanting it raises you to the highest level of consciousness and effects union with the godhead.) Although Reich, on no very clear grounds, excludes radical activists from III, one can see analogous trends in this group. Quite apart from the resort to violence, there is an increasing tendency to believe in such oddities as *radical* truth and *social* logic, in which the ground rules are distinctly non-Aristotelian; further, a belief, almost always implicit, occasionally explicitly stated, in rationality as just one more tool of the military-industrial complex.

These are the spectacular manifestations. Some of the less visible ones are no less striking. Ten years ago, the students of Reed College largely designed a form of community governance, marked by its almost Byzantine structures, for the embodiment of liberal democracy in academe. Until fairly recently, they worked to operate the machinery with a responsible citizenship one should only find in the outside world. Today the machinery creaks badly, battered by the assault of a significant fraction whose political ideas, if any, are anarchistic, and who insist in believing the community government (which would never hurt a fly) is a fascist dictatorship.  The elected Senate is always being referred to as a "self-appointed" body.  Belief in anarchy can hardly in itself be seen as a sign of irrationality; belief in an anarchy simply considered as doing one's thing can hardly be seen as anything else.  To these students, the notion that personal freedom stops when it violates someone else's same-order freedom comes as a novelty, and a foolish one at that.  Last year the campus was briefly terrorized by an armed exhibitionist.  Some students objected to doing anything to discourage his visits on the grounds that he had a neat life-style.  Others urged their fellows holding an assailant for the police to let him go on the grounds that the pigs would just hassle him.

When a year ago this fraction boycotted the college by refusing to pay tuition, and then held a series of meetings to find out for what it was boycotting, regular attendance became painful for the older observer.  Painful, to be sure, as a confrontation with several hundred very unhappy people who were rejecting everything one believed in, but painful *also* because of the pain they appeared to experience in putting the simplest notion into words, and because of the great difficulty being experienced by these people so convinced they were *together* in mediating their differences in detail.  And painful finally because of their conviction that their debates would prove to any disinterested observer their fitness to legislate academic policy.  While I become more and more dubious of the constant assertion that the most malcontent students are the brightest, there is no doubt that the students in question had all the credentials of very considerable intelligence.

Although many of these students exhibited some of the manifestations of Consciousness III (it must be said that no human being, thank heaven, combines the virtues and vices of Reich's construct, as he would admit), the notable quality in common was unreasonable expectation.  That is, expectation unfulfillable in not only a small liberal arts college, but perhaps in any human institution whatever.  Perhaps our catalogs should bear a disclaimer of liability reading something like this: "NOTE: We do not claim that we will make you wise or happy." It would probably be reasonable to include a further disclaimer that the institution has the slightest power—as an institution—to improve or otherwise change society.  The present crisis of higher education is certainly going to prove to the academy's permanent members the limits of its powers; they must convince the temporary members of their own conviction.

Beyond such a retrenchment of expectation, what can we do to accommodate students who bear some of the marks of Consciousness III?  (And what I suspect will be a common phenomenon after the paperback appearance of the *The Greening of America*—the "plastic"

III.   The book has high potential as sacred writ for a secular religion promising effortless salvation.)   Certainly, any attempt at intellectual accommodation will prove suicidal.   One can more easily imagine common ground for a treaty between Bob Hope and Abbie Hoffman.   The academy which tries to play Orpheus will learn—as evidence already begins to suggest—that latter-day Bacchantes have learned to leave the body intact while rending the consciousness.   Although it will be difficult to respond to the symptoms, we may be able to look beyond these manifestations and respond to causes.   Certainly there was never a better time for all colleges and universities to work toward a concept of academic citizenship in which students and faculty are joined together as citizens of the academic city-state.   The persuasive argument for leaving the control of curriculum in the hands of the faculty is of course from the notion of professional competence.   The more rigorously one accepts this notion, the more profoundly one must believe in the social empowerment of students, the realization for students of the personal freedom which their teachers themselves enjoy or aspire to.   What is distressing about life in too many academic communities —if one is a student—is that it is life in a community significantly more bureaucratic than that outside.   In such a context the attractions of Consciousness III must be very considerable.   While Reich's view of the Corporate State is badly distorted by dogmatic assertion and the rhetorical overkill which seems to be endemic in social critics these days, no one can doubt that beneath the perfervid varnish of rhetoric lies a genuinely ugly and depressing picture.   There is no reason why the academic state ought to resemble the corporate state at its worst: a program to make conditions of life on the campuses *livable* could benefit whatever is conscious, in whatever category.

But it is hard, on one's own side, to emulate Reich's cheerful assurance that everything is going to be all right, let alone to be cautiously and tough-mindedly hopeful that intelligence, courage and love will somehow see us through.   Whenever unduly afflicted by optimism, I find it corrective to recall that it is two hundred thousand years between ice ages, and that we are yet only fourteen thousand years from the end of the last one.   The appearance and the acceptance of a Charles A. Reich suggests that the interval between dark ages may be somewhat shorter.

# Chapter 2 Questions

1. Briefly describe Consciousness I, II, and III.  To what extent are they in conflict today in the United States?
2. Identify major allegations that Reich levels at today's socioeconomic system, and evaluate each one according to the following: completely untrue, partly true but distorted, partly true and important, and completely true and highly important.
3. Who, really, is opposed to Consciousness III in principle?  Is it not true, as pointed out in the *Fortune* excerpt, that "the main institutions of American society have been moving very rapidly in the direction of the values and patterns of Consciousness III"?
4. Is it possible, as the comments by Ways and Eisner highlight, that Consciousness III's aspirations are more likely to be aborted by the illusion that the present must be torn down before the future can be born than by the failure of the present system to adapt to changing needs of society?
5. Which of McCracken's major criticisms of Reich's views do you think are unfair and which do you think are fair?
6. Assuming that Reich's Consciousness III were to sweep the nation next year, what major economic, social, political, and philosophical consequences would you predict, good and bad?  (Ideas in the following two articles might also be helpful in answering this question.)

# Three Philosophical Perspectives on Dissent

**3**

# On the nature of man— who's right?

edward bloomberg

**Edward Bloomberg, Assistant Professor of French Literature, University of California Davis, strikes with high accuracy at a major fallacious assumption in the thinking of today's New Left, namely, that man is fundamentally good and we can, indeed, have a paradise here on earth.**

Individuals and societies that try to become angels end up as beasts, Blaise Pascal remarked back in the 17th century. In his day everyone understood what he meant, but today few people get the point, and least of all rebellious students and their sympathizers. To them it is transparently plain that man should insist on angelic conduct, not only from man but even more from the society he creates.

The gap between Pascal and today's counter-culture measures their diametrically opposed views of human nature. To 17th century thinkers, strongly influenced by both Christian thought and the study of history, it was self-evident that man was more evil than good. The ideologists supplying what philosophy underlies the counter-culture— Herbert Marcuse, Richard Lichtman, Richard Flacks, Carl Schorske, Charles Reich and Paul Goodman—hold an underlying belief that man is inherently good.

Many observers would find this idea so preposterous that they would hesitate to attribute it to anyone. Radical critiques and programs make no sense, however, on any other assumption. How, for example, could the removal of literally all constraints in our schools lead to a "beautiful order," as Paul Goodman contends, if man were not good? How could discontinuing law enforcement and punishment eliminate crime, abolishing national defense end war, or dropping competition eliminate poverty if human nature were less than perfect? How could violent action against a democratic and relatively fair society be sanctioned?

In order that man may be good, however, something else must be very evil, for evil plainly exists in the world and must be laid at somebody's door. "Man" is therefore divided up into the "people," who are saintly, and the protectors of a wicked society, who are relegated to subhuman status and called "pigs." In order to sanctify man, radicals

---

Edward Bloomberg, "On the Nature of Man—Who's Right?" *Wall Street Journal*, December 24, 1970. Extracted (with modifications) from *Student Violence*, by Edward Bloomberg, Public Affairs Press, Washington, D. C., 1970.

must, paradoxically, make ogres of the Establishment and all its adherents.

The thesis that man is a noble creature corrupted only by the society surrounding him is not new to history.   Most notably, it was enthusiastically propounded in the 18th century by Jean-Jacques Rousseau, intellectual godfather of the French Revolution.   There is little reason to suppose that its present incarnation, if left unchecked by Pascal's realism, would lead to happier results.

Although assumptions about man's moral make-up are now rarely discussed, they determine a person's political beliefs.   One would expect imperfect man to create imperfect institutions.   Indeed, if perfect, they would not suit him.   The idea of a perfect creature devising anything less than paradise on earth, however, is incongruous to the point of obscenity.

Plainly, if we assume that man is good, the relative merits of the American system are no cause for celebration.   Personal liberty and a high standard of living are to be expected:   Man deserves no less. Anything reprehensible in human conduct, on the other hand, must now be seen as a horrible perversion of the natural order.   Since man is saintly, he cannot be blamed.   All evil must, by elimination, be attributed to "society."

## PLACING THE BLAME

Racism, for example, has no roots in human nature, for racism is bad and man good.   It must be imputed, in America, to capitalism.   The same analysis applies to war.   Virtuous man has no taste for killing, yet we wage war.   It must be the fault of American imperialism.   Depersonalization, the feeling people often have that events are beyond them and that real human contact is absent from everyday life, can no longer be explained by human nature, for man is loving.   American materialism must somehow be responsible.

In brief, all those defects formerly tolerated because they were considered *human* shortcomings are, in fact, intolerable.   Our economic system, based specifically on human defects—self-interest, the competitive urge—is outlandish and immoral.   Angelic man works for the joys of producing for others and cooperating with his fellow workers.

Indeed, once it is presupposed that man is a marvel of righteousness, every American institution becomes monstrous.   Checks and balances in government, for example, are justified only by the idea that power corrupts.   Rousseauistic man, being incorruptible, has no need of petty, legalistic controls.   Power can simply be given to any group, preferably one calling itself "the people," and all will go well.

The very existence of laws indicates mistrust. If man is trustworthy, such suspicions are ignoble. He should be left, as the teeny cliché would have it, to "do his own thing." Situation ethics and the idea that whatever feels good is good are the logical consequences of such confidence. As for the notion of punishing certain acts, it can evoke only horror. It is repression of the individual's right to follow the quasi-divine dictates of his heart.

It would be futile to ask such idolizers of humanity to be reformists. Confronted with a society so depraved, they cannot be expected to suffer the delays of democratic process. One cannot, moreover, repair a machine built on principles which are altogether false. If man is good, America is rotten to the core. It must be transformed—perhaps even destroyed—immediately. Small wonder then that radical calls to revolution are vehement and self-righteous in tone. Given their basic presupposition, extremists are entitled to their fanaticism.

When violence breaks out in America, the usual response by authority—especially in the university—seems to be based on the same postulate. It is because many non-radicals have also come to accept the idea that man is good—and thus that radicals are good—that they attempt to quell riots with concessions. They assume that the perpetrators of violence—idealistic, fair-minded youths—will regard concessions as a sign of good will and abandon the use of force.

## DISARMAMENT AND CONCESSIONS

The same is true in international affairs. If men were good, we could unilaterally disarm, and our Chinese and Russian brothers would hasten to do the same. If, on the other hand, human nature is flawed, appeasement will produce new violence. Non-angelic man does whatever brings reward.

It follows that in order to decide what sort of society man is capable of maintaining, one must find out whether a reasonable case for human perfection can be made. As applied to the examples given here, the theory's weakness is immediately apparent. Concessions have worked neither with radical students nor foreign countries. Economic systems originally built on the principle of cooperation among saints have failed so miserably that even the Russians have accepted the necessity for incentives.

In the realm of government, the Rousseauistic view of human nature has shown itself weaker yet. Its direct result was the French Revolution (the incorruptible Robespierre knew Rousseau by heart), which left us, along with many elevated sentiments and gestures, virtual mountains of corpses. First recalcitrant nobles, then reform-minded nobles, then all monarchists, and finally even dissenting leftists were sent to the guillotine.

Since the new revolutionary state considered itself the embodiment of the "people," all real or imagined enemies of that state were declaring themselves against the people, and thus against goodness. No logical reason for sparing these heartless creatures could be found. Indeed, they were responsible for the unacceptable fact that despite the people's enthronement, a "beautiful order" had not come about. Since the people were angelic, moreover, no restraints were necessary. Their feelings of hatred toward subhumans were good feelings upon which they could act without experiencing any moral qualms. The military dictatorship of Napoleon was the result.

The Russian Revolution, built on the same premise, led to the same result. There are no contrary examples. No government founded on the "man is good" principle has ever ended otherwise than in tyranny and blood.

Does this mean that in order to preserve a free society we must adhere to the opposite view that man is totally evil? Certainly not. This school of thought has also produced dictatorship and easy slaughter (e.g., in Spain, Greece, and much of South America). It is only logical that it should, for if man is evil, he deserves nothing better. Punishment is what he needs.

Fortunately, a third view of man's moral value has come into favor in a few countries in the last 200 years. It is an obvious, inelegant, petty bourgeois solution: Man is that creature your grocer would tell you he is, a mixture of good and evil, reason and madness, love and hate.

Some people at every period in history have, of course, known this. But it is with Montesquieu, John Stuart Mill, and the American Founding Fathers, especially James Madison, that man's mixed moral nature is applied to questions of polity. The American Revolution and the American system of government are founded on it. They presuppose that man will be good only when watched by others, only when threat of punishment exists, only when he knows that he cannot have all the power to himself.

## THE MATTER OF CONTROLS

Governments, made up of men, must be equally subject to controls. On the other hand, man is capable of governing himself, provided he takes his weaknesses into account when fixing upon a form of government. He has a limited, but real, sense of fair play. Most important, he is worth the trouble it takes to organize a system which will not degenerate into despotism.

In economic matters, the applications are obvious. Self-interest plays a substantial, if not predominant, role in the life of man. He will work harder for himself than for the commonweal. The best spur to production is therefore the hope of realizing a profit. What is referred to as free enterprise is the result. If, however, man is allowed to pursue his self-interest without any rules, arbiters, or threats of punishment, he will destroy his competitors; hence the need for laws governing commerce and penalties for violators.

Man's conduct in economic, social, and political matters will be most beneficial to others when restrained by law. Law will be most beneficial when restrained by the vote. The vote must be kept honest by laws which permit people of all factions to supervise the casting and counting of ballots. If there were no goodness in man, this system would fail, for men judge at every step. If there were no evil, checks and balances would be superfluous. Judging from the historical results, the American idea of human nature would seem to be right.

Since the two extremes of depraved and angelic man have been avoided in America, the debate has traditionally been based on more subtle distinctions. Is man 40% evil and 60% good or vice versa? Conservatives see 60% evil, liberals see only 40%. This explains their respective positions on such matters as the size to which government can grow without becoming dangerous and the role of incentive in the economy. The tendency has usually been toward moderation and tolerance, for both sides have realized that they are dealing, not with black and white, but with shades of gray.

Now, however, this moderation seems to be disappearing from the American scene. When confronted with demands that America be perfect, the average enlightened citizen feels vaguely guilty. It no longer occurs to him that because societies are composed of human beings, they have fixed moral limits, well to this side of paradise. The argument from human nature, like so much of the hard thinking underpinning the American political system, has been forgotten.

Today's counter-culture does not really raise the questions its adherents profess, but it does reopen one side of a historical debate American society had previously considered pretty well settled—so well settled, indeed, that most Americans had forgotten it ever existed. At this juncture, plainly, man could do worse than to revive both sides of the debate over his own moral nature.

## QUESTIONS

1. Do you agree with Bloomberg that man is both good and evil, that the mix depends upon many circumstances, and that good will

predominate only when man is controlled by a system of laws?

2. What were the results of past revolutions and reform movements that were based on the Rousseauistic view that man is a noble creature corrupted only by the society surrounding him? Is history in this type of scenario likely to repeat itself?

3. What principles for dissent do you suggest for this day and age that are most likely to maximize orderly change with optimum benefit to society and the individuals in it?

# The politics of dissent · william t. gossett

**William T. Gossett is a distinguished lawyer who made the following commencement address when he was awarded an honorary degree from the University of Michigan. He presents four fundamental frames of reference that, if followed, will help to turn dissent from destruction to constructive directions.**

Mr. President, Regents, distinguished guests, officers and members of the faculty of the University, fellow alumni, students (especially those upon whom a University degree will be conferred today), ladies and gentlemen.

First, let me offer humble thanks for the honor that has been so graciously conferred upon me today by this great university, for which I have so much admiration and respect. To all who are receiving earned degrees today, I bring special words of sincere felicitation. Having met exacting academic requirements, you have been judged worthy of membership in the great world-wide community of educated men and women. For you, and your families and friends, this is, as it should be, a festive day.

This is the university whose students launched the "teach-in" to protest the Vietnam War; this is the university whose student initiative has wrought significant changes in the office of the Vice-president for student affairs; and this is the university that is Tom Hayden's alma mater. It seems entirely appropriate, therefore, that I should address you today. For who more fittingly symbolizes the spirit of protest and the rejection of the Establishment than the President of the American Bar Association?

I am, however, pleased to be here, and pleased to have the opportunity to suggest a frame of reference to the most committed, most intelligent, most idealistic college generation in this nation's history. In the past, all too many commencement speakers have urged their drowsy audiences to go out into the world armed with courage and determination and vigor. Those virtues no one need preach to you. Indeed, it is a measure of your character—the character of your generation to challenge the most fundamental premises about our institutions—that has made the conventional commencement speech itself thoroughly irrelevant.

Reprinted by permission from the November 1969 issue of the *Michigan Business Review*, published by the Graduate School of Business Administration, The University of Michigan.

The conventional commencement address assumes that you share the values of your elders, and attempts to make those values clear and sharp.   In the past three years, from Berkeley to Columbia, a committed minority, at least, of the students of America has flatly repudiated many of those values.

The conventional commencement address assumes that its listeners are at the start of a familiar, predictable journey, and attempts to indicate pitfalls and stepping stones to success.   Yet this year alone—a year of tumult and hope, of violence and tragedy—has shattered traditional assumptions, has made prophecy an occupation for the fool-hardy, and has shown that definitions of success are more sharply at odds than ever before.   Today there is little that we know and still less that is certain.

The conventional commencement address assumes that you and I share the same goals, the same faith, the same assumptions, the same language.   Yet even those limited assumptions may be dubious.   Were I to speak of patriotism, many of you might wonder suspiciously if I were endorsing a war that many of you find morally indefensible. Were I to speak of national obligations, many of you would ask if I was advocating submission to a draft law that you may regard as arbitrary and unjust.   If I were to speak of responsibility for the common good, you might ask what responsibility our great public and private institutions have ever recognized for the consequences of their acts: a polluted environment; an economy in which great affluence co-exists with marked deprivation; a concentration of power at all levels that too often shuts out the individual from power over his own destiny; a legal system that punishes possession of a single marijuana cigarette far more severely than producing a lethally unsafe product.

Although I personally respect most of the institutions that serve American life, the frame of reference that I suggest to you today does not assume anything about those institutions.   It does not assume that they have enriched our lives, promoted equality, expanded personal liberty, or acted justly.   It does not assume that we must adjust to those institutions or that they ought not come under the sharpest of attack.   It does not even assume that they must be saved—even those that pay the largest of fees to lawyers.

The frame of reference for which I speak is for the activist, the morally indignant, the young men and women who have stood up for the kind of world they want.   And it is—and this is most critical—a frame of reference for those who seek to build a strong sense of community, a sense of vital participation and mutual trust and purpose; for those who seek to build it amid what many of you find the impersonal and totalitarian modern world.   It is, fundamentally, a frame of reference for confrontation; not the confrontation of four-letter words and slogans, but the confrontation that can in fact bend and shape institutions to serve the best of human purposes.

The first element of this frame of reference is the awareness on my part that your conduct is at root a manifestation of patriotism and hope. Far too often we have seen those who equate dissent and disaffection with treason, thus branding as unfaithful to America all those who object to an established policy. That view is worse than nonsense; indeed, it is dangerous. For it cuts out the middle ground between the individual's absolute support or his absolute rejection of America. If the members of the committed younger generation ever begin believing that only unswerving acceptance of whatever this nation does qualifies as patriotic, they may well decide that there is no place for them here.

Far more acceptable is the wisdom of Senator Fulbright: "To criticize one's country," he says, "is to do it a service and pay it a compliment. It is a service because it may spur a country to do better than it is doing; it is a compliment because it evidences a belief that this country can do better than it is doing. . . . In a democracy, dissent is an act of faith." That viewpoint is vital to remember against the voice telling you that to dissent is to betray your country; vital to remember against the voice seeking to identify your dissent with a commitment against the United States. To speak according to conscience, consistently and firmly, is the best way for a man to honor the heritage of this nation.

The second element of the frame of reference that I suggest is tentativity. This is an attitude very much out of fashion these days, on campus, in politics; in the media, everywhere. I offer it, nonetheless; because if those who are most articulate and committed do not begin to embrace tentativity as a value, much of what we treasure in this country will be in serious jeopardy.

By "tentativity," I mean what Judge Learned Hand meant in his famous address on The Spirit of Liberty. He said, "The Spirit of Liberty is the spirit which is not too sure it is right." It is what Mr. Justice Holmes said in his brilliant defense of freedom of speech almost half a century ago:

> Persecution for the expression of opinions seems to me perfectly logical. If you have no doubt of your premises or your power and want a certain result with all your heart you . . . naturally sweep away all opposition. . . . But when men have realized that time has upset many fighting faiths, they may come to believe even more than they believe the very foundations of their own conduct that

the ultimate good desired is better reached by free trade in ideas. . . .

Holmes, of course, was speaking of the danger of a government enacting prejudices into iron laws limiting dissenting views. But that same danger is present when any group—majority or minority—assumes that it knows the truth to an absolute certainty. Let me be specific. When a group protests the war in Vietnam, or university affiliation with military research, by shutting down a campus or burning a professor's files, or by other acts of brute force, it has done precisely what every totalitarian government has done; it has assumed the absolute and final truth of its perspective, and has denied any possibility of error.

I ask you to think very carefully about this kind of attitude, not from *my* perspective, but from *yours*.

In the first place, that attitude of certainty is precisely the source of much of what you are attacking. Every opponent of the war in Vietnam, for example, whatever his other views, has found an essential source of this war in the tacit assumption by our government of omnipotence—the assumption that it knew—to the point of committing massive manpower and treasure—what was effective and desirable in a foreign nation. All the attacks made on the war—"the arrogance of power," "the abuse of power," "policeman of the world"—all have argued that a nation cannot arrogate to itself definitive decisions affecting thousands of lives half a world away.

What, then, is the basis behind forceful obstructionist protest if not this same moral absolutism, this same sense not simply of dissent, but of final resolution and ultimate wisdom? That is a strange and simplistic attitude for those so thoroughly convinced that their own government has erred in its belief in omnipotence.

Second, and even more dangerous, lack of tentativity leads almost inevitably to force. Just as Holmes said, "if you have no doubt of your premises or your power" it seems both acceptable and possible to break every rule. Instead of debate, one puts his opponent "up against the wall." Instead of protest, there is forcible resistance; for it is said, "the streets belong to the people." Instead of a peaceful demonstration against a law, there is arson and random destruction on a university campus.

At least you should recognize this: if you resort to force out of confidence in your own wisdom, do not expect others to tolerate your act. Herman Goering, Hitler's trusted lieutenant, once replied to a charge that the Nazis were too quick to use their guns against civilians. Said he, with supreme arrogance: "At least, we shoot!" If "the streets belong to the people," are you sure you know who "the people" are or what "the people" think? Do you mean the 10 million people who voted for George Wallace? Do you mean the people who beat up anti-war demonstrators? Do you mean that questions of right are now to be put aside, so that those with the greatest brute force can determine the limits of public debate?

That may not be what you mean; but it is all too likely to be the consequence of abandoning the sense of tentativity that restrains dogmatism and provides the basis for the fundamental right of dissent so vital to protect.

The third element of my frame of reference is the danger of self-defeat. One of the things that has most impressed me about the dimensions of current student disaffection is its rightful concern with style as well as substance. The theme of "it's the same as it always was" is a frequent description of student dissent; and it is quite inaccurate. There *is* a difference today—not simply in the demand for institutions to account for consequences, but in the insistence on personal integrity among the dissidents. They demand honesty. They seek not simply new answers but a new way of reaching those answers—a way that preserves the humanity and individuality of the participants. They have taken to heart this prophetic account of Lawrence of Arabia:

> We lived many lives in those whirling campaigns, never sparing ourselves any good or evil; yet when we had achieved, and the new world dawned, the old men came out again and took from us our victory and remade it in the likeness of the former world they knew. . . . We stammered that we had worked for a new heaven and a new earth, and they thanked us kindly and made their peace. When we are their age, no doubt we shall serve our children so.

The attempt to avoid that fate—the attempt to break the vicious cycle of retreat and betrayal—is the most ambitious goal that any dissidents have set. But this suggests, even more sharply than reasons of self-preservation, why resort to methods of upheaval and destruction cannot be accepted; they cannot be accepted because they impair the effectiveness of protest even among those who are receptive to change; because they become themselves the focal point for criticism and reaction, thus obscuring legitimate goals and confusing the basic issue.

More than that, what kind of community of love is going to spring from the ashes of violence and disruption? What kind of moral imperatives will remain intact if your conduct denies the essential humanity of your fellow man—even if he did support the Vietnam War? The ancient dictum that "every revolution carries with it the seeds of its own betrayal" is a reflection of this terrible danger that the search for a better way of life and a better society may be abandoned in the rush to tear down the fabric of what now exists. Anarchy is not creative.

That is why Paul Goodman, an eloquent and originative influence on this generation, said:

> I cannot accept the *putschist* use of violence. This is unacceptable, not because it is a fantasy—in a complex technology a few clever people can make a shambles—but because out of the shambles can only come the same bad world.

Put simply, the resort to violence—the tactic of the *putschist*, the acceptance of conspiracy against order—is not the mark of a movement calculated to bring community into modern life. It is the mark of a movement to destroy that possibility in the hearts of those who most deeply believe in it.

The fourth and last element in my frame of reference is that of possibility. I am not one who believes that the "generation gap" is the product of faulty communication. I think the message that many of the dissidents are proclaiming is coming in loud and clear. And at its root is the insistence that the key institutions in American life are corrupt and undemocratic; that they perpetuate injustice and require fundamental challenge. I said at the outset that the frame of reference I suggest does not assume that those beliefs are wrong. But it does insist that a distinction be made between *institutions* and *processes;* and it does insist that this generation have the intellectual honesty to admit the possibility for fundamental, substantial change of *institutions* through orderly and peaceful *processes.*

To ignore that proposition is, bluntly, to ignore our history. It ignores the political change from a government for and by white propertied males to a government fast approaching universal suffrage. It ignores the attempt to change national direction in mid-course and protect the rights of black men once seen only as chattel slaves. It ignores the rescue of labor from economic serfdom. It ignores the astonishing vitality of a nation that could tolerate—and then adjust its course in deference to—a massive protest in time of war by many of those called upon to fight and support that war.

It ignores the present as well. Today there are young lawyers across this country who are posing challenges to injustice far more vital than a frenzied outburst of violent emotion. They have successfully fought for the farmworkers of California against the federal and state governments. They have won battles against medieval welfare laws in New York. They are reaching into the roots of social legislation—into the highway and urban renewal programs, into health care programs; they are demanding that the rights of those minorities affected by those programs be fully protected in their frequently ignored constitutional dimensions. They are struggling against all the elements that have denied the poor equal protection of the law—in criminal cases, against consumer frauds, against slum landlords. They are, in effect, waging a continuing dissent against the *status quo* every single day in the courtrooms of America. And they are bending and reshaping our institutions without tearing them up by the roots, without ripping to shreds the fabric of American life.

Many others who are members of our professionalized institutions—the architects, the engineers, the doctors, the clergymen—are striving hard to assert the importance of humanistic values. I know that if those institutions do change—if we begin to move toward a more just and humane society—the work of those young men and women will be one of the most powerful of reasons why, in fact, we did overcome.

So I ask you, then, not to abandon the fight that many of you have begun, nor to temporize, nor to put aside that sense of indignation at conditions that in fact seem to demand your anger. I ask you instead to place on this indignation a sense of perspective: a perspective that retains love of this nation as an incentive to act; that remembers the need for the restraint that can prevent dogmatism; that avoids throwing away the moral imperatives of dissent; and that recognizes the possibility of prodding our structures effectively through peaceful protest.

What I suggest to you is in no sense a prescription for tranquility. Struggles for humanity are not won quietly, or with ease. The battlegrounds will be turbulent; the struggle will be difficult; the temptations both of resignation and of extremism will seem attractive. But you have in this decade begun what may be the greatest commitment to justice that this nation has ever seen. If the courage, the zeal and the determination that you have shown are fused with responsibility and wisdom, the future of this nation and its people is splendidly bright.

## QUESTIONS

1. Senator Fulbright has said that "to criticize one's country is to do it a service and pay it a compliment. It is a service because it may spur a country to do better than it is doing; it is a compliment because it evidences a belief that this country can do better than it is doing. . . ." Critically analyze and evaluate this statement. Do you agree or disagree with it? Why?
2. Mr. Gossett presents four fundamental frames of reference to guide the thinking of critics of our society. Define and evaluate each one.

# What is a social problem?

neil h. jacoby

Neil H. Jacoby is Professor of Business Economics and Policy, Graduate School of Management, University of California Los Angeles; and Associate, Center for the Study of Democratic Institutions. In the following article he explains that much of the so-called severity of many of our social problems is due to public expectations that soar beyond realities. Indeed, he says this discrepancy has created in the public mind serious crises at the very time the problem is being healed.

It is widely believed that the American nation confronts serious social problems. Many hold that our society is being shaken by a succession of overlapping and interrelated crises, including population growth and concentration, environmental pollution, poverty, crime, drugs, racial enmity, malnutrition, urban blight, and the war in Southeast Asia. Most of those in the New Left aver that unresolved problems are mounting in intensity. Changes in social institutions are occurring too slowly, they say, to accommodate changes in the goals, beliefs, and expectations of the public. Hence, the potentiality of a political revolution—of a sudden drastic restructuring of our social institutions—is rising. Indeed, extremist groups like the Weathermen and the Black Panthers, along with such mentors as Professor Herbert Marcuse, are actively fomenting revolution. They deliberately reject the course of working peacefully within the social system to shape its development along desired lines. The mounting level of violence in American society throughout the Sixties suggests that not a few persons have given credence to this line of thought.

It is therefore timely to examine the meaning of social problems. How do they arise? By what process do they escalate into crises? How can they be ameliorated or resolved?

A basic premise of our inquiry is that peaceful evolution is nearly always to be preferred to violent revolution as a path of social reform. Although revolution may in some circumstances be necessary, man's history shows that it is an extremely wasteful mode of social change. Revolution destroys physical and social capital, and leaves in its wake a large reservoir of wrongs and inequities that require generations to

This article will appear in a forthcoming book by Professor Jacoby tentatively entitled *The Contemporary Corporation: Social Critiques*. It will appear as part of Studies of the Modern Corporation, Columbia University Graduate School of Business Administration, and will be published by the Macmillan Company.

liquidate.  Evolutionary social change can avoid these setbacks.  It can steadily augment social justice and material well-being.  It can yield progress without hiatus.

## THE EXPECTATION-REALITY GAP

Let us consider the nature of a "social problem."  In January 1969 the distinguished Panel on Social Indicators appointed by the Secretary of Health, Education and Welfare reported that, by nearly all measures, the well-being of the American people had improved materially since World War II.  Yet it found that public disaffection had also risen markedly.  The reason was, it wisely observed, that *people's expectations had risen faster than reality could improve.*

The phenomenon noted by the Panel on Social Indicators was the same as that observed by de Toqueville in 18th-century France: "The evil which was suffered patiently as inevitable, seems unendurable as soon as the idea of escaping from it crosses men's minds.  All the abuses then removed call attention to those that remain, and they now appear more galling.  The evil, it is true, has become less, but sensibility to it has become more acute."  (See *Toward a Social Report*, U.S. Department of Health, Education and Welfare, Washington, 1969, pp. xi and xii.)

*A social problem, then, may be defined as a gap between society's expectations of social conditions and the present social realities.*  Social expectations are the set of demands and priorities held by the people of a society at a given time.  Social realities mean the set of laws, regulations, customs, and organizations, along with the appurtenant economic, political, and social processes, that prevail at a given time.

Social problems are created by public awareness of, or belief in, the existence of an expectation-reality gap.  They are basically psychological phenomena—ideas held in the minds of people—about the size of the disparity between what should be, and what is, in our society.  Social problems are not definable solely in physical or biological terms, such as so many calories of food intake per day, or so many square feet of housing per capita.  They must be defined in terms of the size of the expectation-reality gap.

One may illustrate the independence of a social problem from any particular social condition by considering the example of poverty.  Poverty is now perceived by Americans to be an important social problem in the United States, because in 1970 11 percent of the population had incomes under the official poverty level (about $3,500 per year for a family of four), whereas Americans generally believe that no one should live under the poverty line.  Poverty was not perceived to be an important social problem in 1947, although 27 percent of the population then lived under the poverty line by 1970 standards. Despite an astonishing gain in the real incomes of those in the lowest brackets, public expectations outraced realities. Hence the expectation-reality gap with respect to poverty is wider today than it was in 1947. The problem of poverty has become more serious at the same time that the incidence of poverty has been cut 60 percent and continues to decline!

## DYNAMICS OF THE EXPECTATION-REALITY GAP

Once the concept is grasped that a social problem is a gap between public expectations of social conditions and social realities, it becomes clear that our society, and especially its political leaders, must pay as much attention to the forces that determine public expectations as to those that shape social realities. They should seek to keep the gap at a tolerable size and avoid violent or disruptive social behavior.

The expectation-reality gap is, of course, a dynamic system that changes through time. Public expectations change as a consequence of the expanding size and concentration of the human population, of rising affluence, or of technological advances. Thus, the high priority now assigned to the problem of environmental pollution reflects a large elevation in the social expectations of clean air and water and other environmental amenities, by a richer and more crowded population. Public expectations are also shaped by the flow of information, words, and pictures that they receive from the mass media of communication —newspapers, magazines, radio, and television, of which more will be said later on. Expectations are likewise heavily influenced by publicly expressed views of political leaders. For example, President Eisenhower raised the nation's expectations for better highways with his support of the Interstate Highway System in the Fifties; President Johnson boosted public expectations of an end to poverty with his "War on Poverty" in the Sixties.

Changes in social expectations require responsive changes in social realities, if a rise in social tensions—that is, in revolutionary potential —is to be avoided. For example, racial tensions have risen in the United States partly because the rising social expectation of racial integration of the public school system, called for by the 1954 *Brown* decision of the U.S. Supreme Court, has not yet produced a commensurate shift in the racial structure of the educational system. As with the social problem of poverty, the realities of educational integration have improved, but have been outrun by the rise in public expectations.

Revolutionary potential—the degree of public frustration caused by a gap between expectations and realities—is also a function of time. It will rise as the time-lapse lengthens between a given expectation and responsive change in social institutions and processes.  The American Revolution of 1776 exploded when a sufficiently large number of colonials found that the gap between their long-reiterated demands for a larger voice in their own government and the intransigency of the British crown was no longer endurable.  Timely action by the British to delegate powers of self-government would have reduced the revolutionary potential, and even possibly avoided a political revolution.

There have been periods in American history when popular expectations of social improvement have been extremely low.  During the Great Depression of the Thirties, for example, the revolutionary potential was surprisingly weak.  Public expectations of social improvement had become so deflated by 1933 that only a small gap separated them from the grim social realities of those times.  President Franklin D. Roosevelt and his New Deal performed a magnificent act of political leadership in regenerating public expectations.

## MASS COMMUNICATIONS MEDIA AS AMPLIFIERS OF THE GAP

The mass media of communication, printed and electronic, play an important role in the creation and magnification of social problems.  They do this by increasing public awareness of gaps between social goals and current realities, and also by magnifying public perceptions of such gaps.  Today, millions of Americans who would have been oblivious to, or only remotely informed about, these conditions fifty years ago simultaneously read about and see on their television screens crime on the streets, slums in the cities, deprivation in the ghettos, smog in the air, and sewage in the water.  The mass media are frighteningly effective in widening public awareness of the chasms that separate man's expectations of peace, plenty, justice, and stability from the realities of the human condition.  Thus they create social problems where none had existed before; and they escalate minor problems into major crises.

If the mass media operated simply as *transmitters* of faithful printed and pictorial images of society as it is, one could not complain about their effect on the public's perception of reality or the size of the expectation-reality gap.  However, they are more than mere transmitters. They are *selectors* of the information and images presented to people. Because they thrive on the shocking, the extreme, the bizarre, they have little interest in conveying to their audiences the normal life or the quiet incremental progress of society.  "Man bites dog" is news; "dog bites man" is not.  The mass media tend to screen out those words and images that reveal normality, and to transmit those that show deprivation, injustice, suffering, and maladjustment, on the one hand; and those that depict wealth, extravagance, or conspicuous consumption, on the other hand. Thus they function as *magnifiers* or *amplifiers* of the expectation-reality gap that previously existed in the public's mind. Expectations of social improvement are elevated even higher; social realities are seen to be even worse than before.

Art Buchwald recently recounted in his syndicated column that George III had suppressed television in Britain during the latter 18th century, because TV pictures of British mercenaries suppressing colonial Americans were inciting the British public to a state of rebellion against its colonial policies. Buchwald used this imaginary analogy to propose that the U.S. government suppress all television coverage of the war in Southeast Asia! Despite its humorous intention, the proposal has a serious point.

A recent example of journalistic distortion was the statement by *The New York Times* and the *Washington Post* that "the police have killed 28 Black Panthers since January 1, 1968." This "news" statement was widely copied; and followed by editorial speculation that the police were conspiring to wipe out Black Panther leadership. The Negro community reacted in anger. In a carefully researched article in *The New Yorker* of February 13, 1971, Edward J. Epstein showed that the source of this inflammatory statement was Charles R. Garry, counsel for the Panther organization, and that it was both false and misleading. In fact, ten of the 28 Panthers had been killed by their own political opponents. A study of the other 18 deaths showed that in every case the Panthers were armed, threatened the police, and shot first. There was not a shred of evidence to support the conspiracy thesis.

If the mass media are a powerful instrument in the formation of public attitudes and expectations, it becomes vitally important that they present accurate and balanced word-and-picture images of events within their proper historical contexts. No one would suggest governmental censorship of information flows to the public. What is proposed is self-disciplined objectivity, so that the mass media will perform their function of accurate and objective transmission of information that can be the basis of rational and realistic public attitudes and expectations.

## POLITICAL AND ACADEMIC SYSTEMS AS AMPLIFIERS OF THE GAP

Our political system of representative democracy also tends to create or to expand social problems, by raising public expectations of social gains, and by exaggerating gaps between expectations and realities. Politicians generally do not challenge the validity of existing public expectations, or seek to reduce them to realizable levels.  The basic reason for their one-sided influence is clear enough.  It is in the professional interest of the politician to inflate rather than deflate unrealistic expectations.  Politicians are elected by "viewing with alarm" the empty records of their opponents in office; and by leading the voters to believe that the incumbent scoundrels have denied them the good things of life.  If only the electorate turns the rascals out, change will bring great improvements.  Of course, by the time the next election occurs, the roles of politicians in the two parties are often reversed, the "great society" still has not been achieved, and the people are more frustrated than ever!  The expectation-reality gap has widened.

Intellectuals are also traditional "viewers with alarm," because any other attitude would compromise their professional reputations as social critics.  They consider it a duty to decry gaps between the performance of the society and its potential.  Otherwise their colleagues would believe that they had sold out to the Establishment or had lost their critical faculties.  Given the strong propensity to hypercriticize in scholarly teaching and writing, and considering the vast enlargement of youth under academic influence in the higher educational system, it is no wonder that a rising fraction of the U.S. population has become alienated from society and its institutions.

## PUBLIC BODIES AND THE GAP ENLARGEMENT

Presidential Task Forces and Commissions and other public groups often generate or enlarge social problems by attention-getting public statements.  Although such bodies are supposed to provide calm and objective assessments of social problems, their effort to compete with the tidal wave of information that daily inundates us all often leads them to make shocking statements that create distorted impressions or beliefs in the public mind.  Because the whole truth is rarely dramatic, they tend to twist the truth or to convey partial truths in order to create shock value.

An instance of headline-grabbing by distortion is the 1968 Report of the National Advisory Commission on Racial Disorders, commonly known as the Kerner Report.  Although this weighty document contained much wisdom, what stood out when it was issued was the inflammatory headlined statement that "This nation is moving toward two societies, black and white, separate and unequal."  The vast majority of people who read this headline, but who did not read the whole Report, concluded that the Kerner Commission found that racial inequality and separation in America was rising in all dimensions. The implications of the statement were extremely disruptive. By implying that the "Establishment" was failing to improve racial relations, and that the racial gap was widening, the Kerner Report added fuel to the fiery demands of militant groups for revolutionary changes. Seeds of bitterness were sown in the minds of the uninformed. Racial tensions were exacerbated at home. The nation was denigrated abroad.

Yet the truth is that our democratic political institutions and our market economy, despite imperfections, has been making steady progress in narrowing the economic, educational, political, and social inequalities between the races ever since World War II. The median income of non-white families rose from 55 percent of that of white families in 1950 to 63 percent in 1968; and, according to figures cited by Daniel Moynihan, the incomes of black young married couples had become equal to those of white young married couples in 1970. The proportionate reduction in poverty since 1959 has been almost as great among blacks as among whites. Whereas in 1947 black adult Americans completed 34 percent fewer years of schooling than the entire population, by 1969 this difference had narrowed to 19 percent; and, for persons in the age bracket 25–29 years, it had nearly vanished. The difference between the life expectancies at birth of the two races diminished significantly during the postwar era. The steadily rising proportion of black citizens that are registered and vote in elections, and of blacks in public office, show a narrowing of the political gap. Blacks themselves overwhelmingly believe that conditions are improving for their race in this country, as sociologist Gary T. Marx reported in his book *Protest and Prejudice*. All these facts demonstrate impressive postwar progress of the American black toward economic and political equality, although many will understandably say "too little and too late." The correct conclusion to be drawn, however, is to keep public policy on the present course, and to try to accelerate its pace.

## THE LIBERAL LEFT AND THE EXPECTATION-REALITY GAP

The gravity of the nation's social problems is also enlarged by the teachings and writings of the Liberal Left.

Much Liberal Left social thought is based upon illusory concepts of the nature of man and society, well described by Professor Harold Demsetz as the "Nirvana," "other grass is greener," "free lunch," and "people could be different" fallacies. (See *Journal of Law and Economics*, April 1969.)

The "Nirvana" approach to social policy presents a choice between

a theoretical ideal never approached in man's history and existing conditions. The vast distance between the two naturally creates a social
"crisis." The true choice, however, lies between existing conditions
and others that are feasible in the sense of being capable of attainment. Because the expectation-reality gap in the latter case is usually
small, the "crisis" is reduced to a manageable problem.

The "other grass is greener" illusion credits an alternative social
condition, usually in some foreign country, with great virtues said to
be lacking in American Society. Thus atmospheric pollution is said to
be the product of capitalistic enterprise, and its cure is to adopt state
socialism. This idea is repeated by social critics who have not taken
the trouble to ascertain that pollution levels in socialist countries have
risen, along with their GNP's, even faster than in capitalist countries.
When the other fellow's lawn is closely inspected, it is usually found
to be as full of crabgrass as our own!

The "free lunch" fallacy is that there are costless remedies for social ills. Since unemployment is an evil, say the critics, abolish it and
reduce the unemployment ratio to zero. They choose to ignore the
heavy social costs of such a policy in the form of restrictions on individual freedom, lowered productivity, and price inflation. Every decision that produces public benefits imposes costs, and the problem is
to weigh both and determine the balance.

The "people could be different" fallacy is that the Good Society can
be attained by radical changes in the moral and ethical behavior of
people. Thus the "new Communist man," imbued with a totally altru-
istic concern for the public welfare, was seen by the older Marxists as
the condition for the ultimate transformation of socialism into true
Communism. Unfortunately, he has not yet appeared in sufficient
numbers to make this possible; and he shows no sign of doing so.
While moderate changes in men's values and behavior can occur over
time (indeed, changes are essential if our society is to improve), sharp
mutations in human nature are a fantasy. In reforming our society,
we are wise to take human nature as a datum, and to design structures
and processes for imperfect men and women rather than for saints or
philosophers.

## THE PROBLEM OF MULTIPLE GAPS AND CUMULATIVE FRUSTRATION

In his report to the nation on *U.S. Foreign Policy for the 1970's*, President Nixon trenchantly observed: "No nation has the wisdom, and
the understanding, and the energy required to act wisely on all prob-

lems, at all times, in every part of the world." His statement is equally
true and important if we substitute "nation" for "world." The number of different domestic problems that the people of a nation can cope
with effectively at any given time is limited, not only by the stock of
popular wisdom, energy, and understanding, but also by the available
economic resources of the society. In view of the fact that available
economic resources form a severe constraint upon national capability
to improve *real* social conditions, whereas public expectations of social improvement can soar at a virtually unlimited rate, it is far more
likely that a social problem will escalate into a "crisis" through an inordinate rise in expectations than by a failure of real conditions to
improve.

If national political and intellectual leaders ignore the resource constraints upon real social improvements, they may, by dramatizing one
social deficiency after another, stimulate public expectations so powerfully that multiple social "crises" are created in the public mind.
During the administration of President Johnson, for example, a "war
on poverty" was followed by a "war on hunger" and a "war on slums,"
and so on. Faced by a "war" on a new social front every few months,
without having won any of those already in progress, the American
people became progressively confused, frustrated, angered, and alienated from their government. Failure of the national political leadership to hold social expectations within the boundaries of national
capabilities led to the violence and disruptive behavior that marked
the last half of the Sixties.

By the end of 1968 public frustration and social tensions in the
United States had reached a dangerous level. Americans demanded a
quantity and variety of social improvements far beyond the capacity
of this or any other society to produce. People's energies were being
dissipated in dropoutism, absenteeism, and irrelevant protest rather
than utilized in constructive action—as shown by a catastrophic drop
in productivity. Fortunately, the succeeding Nixon Administration applied the remedies of "low profile" and "benign neglect," which succeeded in reducing many social "crises" into manageable problems by
deflating exaggerated public expectations.

It is a mistaken view that real social progress only occurs after a
"crisis" has been generated or that a deflation of exaggerated public
expectations is tantamount to foot-dragging in making necessary social reforms. On the contrary, there is a good deal of evidence that
"crises"—especially if accompanied by violence—are inimical to long
run progress; and that the maintenance of a proper relation between
expectations and realities avoids disruptive social behavior that re-
tards real social progress. Thus, poverty in the United States was being rapidly reduced after World War II and there is no convincing

evidence that the "war on poverty" launched in 1965 speeded up the process.

Our theory of social tensions helps to explain the almost pathological mood of self-criticism and self-deprecation that has descended upon Americans in recent years.  William James said that an individual's self-esteem could be measured by the ratio of his success or achievement to his potential.  By analogy, national self-esteem is the ratio of national achievement to national potential, as they are generally perceived by people.  As national achievements (i.e., social realities) are depreciated, and national potentialities (i.e., social expectations) are exaggerated, the quotient of national self-esteem will fall to the vanishing point.

## ELEMENTS OF OPTIMAL SOCIAL POLICY

Our society is a dynamic system, in which public values and expectations and social institutions and processes change through time. *The central aims of public policy should be to maintain an optimal expectation-reality gap, and to achieve an optimal rate of change in both social expectations and social realities.*

An optimal expectation-reality gap is wide enough to preserve incentive and motive for beneficial changes in social institutions and processes.  ("Man's reach should exceed his grasp, else what is Heaven for.")  Yet it is not so wide as to cause public frustration and diversion of energy from constructive action to inaction or to disruptive behavior.

Public goals and expectations should advance through time, fast enough to maintain social flexibility and adaptability, but not so rapidly as to lose contact with realities.

The real conditions of life should also be improved through time, fast enough to sustain a popular belief in progress but not so fast as to lead to malallocations of resources and social imbalances.

Because the rate of improvement in social conditions is determined within a fairly narrow range by well-known constraints upon the growth of production, whereas the rate of increase in public expectations is virtually unlimited, it is likely that political leaders will more frequently find it necessary to moderate public expectations than to raise them in order to avoid dangerous gaps.  This appears especially probable in our society which, as has been seen, is institutionally organized to magnify expectation-reality gaps, and in which high achievement is the normal goal.

Our simple model of optimum social policy can be displayed in the following figure:

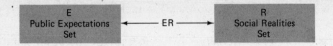

Conditions of Optimal Policy:

1. Optimize ER = (expectation-reality gap)
2. Optimize $dE/dt = dR/dt$

The general strategy for approaching the optimum gap between expectations and realities will include the following elements:

1. *Accelerate* desired institutional changes in the economic, political, and social systems to an optimum rate.
2. *Publicize* the changes that are occurring in the society to reduce poverty, racial discrimination, crime, or to improve health, housing, and other conditions.
3. *Instruct* the public in the political and economic processes of change, and their time-dimensions, so that there will emerge a general appreciation of what is realistically possible.
4. *Develop*, through research, more frequent and reliable *indicators* of social conditions and of the state of public expectations, and of their rates of change through time, as guides to social policy-makers. Social scientists should also try to measure the sustainable rates of change in social institutions. Leonard Lecht's pioneering effort to measure the dollar costs of attaining U.S. national goals, and to compare it with national production capacity, is a type of research that should be expanded. [See his *Goals, Priorities, and Dollars* (New York: Free Press, 1966).]

Managing public expectations has become a vital new dimension of political leadership in the United States, of coordinate importance with the engineering of orderly reform of our social institutions. Political leaders need to observe expectation-reality gaps constantly in order to maintain the proper state of tension in society. The great statesmen of the future will be those who know how to bring about orderly social change, and also to keep public expectations in a productive relationship to realities. Thus they will enable our society to resolve successfully a constantly emerging set of new social problems.

**QUESTIONS**

1. Do you agree with Jacoby's definition that "A social problem . . . may be defined as a gap between society's expectations of social conditions and the present social realities"?

2. How can social problems be "created" or made worse by changes in expectations?

3. Do you agree with the author that the communications media, politicians, and "intellectuals" tend to create and expand social problems? Explain your position.

4. What illusions about the basic nature of man and society does Jacoby say create or enlarge the expectation-reality gap? Do you agree with him?

5. Should social policy seek to maintain an optimum gap between expectations and realities? How might this be done?

6. Do you think we should develop measures of the state of public expectations? How and for what would you suggest this be done?

# Business and Changing Values in Society

**4**

# Conservative is favored label in U.S.

## george gallup

**The results of a Gallup Poll are presented in the following report, and they show that more people today in the United States prefer to be called "conservative" rather than "liberal."**

PRINCETON, N.J.—The American people, by the ratio of 3-to-2, prefer to be labeled "conservatives" rather than "liberals."

However, sharp differences emerge on the basis of the age of the respondent, region and educational background.

To test the grassroots appeal of the terms "conservative" and "liberal," Gallup Poll interviewers talked to a sample of 1,528 adults living in more than 300 localities in a survey conducted between March 20–22. All persons in the survey were first asked: What is the first thing that comes to your mind when you think of someone who is a liberal (a conservative)?

Descriptions of a "liberal" vary all the way from "someone who looks at all sides of a problem" and "a person who believes in mankind" to "someone who is generous with other people's money" and "a drug addict."

The public's image of a "conservative" ranges from "a person who looks before he leaps" and "a decent sort of guy" to "a penny pincher" and "a self-centered square."

The following question was asked of all persons who expressed an opinion on the two questions dealing with the image of a conservative and a liberal:

*Suppose you had to classify yourself as either a liberal or a conservative, which would you say you are?*

Here are the views of this informed group who accounted for 73% of the total sample:

| | | | |
|---|---|---|---|
| Conservative | 52% | No opinion | 14% |
| Liberal | 34 | | |

The liberal label is found to be more popular with college-trained persons than with persons who have had less than college training, but conservatives still outnumber liberals 5-to-4.

---

*Los Angeles Times*, April 17, 1970, Pt. 1 1/N A, p. 8.  Reprinted by permission of The American Institute of Public Opinion (Gallup Poll).

The following tables show in detail the public image of a "conservative" and of a "liberal," with the percentages based on all persons in the sample:

CONSERVATIVE

Favorable

| | |
|---|---|
| Saves, doesn't throw things away | 16% |
| Cautious, careful | 10 |
| General remarks (favorable) | 5 |
| | 31% |

Neutral

| | |
|---|---|
| Mentions Nixon, current administration | 6 |
| Mentions specific person other than Nixon | 5 |
| Mentions political position or party | 3 |
| | 14% |

Unfavorable

| | |
|---|---|
| Does not want to change, does not take a chance | 12 |
| Close-minded, intolerant, self-centered | 9 |
| | 21% |
| Miscellaneous | 3% |
| No opinion | 35 |
| * TOTAL | 104% |

* Total adds to more than 100% because some persons gave more than one response.

LIBERAL

Favorable

| | |
|---|---|
| Open-minded, fair | 12% |
| Generous, good-hearted | 6 |
| Wants change, active in bringing about needed reforms | 5 |
| General remarks (favorable) | 2 |
| | 25% |

Neutral

| | |
|---|---|
| Mentions specific person | 7 |
| Mentions political position or party | 7 |
| Mentions a specific problem (civil rights, etc.) | 3 |
| | 17% |

Unfavorable

| | |
|---|---|
| Gives things away, spends too freely | 8% |
| Negative descriptions (Communists, hippies, drug addicts, etc.) | 5 |
| Gets carried away, wild, too far out | 4 |
| Permissive, indifferent | 4 |
| General remarks (unfavorable) | 4 |
| | 25% |
| Miscellaneous | 2 |
| No opinion | 37 |
| * TOTAL | 106% |

* Total adds to more than 100% because some persons gave more than one response.

## QUESTIONS

1. The words "liberal" and "conservative" are used constantly, but what do they really mean? Do you agree with the definitions expressed in this report?

2. Do you think there is a major difference between the words "liberal" and "conservative" as they are used in this country today?
3. How have the meanings of these two words changed over the history of the United States?

# It's a wyeth, not a warhol, world

## william d. wells

William D. Wells is Professor of Psychology and Marketing, Graduate School of
Business, University of Chicago.  In this article he presents the results of a survey
of attitudes toward the home, family, cleanliness, "swingers," and other topics.

. . .

"The Times they are a-changing," Bob Dylan sings, and the signs of
change are everywhere around us.  Skirts go up, and the bars of censorship go down.  Blacks demand not just equality, but reparations.
Students battle police.  Clergymen battle each other over whether God
is still alive.

The signs of change are nowhere more apparent than in the mass
media.  Magazines publish essays on the new morality, the crumbling
of traditional values, and the anxiety, frustration, and fear of the once-
happy middle-aged middle class.  Advertising pages feature psychedelic art.  Television programs, and especially television commercials,
jump with the new rhythms and the new lyrics of folk-rock.

What impact has all this had on the "average consumer," the "typical
American," the buyer of groceries and payer of rent?  Has the tur-
bulence from the young side of the generation gap loosened traditional regard for hearth and home?  And have "anxiety, alienation,
apathy, and an anarchic repudiation of once precious values" made
apple pie and Mothers' Day obsolete?

If a revolution is indeed taking place, it is important to know this,
because it has profound implications for business.  If a revolution is
not taking place, that is important to know, too.  Many marketing,
public relations, and business planning decisions are based on assumptions about the way people are—and it would take conviction to avoid
being influenced by the unremitting emphasis on change, the high visibility of the "mod" generation, and the assumptions of so many
"thought leaders" that American values have undergone a transformation.

## SAMPLING OF OPINION

How *do* average Americans think?  To separate myths from realities,
two well-known organizations, Market Facts, Inc. and Leo Burnett Co.,
Inc., recently conducted a survey of the activities, interests, and opin-

Reprinted by permission from *Harvard Business Review*, 48 (January–February
1970), 26–32. © 1970 by the President and Fellows of Harvard College; all rights
reserved.

ions of a large sample of people.  An analysis of the results was made possible by a Ford Foundation grant to the Graduate School of Business of the University of Chicago.  In this article we shall look at but one "slice" of the data; many of the findings need not concern us here because they are quite specialized in interest.

---

TEST YOURSELF BEFORE YOU READ FURTHER . . .

One handicap of findings like those presented by Mr. Wells is that once they are in black and white, they seem more obvious than they really are.  "After all," the reader says to himself, "I could have written that!"

Actually, so much has been said about American society that almost any set of findings will meet some preconception, and almost any outcome will sound more predictable than it actually is.  Before you read the findings described by the author, therefore, we suggest you take the following test.  It consists of 30 statements he has chosen from the survey of a cross-section of Americans.  For each statement, he tells us, the average response for both men and women was scored as strong agreement, strong disagreement, or a middle position between agreeing and disagreeing.  How would you expect the scores to turn out?  A line is provided in front of each statement for the recording of your prognostication in indelible ink.  Simply mark A (strong agreement), D (strong disagreement), or M (in the middle).  Then turn to . . . (see p. 93) and see what the actual results of the survey were.

—*The Editors*

_____ 1. A house should be dusted and polished at least three times a week.

_____ 2. My choice of brands for many products is influenced by advertising.

_____ 3. Classical music is more interesting than popular music.

_____ 4. I buy many things with a credit card or a charge card.

_____ 5. The government in Washington is too big and powerful.

_____ 6. I often try new brands before my friends and neighbors do.

_____ 7. I usually look for the lowest possible prices when I shop.

_____ 8. Most big companies are just out for themselves.

_____ 9. Magazines are more interesting than television.

_____10. Every family should own a dog.

_____11. The television set should not be in the living room.

_____12. I exercise regularly.

_____13. I hate to get up in the morning.

_____14. A good mother will not serve her family TV dinners.

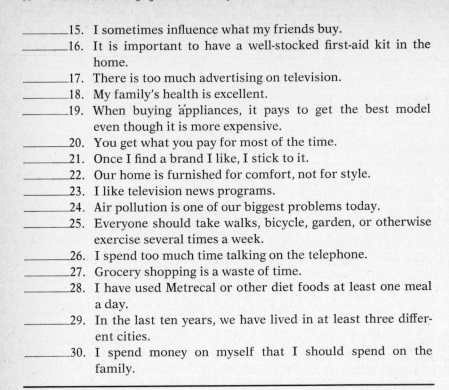

_____15.  I sometimes influence what my friends buy.

_____16.  It is important to have a well-stocked first-aid kit in the home.

_____17.  There is too much advertising on television.

_____18.  My family's health is excellent.

_____19.  When buying appliances, it pays to get the best model even though it is more expensive.

_____20.  You get what you pay for most of the time.

_____21.  Once I find a brand I like, I stick to it.

_____22.  Our home is furnished for comfort, not for style.

_____23.  I like television news programs.

_____24.  Air pollution is one of our biggest problems today.

_____25.  Everyone should take walks, bicycle, garden, or otherwise exercise several times a week.

_____26.  I spend too much time talking on the telephone.

_____27.  Grocery shopping is a waste of time.

_____28.  I have used Metrecal or other diet foods at least one meal a day.

_____29.  In the last ten years, we have lived in at least three different cities.

_____30.  I spend money on myself that I should spend on the family.

The statements gathered in the survey touch on many topics—daily activities, shopping habits, family relationships, hopes and worries, health, sports, reading habits, credit, government, houses, music, and television, to name just a few. The respondents were all married, were predominantly middle-class, and were drawn from all sections of the United States. Although they were respondents to a questionnaire sent in the mail and were not a probability sample, their demographic characteristics (see Table 1) show reasonably close agreement with U.S. census data, and their reports of product and media use conform about as well as their demographics to information from outside sources. They are, then, close to being representative of the "middle majority."

The questionnaire contained 300 statements that allowed respondents to give opinions by rating from "definitely disagree" to "definitely agree" on a 1-to-6 scale. The focus of this article is on those statements to which the average response from both men and women fell below 2.5 or above 4.5—that is, the statements to which the average response showed a *high* degree of agreement or disagreement.

In reporting the findings, I shall give first the statement, then the mean and (in parentheses) the standard deviation for male respondents, and then the similar figures for females. (Standard deviation is

TABLE 1    Demographic Characteristics of Sample and U.S. Census

| Family income (In $ thousands): | Over $15 | $10–15 | $8–10 | $6–8 | $4–6 | Under $4 |
|---|---|---|---|---|---|---|
| Sample | 14% | 26% | 18% | 20% | 11% | 10% |
| Census * | 8 | 17 | 14 | 19 | 17 | 24 |
| Family size: | Over 6 | 5 | 4 | 3 | 2 | 1 |
| Sample | 11% | 10% | 29% | 17% | 33% | 0% |
| Census * | 8 | 11 | 20 | 20 | 32 | 9 |
| Husband's age: | Over 55 | 45–55 | 35–45 | 25–35 | Under 25 | |
| Sample | 29% | 19% | 23% | 24% | 5% | |
| Census | 31 | 20 | 21 | 23 | 5 | |
| Husband's education: | College graduate | Some college | High school graduate | Some high school | Grade school only | |
| Sample | 20% | 24% | 26% | 18% | 10% | |
| Census | 17 | 20 | 27 | 19 | 15 | |

\* U. S. census figures include families with no husband present.

a statistical expression of the range of the answers.)  A rating of 6 is the highest possible expression of "definitely agree."  A rating of 1 is the strongest possible expression of "definitely disagree."  For instance:

The statement, "I like to be considered a leader," is followed by these data, M 3.96 (±1.64), F 3.38 (±1.57).  This means that the mean answer for men is 3.96, with a standard deviation for that response of 1.64 or a range for most answers of from 5.60 to 2.32; the mean answer for females is 3.38, with standard deviation of 1.57 or a range for most answers of from 4.95 to 1.81.

## HAPPINESS AND CONFIDENCE

Are Americans beset by anxiety, worry, frustration, and a loss of confidence and self-respect?  The results suggest that they are not.  Among the statements that receive strong positive responses are these:

○ I am happier now than before: M 4.66 (±1.43), F 4.60 (±1.49).
○ I think I have a lot of personal ability:  M 4.77 (±1.17), F 4.59 (±1.12).

Among the statements that receive a strong negative response is this one:

○ I dread the future:  M 2.01 (±1.44), F 2.07 (±1.45).

Does the picture of happiness and self-confidence reflected here suggest that respondents have been playing the "social desirability game" —that they are uncritically agreeing with all things good about themselves, and disagreeing with all things bad? The answer seems to be *no.* For in some areas where self-concepts are brought into question, the average response is only at the midpoint of the scale, i.e., around 3.0. Examples of such areas are self-assessed leadership, generosity, and neurotic symptoms, like the following:

○ I like to be considered a leader: M 3.96 (±1.64), F 3.38 (±1.57).
○ I have never really been outstanding at anything: M 3.00 (±1.70), F 3.48 (±1.75).
○ I am too generous for my own good: M 3.79 (±1.50), F 3.89 (±1.49).
○ I am just not the nervous type: M 3.81 (±1.67), F 3.35 (±1.71).
○ I eat more than I should: M 3.71 (±1.82), F 3.77 (±1.82).
○ I wish I knew how to relax: M 3.38 (±1.74), F 3.71 (±1.69).

Moreover, with respect to participation in community activities, generally considered a socially desirable trait, the average answers are strongly negative:

○ I do volunteer work for a hospital or service organization on a fairly regular basis: M 1.96 (±1.56), F 2.06 (±1.65).
○ I am an active member of more than one service organization: M 2.03 (±1.67), F 2.73 (±1.78).

And in a general assessment of life so far, neither men nor women say unequivocally that their major choices have been all good.

○ If I had my life to live over, I would sure do things differently: M 3.97 (±1.74), F 3.58 (±1.74).

## FAMILY AND HOME

A second group of statements that draws strong agreement from both males and females attests to the high importance placed on family, especially on the training and nurturing of children:

○ Our family is a close-knit group: M 4.91 (±1.27), F 5.01 (±1.07).
○ My children are the most important thing in my life: M 4.72 (±1.36), F 4.82 (±1.34).
○ I take a lot of time and effort to teach my children good habits: M 4.49 (±1.30), F 5.04 (±1.12).
○ There is a lot of love in our family: M 5.32 (±0.97), F 5.39 (±0.96).

The foregoing attitudes are reinforced by the high regard which most respondents place on the home. Consider the following statements and responses:

○ I would rather spend money on a house than on a car: M 4.81 (±1.28), F 4.88 (±1.27).
○ I take a great deal of pride in my home: M 5.16 (±1.02), F 5.21 (±0.93).

And, despite crabgrass in the lawn and the crack in the picture window, houses are favored over apartments, and suburbs over cities, as locations to live:

○ I would rather live in an apartment than a house: M 1.40 (±1.01), F 1.44 (±1.05).
○ I would rather live in a city than in the suburbs: M 2.01 (±1.57), F 2.15 (±1.68).

Incidentally, the statement, "New York is my favorite city," intended as a measure of cosmopolitan interest in fashion and the arts, was greeted with an emphatic *no*—M 1.58 (±1.21), F 1.70 (±1.32).

## EMPHASIS ON CARE AND CLEANLINESS

What about the "square" American virtues of care and neatness of personal appearance? The very high levels of agreement with the following statements speak for themselves:

○ Good grooming is a sign of self-respect: M 5.47 (±1.00), F 5.61 (±0.84).
○ I do not feel clean without a daily bath: M 4.55 (±1.69), F 4.81 (±1.45).
○ All men should be clean-shaven every day: M 4.94 (±1.44), F 5.19 (±1.21).
○ It is very important for people to wash their hands before eating each meal: M 5.41 (±1.04), F 5.61 (±0.89).
○ Everyone should use a deodorant: M 5.13 (±1.35), F 5.73 (±0.70).

As a way of showing that they have dropped out of American society, hippies could hardly have chosen a better set of symbols than dirty clothes, long hair, and no baths! The extent of their disrepute can be seen in the level of reponse to a statement that appears only on the males' questionnaire: "Hippies should be drafted." The *average* level of response is 5.08.

## PROTECTION OF FOOD

One section of the questionnaire contains a set of items designed to measure the use of various household products. Several of the products—for instance, aluminum foil, plastic wrap, and plastic sandwich bags—protect food, and some attitude statements were included to identify the food-protection fanatic. Somewhat surprisingly, these statements produce some of the highest overall endorsement levels of the entire schedule, both among women and among men. Here are some illustrations:

○ I think dirty dishes should be washed promptly after each meal: M 5.01 (±1.41), F 4.80 (±1.61).

○ Leftovers should be wrapped before being put into the refrigerator: M 5.40 (±1.02), F 5.70 (±0.71).

○ Food should never be left in the refrigerator uncovered: M 5.04 (±1.34), F 5.21 (±1.29).

○ Garbage should be put into a garbage bag before it is thrown out: M 5.05 (±1.41), F 5.35 (±1.18).

"Cleanliness is next to Godliness," the old saying goes. In this survey, three statements testing attitudes toward Godliness—"I often read the Bible," "Spiritual values are more important than material things," and "If Americans were more religious, this would be a better country"—receive solid endorsements from both men and women. But none of these statements create the extraordinary level of consensus that is shown for the cleanliness items just listed. Both cleanliness and Godliness are still important, but cleanliness is first.

## THE SQUARE MAJORITY

Finally, when set against the stereotype of the "now" generation, the middle majority emerges as almost incredibly square. Respondents give a strong "disagree" to these statements:

○ I like to think I am a bit of a swinger: M 2.43 (±1.56), F 2.40 (±1.59).

○ If I had my way, I would own a convertible: M 1.91 (±1.55), F 1.68 (±1.43).

○ I really do believe that blondes have more fun: M 2.22 (±1.60), F 1.91 (±1.45).

○ I would like to be an actor (actress, in the case of women): M 1.94 (±1.51), F 1.62 (±1.34).

○ I often have a cocktail before dinner:  M 2.08 (±1.64), F 1.92 (±1.58).

○ I like danger:  M 2.23 (±1.49), F 1.45 (±1.03).

On the other hand, the respondents agree heartily with the following statements:

○ There is too much emphasis on sex today:  M 4.65 (±1.54), F 5.02 (±1.39).

○ Today most people don't have enough discipline:  M 4.95 (±1.17), F 4.95 (±1.18).


## CONCLUSION

What does all this mean?  First, the findings give little support to those who proclaim that Americans are depressed, confused, and weary, that their traditional ideas have crumbled, and that the "old-fashioned virtues" mean nothing anymore.

Even if the answers to the survey questions show only the way people would like others to see them, rather than the way they "actually are," this point still holds.  A large segment of U.S. society portrays itself as happy, home-loving, clean, and square.

Secondly, the findings confirm and define the wide gap between the bearded, swinging youth and the over-30 "squares" who comprise the large majority of American adults.  Only time will tell whether the "now" generation will settle down and adopt some of the over-30 values once it, too, is over 30 and becomes absorbed with homes, children, and careers.  But one thing now is clear: vocal and visible though they are, "mod" youth have not had much impact on the central values of the average man.

Many businessmen, especially executives in advertising, marketing, and mass communications, live and work in a metropolitan, cosmopolitan subsociety that feeds on and feeds into the mass media and the avant-garde arts.  Living in this ivory tower, executives find it almost impossible to escape the conviction that (to use the vernacular) this world is where it's at; they find it all too easy to assume that the charming, bright, swinging young people so much in evidence in the metropolitan centers are typical of Americans today.

---

Answers to test on pages 87–88
Questions 1–15:  M
Questions 16–25:  A
Questions 26–30:  D

Since "know your audience" is perhaps the most basic of all prerequisites for effective communication, the executive who lives and works in a metropolitan, cosmopolitan environment should keep in mind that:

The typical U.S. citizen doesn't want to own a convertible, doesn't want to think that he or she is even a bit of a swinger, wouldn't like to be an actor or an actress, places a high value on home and family life, thinks that all men should be clean-shaven every day, and thinks it is very important for people to wash their hands before eating each meal.

For the housewife who pushes two loaded shopping carts past the checkout counter every week, home is where it's at, and happiness is what it's all about. The same goes for her husband, who makes a monthly payment at the savings and loan, buys life insurance, says that his children are the most important things in his life, and thinks hippies should be drafted.

For most Americans it is indeed a Wyeth, not a Warhol, world.

# What is the
value system of
the average youth?

## *life* magazine

In the following survey, which *Life* commissioned Louis Harris and Associates to undertake, the younger generation turns out to be interested in change but is not breathing fire for upheaval. It shows that the average youth's value system is surprisingly comparable to that of the older generation.

What will become of this country when the young generation comes of age and takes over? People who expect a cataclysmic rejection of traditions, mores and institutions are in for a shock: the young wouldn't overturn society even if they could. Most of them are much too satisfied with it as it is.

*Life* recently commissioned Louis Harris and Associates to interview a national cross section of the 26 million Americans who are between the ages of 15 and 21. Their views on a broad range of social questions are remarkably moderate, even conservative. In sum, they describe a rather tolerant, relaxed group whose attitudes and expectations on a great many subjects differ very little from their parents'. As Harris reports, "The majority of youth listens to the rhetoric of dissent, picks what it wants, then slowly weaves it into the dominant social pattern."

Within the cross section, college students on almost every issue are strikingly more skeptical and progressive than their younger brothers and sisters in high school. But even here the responses do not forecast a radical future. Change, yes. Revolution, no.

The poll results are depicted here and on the following pages. Where answers total less than 100%, the "not sures" have been dropped. Youth's pantheon of heroes to adorn an imaginary Mount Rushmore represents a variety of philosophies, but the heroes are all from within the mainstream. Nonheroes, on the other hand, are extremists of right or left. The family, apparently, will survive: children will listen if their parents will talk. Like their fathers, young people are willing to work, but they want to enjoy what they do and move around less. Sex doesn't make the young uptight, but many of them cling to some old standards. Even the exploding drug culture—its extent is made frighteningly clear in the statistics—has been absorbed into the new pattern of orthodoxy. Two young people out of three admit knowing someone who has tried marijuana. But asked if pot should be legalized, a majority, as in most other areas of the poll, takes the conservative approach and says no.

## MOTHERS AND FATHERS

| | | |
|---|---|---|
| Has your upbringing been too strict? | | 10% |
| too permissive? | | 8 |
| about right? | | 81 |

Do you accept and agree with your parents' values and ideals? — Yes 73

Have your parents lived up to their own ideals? — Yes 80

Do your parents approve of *your* values and ideals? — Yes 64

Do they approve of the way your generation expresses those ideals? — No 55

| Do you have trouble communicating with your parents? | Yes | 32 |
|---|---|---|
| | No | 66 |
| If so, whose fault is it? | | |
| Parents | | 18 |
| Mine | | 6 |
| Both our faults | | 74 |

## SUCCESS

Do you believe that hard work leads to success and wealth? — Yes 61%

| Is that kind of success still worth striving for? | Yes | 66 |
|---|---|---|
| High school students | Yes | 70 |
| College students | Yes | 52 |

## CAREERS

Do you believe your father has been happy in his work? — Yes 76%

After finishing school, what are your career plans?

| Join armed forces | 9 |
|---|---|
| Get a job | 51 |
| Postpone a decision | 34 |

Would you rather work for

| | HS | COL |
|---|---|---|
| A big company? | 44 | 23 |
| A small company? | 20 | 33 |
| For yourself? | 31 | 38 |

What factors are most important in choosing a job?

1. Enjoyable work
2. Pride in the job
3. Pleasant working conditions
4. Creative satisfaction

Least important factors?

1. Short hours
2. Recognition by society
3. Achieving status

Is it good to change jobs periodically or stick with one?

| Stick | 46 |
|---|---|
| Change | 27 |
| College students | |
| Stick | 31 |
| Change | 35 |

Would you like a job that involves being transferred to different places? — No 63

Would you be willing to work on a factory production line? — No 56

Would you work for a

company that handles
defense contracts? Yes 67

Would you work for a
company that causes
substantial pollution? No 70

If your job paid enough
to take care of basic
needs, would you de-
vote your leisure
time to
A second job? Yes 26
Community work Yes 63
Relaxing and enjoying
life? Yes 88

## HAPPINESS

Has your life been happy
so far? Yes 90%

Why do you say that?
1. I've had a good
home, good family
2. I've had and done
about everything I
wanted

Do you expect your fu-
ture to be as happy or
even happier? Yes 93

## POLITICS

What are your politics?
Conservative 20%
Middle of the road 39
Liberal 23
Radical 5
Other or not sure 13

How do you intend to
vote in the next election
you are eligible to vote
in?
Republican 18
Democratic 35
Wallace 4
Other or not sure 40
Will refuse to vote 3

Can needed changes be
achieved through the
existing parties? Yes 49
No 38

How much confidence
do you have in the
government to solve
the problems of the
'70s?
A great deal 22
Some but not a lot 54
Hardly any 22

## MONEY

Has your family had
enough money? Yes 76%
Blacks only No 59

What would be an ideal
income for you? $17,000

How much do you
realistically expect
to make?
Average $12,000
Males 14,600
Females 9,300
High school students 11,900
College students 14,500
Blacks 10,700

How much money do
you spend on yourself
each week?
High school students $7.50
College students 15.00

Is that enough? Yes 78%
How much of it comes
from your parents?
High school students 26
College students 66

Should young people
earn some of their
own money? Yes 95

Have you saved any
money? Yes 68

If so, how much?

| | |
|---|---|
| Over $100 | 54 |
| Over $500 | 20 |
| Over $1,000 | 8 |

What are you saving for?

| | |
|---|---|
| Education | 42 |
| A car | 20 |
| Travel | 9 |
| Clothes | 9 |

Ideally, at what age should a person have his own car?

| | |
|---|---|
| Between 16 and 18 | 82 |

## EDUCATION

Are you satisfied with your education so far?  Yes  84%

Should everyone who wants to go to college be able to?  Yes  92

Did your father graduate from college?  Yes  17

Do you intend to go to college? (asked of 18 and under)  Yes  66

## THERE OUGHT TO BE A LAW

Penalizing air and water polluters  Yes  90%

Creating an all-volunteer army  Yes  69

Requiring hiring of minorities  Yes  58

Guaranteeing an annual income  No  60

Achieving racial balance in schools by busing  No  66

## RELIGION

Is religion important to you?

| | | |
|---|---|---|
| High school students | Yes | 77% |
| College students | Yes | 56 |

Do you attend church regularly?

| | | |
|---|---|---|
| High school students | Yes | 58 |
| College students | Yes | 43 |

Do liberalized attitudes and new forms of worship make church more interesting to young people?  Yes  69

Do you find more spiritual benefit in nature or in fellowship with others than in going to church?  Yes  47

Would it upset your parents if you married someone of a different

| | | |
|---|---|---|
| religion? | No | 82 |
| of a different race? | Yes | 69 |

## FAMILY PLANNING

Is it important to limit the number of children

| | | |
|---|---|---|
| you have? | Yes | 77% |
| Catholics only | Yes | 71 |

How many children do you want?

| | |
|---|---|
| Two or less | 58 |
| Three | 21 |
| Four or more | 17 |

Is it all right to put children in day-care centers while their mothers work?  No  74

. . .

## TELEVISION

How many hours of TV do you watch in a week?

| | |
|---|---|
| High school | 11 |

| | |
|---|---|
| College | 6 |
| Nonstudents | 12 |

Do you watch more or
less than when you
were younger?

| | |
|---|---|
| More | 11% |
| Less | 77 |
| Same | 11 |

Will you limit the
amount your own
children can watch?

| | | |
|---|---|---|
| | Yes | 36% |
| | No | 55 |

What does TV do best?
1. Sports
2. News
3. Comedy

BOOKS

Have you read any books
for pleasure this year?   Yes   90%
(Read more than 10)   38

Has any one book in-
fluenced your life?

| | | |
|---|---|---|
| | Yes | 45 |
| | No | 51 |

If so, which one?

The Bible led all books
cited by almost three
to one. Others men-
tioned often were
*Black Like Me, Catcher
in the Rye, Christy* and
*The Prophet.*

CINEMA

Do you wish there were
more family-type
movies?   Yes   57%

Have you ever seen a
movie whose explicit
treatment of sex of-
fended you?   No   75

Have you seen a movie
that reflects your own
outlook on life?   Yes   24

If so, which one?
*Easy Rider* was named
twice as often as any
other. *Woodstock,
Getting Straight* and
*M\*A\*S\*H* followed.

# Beliefs of three groups of youth

# *fortune*/yankelovich survey

**The results of a survey made for *Fortune* by Daniel Yankelovich, Inc., are presented in the following article. It shows clearly that on some matters all youth seem to think alike, but concerning some major values there are widespread differences among groups. Of special interest are the views of the so-called forerunners because, presumably, their views are the ones that are most likely to spread in the future. (This fact was partly confirmed in a survey made for *Fortune* by Daniel Yankelovich, Inc., six months after the survey reported here.)**

In the *Fortune*-Yankelovich survey, taken last October, 718 young men and women aged eighteen through twenty-four were interviewed in sessions typically lasting close to an hour. The group was representative as to race, sex, marital status, family income, and geographic region. Those who were attending college at the time of the survey (334) were deliberately oversampled, in order to make possible a more detailed presentation of their attitudes. However, in the comparisons tabulated below, the college and noncollege groups have been reweighted so as to adjust for this oversampling.

The different attitudes registered between those who had and those who had not attended college are clear-cut—but not very surprising. What is perhaps most surprising in the data is the sharp division *within* the college group. All those in the group were shown the following two statements and asked which more closely represented their own views about college and careers:

> (1) For me, college is mainly a practical matter. With a college education I can earn more money, have a more interesting career, and enjoy a better position in society.
>
> (2) I'm not really concerned with the practical benefits of college. I suppose I take them for granted. College for me means something more intangible, perhaps the opportunity to change things rather than make out well within the existing system.

Those who preferred the first formulation were identified as the "practical-minded" students: 58 percent were in this category. For many of them college plainly represented an opportunity to improve their status in society; a third of the practical students came from families headed by blue-collar workers, and a majority (54 percent) were enrolled in business, engineering, or science-oriented programs

Excerpts from "What They Believe," A Fortune/Yankelovich Survey, *Fortune,* Vol. LXXIX, No. 1, January 1969, pp. 70–71, 179–181.

that suggest they have fairly definite ideas about their careers. Those who preferred the second formulation were identified as the "forerunners"—i.e., *Fortune* believes that their attitude toward college and careers will become more prevalent in the years ahead. The forerunners were mostly (80 percent) in the arts and humanities; only a quarter of this group came from blue-collar families.

Both the "practical-minded" and the "forerunner" groups were asked a series of questions designed to elicit their basic values and their beliefs about controversial aspects of U.S. society today. The same questions were also asked of a "control" group of young men and women who had never been to college. The answers are remarkable on two general counts: first, for the extraordinary rejection of traditional American values shown by the forerunner group; second, for the similarities in the beliefs of the practical group and of those who have not been to college. On many questions these two groups are much closer to each other than either is to the forerunners.

The questions and responses included these:

## CURRENT ISSUES

| | No college | Practical college | Forerunner college |
|---|---|---|---|
| Do you agree with those who have called ours a "sick" society? | | | |
| Yes | 44% | 32% | 50% |
| Comments in support of this view (some made more than one): | | | |
| Too much extremism | 34 | 35 | 28 |
| Loss of human concern | 27 | 31 | 34 |
| High crime rate | 25 | 27 | 15 |
| Defiant, rebellious youth | 24 | 17 | 11 |
| Hypocrisy in politics | 9 | 17 | 10 |
| Breakdown of democracy | 7 | 10 | 12 |
| Fear of social or economic change | 1 | 4 | 9 |

## ABOUT PARENTS

| | No college | Practical college | Forerunner college |
|---|---|---|---|
| How would you complete the following sentence? "The main trouble with the older generation is ——————." The most commonly expressed criticisms were: | | | |
| They are reluctant to accept change | 39% | 34% | 41% |
| They do not understand youth | 20 | 27 | 32 |
| They are close-minded, intolerant | 13 | 27 | 32 |
| Some had no criticism to make | 27 | 13 | 4 |

Do you feel that there is a large "generation gap" today, that it exists but has been exaggerated, or that it doesn't exist?

| | No college | Practical college | Forerunner college |
|---|---|---|---|
| There is a large generation gap | 48% | 56% | 69% |
| The generation gap has been exaggerated | 15 | 22 | 20 |
| There is no generation gap | 25 | 20 | 9 |
| No opinion | 12 | 2 | 2 |

Do you feel that the differences between your values and your parents' are very great, moderate, or very slight?

| | No college | Practical college | Forerunner college |
|---|---|---|---|
| Very great | 15% | 11% | 24% |
| Moderate | 41 | 49 | 51 |
| Very slight | 44 | 40 | 25 |

Are the following attitudes more applicable to you or your parents?

| | No college | Practical college | Forerunner college |
|---|---|---|---|
| Likely to compromise with things you don't like | | | |
| Parents | 44% | 45% | 56% |
| Self | 20 | 20 | 16 |
| Respectful of people in positions of authority | | | |
| Parents | 41 | 42 | 56 |
| Self | 16 | 8 | 4 |
| Likely to accept things as they are | | | |
| Parents | 40 | 44 | 52 |
| Self | 31 | 26 | 24 |
| Fearful of financial insecurity | | | |
| Parents | 39 | 40 | 47 |
| Self | 33 | 28 | 18 |
| Have faith in the democratic process | | | |
| Parents | 38 | 30 | 50 |
| Self | 11 | 18 | 13 |
| Tolerant of other people's views | | | |
| Parents | 31 | 20 | 15 |
| Self | 43 | 57 | 60 |
| Honest with oneself | | | |
| Parents | 25 | 19 | 14 |
| Self | 24 | 26 | 39 |
| Interested in other people | | | |
| Parents | 24% | 16% | 11% |
| Self | 37 | 49 | 43 |
| Interested in money | | | |
| Parents | 23 | 28 | 48 |
| Self | 37 | 23 | 12 |
| Likely to do something about what you believe to be right | | | |
| Parents | 22 | 13 | 8 |
| Self | 33 | 36 | 50 |
| Open to the world | | | |
| Parents | 16 | 8 | 7 |
| Self | 55 | 54 | 66 |
| Interested in beauty | | | |
| Parents | 15 | 9 | 9 |
| Self | 40 | 42 | 43 |
| Optimistic about the future | | | |
| Parents | 14 | 17 | 23 |
| Self | 63 | 49 | 42 |
| Self-centered | | | |

| | No college | Practical college | Forerunner college |
|---|---|---|---|
| Parents | 14 | 9 | 17 |
| Self | 36 | 53 | 43 |
| Concerned with what is happening to the country | | | |
| Parents | 14 | 12 | 9 |
| Self | 36 | 35 | 45 |

## BASIC VALUES

*To which of these ideas do you personally subscribe?*

| | No college | Practical college | Forerunner college |
|---|---|---|---|
| Hard work will always pay off if you have faith in yourself and stick to it | 75% | 80% | 59% |
| Everyone should save as much as he can regularly and not have to lean on family and friends the minute he runs into financial problems | 73 | 65 | 51 |
| No matter how menial the job may be, doing it well is important | 73 | 73 | 62 |
| A man should stand on his own two feet and not depend on others for help or favors | 68 | 58 | 50 |

| | No college | Practical college | Forerunner college |
|---|---|---|---|
| The individual who plans ahead can look forward to success and achievement of personal goals | 65 | 64 | 46 |
| Hard work keeps people from loafing and getting into trouble | 54 | 34 | 18 |
| Depending on how much strength and character a person has, he can pretty well control what happens to him. You make your own luck | 52 | 53 | 48 |

. . .

*Which of the following social changes would you welcome?*

| | No college | Practical college | Forerunner college |
|---|---|---|---|
| More emphasis on law and order | 91% | 78% | 39% |
| More emphasis on combating crime | 88 | 95 | 70 |
| More respect for authority | 87 | 73 | 41 |
| More emphasis on work being meaningful in its own right | 85 | 78 | 88 |
| More emphasis on self-expression | 69 | 68 | 90 |

| | No college | Practical college | Forerunner college |
|---|---|---|---|
| More freedom to debate and disagree openly | 68 | 73 | 92 |
| More freedom for the individual to do whatever he wants, provided he doesn't hurt others | 65 | 69 | 84 |
| More acceptance of other people's peculiarities | 60 | 75 | 93 |
| Less emphasis on status—on "keeping up with the Joneses" | 57 | 75 | 80 |
| Less emphasis on money | 57 | 53 | 80 |
| More emphasis on private enterprise | 42 | 55 | 36 |
| More emphasis on the arts | 42 | 55 | 84 |
| More vigorous but nonviolent protests by blacks and other minority groups | 35 | 41 | 64 |
| More sexual freedom | 19 | 35 | 48 |

*Which of these restraints, imposed by society and its institutions, can you accept easily?*

| | No college | Practical college | Forerunner college |
|---|---|---|---|
| The prohibition against marijuana | 77% | 69% | 37% |
| The prohibition against other drugs | 85 | 83 | 63 |
| The power and authority of the "boss" in a work situation | 74 | 60 | 52 |
| Requirement that you be married before you live with someone | 69 | 50 | 36 |
| Conforming in matters of clothing and personal grooming | 65 | 45 | 28 |
| Outward respectability for the sake of career advancement | 54 | 39 | 17 |
| Having little decision-making power in the first few years of a job | 48 | 38 | 23 |
| Abiding by laws you don't agree with | 43 | 35 | 21 |
| Showing respect for people you may not, in fact, respect | 33 | 25 | 17 |
| Pressures to close one's eyes to dishonest behavior | 9 | 3 | 2 |

## ABOUT TECHNOLOGY

*With which of the following statements about technology do you agree?*

| | No college | Practical college | Forerunner college |
|---|---|---|---|
| The problem is not technology—it's what society does with technology | 66% | 81% | 88% |
| Technological progress always involves human problems | 44 | 55 | 58 |
| Technology will permit man to reach his potential and control his destiny | 36 | 39 | 31 |
| Technology is the only means man has of solving existing problems | 30 | 21 | 17 |
| Only good can come from technological advances | 28 | 19 | 11 |
| The bomb is typical of what we can expect from technology | 19 | 7 | 13 |
| Technological advances can only mean more unemployment—it's not worth it | 14 | 7 | 6 |
| Advanced technology could eventually replace human beings | 13 | 11 | 11 |
| Technology is dehumanizing society | 7 | 15 | 24 |

*Would you welcome more emphasis on technological improvement?*

| | No college | Practical college | Forerunner college |
|---|---|---|---|
| Yes | 53% | 75% | 56% |

*Which of the following specific applications of technology do you consider to be a very good thing, which not a good thing at all?*

| | No college | Practical college | Forerunner college |
|---|---|---|---|
| Supersonic airplane | | | |
| Very good | 52% | 59% | 50% |
| Not good at all | 8 | 2 | 11 |
| Computerized instruction | | | |
| Very good | 32 | 22 | 14 |
| Not good at all | 17 | 30 | 40 |
| Genetic control | | | |
| Very good | 22 | 20 | 14 |
| Not good at all | 19 | 38 | 47 |

## ABOUT BUSINESS

*Many persons use the following phrases when they make statements about business. Which of the statements do you consider very true, and which not true?*

| | No college | Practical college | Forerunner college |
|---|---|---|---|
| Competitive atmosphere | | | |
| Very true | 71% | 88% | 86% |
| Not true | 4 | 1 | 1 |

| | No college | Practical college | Forerunner college | | No college | Practical college | Forerunner college |
|---|---|---|---|---|---|---|---|
| Makes a major contribution to America | | | | A 9-to-5 routine | | | |
| Very true | 70 | 74 | 56 | Very true | 31 | 26 | 37 |
| Not true | 7 | 3 | 5 | Not true | 34 | 27 | 15 |
| A key element for the future | | | | High ethics | | | |
| Very true | 65 | 71 | 57 | Very true | 29 | 18 | 7 |
| Not true | 3 | 2 | 5 | Not true | 23 | 36 | 48 |
| A major factor in society | | | | Allows for individuality | | | |
| Very true | 62 | 82 | 80 | Very true | 28 | 19 | 6 |
| Not true | 8 | 5 | 5 | Not true | 18 | 31 | 37 |
| Meaningful | | | | Allows for self-expression | | | |
| Very true | 49 | 43 | 23 | Very true | 25 | 20 | 5 |
| Not true | 8 | 9 | 19 | Not true | 19 | 23 | 26 |
| Allows for self-development | | | | Rigid | | | |
| Very true | 42 | 35 | 16 | Very true | 24 | 33 | 36 |
| Not true | 9 | 14 | 23 | Not true | 25 | 20 | 10 |
| Allows for creativity | | | | Allows individual decision making | | | |
| Very true | 37 | 33 | 13 | Very true | 21 | 27 | 11 |
| Not true | 15 | 19 | 22 | Not true | 18 | 18 | 27 |
| Requires conformity | | | | Would enjoy being involved with | | | |
| Very true | 36 | 40 | 51 | Very true | 32 | 34 | 15 |
| Not true | 17 | 9 | 6 | Somewhat true | 45 | 35 | 36 |
| Large and overwhelming | | | | Not true | 17 | 26 | 46 |
| Very true | 34 | 44 | 54 | . . . | | | |
| Not true | 20 | 12 | 8 | | | | |

# Chapter 4 Questions

1. Compare your values with those reported in these surveys, and indicate where you are in substantial agreement with the "average youth" or with one of the three groups in the second survey. Where are you in major disagreement?
2. Altogether, what do these surveys tell you about changes in the business-society relationship in the future as a result of changing values of people? Are we in for major changes or only evolutionary changes? Where do you think important changes will have been made in the next 15 to 20 years as a result of new values of young people as they move into business or get in positions to influence business?
3. Do these surveys indicate that Reich's Consciousness III will predominate in the future, say in 20 years?
4. Do these surveys indicate that there is great stability among some fundamental values in society?
5. Which of the changing values do you think will have the greatest impact on society and business in the future?
6. Which forces do you think could accelerate changing values of the young, and which ones could slow down change?

# How Much Power Does a Corporation Have?

**5**

# Is there a ruling class in america?

## g. william domhoff

G. William Domhoff is Assistant Professor of Psychology and Fellow of Cowell College, University of California at Santa Cruz. In the following excerpt he lays out the proposition that there is a ruling class in America and describes how he will go about proving it. The question of whether he is correct arises, of course.

. . .

Our starting point, then, must be the demonstration of an observable, differentiated, interacting social group with more or less definite boundaries. In other words, does an identifiable social upper class exist in the United States? This question is closely related to a second empirical question which interests us in the light of Mills's objection that "class" is an economic term: Does this social upper class overlap in membership with any particular economic "class"? The answer to both of these questions . . . is "Yes," thus making Mills's point primarily a semantic one. It will be shown that there is a national upper class made up of rich businessmen and their families, an "American business aristocracy," as Baltzell calls it. Although this national upper class has its ethnic, religious, and new-rich–old-rich antagonisms, it is nonetheless closely knit by such institutions as stock ownership, trust funds, intermarriages, private schools, exclusive city clubs, exclusive summer resorts, debutante parties, fox hunts, charity drives, and, last but not least, corporation boards. This information, when fully elaborated, can be considered a direct answer to sociologist William Kornhauser, who claims that one of the main weaknesses of Mills's work was that he did not sufficiently demonstrate the interaction of the various cliques making up his "power elite." If such a weakness existed, it was in Mills's presentation and not in a lack of such interaction.

In addition to demonstrating the reality of a national upper class, we will emphasize that this social group, whether its members are aware of it or not, has well-established ways of "training" and "preparing" new members. This point must be stressed because it is certainly the case that people are moving into (not to mention out of) this group all the time. "Social mobility" is a distinct reality, and this study will document its occurrence at the highest levels of society as well as at the middle levels where it is usually studied. Social mobility can be looked at from many points of view and in terms of many different questions, but the important thing to keep in mind in understanding this phenomenon in a sociological study of the upper class is the process of "co-optation." For our purposes, we will mean by co-optation the processes whereby individuals are assimilated and committed to the institutions and values of the dominant socioeconomic group. In studying co-optation we want to know which institutions select and prepare those who are assimilated, as well as the ideas and values that make a person acceptable. To anticipate somewhat, the co-optation of bright young men into the American upper class occurs through education at private schools, elite universities, and elite law schools; through success as a corporation executive; through membership in exclusive gentlemen's clubs; and through participation in exclusive charities.

Is this social upper class, with its several institutional focal points and its several means of assimilating new members, also a "governing class"? It is with this question that new ground must be broken, for systematic data are lacking. To begin with, "governing class" must be defined. Our definition is as follows:

> A "governing class" is a social upper class which owns a disproportionate amount of a country's wealth, receives a disproportionate amount of a country's yearly income, and contributes a disproportionate number of its members to the controlling institutions and key decision-making groups of the country.

Disproportionate wealth and income are important in this definition because they imply that the upper class has interests that are at least somewhat different from those of other socioeconomic groups. As we will see, members of the upper class have different sources of income as well as more income than persons of other income levels. By the same token, a disproportionate number of leaders is important because it implies control of these institutions and decision-making groups. . . . these criteria, while not infallible, are at least as good as those used in other approaches to this difficult question. And if, as Dahl says of the decision-making methodology, a group is more or less a ruling elite depending upon how many decisions it controls, we can say that a social upper class is more or less a governing class depending upon the percentage of wealth it possesses, the income it receives, and the leaders it contributes. Finally, we would stress that our minimum definition is valuable because it can be related to empirical data.

Although our definition may not be acceptable to everyone, it does meet Dahl's stricture that the hypothesis contained in such a definition must be capable of disproof as well as support. In fact, the methods we will use in testing the hypothesis are similar to those used by Dahl in his study of New Haven, Connecticut. Since Dahl and one of his former students, Nelson Polsby, have been the most articulate critics of previous studies of the American power structure, we have followed their criticisms and comments with some care. We do not wish to have it pointed out to us, as Dahl did to Mills and Polsby did to Baltzell, that we did not test our hypothesis. Dahl relied primarily on three methods to determine who governed in New Haven. He described them as follows:

1. To study changes in the socioeconomic characteristics of incumbents in city offices in order to determine whether any rather large historical changes may have occurred in the sources of leadership.
2. To isolate a particular socioeconomic category and then determine the nature and extent of participation in local affairs by persons in this category.
3. To examine a set of "decisions" in different "issue-areas" in order to determine what kinds of persons were the most influential according to one operational measure of relative influence, and to determine patterns of influence.

Dahl's first two methods are aspects of what we will call the "sociology-of-leadership" methodology. The essence of this methodology is the study of the sociological composition of leadership groups in order to determine whether or not the leaders come from any given socioeconomic class, ethnic group, or religious group. Dahl used this method in the first six chapters of *Who Governs?* With it he showed quite conclusively that members of the middle class had taken over the decision-making roles he studied in New Haven. Dahl's third method focuses on the decision-making process. With it he showed that different members of the middle class in New Haven were influential in different issue-areas. There was no one "ruling elite" that made decisions on a wide variety of issues.

Unfortunately, the decision-making method is difficult to apply because the "operational measure" of influence is the frequency with which a person "successfully initiates an important policy over the opposition of others, or vetoes policies initiated by others, or initiates a policy where no opposition appears." Inferences about who initiates and who vetoes must be made after "reconstructing" the decision "by means of interviews with participants, the presence of an observer, records, documents, and newspapers." However, we believe with Baltzell and Raymond Bauer, an expert in the study of policy formation, that even when the information with which to reconstruct a specific decision seems to be available, it is a very risky and tricky business. Many aspects of the situation may remain secret, the participants themselves may not be able to correctly assess the roles of the various members, the "real" interests of the participants are complex and often impossible for even them to determine, and the larger context within which the issue arises may be as important in understanding the eventual decision as the decision-making process itself. Thus, we have relied on Dahl's third method somewhat less than on his first two. At the same time we have tried to remain faithful to Dahl's concern with specific issue-areas by studying the sociological backgrounds of members of decision-making groups and by studying institutions and associations which are known to have a great amount of influence in specific issue-areas. Polsby seems to be recommending our approach when he says:

> If there exist high degrees of overlap among issue-areas in decision-making personnel, or of institutionalization in the bases of power in specified issue-areas, or of regularity in the procedures of decision making, then the empirical conclusion is justified that some sort of "power structure" exists.

However, since studying decision-making groups and institutional personnel is not the same thing as studying the decision-making process itself, it is very important in using this method to state explicitly the scope and limits of the powers of the given institution, association, or decision-making group. (One of the main criticisms of Mills's thesis was that he did not spell out the powers of his power elite.) The kind and limits of the powers of the groups and institutions which concern us will be noted as each one is studied . . .

. . . the less than 1 per cent of the population comprising the American upper class, if it is a governing class, does not rule alone. Thus, it will be necessary to demonstrate that most of the non-upper-class leaders are selected and trained by members of the upper class (co-opted), or to say the same thing differently, that the advancement of these non-upper-class leaders is dependent upon their attaining goals that are shared by members of the upper class. This leads to a discussion of our concept of the "power elite," a term borrowed from Mills but defined in a slightly different manner. We agree with Mills in defining the power elite as those who have a superior amount of power due to the institutional hierarchies they command, but we deviate from Mills by restricting the term to persons who are in command positions in institutional hierarchies controlled by members of the American upper class, or, in the case of members of the federal government, to persons who come to the government from the upper class or from high positions in institutions controlled by members of the upper class. By this definition, any particular member of the power elite may or may not be a member of the upper class. It not only allows for co-optation and for control through hired employees, but it agrees that some members of the upper class—what Baltzell calls the functionless genteel—may not be members of the power elite. This definition of the power elite is very similar to Baltzell's concept of an "establishment":

The upper class, in other words, will be a ruling class or, as I should prefer to say, its leaders will form an *establishment*. . . . In a free society, while an establishment will always be dominated by upper-class members, it also must be constantly rejuvenated by new members of the elite who are in the process of acquiring upper-class status.

While our definition of the power elite is somewhat different from that given by Mills, the final result of our research will show that our power elite is very similar to his. This difference lies in the fact that (1) we have not assumed *a priori* that any group is part of the power elite as Mills did in so designating the corporate leaders, military leaders, and political leaders; and (2) we have grounded the power elite in the upper class. Putting it another way, we will attempt to show that Mills's power elite has its roots in Baltzell's "American business aristocracy" and serves its interests. In the case of each institution hypothesized to be a basis of the power elite, control by members of the upper class must be demonstrated empirically. Thus, when we arrive at the crucial institution in this study—the federal government—we will be in a position to show just which parts of it can be considered aspects of a power elite that is the operating arm of the American upper (governing) class. We will not assume, as Mills did, that the Executive branch of the federal government is part of a power elite, but will instead show that its leaders are either members of the upper class or former employees of institutions controlled by members of the upper class. Perhaps several examples from recent Democratic administrations will make this final point clear. Franklin D. Roosevelt, John F. Kennedy, Adlai Stevenson, Dean Acheson, Averell Harriman, Douglas Dillon, McGeorge Bundy, and Nicholas Katzenbach were hereditary members of the upper class, while Robert McNamara was president of the Ford Motor Company, Dean Rusk was president of the Rockefeller Foundation, and John Gardner was president of the Carnegie Corporation. We consider all of these men to be members of the power elite, for they are either old-line members of the American business aristocracy or former high-level employees of institutions controlled by members of that social group. We are quite aware of the humble origins of McNamara and Rusk, whose children may or may not become members of the upper class depending upon the stock accumulations of their fathers, the schools they attend, and the persons they marry. However, we think that the nature of McNamara's and Rusk's previous employment, and the consequent status and income this afforded them, is what is important in understanding their appointment to government.

We believe that the relationship between the concepts of "governing class" and "power elite" is quite straightforward, but it is also true that there can be confusion unless the two are compared and contrasted. To repeat, "governing class" refers to a social upper class which owns a disproportionate amount of the country's wealth, receives a disproportionate amount of the country's yearly income, and contributes a disproportionate number of its members to positions of leadership. However, some of the members of this social group may not be involved in anything more relevant than raising horses, riding to the hounds, or hobnobbing with the international "jet set." The "power elite," on the other hand, encompasses all those who are in command positions in institutions controlled by members of the upper (governing) class. Any given member of the power elite may or may not be a member of the upper class. The important thing is whether or not the institution he serves is controlled by members of the upper class. Thus, if we can show that members of the upper class control the corporations through stock ownership and corporate directorships, the military through the Department of Defense, and the corporate law profession through large corporate law firms and major law schools, we will have gone a long way toward demonstrating that the aims of the American power elite, as defined by either Mills or [us], are necessarily those of members of the upper class.

Perhaps the relationship between "governing class" and "power elite" can be made even clearer by outlining the steps that we will follow in attempting to answer the question: Is the American upper class a governing class?

First, we will show the existence of a national upper class that meets generally accepted definitions of social class.

Second, we will show that this upper class owns a disproportionate amount of the country's wealth and receives a disproportionate amount of its yearly income, and that members of the American upper class control the major banks and corporations, which in turn are known to dominate the American economy.

Third, we will show that members of the American upper class and their high-level corporation executives control the foundations, the elite universities, the largest of the mass media, and such important opinion-molding associations as the Council on Foreign Relations, the Foreign Policy Association, the Committee for Economic Development, the Business Advisory Council, and the National Advertising Council.

Fourth, we will show that the power elite (members of the American upper class and their high-level employees in the above institutions) control the Executive branch of the federal government.

Fifth, we will show that the power elite controls regulatory agencies, the federal judiciary, the military, the CIA, and the FBI through its control of the Executive branch of the federal government. It will be shown also that this control by the Executive branch is supplemented by other lines of control in the case of each of these branches or agencies of the government.

After it has been shown that the power elite does not control but merely influences (1) the Legislative branch of the federal government, (2) most state governments, and (3) most city governments, it will be argued that its control of corporations, foundations, elite universities, the Presidency, the federal judiciary, the military, and the CIA qualifies the American upper class as a "governing class," especially in the light of the wealth owned and the income received by members of that exclusive social group.

It should be added that by "control," we mean to imply dominance, the exercise of "power" (ability to act) from a position of "authority" (the right to exercise power by virtue of some office or legal mandate). Synonyms for control would be rule, govern, guide, and direct. "Influence," for us, is a weaker term, implying that a person can sometimes sway, persuade, or otherwise have an effect upon those who control from a position of authority. Since these vague terms can be the subject of much debate, let us once again make clear that we will try to show that members of the upper class dominate major corporations, foundations, universities, and the Executive branch of the federal government, while they merely have influence in Congress, most state governments, and most local governments. This does not mean that they are never influenced in areas where they have control, nor does it mean that they never get their way where they merely exert influence. However, the interesting thing about "control" and "influence" in a country where the concept of a governing class calls forth notions of sinister men lurking behind the throne, is that members of the American governing class in fact serve their interests from positions of authority. Authority-based control, rather than covert influence, is their dominant mode.

## QUESTIONS

1. Do you agree with Domhoff's claim that the American social upper class is also the "governing class in the country"?
2. If the assertion of the author is indeed true, that is, that less than 1 percent of the American population comprises the upper class and the governing class, how do you suppose we can claim that this is a "political democracy"?
3. Read Domhoff's book, and report on whether or not, in your opinion, he makes his case.

# Business power, today and tomorrow

# leonard s. silk

**Leonard S. Silk, former chairman of the editorial board of *Business Week* and now with the Brookings Institution, discusses the real powers of business in the following article.**

## ONE

Many Americans use the term "business power" pejoratively, implying a usurpation of the rights and liberties of individual citizens and an exercise of authority for selfish pecuniary ends. At the same time, there is widespread recognition that corporate power has had much to do with the economic growth, high living standards, and international strength of the United States. The basic question at issue is how the nation can preserve what is necessary and desirable of business power, but prevent its abuse.

Clearly, no one power element can control the nation on the full range of issues confronting it. The society is held together by a system of rights and duties—or, in Walter Lippmann's words, "a slightly anti-quated formulation of the balance of power among the active interests in the community." Within that somewhat precarious social order, particular interests ordinarily affect only those matters of specific concern to them. When people or groups cannot work out an adjustment of their dispute, public officials may intervene; if the officials fail, public opinion is brought to bear on the issue. Business executives are highly sensitive to the pressures of these other groups, particularly the government, and feel excessively controlled by governmental and public pressure.

Big business actually has less power today than it had in the 1890's and the 1900's, and big labor has more; but neither "dominates" the society. The New Deal years marked a decisive curbing of the power of business, and the post-World War II period witnessed a check on the power of labor. Similarly, we have seen a swelling of the power of the executive branch of the federal government, but there have been unmistakable signs recently that Congress is again asserting its power effectively.

Reprinted by permission from DAEDALUS Journal of the American Academy of Arts and Sciences, Boston, Mass., Volume 98, Winter 1969.

How much power does American business, operating within this system of checks and balances, actually wield?  The customary answer to this question usually offers a statistical table showing what proportions of Gross National Product, or of manufacturing, or of certain selected industries are owned by the largest American corporations.  Comparisons are made between the size of American Telephone & Telegraph or General Motors and that of selected foreign countries or American states.  These statistical measures are so familiar that they have lost their power to astonish and alarm.  Robert Heilbroner, however, presents a fresh and awesome perspective by asking what would happen if the one hundred and fifty largest companies disappeared, by some selective catastrophe:

> To begin with the nation would come to a standstill.  Not only would the Union and the Southern Pacific, the Pennsylvania, the New York Central [the latter two have now merged], and a half dozen of the other main railroads of the nation vanish, leaving the cities to starve, but the possibilities of supplying the urban population by truck would also disappear as the main gasoline companies and the tire companies—not to mention the makers of cars and trucks—would also cease to exist.  Meanwhile, within the nine largest concentrations of urban population, all activity would have stopped with the termination of light and power, as the utilities in these areas vanished.  In addition, communication in all these areas would break down with the disappearance of the telephone company.

But that would be only the beginning.  Virtually all steel production would stop, as would the production of the bulk of chemicals, electrical machinery, cars, trucks, tractors, and other farm implements.  The food processors would be gone, together with the cans into which they put the food.  Distribution patterns would collapse, and a national credit debacle would ensue.  The insurance companies would vanish with $500 million in life insurance, effectively bankrupting a majority of American families.

But to state the matter in this way reveals the true limitations upon the power of these enormous enterprises.  None of these companies is seen to have the right to starve the cities, bankrupt the country, or prevent an individual from getting or using a telephone.  As the late Arnold Rose pointed out, power in the United States is diffused among government agencies, trade unions, farm blocs, civil rights groups, and individual citizens—all aware of their right to oppose and constrain the powers of great corporations.  There is more than symbolic significance in the spectacle of a crusading Ralph Nader bringing to heel the General Motors Corporation, the Ford Motor Company, and the Chrysler Motor Corporation, forcing them to recall hundreds of thousands of cars and spend millions of dollars.  It should also be noted that Mr. Nader assailed the automotive giants with the help of a book-publishing corporation, the mass media supported by advertisers, the Congress, and the American legal system, which protected him from attempts of certain officials of the world's largest industrial corporation to harass him and invade his privacy in efforts to discredit him.

Nevertheless, it cannot be denied that large corporations do exercise considerable power over individual employees, suppliers, and customers, as A. A. Berle has recently observed.  But Berle contends that "these fascinating, frightening, and fantastic institutions will be strengthened rather than weakened by the application of constitutional limitations—and requirements of action—to them." He predicts that a body of rules and doctrines will emerge to prevent or correct abuses of corporate power, such as discriminatory extension of consumer credit, the coercive effect of pension trust agreements, and the invasion of privacy arising from business "data banks."

The laws and procedures of a democratic society (particularly the "equal protection of the laws" guarantee of the Fourteenth Amendment) have already been brought to bear on what had hitherto been the private province of individual businesses with respect to the rights of Negroes and members of other minority groups.  Although we are clearly moving in the direction of greater safeguards against the misuse of corporate powers, we still have a long way to go before we can be sure that businesses cannot curb the rights of individuals or punish them in ways that lie beyond the protection of the Constitution.

### TWO

Large business corporations exercise great influence in American society most clearly in the form of market power—some degree of control over the prices they charge, the wage rates they pay, and the profits they earn.  But this market power, though real, is limited by the checks provided by labor, farm groups, and other power blocs in the American system; by the Antitrust Division, the Federal Trade Commission, and other governmental regulatory agencies; and by traditional pressures of competition, foreign as well as domestic, inter-industry as well as intra-industry.  Those powerful corporations (such as the big steel companies) that underrate foreign and inter-industry competitive pressures can still be badly hurt in the market place.

Given modern technology and the economies of scale, however, some degree of corporate immunity from the pressures of competition is by no means an unmixed evil from the standpoint of the society as a whole.  Monopoly power does seem to have its social uses.  Fritz Machlup, an ardent champion of free markets and vigorous competition, concludes that large corporations, not subject to heavy competitive pressures and enjoying increased affluence and liquidity, are likely to increase their expenditures on investment in new plant development and new equipment, outlays for research and development, or support for pure science and higher education.  Moreover, it is the strong and profitable, not the weak and marginal, companies that can create jobs for unqualified Negroes, train them, and find ways to hold them to the labor force.  How effective business can be in dealing with large social problems remains to be seen.  There is, for example, good reason to worry that the so-called business power structure will prove to have insufficient control over the directly involved forces of urban America to deal successfully with the urban problem.

American business is rapidly coming to understand that cooperation among business, government, and nonprofit organizations is necessary if genuine solutions to complex social problems are to be reached.  The old business ideology is fading, as more and more corporations recognize that "free enterprise" is not an adequate answer to all national problems.  Many companies are, in fact, eager to work with government and community groups in the welfare and educational fields.  Some observers cynically conclude that the heavy degree of corporate involvement in the work of government and society is only a kind of corporate fascism.  Michael Harrington, for example, sees a "social-industrial complex" taking its place beside the "military-industrial complex."

.  .  .

**THREE**

The market economy, as it has evolved in this century, evidently does not lend itself to the emergence of industrial dictators.  It is now three quarters of a century since Henry Demarest Lloyd warned that "this era is but a passing phase" in the evolution of "corporate Caesars."  Robert Heilbroner argues that, instead of corporate Caesars, "we are left with a largely faceless group known as 'management,' whose names the public neither knows nor cares about."  J. Kenneth Galbraith agrees and suggests that corporate power has passed to a bureaucracy of technicians, "the technostructure."  The prediction of a technocratic takeover was first made, of course, by Veblen in 1919; he asserted that the "technologists" were discovering that together they constitute "the indispensable General Staff of the Industrial System" and could, "in a few weeks, incapacitate the country's productive industry."

Heilbroner and Galbraith have, I think, somewhat overstated the case.  Many board chairmen and presidents are far from powerless either outside or within their own organizations, and "the techno-structure" does not make the most important business decisions or provide its own leadership in corporations.  As I observe corporate behavior, organizational achievements or failures are more related to the performance of top management than to the technostructure.

American technologists are as far away today as they were fifty years ago from taking control of the American economic system or the corporations in which they are employed.  Scientists or engineers customarily strive to achieve power within the business world by making themselves into *businessmen*, rather than by remaining technicians.  One route that leads in the direction of genuine corporate power is through graduate work in business or executive training courses paid for by their employers, and schools of business administration endow their graduates not with the values of a new technological elite, but with the attitudes of the existing profit-oriented business management.  Business management does not *fear* the technologists; it needs all sorts of specialists to solve problems not only of production, but of marketing, finance, and accounting and to cope with the corporation's labor, community, and government relations.  Top management is pleased when a specialist shows that he is qualified for general managerial responsibility and has a highly developed sense of the importance of making money.

Business is, at the same time, certainly becoming more demanding intellectually, one reason for business's great concern about the state of American education.  Nevertheless, as much as business today needs educated brains, it retains a certain wariness of "intellectuals," if one defines the intellectual (rather than the technician) as J. P. Nettl does:

> There are three main components to the definition of an intellectual.  In the first place, his concerns tend to be universal.  He is not a specialist, but one for whom any specialist activity always relates to a whole.  He thus necessarily trades in generalizations— at least his views and statements are always intended to be capable of generalization.  Here the idea of the intellectual as the conscience of society becomes relevant. . . . Second, his concern, and therefore the validation of his activities in the eyes of others, is cultural.  He is concerned with the *quality* of life. . . . Finally, an intellectual is always strongly concerned with social and political matters; better, his is a socio-political role.

Intellectuals have often shown a flair for political power, but rarely an ability or a willingness to operate complex organizations, whether governmental, business, or labor.  On the whole, business has done a better job than organized labor in attracting and retaining intellectuals as well as technicians.  It has done this in part by rewarding them well and in part by granting them a relatively greater degree of freedom than do labor unions.  As academic pay and perquisites have risen, however, it has become more difficult than it once was for business to attract intellectuals.

A number of thoughtful observers of the American scene have con-cluded that the era when creativity and innovation were centered in the world of business is now passing, and that the locus of power is shifting from the business world to other sectors of the society, espe-cially to the universities and research centers.  Daniel Bell, for exam-ple, writes:

> Perhaps it is not too much to say that if the business firm was the key institution of the past hundred years, because of its role in organizing production for the mass creation of products, the uni-versity will become the central institution of the next hundred years because of its role as the new source of innovation and knowledge.
>
> To say that the primary institutions of the new age will be intel-lectual is not to say that the majority of persons will be scientists, engineers, technicians, or intellectuals.  The majority of individuals in contemporary society are not businessmen, yet one can say that this has been a "business civilization."  The basic values of society have been focussed on business institutions, the largest rewards have been found in business, and the strongest power has been held by the business community, although today that power is to some extent shared within the factory by the trade union, and regulated within the society by the political order.  In the most general ways, however, the major decisions affecting the day-to-day life of the citizen—the kinds of work available, the location of plants, investment decisions on new products, the distribution of tax burdens, occupational mobility—have been made by business, and latterly by government, which gives major priority to the wel-fare of business.
>
> To say that the major institutions of the new society will be intellectual is to say that production and business decisions will be subordinated to, or will derive from, other forces in society; that the crucial decisions regarding the growth of the economy and its balance will come from government, but they will be based on the government's sponsorship of research and development, of cost-effectiveness and cost-benefit analysis; that the making of deci-sions, because of the intricately linked nature of their conse-quences, will have an increasingly technical character.  The hus-banding of talent and the spread of educational and intellectual institutions will become a prime concern for the society; not only the best talents, but eventually the entire complex of social prestige and social status will be rooted in the intellectual and scientific communities.

Robert Heilbroner worries that the shift of power to the intellectuals and technicians may assume a nasty, authoritarian character before it eventually grows gentler and more humane.  He fears that we may first experience a dictatorship of the intelligentsia and technicians: "There lurks a dangerous collectivist tinge in the prospect of controls designed for the enlargement of man but inherently capable of his confinement as well." Nevertheless, he believes that all advanced industrial states —the U.S.S.R. as well as the U.S.—must make way for "the scientific cadres, the social scientists, the skilled administrators, and the trained brains." Admittedly, says Heilbroner, the intellectuals and technicians have not yet "divorced their social goals from those of the society to which they are still glad to pay allegiance, and no more than the thirteenth-century merchants huddled under the walls of a castle do they see themselves as the potential architects and lords of a society built around their own functions. But, as with the merchants, we can expect that such notions will in time emerge and assert their primacy over the aims of the existing order."

Herman Kahn and Anthony Wiener also anticipate a "shift from private business enterprise as the major source of innovation, attention, and prominence in society," as the work of society becomes increasingly concentrated in the government, the professions, the nonprofit private groups, and the like. Zbigniew Brzezinski observes that "in the post-industrial technetronic society plutocratic pre-eminence comes under a sustained challenge from the political leadership which itself is increasingly permeated by individuals possessing special skills and intellectual talents. Knowledge becomes a tool of power, and the effective mobilization of talent an important way for acquiring power." Brzezinski thinks that, unlike the revolutions of the past, the developing scientific-intellectual metamorphosis of society "will have no charismatic leaders with strident doctrines, but its impact will be far more profound."

J. Kenneth Galbraith ends his *New Industrial State* with this manifesto: "We have seen wherein the chance for salvation lies. The industrial system, in contrast with its economic antecedents, is intellectually demanding. It brings into existence, to service its intellectual and scientific needs, the community that, hopefully, will reject its monopoly of social purpose." That new community—the "educational and scientific estate"—will wax in power, Galbraith contends, as the financial community wanes and "the trade unions retreat, more or less permanently, into the shadows." Although some writers, such as Brzezinski, seem to think that the metamorphosis of society will be gradual and gentle and may not involve an actual push for political power by the scientists and intellectuals, Galbraith implies that they will have to mold themselves into a conscious, new political force:

> The educational and scientific estate is not inhibited politically by the ties of organization. It is also growing rapidly in numbers. It still lacks a sense of its own identity. It has also sat for many

years under the shadow of entrepreneurial power. A seemingly respectable measure of cynicism as well as a residual Marxism join in deprecating any political power not founded firmly on the possession of money. Yet it is possible that the educational and scientific estate requires only a strongly creative political hand to become a decisive instrument of political power.

I do not feel that a realistic model of the structure of the society and the economy emerges from the speculations of scholars who prophesy the decline of American business as a central institution. Their prognostications greatly underestimate the flexibility and adaptability of American business. Their culture-heroes are anti-bourgeois, but there are paradoxes in the situation they describe. Business has great power today, but only as one important element in a pluralistic society. It is less dominant than either Marxist ideology or Post-Industrial Society reasoning would imply. The sustaining source of business power has been its ability to innovate and to keep developing.

It is incontrovertible that there are many intellectuals and specialists who are hostile to business. Others—in great number—work for business corporations and even invest in business enterprises. Stock ownership, for example, has risen enormously in America, even on university campuses and in research centers. As A. A. Berle notes:

> Directly, there may be 23 million owners of stock in the United States. Indirectly, through pension and similar funds, some 30 or 40 million more Americans have a beneficial interest in the market value assigned by share quotations to the accumulated corporate assets—and a still more direct interest in the income generated and partly distributed by them.

The capitalist system, as Father Harbrecht has said, "seems well on the way to digesting itself." Already vast and rapidly growing sums of money are flowing into financial institutions out of the weekly and monthly pay packets of individuals and then moving into the market to buy up ownership of American industry. In 1955, all these financial institutions—such as pension funds, state and local retirement funds, life insurance companies—increased by $1.5 billion their purchases of common stocks of corporations; in 1967, these institutional purchases increased by $7.4 billion. In the year 1973, according to estimates of Scudder, Stevens, and Clark, an investment counseling firm, the new institutional demand for equities will climb by $13 billion. In addition, of course, as Americans' incomes rise, individuals will be buying more and more stock directly and through mutual funds. A huge bidding up of equity values over time appears in prospect. This growing involvement of Americans in the ownership of stock, directly or indirectly, is likely to have subtle but profound effects in strengthening the foundations of American capitalism. It will provide a kind of political barrier to moves by government that could seriously undermine business profits or growth.   Will masses of affluent Americans be responsive to some future call that they unite to change the system radically, since they have nothing to lose but their stocks, mutual funds, and pension rights?   It seems unlikely.

Moreover, one of the most striking trends of our time has been the extremely effective performance of American corporations as they have moved into international markets.   The huge sale of Jean-Jacques Servan-Schreiber's *Le défi américain* is one indication of Europe's recognition of and concern over the remarkable drive of American business management.   The Europeans do not lack scientific and technological prowess; on the contrary, as they themselves like to point out, Europeans did most of the basic work in such major fields as nuclear energy, antibiotics, jet propulsion, radar.   The American business advantage comes from the application of significant ideas and discoveries; it has to do fundamentally with the capabilities of industrial management, engineering, finance, marketing—the willingness to take risks and the willingness (indeed the zeal) to change.

This is not a new phenomenon in America.   The prophetic de Tocqueville wrote in 1835:

> I accost an American sailor and inquire why the ships of his country are built so as to last for only a short time; he answers without hesitation that the art of navigation is every day making such rapid progress that the finest vessel would become almost useless if it lasted beyond a few years.   In these words, which fell accidentally, and on a particular subject, from an uninstructed man, I recognize the general and systematic idea upon which a great people direct all their concerns.

This general and systematic idea gave rise to other characteristically American institutions: mass public education and a labor force that (though far from ideal, especially in old crafts) largely recognizes its own stake in technological progress.   American business corporations have shown in recent years that they have not lost their creativity and adaptability, but increased them by their liaison with the learned world.   The new intelligentsia is helping to change the style and mood of our society, but it is not producing a radical change in the structure of the society or the economy.   Business will, I think, prove to be flexible enough to adapt to these shifts in style and mood.   Indeed, American businesses have shown a remarkable ability to ride the trends of the times—to produce the instruments and tools of learning, loafing, calculation, reasoning, fighting, extending life and curbing fertility, traveling through space (inner and outer), or whatever it is the human race wants to do. . . .

. . .

To do the job that needs to be done, business must, however, achieve a new conception of its role in the society. In the past the essence of American business power has been ideological—that is, it has provided the value conceptions and set the limits upon what the nation is doing or trying to do. Those conceptions must now be made more humane and sensitive to the needs and aspirations of all people, but especially to those at the bottom of society. The ideological limits that have prevented us from using our matchless resources of energy and imagination for improving the quality of American life need to be widened. If business plays its full role in this effort, it will help the society to avoid chaos and stagnation, on the one side, and an excessive concentration of power in the hands of government, on the other.

## QUESTIONS

1. Silk argues that big business today actually has less power than it had in the 1890s and 1900s. How could one prove or disprove this hypothesis? Do you believe it? Explain.
2. What important checks and balances restrain the use of business power?
3. Contrast the power of business over markets and individuals.
4. What sort of safeguards would you suggest against the misuse of corporate powers?
5. Do you believe, as does Daniel Bell, that the locus of power is shifting from the business world? Explain your position.
6. Would you say that a major source of business power is its ability to adapt to the changing environment? Explain.

# The two faces of economic concentration

### m. a. adelman

**M. A. Adelman, Professor of Economics, Massachusetts Institute of Technology,**
**points out in the following article the dangers in using market structure ratios to**
**draw conclusions about the power of large companies in society.**

Last year, in a widely publicized speech, Attorney General John N. Mitchell professed alarm over the rapidly increasing concentration of American industry. In a less publicized article, Professor Pashigian of the University of Chicago suggested various methods of explaining the familiar fact that industrial concentration had been so stable for so long. Oddly enough, the Attorney General and the professor were not really contradicting each other; they were not referring to the same thing.

"Economic concentration" or "concentration of economic power" calls up a vision of a corporation, with billions in assets, thousands of employees, elaborate staff planning, etc., etc. It "dominates" its market and decides prices and outputs, either alone or in concert with one or two of its fellow giants. Such concentration and domination, presumably, is the typical pattern, or at least the wave of the future. The grand sweep of the 20th century is away from competition and into the new era of the big firm, etc. All this is a good story but not necessarily a true story. An effort to see and analyze what is actually happening in the world makes it apparent that "economic concentration," so far from being a simple, massive phenomenon, is actually a vague phrase applied to two different kinds of measurement of two different phenomena. One is that of bigness, the other of market concentration, but the relation between the two is quite complicated.

## CONCENTRATION RATIOS

The statistics of *market concentration* exist because economists have tried to put numbers into their analysis of monopoly and competition. Theory and observation seem to prove that it does make a difference

From *The Public Interest*, 21 (Fall 1970), 117–126. © National Affairs, Inc. 1970. Reprinted by permission.

whether there are few or many firms in a market. The ultimate in fewness is monopoly, where a single firm can do what is best for the industry as a whole because it *is* the industry as a whole. It has the power to control output: to let only so much of production on to the market as will yield the greatest money profit, or perhaps the most quiet managerial life. Short of actual monopoly, the fewer the firms, the easier it is for them to collaborate, to align prices and production so as to travel much or all the way toward monopoly. The more firms, the harder is such collaboration, and the more are they forced willy-nilly to act independently. At the extreme of such competitiveness, each firm always seeks its own profit, neither trying to serve the group industrial interest nor expecting anyone else to do so. Of course, even a very large number of firms can be regimented into monopoly through detailed agreements tolerated or enforced by government. But if these cannot be made, there is no control of supply, and no market power. Output is higher, prices are lower, and resources [are] better used. It is less clear that the *long-run* performance of a competitive market is also superior to one where a small group has market power and controls supply. I think it is, but discussion would take us too far afield.

All this seems simple enough. But it isn't. To begin with, trying to measure the manyness or fewness of firms in an industry is difficult. Companies are usually of such unequal size that a simple head-count is useless. Suppose one firm had 95 per cent of a market and 100 other firms have the other 5 per cent. There would be literally 101 sellers. But it would be nearer the truth to call this a one-firm industry. Both statements would be imprecise, but the first would be wildly wrong in its implications.

In the 1930's, the Census Bureau first tabulated something called the "concentration ratio": the sales of the largest four companies in each industry as a percentage of total sales of all companies in that industry. (The number four had no particular justification; it was only that Census regulations forbid separate publication of the sales of smaller numbers of companies. Fortunately, it turns out that it does not seem to make much difference if we use the largest eight or twenty; industry rankings are hardly changed.) Since 1947, the Census of Manufactures has regularly collected and published concentration ratios for each of 450-odd manufacturing industries, further subdivided into about a thousand product classes.

Now, manufacturing is certainly the heart of what is usually called "the industrial economy." But it is well to keep in mind that manufacturing represents only about 35 per cent of the private economy; we have no such systematic data for mining, construction, wholesale and retail trade, services, or the "public utilities" of transportation, communication, and electric power. Thus, the very biggest (e.g., A.T.&T.) and the very smallest companies fall outside of the range of what is periodically canvassed and reported by the Census.

Moreover, the concentration ratio—the sales of largest four as a per cent of the total—is no precise measure. A concentration ratio of 50 could mean that the single largest company had 49 per cent of the sales, while the three next largest had ⅓ per cent each. A concentration ratio of 50 could also mean that the largest four had respectively 13, 13, 12 and 12. True, some more refined measures have been devised; at least one of them, the so-called Herfindahl index, seems much superior, but it has not been applied widely.

Even if it were, it might not help much. A far more important limitation of the concentration ratio is the uncertain denominator, "total industry sales." The boundaries of the "industry" or "market" are often fuzzy. Any official definition is a rough approximation at best, and often has little to do with buyers and sellers whose offerings and demands interact to make a price. The basic idea of "a market" in economic analysis is: a discrete area of economic activity, with a clear-cut boundary between it and the rest of the economy. What is produced outside this area cannot easily and quickly be substituted for what is produced within. In the real world, however, such boundaries are never all that clear-cut. If much of a product used in this country is imported or exported, the American sellers and customers are part of a world-wide market, and figures on domestic activity are only a truncated fragment of a larger whole. (Large imports or exports do not necessarily mean that the concentration ratio overstates true market shares; the big American companies may account for some or even most of what is produced abroad. Hence the true world-wide concentration ratio could be greater or less than the false national ratio.) Inside the United States, there may be a substitution from similar or identical products which happen to be classified as belonging to another industry, or from facilities which can easily be converted. "Industries" are collections of similar plants which may produce a varied assortment of products. (Fortunately, there are separate tabulations of product totals regardless of what industries they happen to be produced in. The result is a valuable opportunity to cross-check and get a stereoscopic view.) It might at first seem that because of substitution across product lines or industry lines, concentration is usually overstated; as with foreign trade; however, it can work both ways—the "substitute" may itself be produced by a large manufacturer of the original. But one limitation of the data works always in a single direction; where products are sold in regional or local—i.e., "insulated"—markets, concentration ratios come out higher, sometimes much higher, than the national average.

Finally, a concentration ratio is a snapshot and gives no indication of the way an industry is going.  In a concentrated market, but a growing one to which entry is relatively easy, rewards to those who grab the largest share may be so great that an attempt to hold the line on prices cannot succeed.  Prices and outputs may be highly competitive.  But if entry into this growing market is difficult (e.g., because of patents), there may be less competition than there seems.

## THE FACTS OF MARKET CONCENTRATION

In any given instance, therefore, a concentration ratio may not mean anything.  But what cannot be said of any individual in a group may be truthfully said of a group.  A single concentration ratio tells us little about a given industry at a given time, but much may be learned from analysis of groups of industries over time, or among countries or regions.  So the close attention to dusty detail is bound together with broad comparisons in time and space.  The most important contribution of the statistics is perhaps not in the detailed numbers but the way of looking at industries.  We see some familiar terrain in a new light and the single stereotype of "big business" disintegrates into a more difficult but more interesting universe.

For example, the "third world" of the less-developed countries is almost surely the most highly concentrated and monopolized.  Because incomes are low, most markets are extremely small, with room for few rivals.  Capital, skilled labor and know-how are scarce, innovation is risky, and starting new enterprises is that much harder.  Hence, vested interests are that much more safe from new entrants.  Growth and development would entail the breakdown of a host of miniscule monopolies.  But economic development is usually planned and controlled by government, which restricts imports to conserve foreign exchange, protects nationalized enterprise against either foreign or domestic rivals, etc.—all to the effect, if not always for the purpose, of narrowing the circle of possible rivals.

In such countries as Great Britain and France, companies tend to be much smaller than in the United States, but markets are very much smaller, so that in any given market, concentration tends to be higher than in the United States.  (The European Economic Community is now providing much bigger markets, within which the rivals will be bigger but also more numerous and hence more competitive.)  Japan is, as in so many other respects, in a class by itself.  Concentration seems to run higher than in the United States, but the importance of foreign trade is so much greater that the conclusion is in doubt.

In the United States, one can study concentration over time.  A comparison between manufacturing around 1900 and in 1947 seems to show a substantial drop.  But given the unsystematic data for 1900, it seems better to make a sure bet on a milder proposition: concentration could not have increased.  Between 1947 and 1966, individual industries or products often change, but the ups balance the downs, and there is no net total change in industrial concentration.

But as the stability becomes obvious, it also is less satisfying.  Why should there *not* be a change up or down?  If we could explain the past stability, and identify the causes thereof, we might make an educated guess at the future.  But since we have not yet reached the first stage, we ought to resist the impulse to extrapolate and predict that what has been will be.  Mark Twain said somewhere that the Mississippi River is an alluvial stream which often cuts its bank  and has in the course of years shortened its total length—hence any fool could see, and some fools would say, that in a thousand years Minneapolis would be a suburb of New Orleans.

One plausible theory for the steady level of concentration is that the larger the industry, and the faster its growth, the better the odds that concentration decreases.  The bigger market works in two opposed ways: there is more scope for economies of scale, and the companies therefore tend to be bigger; but there is also more room for rivals, and the latter tendency seems on the whole to be a little stronger.  For example, in 1963 there were 52 product classes with sales of more than a billion dollars each.  Three of these products had a concentration ratio of over 80 (the largest four made 80 per cent of the sales) and 16 of them had a concentration ratio of over 50.  At the other extreme, there were 96 product classes with sales of less than $50 million apiece.  Fourteen had concentration ratios of over 80, and 47 of over 50.  Thus, the bigger the industry and the bigger the companies, the lower the concentration.  But the tendency is very mild.

The stereotype that the big company has a big market share is obviously supported by many examples.  Only, it is refuted by even more.  The association of rapid growth with lower concentration is somewhat stronger, but even so it is not very marked.

Yet if size of market and economic growth are on the whole favorable to lower concentration, one would expect a slow downdrift over time; in fact, there has been none since 1947.  Perhaps the reason is that in earlier years the growing markets increased company size faster than market size.  That, of course, is the problem with which we started!  As in most fields of study, the more we learn, the more questions we encounter.

Attempts have also been made to relate concentration to other economic variables.  The more concentrated an industry, for instance, the less competitive it presumably is, and the more profitable it ought to be. And so it appears in fact. But the relation is a weak one at best, and the odds are only a little over 50–50 that a more concentrated industry will be more profitable than a less concentrated one. This mild signal is actually reassuring. For if higher industry concentration were associated with *lower* profits, one would have to ask—on the assumption that businessmen are not as a class insane—whether concentration data made much sense.

## THE LARGEST 100–200–ETC.

These facts on industry concentration get no headlines, and they are not what Mr. Mitchell professed to view with alarm. What we mostly hear about is "aggregate concentration" (or "overall concentration" or "superconcentration"), which is the percentage of total manufacturing —all industries added together—that is accounted for by the largest 50 or 100 or 200 firms, regardless of industry.

A few comparisons over time are possible. In 1935, the largest 50 companies accounted for somewhere around 22 per cent of total Census manufacturing "value-added" (i.e., the margin between purchases and sales); in 1947, only 17 per cent; in 1954, 23 per cent, and in 1967, 25 per cent. Another way to measure big-company participation is by the proportions of corporate assets owned. Assets are harder to measure and more risky to compare, because of variations in accounting rules, which moreover have changed over time. (In addition, it is necessary to splice together various statistical series.) But the figures on assets show a parallel movement to the figures on "value-added." According to the statistics of the Internal Revenue Service, the largest 139 manufacturing corporations had 47 per cent of all corporate assets in 1931 and the largest 141 had 48 per cent in 1963. (Technical adjustments, for noncorporate manufacturing and for greater consolidation of corporate reporting, work both ways and make little net difference.) Measuring on a different basis, Professor Charles Berry has estimated the share of the largest 100 at 44 per cent in 1948 and 48 per cent in 1964; applying his methods to later years, the figure is seen to be 50 per cent in 1968.

It is reassuring that both value-added and asset figures agree in broad outline: a decrease from the early 1930's to the late 1940's; then a restoration; then an even further increase.

The trend can be embellished, for polemical purposes, by measuring from low to high, i.e., comparing 1948 with 1968, rather than from high to high (or at least earliest to latest), i.e., comparing 1931 with 1968. It is a bit like comparing department store sales, August with December, to show that sales are doing fine. Extrapolate the 1948–1968 "trend" by twenty or fifty years, and there is as much to view with alarm as there was decades ago; only a spoilsport would ask what happened to those earlier predictions of an imminent monopolistic economy.

The increased share of the largest 50 or 100, etc., has come about largely because the industries composed of big companies have grown faster than industries with smaller companies. (These industries of big companies, it should be noted, are *not* the industries with the highest concentration ratios. And within these big-company industries, there was actually some decrease in concentration ratios during 1947–1966.) The minor reason for the higher aggregate concentration has been mergers, some conglomerate some not, though such terms are highly imprecise.

But the most important question is the relevance of "superconcentration." Statistics do not speak for themselves. One needs a theory to show that a given set of numbers has a given meaning. A private-enterprise economy works well or badly through the network of markets which compose it. But there is no linkage between "aggregate concentration" and any market in the real world. At the limit, concentration ratios could be declining in every industry, and the less concentrated industries growing more rapidly, yet if those were big-company industries, "aggregate concentration" would increase.

The two biggest manufacturing companies are Standard Oil (New Jersey) and General Motors, with respectively $17 billion and $14 billion of assets. GM has about 55 per cent of U.S. automotive production. (The largest four automobile producers account for practically all domestic output. Yet as we warned earlier, a concentration ratio of 100 *exaggerates*. GM, Ford, Chrysler, and American Motors do not in fact have the entire market. Imports are 13 per cent of car sales, and if we are to believe some auto executives quoted in *The New York Times* last May 22, imports will be 19 per cent if the industry does not change its offerings.) Jersey Standard, although bigger than GM, has only about 9 per cent of domestic oil refining, and less of production. (It is larger in the world market than in the United States, but the two are altogether separate.) *The huge size of a given company tells nothing about the rivalry it faces, the kind of market it lives in, or its price-output pattern.*

A useful mental experiment is to imagine that the largest 100 industrial corporations have all doubled in size and now account, not for about 50 but for 100 per cent of all manufacturing. In addition, they have completely diversified; every one of these companies operates in every market, in the same proportion as in total manufacturing. Then every market would have 100 sellers, of whom the largest would be only 7 per cent of the total.   Few manufacturing markets show so little market concentration today.

Alternatively, suppose that 1,000 rather than 100 corporations account for all manufacturing activity, and that each one of the thousand is all alone in each of the 1,000 product classes (the so-called five-digit groups) enumerated by the Census.   This would be, loosely speaking, universal monopoly.   Strong competition with 100 firms and universal monopoly with 1,000 firms would seem to indicate that the number of the largest firms, regardless of industry, and the per cent of production which the largest firms account for, gives us no basis to say anything about competition or monopoly.

Assertions are made from time to time that somehow, somewhere, there is a connection between bigness and concentration.   A recent 730-page report by the staff of the Federal Trade Commission makes the assertion in many different ways; but one can find only one table which has some claim to relevance and at least asserts a slight connection between market concentration and the participation of the largest 200 firms.   Were the table valid, it would mean that, e.g., an increase from 35 to 45 per cent in the participation of the top 200 in an industry would increase the concentration ratio in that industry from 42 to 44 per cent.   The effect is too mild for discussion, and this is not the place to scrutinize technical defects, however grievous.   But one general comment is unavoidable.   The foundation of physical science is the reproducible experiment; that of economic statistics is the reproducible table.   It is impossible to say how this particular table—like many other tables in the FTC report—was constructed.   The lawyers would call it void for vagueness.   And this is the sum total of evidence on the subject in the report.

The attention and publicity given to "aggregate concentration" derives partly from the belief that "the big firm" has basic advantages in the market place.   It can outlast, outlose, outfight, outspend, etc., and thereby drive smaller rivals out of its respective markets without resort to anything so crude and costly as predatory warfare.   (The belief is even stronger in Europe, despite the loss of export markets by American companies to much smaller European and Japanese firms.)   The theory is general, and presumes to hold as well for the United States 70 years ago as for now.   If it is correct, one should see an updrift in concentration ratios, as the firms which were largest in total size took over more and more of the markets in which they operated. The tendency would be stronger in some places, weaker in others, but over a long period of time it would be a tide lapping steadily upward and onward over the land.   But as seen earlier, there is no such tendency; the chief problem is why industry concentration has remained so stable for so long, through stronger and weaker antitrust enforcement; through war, depression, and boom.

Plainly the theory is wrong, and size alone does not convey an inherent advantage.  There are two mistakes in supposing that big and richer companies can elbow smaller rivals out of the market merely because they are big.  First, investment for profit is not like spending for personal need or pleasure.  If Mr. A and Mr. B both bid for the same painting, and Mr. A has ten times as much income and assets, he has the power to outbid and take the picture.  But if Corporation X has a cash flow ten times that of Corporation Y, it has about ten times as many claims on it.  There is no presumption that Corporation X can obtain more money more easily than Corporation Y for the particular purpose of improving its position in Y's market.  Other markets may offer more lucrative opportunities—and such a comparison is bound to be made by management, the firm's creditors, and the investing public.  Possibly the big firm can borrow more cheaply, though the advantage is never great and above a certain point, perhaps $50 million in assets, it goes to zero.  Furthermore, most capital is equity capital, and the more profitable company can sell equity securities on better terms.

This brings us to the second and perhaps more basic mistake in supposing that larger companies can outlose or outbid smaller ones.  Business firms only want money in order to make more.  The firm which stands to gain more from an expenditure can offer more for the use of money.  In any given market, therefore, the more efficient firm will tend to outbid its less efficient rival.  The more profitable companies will tend to grow faster than the less profitable.  If the process continues for some time, the biggest companies in any given industry may well end up being the ones who are the most profitable—but this hardly proves that size as such brings high profits.

But although "superconcentration" has nothing to do with market concentration, nor with monopoly and competition, it may be much more important.  There may be strong *non*economic reasons for paying so much attention to the biggest companies simply because they are big.  The feeling goes back a long way.  A grandfather of the current Mr. Justice Harlan, who bore the same name, is best remembered today for his dissent in an early segregation case; his opinion that our Constitution is color blind was vindicated sixty years later.  In 1911, shortly before his death, Justice Harlan wrote an opinion recalling the fear just after the Civil War that, with human slavery just abolished at appalling cost, there might be a new subjection to big corporations.  There is a recent much-acclaimed biography of Huey P. Long, the brilliant and dangerous Louisiana Kingfish, who suited the action to the word that large corporations were wonderful to run against.

Public opinion has been, not hostile to big business, but at least cool and critical of it.   It is no bad thing, in my opinion, that generations of big business executives have learned that they live in a goldfish bowl, more subject to taxes and regulations and prohibitions than smaller firms.   But like all good things, this public opinion has its price, which is confusion and ambivalence, admiration and mistrust often equally misplaced.   Like Huey Long, Mr. Dooley knew his America.   The words he put into President Theodore Roosevelt's mouth would have been as true and apt twenty years earlier as they are now 65 years later: "Th' thrusts are heejous monsthers, built up be th'enlightened intherprize of the men who've done so much to advance progiss in our happy country.   On the wan hand, I wud stamp thim undher fut; on th'ither hand, not so fast."

Perhaps bigness is much more important, sociologically or politically, than is revealed by measuring economic quantities to understand market facts.   If that is the case, it should be studied directly, and not be confused with economic concentration, a market phenomenon.


## QUESTIONS

1. Does the fact that the largest companies own today a larger proportion of total corporate assets than in the past indicate that business today has greater power in the society than it had in the past? Explain.
2. Adelman says that "size alone does not convey an inherent advantage." Why?
3. Do you think you can predict the behavior of a corporation on the basis of the concentration ratio of the industry in which it is located? Explain.
4. There are some arguments to support the notion that bigness in corporations is a good thing from the standpoint of social welfare. On the other hand, there are arguments against this notion. What are the pros and cons?
5. Argue the case pro and con that small business has more political power than large business.

# The hidden executives    ralph nader

**Ralph Nader, the well-known critic of both corporate and governmental institutions, asks some questions about the visibility of the modern corporate executive.**

Last year a group of Princeton University seniors wrote to the heads of fifteen large corporations requesting the participation of either the Chairman, President or Executive Vice-President on a panel of business leaders to discuss in open forum some problems of corporate responsibility. The students added that the forum's format would provide for audience questions and comments on the positions taken by the executives.

The response to this letter was strongly negative, with only two companies agreeing to send a public relations man. The students were dismayed. But it is standard operating procedure for large companies to avoid exposing their top executives to any college audiences that can ask questions. The last time the chief executive of one of America's 50 largest companies spoke to and with students in an open forum may not be within the memory of man. Presidential candidates, Cabinet officers, Senators, Governors have all entered into unstructured dialogues on basic issues with students. But this has not been the case with corporate moguls.

Such a strict policy of avoidance cannot be explained away on the basis of time pressures but rather is rooted in the desire to be insulated from bilateral communication on issues deemed too controversial for public airing. The principle is as old as politics: if the arena of exposure can be limited, then the control over policy and dissent can be maximized. Perhaps the best indication of this policy's success is that students have settled for low echelon, public relations or trade association employees speaking for companies and industries in the most bland terms. Indeed, there are probably few students who can name the Chairman and President of the five largest corporations; yet many can reel off the names of Governors of states most of whom are smaller than these companies.

Anonymity of mega-corporate leaders outside the business world is actively pursued as a shield against public scrutiny of their massive and pervasive economic power. When General Motors Chairman Frederic Donner and President James Roche were asked to testify in July 1965 before Senator Abraham Ribicoff's Subcommittee inquiring into auto safety, few newsmen or Washington hands in that hearing room had heard, much less seen, the managers of a company grossing more annually than all but two foreign governments ($2.3 million an hour). GM was personalized that day and the nation was given a glimpse into the unresponsiveness and laggardness of a company's auto safety policy and investment—a glimpse that soon grew into outrage and safety legislation. The weekly program—"Meet the Press"—tried repeatedly to interview Henry Ford II during the auto safety controversy in 1966, but he declined.

As long as corporate giants remain faceless institutions garnished with a few slogans and trademarks, the public will receive few glimpses into decisions or inaction that affect the course of the economy and the health and safety of a society.

It is interesting to note how General Motors, as one large corporation, tries to reconcile the need to "appear" before the public and the demands of insulation from an inquiring public. The company maintains a guest lecture list which organizations can draw upon for speakers. Illustratively, a former Miss America, Marilyn Van Derbur, is presently a guest lecturer for General Motors and speaks before groups around the country. Presumably, providing the public with a list of celebrities ready to speak conserves valuable time of top executives who restrict their addresses to business and trade groups.

It would seem reasonable to recognize a public right of access to corporate leaders. In January 1966, the Attorney General of Iowa invited the heads of GM, Ford and Chrysler to testify at a public hearing on auto safety open to citizens of Iowa who were given the opportunity to ask questions. All three companies turned him down and a trade representative of the Automobile Manufacturers Association took their place. He declined to answer any questions dealing with the companies because he was not authorized to speak for any company's policy. The AMA does not build and sell automobiles; it could not substitute for the auto companies. Yet these companies stated that they would have to decline any and all such invitations. The officials of Los Angeles County still have not succeeded, for example, in having auto company heads publicly tour the besmogged city and engage in a public exchange of views with the citizenry in an orderly public forum. Making sales and taking our profits from a region polluted by the companies' products incur no responsibility to meet the consumer, in the stiff judgment of corporate management.

Only once a year do corporate leaders have to expose themselves to a two-way communication process. This occasion is the stockholders' meeting. But this dialogue is conducted under the most abbreviated, authoritarian manner with a stacked audience of highly partisan and vocal employees and luncheon-oriented shareholders who usually hoot down anyone trying to engage in a sequentially rational exchange involving a point critical of the company. Arbitrary rulings by the Chairman are cheered and only the threat of turning oneself into a spectacle —as do the few professional corporate quizzers—ensures a minimum hearing.

The rules and rationale behind economic (and corporate) democracy are much the same as those underlying a democratic politics. The contempt accorded rights of access and duties to confront citizens by corporate management has been costly to the public interest. For the variety of values and urgencies, rarely communicated to top corporate echelons by subordinates and other filters of communication, are denied a chance to enrich the company's vision and provide it with a close sense of the community's moral imperatives which a just economy must always reflect.

## QUESTIONS

1. Do you think the chief executive of a large company, or any company, is obliged to appear before a legislative committee or a group of citizens whenever they want to question him? Explain your position.
2. What valid reasons do you see for chief executives being rather careful about the invitations they accept to speak or to engage in dialogues with persons and groups outside the corporation?
3. If corporations are to conduct meaningful and fruitful dialogues with their critics, how do you think this can best be done?
4. Do you believe the larger corporations tell as much about their affairs as they should? Explain your position.
5. Are the rules and rationale of corporate life much the same as those underlying a political democracy, as Nader claims?

# Pros and Cons
# of Business Social
# Responsibilities

**6**

# The social responsibility of business is to increase its profits

## milton friedman

Milton Friedman, Professor of Economics at the University of Chicago, presents in this article a strong defense of the view that the only social responsibility of business is to maximize its profits.

When I hear businessmen speak eloquently about the "social responsibilities of business in a free-enterprise system," I am reminded of the wonderful line about the Frenchman who discovered at the age of 70 that he had been speaking prose all his life. The businessmen believe that they are defending free enterprise when they declaim that business is not concerned "merely" with profit but also with promoting desirable "social" ends; that business has a "social conscience" and takes seriously its responsibilities for providing employment, eliminating discrimination, avoiding pollution and whatever else may be the catchwords of the contemporary crop of reformers. In fact they are—or would be if they or anyone else took them seriously—preaching pure and unadulterated socialism. Businessmen who talk this way are unwitting puppets of the intellectual forces that have been undermining the basis of a free society these past decades.

The discussions of the "social responsibilities of business" are notable for their analytical looseness and lack of rigor. What does it mean to say that "business" has responsibilities? Only people can have responsibilities. A corporation is an artificial person and in this sense may have artificial responsibilities, but "business" as a whole cannot be said to have responsibilities, even in this vague sense. The first step toward clarity in examining the doctrine of the social responsibility of business is to ask precisely what it implies for whom.

Presumably, the individuals who are to be responsible are businessmen, which means individual proprietors or corporate executives. Most of the discussion of social responsibility is directed at corporations, so in what follows I shall mostly neglect the individual proprietor and speak of corporate executives.

*The New York Times Magazine*, September 13, 1970, pp. 33, 122–126. © 1970 by The New York Times Company. Reprinted by permission.

. . .

In a free-enterprise, private-property system, a corporate executive is an employe of the owners of the business.  He has direct responsibility to his employers.  That responsibility is to conduct the business in accordance with their desires, which generally will be to make as much money as possible while conforming to the basic rules of the society, both those embodied in law and those embodied in ethical custom.  Of course, in some cases his employers may have a different objective.  A group of persons might establish a corporation for an eleemosynary purpose—for example, a hospital or a school.  The manager of such a corporation will not have money profit as his objective but the rendering of certain services.

In either case, the key point is that, in his capacity as a corporate executive, the manager is the agent of the individuals who own the corporation or establish the eleemosynary institution, and his primary responsibility is to them.

Needless to say, this does not mean that it is easy to judge how well he is performing his task.  But at least the criterion of performance is straightforward, and the persons among whom a voluntary contractual arrangement exists are clearly defined.

Of course, the corporate executive is also a person in his own right.  As a person, he may have many other responsibilities that he recognizes or assumes voluntarily—to his family, his conscience, his feelings of charity, his church, his clubs, his city, his country.  He may feel impelled by these responsibilities to devote part of his income to causes he regards as worthy, to refuse to work for particular corporations, even to leave his job, for example, to join his country's armed forces.  If we wish, we may refer to some of these responsibilities as "social responsibilities."  But in these respects he is acting as a principal, not an agent; he is spending his own money or time or energy, not the money of his employers or the time or energy he has contracted to devote to their purposes.  If these are "social responsibilities," they are the social responsibilities of individuals, not of business.

What does it mean to say that the corporate executive has a "social responsibility" in his capacity as businessman?  If this statement is not pure rhetoric, it must mean that he is to act in some way that is not in the interest of his employers.  For example, that he is to refrain from increasing the price of the product in order to contribute to the social objective of preventing inflation, even though a price increase would be in the best interests of the corporation.  Or that he is to make expenditures on reducing pollution beyond the amount that is in the best interests of the corporation or that is required by law in order to contribute to the social objective of improving the environment.  Or that, at the expense of corporate profits, he is to hire "hard-core" unemployed instead of better-qualified available workmen to contribute to the social objective of reducing poverty.

In each of these cases, the corporate executive would be spending someone else's money for a general social interest. Insofar as his actions in accord with his "social responsibility" reduce returns to stockholders, he is spending their money. Insofar as his actions raise the price to customers, he is spending the customers' money. Insofar as his actions lower the wages of some employes, he is spending their money.

The stockholders or the customers or the employes could separately spend their own money on the particular action if they wished to do so. The executive is exercising a distinct "social responsibility," rather than serving as an agent of the stockholders or the customers or the employes, only if he spends the money in a different way than they would have spent it.

But if he does this, he is in effect imposing taxes, on the one hand, and deciding how the tax proceeds shall be spent, on the other.

This process raises political questions on two levels: principle and consequences. On the level of political principle, the imposition of taxes and the expenditure of tax proceeds are governmental functions. We have established elaborate constitutional, parliamentary and judicial provisions to control these functions, to assure that taxes are imposed so far as possible in accordance with the preferences and desires of the public—after all, "taxation without representation" was one of the battle cries of the American Revolution. We have a system of checks and balances to separate the legislative function of imposing taxes and enacting expenditures from the executive function of collecting taxes and administering expenditure programs and from the judicial function of mediating disputes and interpreting the law.

Here the businessman—self-selected or appointed directly or indirectly by stockholders—is to be simultaneously legislator, executive and jurist. He is to decide whom to tax by how much and for what purpose, and he is to spend the proceeds—all this guided only by general exhortations from on high to restrain inflation, improve the environment, fight poverty and so on and on.

The whole justification for permitting the corporate executive to be selected by the stockholders is that the executive is an agent serving the interests of his principal. This justification disappears when the corporate executive imposes taxes and spends the proceeds for "social" purposes. He becomes in effect a public employe, a civil servant, even though he remains in name an employe of a private enterprise. On grounds of political principle, it is intolerable that such civil servants—insofar as their actions in the name of social responsibility are real and not just window-dressing—should be selected as they are now. If they are to be civil servants, then they must be selected through a political process. If they are to impose taxes and make expenditures to foster "social" objectives, then political machinery must be set up to guide the assessment of taxes and to determine through a political process the objectives to be served.

This is the basic reason why the doctrine of "social responsibility" involves the acceptance of the socialist view that political mechanisms, not market mechanisms, are the appropriate way to determine the allocation of scarce resources to alternative uses.

On the grounds of consequences, can the corporate executive in fact discharge his alleged "social responsibilities"? On the one hand, suppose he could get away with spending the stockholders' or customers' or employes' money. How is he to know how to spend it? He is told that he must contribute to fighting inflation. How is he to know what action of his will contribute to that end? He is presumably an expert in running his company—in producing a product or selling it or financing it. But nothing about his selection makes him an expert on inflation. Will his holding down the price of his product reduce inflationary pressure? Or, by leaving more spending power in the hands of his customers, simply divert it elsewhere? Or, by forcing him to produce less because of the lower price, will it simply contribute to shortages? Even if he could answer these questions, how much cost is he justified in imposing on his stockholders, customers and employes for this social purpose? What is his appropriate share and what is the appropriate share of others?

And, whether he wants to or not, can he get away with spending his stockholders', customers' or employes' money? Will not the stockholders fire him? (Either the present ones or those who take over when his actions in the name of social responsibility have reduced the corporation's profits and the price of its stock.) His customers and his employes can desert him for other producers and employers less scrupulous in exercising their social responsibilities.

This facet of "social responsibility" doctrine is brought into sharp relief when the doctrine is used to justify wage restraint by trade unions. The conflict of interest is naked and clear when union officials are asked to subordinate the interest of their members to some more general social purpose. If the union officials try to enforce wage restraint, the consequence is likely to be wildcat strikes, rank-and-file revolts and the emergence of strong competitors for their jobs. We thus have the ironic phenomenon that union leaders—at least in the U.S.—have objected to Government interference with the market far more consistently and courageously than have business leaders.

The difficulty of exercising "social responsibility" illustrates, of course, the great virtue of private competitive enterprise—it forces people to be responsible for their own actions and makes it difficult for them to "exploit" other people for either selfish or unselfish purposes. They can do good—but only at their own expense.

Many a reader who has followed the argument this far may be tempted to remonstrate that it is all well and good to speak of government's having the responsibility to impose taxes and determine expenditures for such "social" purposes as controlling pollution or training the hard-core unemployed, but that the problems are too urgent to wait on the slow course of political processes, that the exercise of social responsibility by businessmen is a quicker and surer way to solve pressing current problems.

Aside from the question of fact—I share Adam Smith's skepticism about the benefits that can be expected from "those who affected to trade for the public good"—this argument must be rejected on grounds of principle. What it amounts to is an assertion that those who favor the taxes and expenditures in question have failed to persuade a majority of their fellow citizens to be of like mind and that they are seeking to attain by undemocratic procedures what they cannot attain by democratic procedures. In a free society, it is hard for "good" people to do "good," but that is a small price to pay for making it hard for "evil" people to do "evil," especially since one man's good is another's evil.

I have, for simplicity, concentrated on the special case of the corporate executive, except only for the brief digression on trade unions. But precisely the same argument applies to the newer phenomenon of calling upon stockholders to require corporations to exercise social responsibility (the recent G.M. crusade, for example). In most of these cases, what is in effect involved is some stockholders trying to get other stockholders (or customers or employes) to contribute against their will to "social" causes favored by the activists. Insofar as they succeed, they are again imposing taxes and spending the proceeds.

The situation of the individual proprietor is somewhat different. If he acts to reduce the returns of his enterprise in order to exercise his "social responsibility," he is spending his own money, not someone else's. If he wishes to spend his money on such purposes, that is his right, and I cannot see that there is any objection to his doing so. In the process, he, too, may impose costs on employes and customers. However, because he is far less likely than a large corporation or union to have monopolistic power, any such side effects will tend to be minor.

Of course, in practice the doctrine of social responsibility is frequently a cloak for actions that are justified on other grounds rather than a reason for those actions.

To illustrate, it may well be in the long-run interest of a corporation that is a major employer in a small community to devote resources to providing amenities to that community or to improving its government. That may make it easier to attract desirable employes, it may reduce the wage bill or lessen losses from pilferage and sabotage or have other worthwhile effects. Or it may be that, given the laws about the deductibility of corporate charitable contributions, the stockholders can contribute more to charities they favor by having the corporation make the gift than by doing it themselves, since they can in that way contribute an amount that would otherwise have been paid as corporate taxes.

In each of these—and many similar—cases, there is a strong temptation to rationalize these actions as an exercise of "social responsibility." In the present climate of opinion, with its widespread aversion to "capitalism," "profits," the "soulless corporation" and so on, this is one way for a corporation to generate good will as a by-product of expenditures that are entirely justified in its own self-interest.

It would be inconsistent of me to call on corporate executives to refrain from this hypocritical window-dressing because it harms the foundations of a free society. That would be to call on them to exercise a "social responsibility"! If our institutions, and the attitudes of the public make it in their self-interest to cloak their actions in this way, I cannot summon much indignation to denounce them. At the same time, I can express admiration for those individual proprietors or owners of closely held corporations or stockholders of more broadly held corporations who disdain such tactics as approaching fraud.

Whether blameworthy or not, the use of the cloak of social responsibility, and the nonsense spoken in its name by influential and prestigious businessmen, does clearly harm the foundations of a free society. I have been impressed time and again by the schizophrenic character of many businessmen. They are capable of being extremely far-sighted and clear-headed in matters that are internal to their businesses. They are incredibly short-sighted and muddled-headed in matters that are outside their businesses but affect the possible survival of business in general. This short-sightedness is strikingly exemplified in the calls from many businessmen for wage and price guidelines or controls or incomes policies. There is nothing that could do more in a brief period to destroy a market system and replace it by a centrally controlled system than effective governmental control of prices and wages.

The short-sightedness is also exemplified in speeches by businessmen on social responsibility. This may gain them kudos in the short run. But it helps to strengthen the already too prevalent view that the pursuit of profits is wicked and immoral and must be curbed and controlled by external forces.  Once this view is adopted, the external forces that curb the market will not be the social consciences, however highly developed, of the pontificating executives; it will be the iron fist of Government bureaucrats.  Here, as with price and wage controls, businessmen seem to me to reveal a suicidal impulse.

The political principle that underlies the market mechanism is unanimity.  In an ideal free market resting on private property, no individual can coerce any other, all cooperation is voluntary, all parties to such cooperation benefit or they need not participate.  There are no "social" values, no "social" responsibilities in any sense other than the shared values and responsibilities of individuals.  Society is a collection of individuals and of the various groups they voluntarily form.

The political principle that underlies the political mechanism is conformity.  The individual must serve a more general social interest— whether that be determined by a church or a dictator or a majority. The individual may have a vote and a say in what is to be done, but if he is overruled, he must conform.  It is appropriate for some to require others to contribute to a general social purpose whether they wish to or not.

Unfortunately, unanimity is not always feasible.  There are some respects in which conformity appears unavoidable, so I do not see how one can avoid the use of the political mechanism altogether.

But the doctrine of "social responsibility" taken seriously would extend the scope of the political mechanism to every human activity. It does not differ in philosophy from the most explicitly collectivist doctrine.  It differs only by professing to believe that collectivist ends can be attained without collectivist means.  That is why, in my book *Capitalism and Freedom,* I have called it a "fundamentally subversive doctrine" in a free society, and have said that in such a society, "there is one and only one social responsibility of business—to use its resources and engage in activities designed to increase its profits so long as it stays within the rules of the game, which is to say, engages in open and free competition without deception or fraud."

## QUESTIONS

1. Do you accept Friedman's thesis that an executive in a large company is the employe of the owners?
2. Do you accept Friedman's views that social responsibilities refer to actions taken by executives that result in the expenditure of money in a different way than stockholders, customers, or workers would choose to spend the money?
3. Do you think that Friedman is correct when he says that spending

money for social responsibilities raises a major political issue, namely, taxation without representation?

4. What do social responsibilities of business mean to you?

5. If an executive chooses to assume social responsibilities, there is no clear formula for telling him what he can or should do like that of the old MR = MC rule. Does the absence of such a formula necessarily mean that a businessman should assume no social responsibilities?

6. Is the business system more likely to collapse if it follows Friedman's rigid doctrine of absolutely no business social responsibilities (except to use resources efficiently to maximize profits) or if it follows a moderate program to adapt its activities to social needs while still retaining a primary economic objective?

# A case for social responsibility

## douglas a. hayes

Douglas A. Hayes, Professor of Finance, Graduate School of Business Administration, University of Michigan, presents several reasons why he is in favor of modifying the classical economic optimal decision-making concepts and why vigorous programs to meet social needs are not incompatible with long-run business profit goals.

It is difficult to argue with the proposition that the basic objective of corporate business in the private sector is to maximize the long-term return opportunities for the shareholders within the constraints imposed by law and generally accepted ethical standards. However, as certain problems have become more complex and more critical in their implications for the long-run future of society, it no longer seems sufficient to hold that the operational policies instituted to implement this objective should be based on the simplistic notion of earnings potentials in relation to risks assumed. This notion is specifically incorporated into the capital budgeting models used in business school finance courses and as a guide for resource allocation by many industrial corporations. Therefore, at the outset I confess to being a heretic. The heresy, however, is finding support. For example, an increasing number of corporations are taking the view that satisfactory pollution control policies are desirable, if not essential, despite the fact that the diversion of scarce resources to these ends may promise lower returns than alternative uses.

The rationale for policies which are nonoptimal from an economic standpoint but are designed to contribute to the solution of environmental and social problems can be based on the view that corporations have instituted social welfare goals that are completely independent of the profit goals. Indeed, some academic behavioral scientists have advanced this notion as exemplified by the following statement:

> The norms and roles of big business include a conglomeration of profits, efficiency, democratic human relations, freedom and justice. Big business is not cast in the simple molds of profit maximization or of pursuit of public welfare.

Douglas A. Hayes, "Management Goals in a Crisis Society," XXII (November 1970), 7–11. Reprinted by permission from the November 1970 issue of the *Michigan Business Review*, published by the Graduate School of Business Administration, The University of Michigan.

However, because managerial performances are largely evaluated in terms of their current results and long-term prospects, it is doubtful if purely "public welfare" considerations bulk large in their decision-making process beyond a modest concern with a favorable "public relations" image. A possible exception may be those unusual corporations that have been highly successful because of a unique product line or for other reasons. In these cases, even if significant resources are diverted to social purposes, their stockholders and employees may still enjoy returns well above average. Xerox Corporation, for example, is well known for its concern and expenditures on educational and cultural programs, but its exceptional growth and profitability give its management a degree of flexibility not enjoyed by most private sector firms. It is particularly known for sponsorship of public interest television programs at prime time costs with probably less than commensurate marketing rewards.

A second rationale advanced to justify policies that are socially rather than profit oriented is that they are a necessary defensive reaction to pressures from governments and organized public interest groups. The public sector, it is noted, has assumed an increasingly aggressive posture in their attitudes toward the apparent deficiencies of corporate enterprises, particularly large companies. Therefore, it is argued, in order to avoid punitive regulations which might seriously erode profit potentials, it is necessary to introduce some policies aimed at the mitigation of social problems, although reluctantly and minimally as they are essentially regarded as conflicting with the main goals of the corporation.

Probably some managements are oriented to the defensive view of those policies which commit corporate resources to projects not directly related to immediate profit potentials. But a third rationale is also possible. It is that the long-term profit prospects of many, if not most, corporations may be eroded unless adequate solutions are found within a reasonable time to the pressing environmental and social problems. For example, as a major segment of corporate resources is committed to large metropolitan areas, the preservation of the value and productive usefulness of these resources may well depend on maintaining a stable society and tolerable environmental conditions in these areas. It has become apparent that urban decay has seriously impaired the progress of many companies, particularly where both employees and customers are largely concentrated in these areas.

Enterprises dependent on urban markets, such as retailers and banks, would seem particularly exposed to deterioration in the condition of the cities. Therefore, it is not surprising that Mr. Charles

Lazarus, the head of a leading department store chain, made the following statement concerning the need for enlightened social policies:

> . . . whether you are a part of a national, a regional or a local business, the great urban center—whatever its name—is where most of our business is done. The city is where, when we speak of the future, we will either grandly win or meanly fail. That will depend, more than perhaps on any other group, on the business leaders, and particularly the retail leaders, of each great urban community.

The clear recognition that policies instituted to alleviate environmental and social decay are not dictated by a peripheral concern for "public welfare" outside the mainstream of corporate goals would seem salutary rather than deplorable. If corporate managements generally accept the view that such policies are not only compatible with, but may be essential to, their goals of long-term profit maximization, then they will probably be more forcefully conceived and implemented. Until recently, there seemed to be no more than a rather vague conceptual justification for policies not related directly to earnings performance. These policies were, therefore, often tentative and minimal in character. The concept that long-term profit goals may depend on solving problems ordinarily considered beyond the concern of individual private companies may seem a self-serving approach, but it might well provide the incentive to more dedicated action with respect to these problems than has been evidenced in the past.

As my major direct interest in teaching and research is banking, let me observe that large metropolitan banks have reason to be particularly sensitive on this score. While most have penetrated into regional, national, and even international markets, a substantial proportion of their business is still generated locally. They have, therefore, a substantial stake in the maintenance of a viable metropolitan community. In addition, because they have been given the privilege of providing society with its major monetary mechanism, demand deposits, they are subject to special public regulation by both State and Federal jurisdictions. Favorable political relations are highly important to banks. As a result, clear evidence of operational policies concerned with the social problems of their communities would seem desirable, if not imperative, in order to preserve the economic base of their major markets and to convince political bodies that their activities are positively in the public interest and not insensitive to it. For example, vigorous programs to render financial and even management aid to businesses operated by minority groups in the inner-city would seem particularly relevant for major urban banks.

Therefore, despite the increasingly serious environmental and social problems plaguing society, it is arguable that the basic management goals remain intact.  These are (1) maximizing long-term total returns to the shareholders and (2) maintaining the integrity of their investment.  However, the policy spectrum related to achieving these goals has changed.  Whereas a decade or so ago, most policy decisions might have been based almost entirely on their probable effects on earnings relative to risks assumed, the policy parameters now appear more complex.  For large urban corporations, the additional dimension of the impact of policies on the environmental and social quality of their communities should become, if it has not already, a more important factor in future policy decisions.

It should not be concluded that major corporations in the past have lacked any concern for the social problems of their communities.  Most have cooperated in civic charitable and developmental projects, but these activities have usually been peripheral to the mainstream of corporate activities.  Trade-offs between socially oriented policies and earnings oriented policies have not been typical, but looking ahead to the remaining decades of the twentieth century, a real question can be raised as to whether such trade-offs might not become increasingly necessary in order to preserve large corporations as viable private sector institutions.

But in view of their obligations to their stockholder constituents, some managements hold that corporate enterprise cannot make major sacrifices in their earnings potentials in order to solve these problems.  Consequently, it is further argued, to achieve the massive resource commitments, social and environmental programs should include the profit motive in their program parameters; otherwise, it is doubtful if the real and managerial resources will be made available on the scale required.

Mr. Tilford Gaines, senior economist of a New York bank, argued in this vein as follows:

> Programs of the type proposed in the Master Plan must be heavily weighted with government participation, since many are by their nature essential functions of government.  At the same time, the compatibility of the overall programs with the economic and social structure of the country and, therefore the likelihood of success for the program demand that private enterprise should be employed wherever possible.  To enlist *maximum* [italics mine] support from private industry, it will be necessary that there be a realistic prospect of profits and a minimum of interference from government in the form of surveillance, unnecessary requirements, and an atmosphere of suspicion toward the motives of private business.

While one might agree in principle with these comments, it is probably sanguine to expect that they will be fully implemented in practice.

Since the Great Depression, it has been fashionable in liberal political circles, and to some extent in the communications media, to regard the "profit motive" as crass and somewhat suspect. To expect politically oriented policies to embrace the efficacy of profit incentives solving the pressing problems of society may prove to be a difficult proposition. Despite the logic of the matter, politically initiated programs have tended to emphasize compulsory controls to achieve the necessary resource allocations rather than indirect inducements through profit prospects.

Clearly, it would be intolerable for behavioral biases to interfere with the solutions to these problems, because they must be solved one way or another if existing social and economic structures are to persist. Compromise would seem essential and this might suggest two courses of action. First, corporate goals and related policies, particularly those of large corporations, should be made compatible with the vital goals of society at large. Second, because it would seem highly inequitable to allow a minority of insensitive managements to ignore their responsibilities and thereby enjoy a competitive cost advantage, public controls to achieve the necessary resource allocations and to distribute costs in an equitable manner should be welcomed and even initiated rather than reluctantly accepted.

One further point, implicit in the above comments, should be emphasized. An increasing number of active, concerned, and intelligent groups, including the communications media, are constantly evaluating the performance of the private sector on these matters. As a result, corporations would be well advised not to yield to the temptation of making the rhetoric of their public relations statements in excess of true performance. The media and the public are becoming increasingly sensitive to "credibility gaps," and the corporate sector must expect that any differences between their public statements and operational policies are likely to be critically exposed to public view. A serious "credibility gap" could prove disastrous. This would invite public support, if not agitation, for punitive regulations and controls on the grounds that corporations cannot be trusted to act vountarily in a socially responsible manner, and in fact will attempt to evade their responsibilities through hypocritical smoke-screens.

Thus it is my opinion that vigorous programs to meet the crucial social and environmental problems of our society are not incompatible with the long-run profit goals of business. Such programs may, however, require significant near-term sacrifices of optimal resource allocations. But unless these sacrifices are made, the corporate sector can expect increasingly hostile responses from activist groups and ultimately the free enterprise system itself may be endangered. Some argue that these matters are largely the concern of the government and that the private sector should merely cooperate with governmental programs. Now hopefully, some of the real costs involved in allocating scarce resources to these programs can be met partially through a shift in government spending priorities, particularly through a massive shift in expenditures from defense and subsidy programs to social programs. But to default leadership on these matters to the government would be, in my opinion, a serious mistake; it would suggest that the private sector is for all practical purposes inept in responding to the basic problems of society.

There is no doubt that under a competitive free enterprise system, a creative and industrious people will maximize the traditional measures of economic performance, such as per capita output and growth thereof. The question is whether such a system can adapt itself to other measures of performance, such as preserving the quality of the environment and alleviating urban decay. If it cannot, then the critics who argue the system is out of control may be right. But the system has proven to be remarkably adaptable in the past and I feel that management goals will increasingly recognize the need for enlightened long-term policies in order to avoid self-destruction. But it will not be easy, because such policies will require major changes in the traditional patterns of management decision-making that will be difficult to bring about. Therefore, it is not a time for complacency. Unless the system is responsive, history may show that the last half of the twentieth century witnessed the demise of the free enterprise system as we know it, and this would be a tragic event.

## QUESTIONS

1. Do you agree with the rationale that Hayes presents to support business decisions that are "nonoptimal"? Explain your position.
2. It is argued that current socially oriented business activities may be justified because they will result in long-range profit maximization. Is this really justified if the connection between the action today and the long-range profit maximization of a company is not clear? For example, can a corporation trace the future impact on its profits of a current decision to increase its community welfare contributions?
3. What limits does Hayes put on the assumption of social responsibilities by a business? Do you accept them as appropriate for this day and age?

# Social responsibility schools of thought

## william c. frederick

William C. Frederick, Professor of Business Administration, Graduate School of Business, University of Pittsburgh, in this article critically examines five schools of thought concerning social responsibility and presents his own criteria for the development of an acceptable theory.

. . .

It is the contention of this paper that the heightened interest in the problem of business responsibility can be explained in terms of two developments of the twentieth century. One of these developments is intellectual, the other is institutional in character—and both of them are related to the collapse of *laissez faire* as a philosophy and as an economic order.

## THE RELEVANCE OF LAISSEZ FAIRE

The disintegration of the world economy, starting early in the present century, signaled the beginning of the end for the *laissez-faire* philosophy and all its supporting institutions. The trend, accelerated by the First World War and the subsequent monetary panics of the 1920's, culminated in the early 1930's in what Karl Polanyi has characterized as "The Great Transformation." Free economy was transformed into regulated economy in all of the advanced nations that stood in the capitalist tradition, including Soviet Russia, where the 5-year plans were initiated; Germany, where National Socialism was in the ascendant; Italy, which was in the throes of corporate Fascism; and the United States, where the New Deal was the symbol of institutional transformation on a grand scale. These and other domestic economies, seeking to protect themselves from the ravages of a self-regulating market mechanism, were transformed to an economy in which centralized state planning and regulations were increasingly the rule rather than the exception.

At the same time, it became more and more obvious that the world of business itself was the scene of growing economic power. Moreover,

William C. Frederick, "The Growing Concern Over Business Responsibilities." © 1960 by The Regents of the University of California. Reprinted from CALIFORNIA MANAGEMENT REVIEW, Vol. II, Summer 1960, pp. 54–61, by permission of The Regents.

the growth of the large-scale corporation, with its tendency to divorce legal ownership from actual control of operations and with its technique of feeding upon itself for growth capital, freed the giants of business from the checks formerly put upon them by stockholders and capital investors.  In addition, business had combined two forces to dilute what could be considered "consumer sovereignty": a refined and sophisticated advertising program and what amounted to programming control of one of the nation's mass media of communication, thereby making possible the massive tailoring of consumer tastes to the standards of mediocrity that have become so common in our times.   ·

All of this institutional transformation was remarkable enough. Even more remarkable (though far less spectacular) was the intellectual revolution that accompanied the institutional change of the old order.  It was to be expected that the maxims that had guided economic thinking for over a century would undergo change as the institutions themselves were transformed, and as early as 1933, Robinson and Chamberlin had written economic treatises discussing the impact of the large-scale corporation on traditional forms of competition.  Three years later Keynes published *The General Theory of Employment, Interest and Money.*

But the real revolution in ideas came from without—primarily from the social sciences.  Psychology challenged the concept of a rational "economic man" who always pursued pleasures and avoided pains. Sociology questioned the individualistic "Robinson Crusoe" theory of behavior which had been an article of faith with economists for years. And comparative anthropology brought into serious question the belief in natural rights and natural order—a belief basic to the philosophy of *laissez faire.*

In a few words, the philosophy of *laissez faire* had collapsed as thoroughly as had its supporting institutional framework.  All of the major foundation stones were disintegrating.  Gone, or seriously weakened, was the invisible hand of free competition which was to guide selfish interests into socially-useful channels.  Displaced from the center of the stage were the old forms of business organization—the proprietorship and the partnership—through which competition was to work.  Gone was the theory of behavior which posited a free and rational individual capable of promoting his own interests if only allowed to do so by a meddlesome government.  Gone was the theory of social institutions which found at [their] core a rational desire of man to solve his problems.  Gone was the theory of a harmony of interests which was to be the automatic outcome of the self-seeking interests of a society of rational men checked in their selfishness by the invisible hand of competition.  A type of civilization and a way of thinking were truly "gone with the wind."

The collapse of the *laissez-faire* philosophy created a philosophical vacuum. It is this vacuum that businessmen and others interested in the issue of business responsibility have been trying to fill since the end of World War II. Under the *laissez-faire* philosophy private interests were supposed to be channeled into publicly useful pursuits, but now such institutions as had been responsible had fallen into disuse. Under the *laissez-faire* philosophy, there had been a social theory by which private interests could be harmonized with the interests of society at large. This meant that there was no need to be concerned deliberately with the social responsibility of private businessmen; it would be produced automatically. But now there was no such theory. Quite plainly, the older rubrics no longer furnished an adequate intellectual system for explaining the social consequences of business activities. Hence, the collapse of *laissez faire* posed a giant intellectual conundrum for social theorists: How could a society with democratic traditions and democratic aspirations rationalize the growing amounts of power accruing to businessmen? And how could that power be channelled into socially-useful functions without driving the populace into some Orwellian nightmare of *1984* proportions?

Several events conspired to cloak the true nature of the crisis until after the Second World War. It is true that a few questioning voices were raised during the 1930's and the 1940's—most notably those of Adolf A. Berle and Gardiner C. Means in their monumental study, *The Modern Corporation and Private Property,* and James Burnham in his analysis, *The Managerial Revolution.* But preoccupation with the Great Depression and with the impending World War II served to postpone a consideration of the major problems of business power that had developed out of the broad-scale institutional changes in the 1930's.

However, with the resumption of peacetime production, and after it became evident that the American economy would not be subjected immediately to another large-scale depression, and particularly after studies which revealed the very great concentration of economic power that had occurred during the Second World War, all of the same worrisome questions were asked once again. Since 1950, as a result, five major currents of thought about business responsibility in American society have developed. Each of these currents attempts to grapple with the problems of power in a complex society and with the resultant issue of business responsibility to the society at large.

## MANAGEMENT AS TRUSTEE

The first of these currents of thought, and one that has gained increasing favor, is the idea that corporate managers should voluntarily act as trustees of the public interest.  They should police themselves and their use of the tremendous amounts of power they possess.  The keynote of this concept is the deliberate and voluntary assumption of public responsibility by corporate managers, even though at times such a trusteeship might cause a managerial group to forego immediate profits for the sake of the public good.  Management, according to this concept, has a multiplicity of obligations—to the stockholders, to the employees, and to the public at large.  This viewpoint, therefore, appeals to the conscience of individual managers to wield their power in a publicly responsible manner.  One student of the problem has even called for the development of the "conscience of the corporation" to protect the public against possible abuses of corporate power.

## THE RELEVANCE OF CHRISTIAN ETHICS

Easily the most appealing and the most emotional of these five viewpoints is the notion of relating Christian ethical principles of conduct to the problems of business enterprise.  The basic idea seems to be that the businessman needs to think of himself as something more than a simple moneygrubber.  He needs to have a nobility of purpose that overarches his corporate activities and day-to-day duties.  He needs "skyhooks" to orient him toward the nobler ideals of Christian ethical conduct so that he might become a practicing Christian businessman on the job.  One spokesman for this viewpoint even argues the direct applicability of such Christian doctrines as the idea of original sin, forgiveness, creation, and the general concept of God to the problems of business.  Christian ideals and doctrines are said, therefore, to furnish the Christian businessman with a framework of ethics by which he can approach and grapple with problems of finance, personnel, production, and general decision making.

## BALANCE OF POWER

One of the most intriguing ideas to reappear in the postwar period is the notion that the answer to concentrated business power is more power.  The central theme of this argument is that business power is here to stay and that the answer to this problem is to build up countervailing power in the hands of the other major groups in the society so that a balance of power is struck between the contending members of society.  Only by actively participating in the race for power can the various sectors of society protect themselves from the overweening power held by others.  Government, according to this viewpoint, should play a major role in establishing a balance of power between the major functional segments of the economy, even if it means taking the side of one group against all the others while a sufficient amount of countervailing power is being developed.  Thus, the balance of power doctrine handles the problem of business responsibility by permitting all parties, including the business interests, to look out for their own economic and social interests.  The public welfare is presumed to be the outcome of the balanced sum of interests represented in the power struggle.  This relieves businessmen of deliberately and consciously promoting public responsibility, often in contradiction to their own private interests.

## THE VIEWERS WITH ALARM

Perhaps the strongest of the currents that have attempted to fill the philosophical vacuum left by the collapse of *laissez faire* consists of the ideas of the group that "views with alarm."  Often these spokesmen see the problem of business power as only one facet of a larger process, namely, the drift of the total society toward monolithic and totalitarian control of the human mind and spirit.  Huxley, Orwell, Riesman, Whyte, and Mills—all basically humanistic in their philosophical predilections—are dismayed by the press of technology and organization upon the traditions of a free society.  They express grave doubts about concentrating so much power in the hands of so few bureaucrats, whether of the industrial, the governmental, or the military type.  The members of this group have no clear-cut answer to the problem of concentrated power, counseling a resistance of the spirit against the ravages of organization and mass technology.  Business responsibility, they seem to say, will be achieved only when there is a general recognition by businessmen and others of the perils to the individual personality that accompany great aggregations of power.

## CAPITALIST ETHIC REFORMULATED

The fifth major current is actually composed of many smaller rivulets of thought, all of them related to an attempt to reformulate and restate the capitalist ethic in terms that will be acceptable in the changed institutional situation that now confronts those of us living under the capitalist tradition.  Perhaps the most notable attempt to reformulate the capitalist ethic can be found in *The Capitalist Manifesto*, by Louis O. Kelso and Mortimer J. Adler.  This manifesto argues that the capitalist revolution will not be fully realized until some of the basic capitalist principles—ownership, for example—have been extended to embrace ever larger numbers of citizens. As ownership is more widely diffused, so will the citizen's stake in the prevailing system increase. As a result, his interest and loyalty to the modified capitalist system will increase. Thus, a higher degree of responsibility on the part of capitalist-owners will be achieved by modifying and extending one of the basic capitalist institutions. Clarence B. Randall, formerly chairman of the Inland Steel Company, has also tried to restate a more realistic ethic for the capitalist system in his book, *A Creed for Free Enterprise.*

## A CRITIQUE

There is a surprising shortcoming shared by these five schools of thought: not one of them offers a clear-cut, substantive meaning of the social responsibilities of businessmen. That is, none of them explains in unequivocal terms what would constitute socially responsible business behavior. The public trustee theory and the Christian theory have been heavily influenced by the remnants of the *laissez-faire* philosophy in which "the greatest good of the greatest number" seems to have been a major criterion of social responsibility, although we are still left in some doubt as to the precise nature of the "good" to which the formula refers. The balance of power theory generally suffers from the same shortcoming, although in the case of John Kenneth Galbraith's version of countervailing power it is rather obvious that total over-all economic production constitutes the criterion of value, especially as revealed later in *The Affluent Society.* The basic value assumptions of the "viewers with alarm" are those of individualism and humanism; therefore, socially responsible business behavior presumably would protect the integrity of the individual and humanist qualities generally. But it does seem amazing that throughout most of these writings there appears no precise formulation or description of behavior that clearly bears the label of social responsibility.

The real explanation, of course, is to be found in the precise nature of the intellectual vacuum created when the *laissez-faire* system collapsed. For that vacuum, more than anything else, is a vacuum of values. It is our value systems that have been most sorely bruised in the transformation to the world of large-scale organization and technology. Older value systems have been rendered useless by the advance of knowledge and by vast institutional transformation. And new value systems have not yet had time to emerge. We stand too close to the older systems and to the dust that still rises from the ruins of the fallen order. And as the five major schools of thought seem to demonstrate, the temptation to dart back into the murky ruins of the old order and to snatch at the weakened timbers for use in constructing a new philosophical framework is still great.

Moreover, the public trustee theory and the Christian theory are startlingly naive in some respects. They seem to ignore some of the basic and fundamental realities of historical development and of the contemporary institutional setting in which business enterprise operates. To the extent that they are based on a theory of history at all, that theory is an idealistic or a romantic one. Such a historical theory ignores the essentially materialist and self-seeking basis of business enterprise as it emerged in Western culture. Further, both the trustee and the Christian theories seem to ignore the force of historical tradition and custom in determining the basic value elements of contemporary business institutions and the force that these traditions still exert upon the behavior of businessmen caught up within such a historically determined system. Both theories seem to imply, for example, that private gain can be simply pushed to one side by the force of will of public-spirited businessmen or of those who have been inspired by Christian ethics.

In addition, the theory of behavior that underlies both of these positions on business responsibility ignores some of the basic and most significant findings made by social scientists in the past fifty years. Little or no use is made, for example, of the concept of the social role, which explains the behavior of any given individual in terms of a pattern of interrelated actions drawn from a variety of sources within the contemporary institutional setting. Such a social role defines for an individual a pattern of behavior to which he is expected to conform in order to carry out his socially approved functions within the society. The businessman's role is defined largely, though not exclusively, in terms of private gain and private profit. To ignore this important fact, or to assume that the businessman himself can ignore it simply by force of will inspired by Christian ideals or by public spiritedness, is preposterously naive.

Therefore, we find that the businessman, by virtue of historical traditions and contemporary institutional forces, is in a sense "locked into" a going system of values and ethics that largely determines the actions he will take. There is no question that the system itself is subject to change over a period of years. Neither is there any doubt that the force of an individual personality can wield a great influence over the manner in which a person acts out his socially defined role. But there also seems to be little question that at any given time individuals who are active within the system of social roles and institutions are subject in large measure to its prevailing characteristics. This means that businessmen *must* be concerned primarily with private gain and profits, for they are a prime value within the presently existing system of business enterprise.

The balance of power theory, on the other hand, is a grown-up version of the automatic institutional forces that allegedly worked for the social good under the *laissez-faire* order.  The argument is basically the same:  When countervailing power is brought to bear against the holders of original power, such privately wielded power will be deflected into channels that are not so harmful to the interests of society as would otherwise be true in the absence of such a power struggle.  Under the *laissez-faire* order, competition between self-seeking business firms was said to have produced the same effects.  Countervailing power in the Twentieth Century substitutes for the free competition of the Nineteenth Century.  As Galbraith himself has been careful to point out, there are certain institutional situations, particularly inflation, in which the whole balance of power system breaks down and does not in fact channel private power into socially desirable uses.  Moreover, in *The Affluent Society,* Galbraith seems to be saying that the entire institutional order, including the balance of power system, is outmoded and unserviceable with respect to the utilization of society's resources for socially intelligent ends.

Some of the most powerful statements on business responsibility have been made by the "viewers with alarm," who, like Galbraith, at least are cognizant of some of the realities of the contemporary scene.  They are aware, for instance, that power is now drawn up in different configurations and different proportions than was true of the older order; and they sense that these changed dimensions of power have shifted the nature of the problems.  But since the alarmists are basically individualistic and humanistic in their predilections and since both individualism and humanism are products of an age before the fantastic aggregations of power that we know today, there is very little the alarmists can do except object to what is going on and to what power accumulations are presumably doing to individuals and to human values generally.  For them, there is no way out save by some brand of passive resistance to the organizational society and its many bureaucratic institutions.  It is characteristic of this group of thinkers that they have little or nothing to offer in the way of an institutional system that will lead us out of our present difficulties with respect to promoting the social responsibilities of private businessmen.

## THE BASIS OF AN ADEQUATE THEORY

An adequate theory of business responsibility must meet several requirements.  First, its criterion of value should be drawn from our increasing awareness of the requirements of socially effective economic production and distribution, and particularly the necessities of economic growth and development on a broad social scale. Some such value criterion has been a part of American thinking since the Great Depression of the 1930's, and it was reinforced by the great emphasis that the Second World War placed upon the value of high production and the efficient allocation and distribution of economic resources. In the current race with the Soviet Union to dominate the world economic scene, we see once again that economic production and distribution constitute a major criterion of value. Further, such a value assumption underlies the Employment Act of 1946. Also, such an assumption has caused the nation's two major political parties to pledge themselves to use all of the resources of government at their command to offset the fluctuations of the business cycle.

All of this suggests strongly that when we invoke the phrase "the social responsibilities of the businessman," we mean that businessmen should oversee the operation of an economic system that fulfills the expectations of the public. And this means in turn that the economy's means of production should be employed in such a way that production and distribution should enhance total socio-economic welfare. Social responsibility in the final analysis implies a public posture toward society's economic and human resources and a willingness to see that those resources are utilized for broad social ends and not simply for the narrowly circumscribed interests of private persons and firms. The television quiz show scandal is a case in point.

The second requirement of an adequate theory of business responsibility is that it be based upon the new concepts of management and administration that are now emerging. There is an increasing awareness of the usefulness of scientific methodology in defining and solving problems within the management environment. The "Great Man" theory of management is being replaced with a concept of the manager as coordinator and planner, as a team member whose main play consists of making significant links between relevant pieces of information. This means that managers need to reconstruct their self-images and to de-emphasize the role that status and authority play in the management function. And finally, the study of human relations is convincing managers that careful treatment must be accorded employees if they are to be fully effective in the work situation and if their jobs are to form a part of the "good life." Any theory of business responsibility that ignores these recent developments in management science would be seriously deficient.

Third, an adequate theory of business responsibility will recognize that the present business system is an outgrowth of history and past cultural traditions. It will recognize that what we are today is, to a very large extent, a function of what we were yesterday. In more specific terms, this means that there is not likely to be any escape from the very powerful motive of private gain and profit which is often at variance with social interest. Rather than denying the importance of this force or wishing it away in an idealistic fashion or assuming that businessmen can or will ignore it as they make decisions, the new theory of business responsibility will attempt to find institutional means for hedging about this motive and for directing it into socially useful channels. This, of course, is the hope of Galbraith in his theory of countervailing power. It is also a hope expressed by Berle in *The Twentieth Century Capitalist Revolution* in which he speaks of the need to develop "the conscience of the corporation."

The fourth requirement of a theory of business responsibility is that it recognize that the behavior of individual businessmen is a function of the social role they play in business and in society. This means two things: (a) that the individual businessman, however noble may be his intentions, is often unable to influence significantly the total business configuration within which he works; and (b) that many times the individual businessman will be motivated to take action or make decisions that are not at all consistent with the ideals of social responsibility that he may hold in the abstract. Both forms of behavior are understandable when we realize that the businessman does not operate in a cultural vacuum but within a social role whose total pattern is fairly well defined for him by the mores of his society.

Fifth, there should also be a recognition that socially responsible business behavior is not to be produced automatically but is rather to result from deliberate and conscious efforts of those institutional functionaries who have been given this task by society. There are no magic formulas and no automatic mechanisms which by themselves will guarantee the results that the public desires. Conscience alone, whether of public trustee or of Christian businessman, is not enough. A balance of power is likewise insufficient. Nor is courageous action by public servants enough. The task requires a constant tinkering with the institutional mechanisms of society, employing more and more of the fruits of scientific methodology and the scientific attitude. The job, though difficult, should become easier as social scientists increase their knowledge of human behavior and human institutions. It is true that we cannot totally escape the impact of our cultural heritage, but we are slowly accumulating a storehouse of knowledge about ourselves and about businessmen that should enable us to resolve some of the problems and issues of business responsibility.

## QUESTIONS

1. Which of the five schools of thought presented by Frederick concerning social responsibilities of business do you think has the most relevance for today and tomorrow? Justify your beliefs.
2. Do you agree with Frederick that they all are deficient?
3. Would you say that the swifter and better solutions to the great problems of today and tomorrow will come from a continuing pressure on business to use its resources efficiently and thereby to expand the wealth of the society more rapidly?
4. At what point will increased assumption of social responsibilities result in a reduction of efficiency in business? Illustrate.
5. What is your reaction to the following question: "One of the greatest problems that the United States must face today and in the near future is this: Shall private enterprise function in a comparatively free market within a broad framework of law? Or shall business be considered an instrument to be used by the state to achieve social objectives that people generally feel have the highest priority?" Are we really left with this "either-or" proposition?
6. Do Frederick's bases for an adequate theory of social responsibility help in answering this problem? Why or why not?
7. What limitations do you suggest be placed on the assumption of social responsibilities by business?

# Business and society's problems

## henry ford II

**Henry Ford II, Chairman of the Board of the Ford Motor Company, in the following remarks rejects both the position of the right and the left concerning the pursuit of profit.**

. . .

. . . How much business can and should do to solve the problems of society is currently the subject of a lively debate. The answers range from everything to nothing. The real answer, in my opinion, is somewhere in between. Business can and should do something, but far from everything.

Like governments and universities and other institutions, business is much better at some tasks than at others. Business is especially good at all the tasks that are necessary for economic growth and development. To the extent that the problems of society can be solved by providing more and better jobs, higher incomes for more people and a larger supply of goods and services, the problems can best be solved by relying heavily on business.

On the other hand, business has no special competence in solving many other urgent problems. Businessmen, for example, know little about the problems involved in improving the education of ghetto children, the quality of ghetto family life, the relations between police and minority citizens or the administration of justice. Solutions to problems such as these will be more effective if they are left to political, educational and social agencies. In short, our society will be served best if each of its specialized institutions concentrates on doing what it does best, and refuses either to waste its time or to meddle in tasks it is poorly qualified to handle.

I can best illustrate these broad generalizations by discussing the role of business in solving one of the nation's most urgent problems—the problem of providing equal economic opportunity for Negroes, Indians, Spanish-speaking Americans and other disadvantaged peoples. Since this is largely an economic problem, I believe that business has a large role in solving it.

Not everyone agrees with me. Oddly enough, the extreme left and

Remarks delivered before the Yale Political Union at Yale University, April 7, 1969. From *The Human Environment and Business* by Henry Ford II. Copyright © 1970 by Weybright & Talley, Inc. Used by permission of Weybright & Talley, Inc., a division of David McKay Company, Inc.

the extreme right agree with each other that the profit motive rules out any significant contribution by business to the solution of the economic problems of disadvantaged peoples.  The right says that business *should* concern itself exclusively with maximizing profit.  It regards any special effort to help minorities as discrimination in reverse and a violation of management's obligations to the stockholder.

The left, on the other hand, says that business *does* concern itself exclusively with profit and therefore will never really do anything to help people who need help.  Many on the far left go on to say that business deliberately exploits and oppresses the disadvantaged in order to increase its profits.  Colonialism at home, they believe, is the main reason for poverty and the main bulwark of prejudice.

Both of these views can be refuted by the same answer.  I agree with the right that business *should* concern itself primarily with profit.  I agree with the left that business *does* concern itself primarily with profit.  But neither premise supports the conclusion that business has no role in promoting equal opportunity.  On the contrary, even if there were no other reason, business should have a role because equal opportunity is profitable.

There are, of course, some businessmen who profit from prejudice and poverty.  Blockbusting real estate operators, loan sharks, and unscrupulous landlords are among the obvious examples.  These, however, are the exceptions rather than the rule.  The rule is that people who have money, education, and opportunity make better customers, better employees, and better neighbors for business than people who are poor, ignorant, and oppressed.

It is clearly in the self-interest of businessmen to enlarge their markets by selling housing, insurance, credit, restaurant meals, haircuts, automobiles, and all other products and services to all comers on equal terms.  Any businessman who discriminates against certain classes of customers automatically reduces his sales and profits.  Whenever discrimination against disadvantaged customers is widespread, the only people who benefit, as I've just pointed out, are the few businessmen who specialize in serving such markets at higher prices.

It is clearly in the self-interest of business both to enlarge its markets and to improve its work force by helping disadvantaged people to develop and employ their economic potential.  Good employees are any company's most valuable resource.  Good employees are also hard to find.  Any company that limits its access to good employees by imposing such irrelevant criteria as race or color is also limiting its profit potential.

Likewise, it is in the self-interest of business to help reduce dependency, frustration, crime and conflict in the community by treating all people on their merits as individuals.  The costs of occasional civil disorder are impossible to overlook, but are far smaller than the continuing costs of welfare, crime, disease and waste of human potential —costs which are borne by business as well as by the rest of the community.

In short, the profit motive provides abundant incentive for businessmen to help solve the economic problems of the disadvantaged.

I will readily admit that business did not move soon enough and has not moved far enough to provide full equality of opportunity.  But we have not lagged *because* of the profit motive.  We have lagged *in spite of* the profit motive and in opposition to our own best interests.

Businessmen have lagged because they are people who share the prejudices and preconceptions of the society around them.  Like other people, businessmen are reluctant to change the way things have always been done.  In a community where Negroes have never been hired except as janitors or sweepers, it takes an exceptional man to break the pattern.

If businessmen are no better than other people, they are also no worse.  Like the rest of American society, American business is now waking up to its own self-interest in doing what is right.  The stirrings of conscience have led us to see our own interests in a clearer light and we are now acting more decisively.

The idea that conscience and profit pull in the same direction is a difficult one to accept.  There is something in human nature which makes us feel that profit is a poor reason for helping others.  But this is a feeling we should resist.  To help a man because we think it is good for him is to treat him as an inferior.  It is difficult to do good without being condescending and paternalistic and perpetuating dependence.  To hire a man because he needs a job rather than because the job needs him is to assure him that he is useless.

On the other side of the coin, to help a man because it is in your own interest to help him is to treat him as an equal.  It is a way of telling him that you have confidence in him and in his ability to stand on his own feet and take care of his own interests.

Self-interest is also a more reliable motive than altruism.  Negroes and other disadvantaged people have learned from bitter experience that promises of help are often much bigger than performance.  They are justifiably suspicious of white liberals who are better at starting programs than they are at finishing them.  Today they suspect that business programs to hire and upgrade the disadvantaged are a fad that will fade away with little accomplishment.  The best assurance that this will not happen is the recognition by businessmen that equal opportunity is profitable.

What I am suggesting is simply that good results are much more valuable than good intentions.  Like most other big companies Ford has established its good intentions with respect to equal opportunity and made them a part of its basic corporate policy. We have devoted much effort to carrying out that policy, but our results, like those of most other companies, are still very mixed.

Our biggest results have been in providing entry-level production jobs for the so-called hard-core unemployed. Negroes and other disadvantaged people have always been an important part of our work force, but since late 1967 we have deliberately recruited people who would have been rejected as poor employment risks in the past. So far, we have hired some 12,000 of them. We have found among them some outstanding employees and on the average they have been about as satisfactory in most respects as other new employees hired during the same period. Negroes and other minorities now make up more than 25 percent of our hourly work force in the U.S. compared with 18 percent five years ago.

Many other employers have achieved similar results. The National Alliance of Businessmen was formed early in 1968 to work with the federal government to encourage employers to hire the hard-core unemployed. By the end of the year, the Alliance had placed 125,000 people in jobs with 12,500 firms and 85,000 of those hired were still on the job.

At Ford, we have also done fairly well in giving minorities access to entry-level salaried positions. We have done less well in raising them to positions as plant foremen and skilled workers.

In other areas, we have barely scratched the surface. We have very few Negroes and other minorities in the higher salaried positions. We have only four Negro dealers—which is four more than we had a couple of years ago—and there are very few in the dealer sales force. We have a program to support the development of minority businesses through our purchasing activities, but so far it has hardly gotten off the ground. In each of these areas, although our results are still small, our progress is accelerating.

We intend to continue increasing our rate of progress, but our results will depend more on hard work and good management than on good intentions. To translate any set of intentions into results, programs have to be developed and built into the structure of the organization and its operating procedures. We need to make changes in our organization, to allocate responsibility and authority, to determine priorities, establish targets, timetables and reporting procedures, make up budgets, provide incentives and do all the numerous things a big organization needs to do to reach any goal. In the past, our equal opportunity efforts have been scattered and largely uncoordinated. Now we are getting ourselves better organized to translate our intentions into accomplishments in every aspect of our business.

There has been a great deal of discussion about whether or not it is proper to discriminate in favor of minorities in order to make up for generations of discrimination against them. In my opinion, much of this argument is academic. There is still a long way to go in eliminating discrimination *against* before we have to start worrying too much about discrimination *for*.

I am not talking so much about out-and-out racial prejudice, which is no longer the main problem in most big companies. Rather, I am talking about a variety of practices and procedures which have the effect of discriminating against even though their purpose is pure.

The purpose of educational requirements for employment, for example, is to select employees who will be able to perform well in particular jobs. The theory is that a man's future job performance can be predicted from past performance and experience in school. In practice, however, the predictions often turn out to be wrong. Some people who have the required education can't do the work, and some people who can do the work don't have the required education. In routine jobs, too much education may even be a handicap, and the man with less schooling may be a better risk.

In practice, therefore, minimum educational standards for jobs always discriminate against people who could meet the job standards even though they cannot meet the education standards. Discrimination of this kind has its biggest impact on Negroes and other groups of people whose educational achievement is relatively low. Obviously, the answer to this problem is to develop innovative personnel practices which make it possible for a man to show what he can really do in spite of apparent handicaps. That's not discrimination for or against anybody. It's just common sense and fair play and self-interest.

Even when this point is reached, however, it will still be difficult to achieve big gains in minority employment in the better jobs. There is no escaping the fact that minority group members who are really qualified by skill and knowledge to handle the better jobs are very hard to find.

Industry can do something through training programs to make up for the shortage, but industry cannot handle this whole job by itself. The shortage is a reflection of the deficiencies of ghetto schools, ghetto medical care, ghetto housing and ghetto life. Before these deficiencies can be remedied, school systems, city governments and other community organizations will have to organize themselves in the same way that business is now getting organized to translate good intentions into good results.

The success of these efforts to get organized for good results will depend, in turn, on the kinds of people who are managing the organizations. No organization can be more progressive or more effective

than its people.  This is just as true of school systems and governments as it is of business.

This brings me, in conclusion, to your generation, to the students of
today and what they can do to make the world somewhat better.  Your
generation seems intensely disillusioned not only with big business but
also with big universities, big government and big organizations in general.  If you feel that way, I don't blame you.  I can assure you . . .
that big organizations are at least as frustrating to the people who administer them as they are to the people who are affected by them.

On the other hand, we have to accept the fact that big organizations
are here to stay.  We cannot turn back to a simpler age and a smaller
scale.  We cannot decide whether or not to rely on big organizations;
our only choice is whether they shall be better or worse.  If the big
ideals of our time are not achieved through our major institutions, they
will not be achieved at all.

The great opportunity your generation faces is the opportunity to
transform our major institutions and make them serve your highest
ideals.  If the best and most idealistic people of your generation accept
this opportunity, then there is hope for a better future.  But if the best
of you reject business and other large organizations, then our national
institutions will surely become even less effective and more stagnant
than their worst critics claim they are.

In business, in government, in school systems and in all our major
institutions, we need people who are convinced that the way things are
is a shame and a disgrace.  It is easy to stay outside the system and
protest the way it works.  Protest has its place, but right now our
country seems to have all the protestors it can use.  What we really
need are more people who are willing to come inside the system and
fight and work to make the system better.

If any of you believe that our present institutions are not worth
fighting and working for, let me remind you of one thing.  In the perspective of history, the astonishing thing about our American institutions is not that they work so poorly.  The astonishing thing is that
they work as well as they do.  We should count it as our great good
fortune that our present institutions—for all their grave deficiencies—
are perhaps the most effective that any society has ever inherited.  To
give up on the best because it is not better is not the counsel of idealism.  It is the counsel of despair.

If any of you believe that the struggle for a better society would be
hopeless and the work useless, let me remind you of another thing.
It is natural for youth to be impatient for faster progress.  To those of
you who may feel discouraged by the slow pace of reform, I would respond that it's always hard to teach an old dog new tricks.  Major
progress in any field of endeavor seldom comes because people change

their minds and their way of doing things. It comes because one generation grows old and leaves the field and another generation takes over.

The correct measure of possible progress in the future is not the actions of my generation, but the ambitions of yours. The size of the generation gap today suggests that when your generation takes over, the progress could really be major. How much progress big organizations can make toward building a better world is not fixed in the nature of organizations. It depends on you.

## QUESTIONS

1. Do you agree or disagree with Ford's views that the profit motive provides abundant incentive for businessmen to help solve the economic problems of the disadvantaged? Why or why not?
2. Ford asserts that business has not moved soon enough and far enough to solve social problems, not because of the profit motive, but in spite of it. Critically analyze and evaluate this statement.
3. Do you agree or disagree with Ford that our present institutions—despite their grave deficiencies—are probably the most effective that any society has ever inherited? Which institutions does he have in mind?
4. Ford further asserts, "How much progress big organizations can make toward building a better world is not fixed in the nature of organizations. It depends on [this generation and what it does]." What do you think he has in mind in making this statement?
5. Do you get the impression, after reading this article, that Ford is trying to "make excuses" for the business community? Or do you think he is really sincere and is "telling it like it is"?

# Beyond profitability: a proposal for managing the corporation's public business

## william c. stolk

**William C. Stolk, former Chairman of the Board of the American Can Company and now Chairman of the Board of the Committee for Economic Development, calls for a definition of corporate goals beyond profitability.**

It has become imperative for business to undertake social responsibilities on a major scale. This is urgently required because of government's demonstrated inability to deal with many of these problems effectively—under conditions of political influence, inexperience, and profligate use of tax money. Business has the talent and experience to lead the way by enlisting the resources of our economy in solving our national problems. And there isn't the slightest doubt in my mind that business must now assume the responsibility of this leadership if we are to avoid chaos. The question is how to do it.

I have much sympathy with the plight of my colleagues in business. A chief executive who really would like to commit enough corporate resources to help solve our major social problems faces the prospect that the directors will consider him a starry-eyed philanthropist—the stockholders will feel he is wasting their money—the investment funds will dump his stock because such crackpot management may reduce earnings—the competitors will take advantage of their lower costs to undermine him in the market—and even if he surmounts all these the government may foul it all up for him anyway. So it is no wonder that many chief executives are testing the water gingerly and looking around to see who is getting his feet wet.

As one who has been thoroughly immersed in these problems, I am going to suggest some ways in which corporations can organize and carry out their social responsibilities more effectively.

## VICE PRESIDENT FOR PUBLIC BUSINESS

The first step, I believe, is for the chief executive officer to appoint a qualified senior executive to manage the corporation's *public* business

From *The Conference Board Record*, December 1968, pp. 52–54. Reprinted by permission.

just as systematically as its *private* business. This man should be an executive vice president and a director. Public business is an ideal area for the man who has risen through the corporate hierarchy to become a finalist in the competition for the presidency, and who might be lost to the company unless he has a fresher and more challenging assignment than a secondary spot in the new executive setup.

One executive vice president for public business should be a director because this area of corporate activity deserves the involvement of the board. The qualification for outside directors should include knowledge and competence in the broader social, political, and economic affairs that affect the company. Two or three of these directors could constitute a public business committee of the board along with the chief executive officer and the executive vice president for this activity.

Within the company, the executive vice president for public business must have the corporate resources necessary to do the job. This means *staff*—particularly some of the bright, young tigers who are often bottled up in the more rigid line bureaucracies, and the idealistic college graduates who have been passing up business for the Peace Corps and the Job Corps.

And it means *money*. Since the company has a clear self-interest in improving its social environment, this activity should be considered just as much a part of the true cost of doing business as any other costs—raw material, sales expense, power and light. The monies required for improving the social environment should be budgeted and managed as any other operating budget.

The *public business* of the corporation is, in fact, a *line* not a *staff* function—on exactly the same level as manufacturing and marketing. This approach completely changes the meaning of corporate execution of its social responsibilities. As a working line department of the company, the public business group must be equally accountable for its performance and produce satisfactory results.

Now that we are organized, how do we tackle the job?

## DEFINING THE JOB

The public business group, including particularly business economists, should start by making an inventory of all the problems and opportunities. One type of problem, for example, is that which the corporation has actually created—such as air and water pollution. It is fair to say that most corporations now understand that they have the primary responsibility to clean up their own "messes"—and to use natural resources in such a way as to maintain their value for others.

The opportunities for corporations to apply their resources to help solve broader social problems is less clear because, for the most part, they have not been examined either imaginatively or systematically.

Looked at this way, there is almost no social task to which some corporation could not make a significant contribution.  This is because our corporations have absolutely unique capabilities in research, technology, and managerial skills—and these are precisely what is needed.  If Aerojet General and North American Aviation can apply systems analysis to pollution abatement and public transportation for the State of California; if Litton and ITT can run education and job-training camps for the Job Corps—why should not every corporation find an area of social improvement that matches its capabilities.

After completing the inventory of social problems and opportunities, the public business group should develop a strategic plan—the corporate resources, both money and talent, that would be required; the priorities; the relationship between the company's piece of the problem and the responsibilities of others in industry and in the governmental sector; and the results to be attained, both for the corporation and for society.  This provides the basis for establishing a public business budget and going into operation.

At this point, we face three important considerations—profitability, burden-sharing, and the private-public sector relationship.

## COSTS AND PROFITS

I think there are two ways to deal with the profitability problem.  One is for the corporation to be clear about what it requires to do the job —including tax benefits, specific types of government assistance, or other inducements.  The appropriate public authorities then could determine whether the results would be worth the costs, in light of alternative ways of getting the job done.

The second is to reexamine our traditional concepts and measurements of "profit," many of which haven't changed since Adam Smith.  We have all heard speeches by heads of companies—I have made some myself—stressing the fact that people are the company's most valuable asset.  The speech goes something like this: "We can build factories, build machines and laboratories but we must have people to manage them profitably."  Yet, we capitalize the buildings and machinery but the investment in aid to education is treated as a philanthropic activity —and we don't even bother to measure the benefits.  If we treated it as a capital investment, the money put into education would go up dramatically.

Another factor to consider is what it costs *not* to do the job.  The cost is corporate, employee, and shareholder taxes to pay for the efforts of public agencies.  In many instances, the corporation probably could enhance its profitability by doing the public business job at lower margins, or it could break even, instead of paying the taxes for somebody else to do it—perhaps badly.

The problem of burden-sharing is very closely related to profitability.  Industry is spending more than $3 billion a year on air and water pollution abatement, and it is estimated this would have to be increased manyfold to bring the problem under control.  I'm sure there are very few chief executive officers—even with strong social consciences—who would relish the notion of quadrupling their company's expenditures on pollution control unless they were sure all their competitors would be just as public spirited.

The result is that business generally proceeds by the lowest common denominator of industry action—or inaction.  Government then has to take over and set the standards that industry could have established for itself.  Business pays most of the bill, which is almost always higher than if industry had done the job in the first place, and it gets the blame for foot-dragging while the government gets the credit for acting in the public interest.

It doesn't take much intelligence to figure out that this is self-defeating.  And it isn't too difficult to find a better way.  The machinery is already in place—the industry or trade associations.  All we have to do is turn them around: convert them from rear-guard defenders of the *status quo* into instrumentalities for collective industry action in the public interest.

The industry association is the place where corporate public business executives can bring their proposed action programs—sort out who does what—decide on a fair apportionment of the costs—and work out a detailed industry plan and time schedule for solving the problem.  There need be no antitrust difficulty, and there is every indication that government, as well as public opinion, would welcome such initiatives.

If one or two leading companies in our major industries would take strong leadership in this direction, we could get results very quickly.  I had some personal experience in helping set up "Keep America Beautiful" when my company and other packaging producers were threatened with legislation that would have outlawed disposable containers to prevent unsightly litter.  It was fairly easy to persuade all diverse segments of the industry to adequately finance the program to deal with the problem.  The service clubs, national parks association, state and local organizations, all understood we would see the job through because it was in our self-interest to do so.

I believe this approach has very great possibilities—not just for burden-sharing but more positively for effectively mobilizing the economic resources required to help solve major social problems which are too big and costly for any single company.  In some areas we are beginning to apply the industry-wide approach to the hiring, specialized education and training of unemployables.  Similarly, corporations in the construction and related industries might jointly supply materials for ghetto rebuilding projects—or for the new, stepped-up low income housing program—at much lower margins than would be the case in their regular course of business.

## MOBILIZING FOR EMERGENCY IN PEACETIME

Most of the trade associations have done this sort of resource mobilization job in wartime, and the government facilitated it by permitting the lifting of certain peacetime restrictions.  There is every reason why we should do the same thing in the comparable kind of national emergency we now face.

The resources are available in the private sector to make the critical contribution to solving our urban, civil rights, and educational problems.  Total business sales last year, for example, were more than $600 billion.  Just a few percent of that, applied to the operating costs of those businesses, and added in an organized and equitable fashion to our present efforts to improve our social environment, would make a massive difference without impairing the economic strength of American business in the slightest.  And it would be money well invested.  It would come back in increasing long-term profitability, in holding down the tax burden, and in assuring an environment for business prosperity.

Regarding the private-public sector relationships, I think it is obvious that business and government must develop the same kind of effective partnership in social problem-solving that has been achieved in wartime.  This will be helped enormously by business organizing itself for effective action on those aspects of the problems it can best handle —by being quite clear about what it will take in the way of reasonable profit incentives—and by measuring the results of its social investments.  We must insist that government do likewise—develop an effective organizational structure out of the present hodgepodge of agencies, define its areas of greatest competence, and also measure its results.

## QUESTIONS

1.  What do you think of Stolk's proposal?
2.  Do you agree with him that "there is almost no social task to

which some corporation could not make a significant contribution"?

3. How does Stolk's proposal compare with the positions of Friedman, Hayes, and Frederick? Do you think that most businessmen agree with Stolk?

4. It has been alleged that business pays most of the bill in solving social problems, and the bill is almost always higher than if business did the job alone. Yet business gets blamed for dragging its feet while the government gets the credit for acting in the public interest. How do you view this?

# Campaign GM                    george a. steiner

In 1970 the Committee on Corporate Responsibility was created in Washington, D.C., and leaped into prominence with its "Campaign GM." Two demands were made on the General Motors Corporation at its annual stockholders' meeting in May 1970: (1) to place three "public interest" directors, and (2) to set up a committee on corporate responsibility to study GM's performance in dealing with social and environmental issues and recommend changes "to make GM responsible."

The committee requested large holders of GM stock to give it proxies to be used at the annual stockholders' meeting to enforce its demands. Those requested included various university boards of trustees—Harvard, California, Michigan, and Texas, for instance—and charitable foundations. No large holder gave the committee its proxies. Some, however, sympathized with the views of the committee.

James Roche, Chairman of the Board of General Motors, said that "The project is using General Motors as a means through which it can challenge the entire system of corporate management in the United States." The company argued that "special interest" groups on the board would introduce "partisanship," which would be bad. Also the formation of a special shareholders' committee "would do serious damage to General Motors and to its stockholders and to the general public," because it would be "structured for harassment and publicity."

The Rockefeller Foundation (with 195,000 out of 1,400,000 outstanding shares), while casting its vote with management, criticized the corporation in explaining its position. Some excerpts of the criticism follow:

> There are constituents other than stockholders to whom corporations are also obligated. There are battles to be waged against racism, poverty, pollution, and urban blight which the Government alone cannot win; they can be won only if the status and power of American corporate industry are fully and effectively committed to the struggle.
>
> What is needed from business today is leadership which is cou-

rageous, wise and compassionate, which is enlightened in its own and the public's interest, and which greets change with an open mind. In our judgment, the management of General Motors did not display this spirit in its response to the two proposals offered by Campaign GM (a subgroup of the Committee on Corporate Responsibility).

We recognize that these proposals are, from management's viewpoint, unwieldy and impractical; Campaign GM itself conceded the difficulty it encountered in trying to determine a method of selecting members of a Committee for Corporate Responsibility. Because of these inadequacies we are prepared, this time, to sign our proxy as requested by management. But we are not prepared to let the matter rest there.

We do not share the view which was expressed by management that the Campaign GM proposals represent an "attack" on the corporation. . . . We believe the language of the Campaign GM proposals is more reasonable and temperate than the response of management. We also believe the goals of the proposals have been designed to serve the public good by increasing the corporation's awareness of the major impact of its decisions and policies on society at large.

Editor's Note: In September 1970 the General Motors Corporation announced that it was responding to criticism that the company's decisions sometimes did not take the public welfare into consideration by forming a "public policy committee" of five GM directors. Mr. Roche said that matters associated with community action and corporate citizenship will, therefore, have "a permanent place on the highest level of management." He said that he anticipates that the committee "will demonstrate their understanding of General Motors and its industry, their awareness of the expanding role of business in society and their comprehension of the responsibilities of the board of directors, who are charged with the successful operation of the business." The committee "will inquire into all phases of General Motors' operations that relate to matters of public policy and recommend actions to the full board" (*Wall Street Journal*, September 1, 1970). None of the members of the committee are officers of GM.

## QUESTIONS

1. Do you think Roche's response was appropriate?
2. If you were a shareholder of the company, would you give your proxy to management or to the committee?
3. If GM does take leadership in assuming the kind of responsibilities the committee wants, how far should it go in doing what?
4. If the so-called public members were presumed to act only in the

public interest, would they be held liable in stockholders' suits for actions of the board that might jeopardize stockholder investment?

5. Do large philanthropic institutions, like the Rockefeller Foundation, that own shares of stock in America's corporations have the same objectives concerning decision making of companies in which they own stock as do other common stockholders who purchase shares for capital gain and dividends?

6. Would you say that it would be a good thing for business and society if large holders of corporate shares, like universities and philanthropic institutions, gave their proxies to minority stockholder groups?

# Issues in Our Polluted Environment

**7**

# The environmental crisis

### neil h. jacoby

Neil H. Jacoby in this article explains the basic causes of environmental degradation, schools of thought developed to deal with the problem, and his recommendations on how to come to grips with the crisis.

Who would have predicted, even as recently as a year ago, the strong ground swell of public concern about the environment that now preoccupies Americans? The great silent majority as well as activists of the left have discovered that our country is running out of clean air and pure water. Suddenly, we all understand that smog, noise, congestion, highway carnage, oil-stained beaches, junk graveyards, ugliness, and blatant commercial advertising not only offend our senses but threaten our health and our very lives.

Now we are trying to identify the culpable parties and to demand corrective action. What are the basic forces behind environmental deterioration and why has a crisis emerged so swiftly? What are the merits of the diagnoses and prescriptions that have been advanced for the environmental problem? How can the environment be improved, and who should pay the costs? What are the respective roles and responsibilities of business and of government in restoring environmental amenities? Above all, what lessons does the environmental crisis teach about the functioning of our political and market systems, and about reforms needed to forestall other crises in the future?

We focus attention upon the urban physical environment, that is, upon the spatial and sensory qualities of the land, air, water, and physical facilities that surround the three out of four Americans who live in towns and cities. This milieu deteriorates as a result of air and water pollution, noise, industrial and household waste materials, declining quantity or quality of housing per capita, crowding, congestion, loss of privacy and recreational facilities, rising accidents and loss of time in urban transportation, and, not least of all, drabness and ugliness.

The physical environment is, of course, only one dimension of the

From *The Center Magazine*, 3 (November–December 1970), 37–48. Reprinted by permission.

quality of human life.  In focusing upon physical factors, one excludes important social and psychological factors such as order and security, social mobility, and the social participation or alienation of the individual.  All of these environmental factors, along with per capita income, wealth, health, and education, need enhancement.

Spatially, the urban environment must be viewed as one subdivision of the entire global ecosystem, which also embraces rural lands, the oceans, the atmosphere surrounding the earth, and outer space.  Since all parts of this system interact, ideally it should be analyzed, planned, and managed as a whole.

The urban physical environment nevertheless merits a top priority because it affects the majority of our population and, by general assent, its qualities are below the threshold of tolerability.  In addition, physical factors powerfully influence the health, mental attitudes, and life-styles of urban residents, and their enhancement will elevate the social and psychological qualities of American society.  One is therefore justified in focusing attention upon the physical characteristics of urban life, notwithstanding that it is a partial analysis of the global ecosystem.

Three basic forces have operated to change the urban physical environment for the worse: population concentration, rising affluence, and technological change.  The overwhelming tendency of people to concentrate in cities has worsened the environment in many ways.  Traffic congestion, crowding, overloading of transportation, marketing and living facilities, delays and loss of time, along with rising levels of air, water, and noise pollution, have been among the social costs of urbanization.  During the half-century between 1910 and 1960 the percentage of Americans living in urban areas of 2,500 or more rose from 45.7 to 70, while the number of urbanites tripled from 42 to 125 million.  Beyond doubt, the 1970 census will reveal an accelerated urbanization.  Urbanization clearly brings benefits to people—wider job opportunities, richer educational and cultural fare, more individual freedom from social constraints—or else it would not have been so powerful and enduring a movement.  Yet, beyond some levels of population size and density, the total costs of urbanization begin to exceed the total benefits.  Discovery of the optimum size of cities and optimum density of their populations [is a] vitally important [task] confronting national planners.

A second prime mover in environmental change has been rising affluence—the expansion of annual real income and expenditure per capita.  Real income per person (measured in 1958 dollars) more than doubled during the eighteen years, 1950–1968, from $1,501 to $3,409.

As real incomes have mounted, each person has bought and consumed more tangible goods, thrown them away more quickly, and generated solid waste.  Each person has traveled more miles per year, multiplied his contacts with other people, and rapidly expanded his usage of energy.  All of this has increased air, water, and noise pollution, crowding and congestion, traffic accidents.  With the number of urbanites doubling and per capita real incomes quadrupling every forty years, the problem of supplying urban amenities is exploding.  One shudders to contemplate the environmental degradation that would occur if 525 million Indians, now crowded 417 per square mile, were each to spend as much as 200 million Americans living only 60 per square mile.  India seeks affluence, but could she stand it?

Environmental degradation is not, of course, inherent in rising affluence.  Only the particular forms and methods of production and consumption to which our society has become accustomed degrade it.  Rising affluence can and should be a source of environmental enhancement.

It is often overlooked that rising per capita income results in an increased demand for environmental amenities.  People naturally demand better public goods—more comfort and convenience and beauty in their communities—to match the better private goods and services their rising incomes enable them to buy.  One reason for the environmental "crisis" is the frustration felt by the public with a short supply of environmental amenities available to meet a rising demand for them.

The physical environment of large American cities has not degenerated absolutely in an overall sense, but probably has been improving.  People easily forget amenities taken for granted today that were lacking half a century ago.  Examples are air-conditioned offices, restaurants, and homes; thermostatically controlled electric and gas heat; underground utility wires and poles; paved boulevards and auto freeways.  These have widely replaced the crowded slums, the filth of unpaved streets, the drafty cold-water flats and belching chimneys of winter, and the steaming miseries of unrefrigerated summers.  Even in the inner city, people today live longer, healthier, and more comfortable lives—if not happier ones—than they did before World War I.  What has happened is that the overall supply of urban amenities has fallen far short of the rising effective demand for them, and the supply of certain critical goods, such as pure air and water, has virtually vanished.

The third source of the environmental problem is technological change.  Advancing technology has expanded the variety of products available for consumption, made products more complex, raised rates of obsolescence and thereby added to waste disposal. It has also added immensely to the per capita consumption of physical materials and energy, with consequent increments of waste and of pollution. It has expanded the amount of information required by consumers to make rational choices in markets, thereby creating market imperfections that are the source of the contemporary "consumerism" movement. Technological change, however, is, like rising affluence, a two-edged sword; it can be used to improve as well as to degrade the environment. Technology can *reduce* material consumption and recycle harmful wastes. Examples are the replacement of bulky vacuum tubes by microminiaturized circuits in computers, or the conversion of sewage into pure water plus fertilizers. Environmental preservation calls for a redirection of our technological efforts, as well as a restructuring of patterns of consumption.

One conspicuous aspect of environmental deterioration has been the disappearance of "free goods"—amenities such as clean air, pure water, and open space—that are in such ample supply relative to the demand for them that they are not economized. Pure air is no longer free. To obtain it one must buy air-conditioning equipment and acquire a home in which to install it. Pure water must be purchased by the bottle, now that the product of many municipal water systems is barely potable. Most urban dwellers must spend large sums of money for travel in order to gain the privacy and recreation of a natural environment unavailable at home.

A second aspect of environmental change is the fast-rising importance of spatial relationships in the cities. Such factors as building heights and population densities, street layout, park location, and zoning patterns largely determine the life-styles of urban residents and the supply of amenities available to them. The atrociously bad planning of most American cities and the abject perversion of zoning and building requirements to serve short-term commercial interests are well documented. The flagrantly over-dense building on Manhattan Island has been permitted only because of popular ignorance and apathy. Now, the public is belatedly recognizing the heavy social costs that its neglect has created. Popular concern with city planning, zoning, and building development is rising. The heavy stake of the individual in the physical attributes of his community is finally being appreciated.

A third aspect of environmental change is the multiplication of interdependencies among individuals. To an increasing extent the activities of each of us impinge upon others. This is so not only because more people live in cities, but also because the scale and variety of each person's activities rise with the amount of real income he produces and consumes. Thus, no one suffered disamenity a generation ago when his neighbor played a phonograph in a suburban home; but many suffer when a neighbor's son now turns up the sound volume of his hi-fi instrument in a high-rise apartment building.

Increasing interdependency is one way of looking at what economists call the "spillover effects" or external costs of production or consumption. For example, paper mills emit chemical wastes into lakes and streams, copper smelters inject sulphur dioxide into the air, and electric generating stations throw off carbon monoxide, radioactive wastes, or hot water, depending upon their fuels. Motor vehicles cause massive air and noise pollution, traffic accidents, and vast expenditures on medical, legal, policing, and engineering services and facilities—all borne mainly by the public. These industries all generate external costs, thrust upon society in the form of loss of environmental amenities. Although reliable estimates are lacking, total external costs in the U.S. economy are of the order of tens of billions of dollars a year.

The speed with which public interest in the environment has mounted may be explained primarily by the swift decline in certain amenities below thresholds of tolerability. Although certain critical amenities, notably pure air, have been diminishing for many years, the public has suddenly become aware of critical deficiencies. Thus, the quality of air in the Los Angeles Basin deteriorated steadily after 1940. Yet only by the mid-nineteen-sixties, after school children were being advised not to exercise outdoors on smoggy days and when smog alerts were being sounded on many days each year, was decisive action taken to reduce air pollution from motor vehicles. By the sixties, people saw that the "capacity" of the atmosphere over the basin to disperse pollutants had been intolerably overloaded.

After the design capacity of any facility has been reached, amenities diminish exponentially with arithmetic increases in the load. For example, when a twenty-first person enters an elevator designed to hold twenty persons, everyone in the elevator suffers loss of comfort; and when a twenty-second person enters, the percentage loss of amenity is much greater than the 4.8 per cent increase in the number of passengers. Similarly, when the five thousand and first automobile enters a freeway designed to carry five thousand vehicles per hour, it puts pressure of inadequate space upon five thousand and one drivers, and not only upon the new entrant.

Another reason for current public concern with the environment is the gathering appreciation of inequity as some groups in society gain benefits at the cost of other groups. The automobilist whose vehicle spews out air pollution gets the benefits of rapid and convenient travel; but he imposes part of the costs of that travel upon people who are forced to breathe bad air and hear deafening noise and who must bear the costs of painting and maintaining property corroded by pollutants.

Because this is manifestly inequitable, upgrading the environment by eliminating this kind of pollution will not only add to aggregate real income, but will also improve its distribution.

Before examining effective measures for enhancing the environment let us dispose of a number of partial or superficial diagnoses of, and prescriptions for, the problem. Several schools of thought have arisen.

First, there is the Doomsday School. It holds in effect that the problem of environmental degradation is insoluble. For example, Paul Ehrlich argues in his book *The Population Bomb* that it is already too late to arrest man's inexorable march to racial extinction through overpopulation, malnutrition, famine, and disease. Other criers of doom are the natural scientists who predict changes in the earth's temperature, as a result of accumulating carbon dioxide in the atmosphere, with consequent melting of the polar ice and other disasters. Although laymen are incompetent to judge such matters, they remain moot issues among natural scientists and therefore call for at least suspended judgment. Accumulating evidence suggests that population growth in the advanced nations has already slowed appreciably, and is starting to do so in many less developed lands. In any event, an apocalyptic view of the future should be rejected if only because it leads to despair and inaction. If one really believes that the future is hopeless, one will cease making an effort to improve society.

At the opposite pole is the Minimalist School. It holds that environmental deterioration is a minor problem in comparison with such contemporary issues as poverty, civil rights, and school integration. Its members argue that political leaders calling for a better environment are "eco-escapists," seeking to divert public attention from their failure to resolve these primary issues. What the Minimalists overlook is that the United States is already making progress in reducing poverty, expanding civil rights, and achieving educational integration, while it is still losing ground in arresting the decline of the urban environment. They also forget that attention to the environment does not mean neglect of poverty. On the contrary, central-city areas generally have the worst physical conditions of life and are populated mainly by low-income families. Because the poor stand to gain most from environmental enhancement, a war on pollution is one battlefront in a war on poverty. A vigorous attack on that front need not inhibit action on other fronts.

There is also a Socialist School. Its members view environmental deterioration as an inescapable consequence of capitalist "exploitation." If only private enterprise, market competition, and profit incentives were replaced by central planning and state ownership and management of enterprises, they contend, the problem would disappear. However, the socialist countries are facing more serious problems of pollution as their per capita G.N.P.'s are rising. Managers of socialist enterprises are judged by the central planners on the efficiency of their operations, and are under as much pressure to minimize internal costs and throw as much external cost as possible on the public as are the managers of private firms in market economies who seek to maximize stockholders' profits. Moreover, because a monolithic socialist society lacks a separate and independent mechanism of political control of economic processes, it is less likely to internalize the full costs of production than a market economy, with its dual systems of market-price and governmental controls. Pollution has arisen primarily from the failure of our political system, acting through government, to establish desired standards of production and consumption. If government performs its unique tasks, the competitive market system will operate within that framework to produce what the public demands without harming the environment.

The largest group of new environmentalists appear to be associated with the Zero Growth School. Its thesis is simple: since environmental degradation is caused by more people consuming more goods, the answer is to stop the growth of population and production. Nature has fixed the dimensions of the natural environment; therefore man should fix his numbers and their economic activities. We must establish a stable relationship between human society and the natural world.

Zero economic and population growth could arrest the process of environmental degradation, but could not, per se, restore a good physical environment. Were real G.N.P. constant through time, current levels of air and water pollution, noise, crowding, ugliness, and other negative elements would continue as long as present patterns of production and consumption are maintained.

Zero growth of population and production is, moreover, impossible to achieve. Because economic growth is a product of expanding population, higher investment, and advancing technology, zero growth would call for stopping changes in all three variables. This cannot be done in the proximate future, if at all. A leading population analyst has shown that even if, beginning in 1975, every family in the United States were limited to two children—an heroic assumption—population dynamics are such that this nation would not stop adding people until about 2050 A.D., when it would contain nearly 300 millions. (See Stephen Enke, "Zero Population Growth—When, How, and Why," TEMPO Publication 70TMP35, Santa Barbara, California, June 2, 1970.) While a decline in net savings and investment to zero is possible, it is extremely unlikely in view of the savings and investment rates Americans have maintained during the present century in the face of enormous increases in their real wealth and incomes. (See *Policies for*

*Economic Growth and Progress in the Seventies,* Report of the President's Task Force on Economic Growth, U.S. Government Printing Office, Washington, D.C., 1970.) A static technology of production is inconceivable. As long as Americans remain thinking animals they will increase the productivity of work.

Finally, zero growth is undesirable. A rising G.N.P. will enable the nation more easily to bear the costs of eliminating pollution. Because zero growth of population is far in the distance, and zero growth of output is both undesirable and unattainable, it follows that the environmental problem must be solved, as President Nixon stated in his January, 1970, State of the Union Message, by redirecting the growth that will inevitably take place.

The Austerity School of environmental thought is related to the Zero Growth School. Its members assert that environmental decline is produced by excessive use of resources. They are outraged by the fact that the United States consumes about forty per cent of the world's energy and materials, although it contains only six per cent of the world's population. Believing that asceticism is the remedy, they call for less consumption in order to conserve resources and to reduce production and pollution. We should convert ourselves from a society of "waste-makers" into one of "string-savers."

The basic error here is that it is not the amount of production and consumption per capita that degrades the environment, but the fact that government has failed to control the processes of production and consumption so as to eliminate the pollution associated with them. Without such political action, consumption could be cut in half and society would still suffer half as much pollution; with appropriate political control consumption could be doubled while pollution is radically reduced. The second error of the Austerity School, which distinguishes it from the Zero Growth School, is a notion that the world confronts a severe shortage of basic natural resources. Exhaustive studies by Resources for the Future have shown the contrary: there are no foreseeable limitations upon supplies of basic natural resources, including energy, at approximately current levels of cost. Technological progress is continually opening up new supplies of materials that are substitutable for conventional materials (e.g., synthetic rubber and fibers) and lowering the costs of alternative sources of energy (e.g., production of petroleum products from oil shales, tar sands, and coal). Austerity theorists do make a valid point, however, when they observe that governmental regulation to internalize external costs can cause business enterprises to develop ways of recycling former waste materials back into useful channels.

Finally, there is the Public Priorities School. Its adherents see the problem as one of too much governmental spending on defense and space exploration, leaving too little for environmental protection. The solution, as they see it, is to reallocate public expenditures. There are two responses to this line of reasoning: public expenditures are already being strongly reordered, and in any event reallocations of private expenditures will weigh far more heavily in a solution of the environmental problem. Thus between the fiscal years 1969 and 1971 federal budget outlays on defense and space are scheduled to shrink by ten per cent, from $85.5 billions to $77 billions, whereas outlays on social security and public assistance will rise by twenty-six per cent, from $46 billions to $60 billions. The President has announced plans for further contractions of defense outlays and expansions of expenditures on the nation's human resources.

Environmental restoration does require large increases in public expenditures upon sewage disposal and water purification, parks, housing, urban development, and public transportation. Even more, however, it calls for a reallocation of private expenditures as a result of governmental actions to internalize external costs in the private sector. For example, the purchase price and operating expenses of an automobile that is pollution-free will undoubtedly be higher than for a vehicle that degrades the environment, because the auto user will be paying the full costs of his private transportation. With internalization of costs, spending on private auto transportation may be expected to decline relatively. At the same time, spending on education and housing, which produce external benefits, will increase relatively. In the aggregate, readjustments in patterns of private expenditure will far outweigh reallocation of public expenditure in a total program of environmental restoration.

Because the environmental problem is critically important and is soluble, and neither socialization of the economy, zero growth, austerity, nor new public spending priorities offer a satisfactory solution, a more basic approach must be made. A good policy for environmental improvement should improve the distribution of income among people as well as the allocation of society's resources. Governmental intervention is necessary to attain both ends.

Environmental degradation occurs, as has been shown, when there are significant external costs involved in producing or consuming commodities. A social optimum cannot be achieved when there is a divergence between private (internal) and social (external plus internal) costs. An optimal allocation of society's resources requires that the full costs of production of each good or service be taken into account. The internalization of external costs must therefore be a pivotal aim of environmental policy. (A trenchant description of the external costs of economic growth is given by E. J. Mishan, *The Costs of Economic Growth*, New York: Praeger, 1967.)

Theoretically, perfectly competitive markets in which there are no transaction costs will lead to an optimum reallocation of resources in cases of pollution via bargaining between the polluter and the person harmed by pollution, no matter which party is legally responsible to compensate the other. (See R. H. Coase, "The Problem of Social Costs," *Journal of Law and Economics*, III, October, 1960.) In practice, however, the transaction costs of education, organization, and litigation are excessively high when pollution affects large numbers of people, as it usually does. For this reason it is more efficient for government to resolve pollution problems by legislation or regulation, rather than to leave them to bilateral market bargaining. For example, government can order air polluters to reduce their emissions by x per cent. Polluters then incur (internalize) costs in order to conform to the public regulation, thereby relieving the public of even greater costs of maintaining health and property damaged by pollution.

Prior governmental action is essential because the competitive market system is incapable, by itself, of internalizing the costs of anti-pollution measures. Suppose, for example, that the automobile could be made pollution-free by installing a device costing x dollars. An automobile owner would not voluntarily install the device, because other people would reap the benefits of the cleaner air made possible by his expenditure. General Motors proved this in 1970 by a well-advertised effort to sell motorists in the Phoenix, Arizona, area a pollution-reducing kit costing only twenty-six dollars. During the first month only a few hundred kits were sold in a market with several hundred thousand potential buyers. Auto makers would not voluntarily install the device because to do so would add to their costs and put them at a disadvantage in competition with other manufacturers who did not install it. And antitrust laws prohibit any agreement among all auto manufacturers simultaneously to install, or not to install, pollution-reducing devices. Where large external costs or benefits are involved, there is a conflict between the decision that serves the self-interest of the individual and that which serves the collective welfare of the community. Community welfare can only be given the precedence it deserves by a prior governmental action regulating private behavior, followed by corporation actions to modify products, prices, and allocations of resources in order to conform to the public regulation.

Society cannot reasonably expect individual enterprises or consumers to shoulder external costs in the name of "social responsibility," because the competitive market system puts each firm and household under strong pressure to minimize its costs in order to survive. What is needed is a prior political decision that leaves all producers or consumers in the same relative position.

There are usually alternative solutions to pollution problems; each alternative should be evaluated in order to identify the least costly of them. Consider again the example of smog in the Los Angeles Basin. Among possible ways of coping with this problem are the following: controlling emissions of pollutants from motor vehicles and stationary sources by public regulation; moving people out of the basin; rezoning to reduce building density; building a rapid mass-transit system; imposing heavy taxes on private automobile operation; or subsidizing motorists to limit their auto mileage. The costs and benefits of each alternative, and combinations thereof, should be evaluated before an anti-pollution policy is adopted. The goal should always be the most efficient use of scarce resources.

All desirable things in limited supply have a cost, and there are trade-offs between desirable things. People may gain more of one thing only by sacrificing something else, and the optimum situation is reached when no additional benefits can be obtained by further substitutions. These principles apply to environmental amenities. For example, noise pollution can be reduced with benefits to health and well-being, but at the cost of larger expenditures for insulation or noise-abatement devices or a reduction in the speed or power of engines. Conceivably, utter silence could be achieved by incurring astronomical costs and by making great sacrifices of mobility, power, and time. The public decides the optimum noise level by balancing the benefits of less noise against the costs of attaining it. Government then fixes a noise standard at that point where the costs of reducing noise further would exceed the additional benefits to health and well-being. Although the calculus is necessarily rough, this is the rationale of determining standards to reduce pollution of all kinds.

Just as governmental intervention is needed to bring about the reallocations of resources needed for environmental improvement, so it is also required to levy the costs of such improvement equitably among individuals and groups in society so as to improve—or at least prevent a worsening of—the distribution of income.

There are opposite approaches to the problem of cost allocation. By one principle, polluters should pay the costs of suppressing their pollution; by another, the public should pay polluters to stop polluting. The second principle is defended on the ground that the public benefits from the reduction of pollution and should pay the costs of this benefit. Those who espouse this view hold that tax credits and public subsidies are the proper instruments of a policy for environmental betterment. Libertarians usually favor this approach because of their preference for the "carrot" versus the "stick," and their belief that public boards often come under the domination of those they are supposed to regulate.

Advocates of the first principle argue, to the contrary, that society initiates an anti-pollution policy from a current status of inequity. The problem is to restore equity as between polluters and those damaged by pollution, not to compensate polluters for a loss of equitable rights. They also observe that persons with large incomes generally generate disproportionately more pollution than those with low incomes, so that a policy of internalizing costs in the polluter will tend to shift income from richer to poorer people, with resulting gains in social well-being. The appropriate instruments for dealing with pollution are, in their view, public regulations to reduce harmful activities, or taxes and fines on polluters.

Equity requires that the costs of suppressing environmental damage be borne by those responsible for it. Public restraint of private actions harmful to the environment thus should be the dominant instrument of environmental policy. Assertion of this principle does not, however, preclude the use of taxes, fines, or lawsuits, nor does it rule out the use of public subsidies to enterprises which, through long-continued tolerance of harmful activities vital to their survival, have acquired a certain equity in them. For example, a city council might prohibit billboard advertising of off-premise goods or services, on the ground that the visual pollution costs borne by the public exceed the benefits. To enable outdoor advertising companies to finance an adjustment into other activities, a city might reasonably offer to pay them subsidies over a period of years on a descending scale.

Since the quality of the urban environment is a function of many variables, public policies to enhance the environment must utilize many instruments.

Direct governmental control of emissions of pollutants—[aural], atmospheric, olfactory, visual, or health-affecting—is now exemplified in federal and state laws governing air and water pollution, and in federal standards of noise emissions from aircraft engines. Assuming that reduction of emissions is the least costly solution, the main problems are to determine appropriate standards and enforce them. In fixing standards, the state of pollution-control technology is an important consideration. Where such technology exists and can be applied at reasonable cost, the law should simply ban emissions and enforce compliance. This appears to be true of much air and water pollution from fixed sources, such as the chimneys of manufacturing and power-generating plants. Where pollution technology is in process of development, as in the case of automobile emissions, government should fix standards that are progressively raised as time goes on.

Another way to internalize external costs is to guarantee each property owner legal rights to the amenities pertaining to his property. A California court recently awarded substantial damages to home owners near the Los Angeles International Airport to compensate them for demonstrated loss of property values because of excessive noise from airplanes. A constitutional amendment should be enacted guaranteeing every property owner a right to environmental amenities, because this would induce business enterprises to reduce or eliminate pollution in order to escape legal liabilities. However, judicial processes are so costly, time-consuming, and uneven in their results as to make other solutions to environmental problems preferable.

Governments—federal, state, and local—themselves contribute to air and water pollution, especially by discharging untreated sewage into rivers and lakes. They should internalize these costs by massive public expenditures on sewage-treatment and water-purification plants. Such outlays will, of course, ultimately be paid for by a public that presumably values a clean environment more highly than the money paid in taxes to finance such facilities.

Urban planning, zoning, and building regulations are powerful instruments for enhancing the amenities of space, privacy, recreation, housing, transportation, and beauty in our cities. If American cities are to offer ample amenities for living, much stronger governmental controls of the design, quality, height, and density of buildings, and of the layout of transportation, recreation, and cultural facilities will be necessary. Americans will have to put a much higher priority on urban amenities, if strong enough instruments of social control over property usage are to be forged. Such controls will be opposed by builders, accustomed as they are to permissive public regulation that can be bent to their purposes. Yet firm public control of land usage under a long-range metropolitan plan is one reason why such cities as London hold a strong attraction for their residents as well as for millions of foreign visitors.

Enlargement of the supply of urban amenities also calls for immense public and private expenditures on recreational and cultural facilities, housing, and public transportation systems. The many programs coming under the auspices of the federal Departments of Transportation and of Housing and Urban Development serve this end. A whole battery of incentives for the participation of private enterprise in the gargantuan tasks will need to be fabricated, including tax credits, accelerated depreciation, credit guaranties, cost-plus contracts, and direct governmental subsidies. The naive idea that private corporations can or will undertake urban rehabilitation out of a sense of "social responsibility" denies the ineluctable fact that in a competitive market economy the firm cannot devote a material part of its resources to unprofitable activities and survive. Just as government must first create a market for pollution-reducing devices before the enterprise system will produce them, so it must first create adequate incentives to induce enterprises to produce urban housing and transit systems. That the responses are swift when the incentives are strong is shown by the great strength of the housing boom after World War II, triggered by liberal F.H.A. mortgage insurance and Veterans Administration home-loan guaranties.

Above all, a high-quality urban environment requires the public to assign high values to urban amenities—to appreciate them greatly and to work hard and pay for them. So far, too few American urbanites have held such values with sufficient intensity to bring about the necessary political action. Whether recent public outcries for a better environment will be sufficiently strong, sustained, and widespread to change the historical American posture of indifference remains to be seen.

The sudden emergence of the environmental problem raises profound issues about the functioning of our social institutions. Does it betoken an institutional breakdown—a failure to respond to new demands of the public? Has the social system responded, but been seriously laggard in its responses? Does the fault lie mainly in the political or in the market subsystem of our society, wherein there are two methods by which social choices of the uses of resources are made—voting in elections and buying in markets?

Although these questions cannot be answered finally, the most defensible positions appear to be the following. First, the social system has been sluggish in responding to the higher values placed by the public on environmental amenities, but it has not broken down and the processes of resource reallocation have begun. Second, the environmental crisis was generated primarily by tardy responses of the political system, and only secondarily by faults in the market system.

If American society is to attain optimal well-being, its dual set of political and market controls must operate promptly and in the proper sequence in response to changes in social values. Political action is first needed to create a demand for environment-improving products; market competition can then assure that this demand is satisfied economically. Measures are needed to improve both political and market processes.

Our model of the dynamic relationships between changes in social

values, government actions, and corporate behavior is shown in the
chart below. The primary sequential flow of influence runs from
changes in social values, via the political process, to changes in governmental regulation of the private sector and reallocation of public
resources; thence, via the market process, to corporate reallocation of
private resources. However, changes in social values are not wholly
determined by shifts in levels of income and other autonomous factors.
They also respond to political leadership in the legislative and executive branches of government and to the public advertising and selling
efforts of corporations. Similarly, governmental actions are not re-

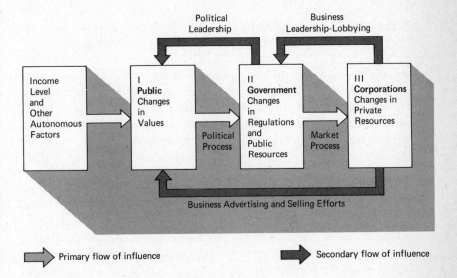

sponsible exclusively to shifts in the values of the public. They are
also influenced in some degree by the political activities of businessmen and by corporate lobbying. These secondary flows of influence
also help to determine the performance of the social system.

The model enables us to identify salient points of improvement in
the system. They are to reform the political process so that government actions will more rapidly and accurately reflect significant shifts
in social values, to reform the market process so that corporate behavior will more rapidly and accurately reflect changes in governmental regulation, and to reform political and business behavior so that
their secondary influences will help rather than hinder. Specifically,
what changes are needed in each of these three areas?

The environmental problem emphasizes once again the need for a
political system capable of translating changes in social values rapidly

and accurately into governmental actions. The political apparatus for sensing, recording, mobilizing, transmitting, and acting upon millions of changes in individual preferences must be improved. Our representative system of government must be made more representative. This raises anew the old dilemmas of participative democracy, the weaknesses of political parties, the unrepresentativeness of legislatures, and the inordinate influence of pressure groups in an age of accelerating technological, demographic, and economic change. The basic requirements for greater efficiency of the political system are better education and sustained participation in political affairs by citizens. While one may easily be pessimistic in the light of the past, there is ground for hope of improvement. Americans generally spend only a small fraction of the time and effort they devote to private goods in making choices of the public goods they purchase with their taxes. Yet purchases of public goods and services are now nearly one-third as large as purchases of private goods. During 1969 government purchases amounted to $225 billions or twenty-three per cent of a total G.N.P. of $923 billions, whereas private purchases were $698 billions or seventy-seven per cent. Rational behavior in resource allocation requires a massive increase in the time and effort devoted to public decisions. Hopefully, the present egregious under-allocation of time represents a cultural lag which will be rectified in due course.

Changes should be made in the voting process to make it function more like a market. Just as consumers record the relative intensities of their demands for different private goods by the amounts of their expenditures in markets, so voters could be enabled to record the relative intensities of their demands for public goods. Each voter could be given, say, one thousand votes, which he could cast in whatever numbers he chose for alternative aggregate levels of public expenditures and alternative patterns of allocation of each level among different objects. Finally, a maximum usage of direct links between public expenditures and the taxes levied to finance them could help to make the political system more responsive.

The competitive market system must also be made more responsive to shifts in public values and governmental regulations. Despite its undoubted superiority as a device for gauging consumers' wants, the recent rise of the "consumerism" movement reflects, among other things, a disturbing insensitivity of the business corporations to changing public demands and expectations. The foot-dragging behavior of the auto makers in regard to safety and air pollution and of the oil companies in regard to air and ocean-water pollution are symptomatic. Business corporations generally have been reluctant, if not obstructive, reactors to new social values instead of innovative leaders in satisfying them. Either their market researchers have been unable to detect them, or else correct market intelligence has not been utilized by their engineering, manufacturing, and marketing executives.

A reorientation of corporate organization is needed, from the board of directors down through corporate and divisional managers to individual plant and store executives. The board should include one or more "outside" directors chosen especially for their knowledge of corporate relationships to society, including the environment. This need should be met by the normal process of including such nominees in the slate of directors presented by management for stockholder vote, rather than by augmenting the board by special stockholder nominees, as Ralph Nader proposed to General Motors Corporation. The normal procedure is more likely to result in effective board action to improve the environment, because it avoids "bloc" politics within the board. Every single policy and action of the firm should be reviewed for its effect upon the environment. An environmental analyst, assigned to this task as a staff adviser to the chief executive, would help to assure good corporate behavior. Standard corporate policy should require all managers to include in their proposals for new operations of facilities measures for preventing adverse environmental effects. Corporations should also make more penetrating use of consumer surveys and public-opinion polls in order to keep informed of shifts in public tastes and priorities.

Reforms are also needed to ensure that the secondary influences upon social values exercised by political and business leaders are facilitative rather than obstructive. These influences are significant. For example, President Eisenhower's sponsorship of the Interstate Highway Act in 1956 and President Kennedy's proposal of a manned round trip to the moon in 1961 mobilized and activated changes in the values of the American people which led to highway and space programs each of the order of five billion dollars a year. President Nixon's leadership in 1970 in a national effort to improve the environment will probably produce even larger reallocations of resources. All three Presidents discerned deep changes in public priorities to which they gave form and implementation. Without such political leadership, readjustments would have been delayed amid mounting public tension and frustration.

American corporate leadership generally has not played a helpful role in implementing changes in social values. Whereas business lobbyists should be informing legislators of new environmental regulations desired by the public, they usually oppose such changes. Most corporate advertising is narrowly focused upon expanding public demand for existing products rather than for new products with superior environmental effects. As Henry Ford recently advised, corporate managers should "stop thinking about changing public expectations as new costs which may have to be accepted but certainly have to be minimized. Instead, we should start thinking about changes in public values as opportunities to profit by serving new needs."

This analysis of deterioration in the urban environment and of means to restore it has unveiled neither a master culprit nor a panacea. It has delineated a complex public problem requiring many instruments of policy for its solution. It has shown that the basic requirement is a citizenry that assigns higher values to urban amenities than it has in the past, and will work harder and pay more to get them. Given new social preferences, new regulations will be imposed and those long-neglected regulations on the statute books will finally be enforced. It is disturbing to reflect that a lawsuit brought by the Attorney General of the United States early in 1970 against several large corporations for polluting the southern end of Lake Michigan was to enforce a federal statute enacted in 1899. Here—as in the administration of urban zoning codes—Americans have not put high enough values upon environmental amenities to insist that private actions conform to existing public laws.

Environmental improvement will call for annual public and private expenditures of tens of billions of dollars indefinitely into the future. Profound changes will be necessary in the structure of relative costs and prices of goods, and in patterns of production and consumption. These readjustments will cause difficulties for individual companies operating on the margin of profitability and unable to pay the full costs of their products. Yet the ability of our profit-oriented enterprise system to adapt to a massive internalization of costs cannot be doubted, when one recalls its successful assimilation of the technological revolution since World War II. Over a period of time the costs and prices of products with large external costs (e.g., automobiles) would rise relatively, while those with large external benefits (e.g., homes) would decline relatively. While consumers would spend relatively less on autos and relatively more on housing, in a growing economy this would mean changes in the growth rates of different industries rather than an absolute decline in the output of any one. Also, new industries would emerge to supply the growing demand for pollution-controlling equipment and services. Profit rates and market signals would continue to guide resources in the directions desired by consumers.

The effects of environmental improvement upon the overall growth of the U.S. economy depend mainly upon how "economic growth" is defined and measured. There is a growing recognition that the true end of public policy is a steady expansion of social well-being, and that a rising G.N.P. is only a means to this end. G.N.P. is simply a measure of the aggregate output of the economy, whereas social well-being is also directly related to the composition of output, its full costs, and the uses to which it is put. If, as has been true during the past twenty years, much production included in the G.N.P. has been associated with national defense and environmental degradation, growth of the G.N.P. can be a highly misleading index of gains in social well-being. Indices of well-being should be developed to help guide long-term public policy, and G.N.P. also should be recast to provide a more meaningful measure of total output.

Assuming the existence of a strong effective demand by the public for a better urban environment, it cannot be doubted that a redirection of production to supply that demand will expand the well-being of American society. A better environment would enable people to reduce many other costs they now incur for health, property maintenance, recreation, and travel to leave uncongenial surroundings. Rising social well-being is not in conflict with an expanding G.N.P., provided that the increments of production improve the quality of life. On the contrary, growth of production is needed for that purpose. As President Nixon said in his 1970 State of the Union Message: "The answer is not to abandon growth, but to redirect it."

## QUESTIONS

1. What three basic forces does Jacoby identify as causing our environmental degradation? Discuss them.
2. What schools of thought have arisen to tell us what to do or not to do? Explain their reasoning, and comment on the extent to which they promise to meet the crisis.
3. Jacoby says, "The internalization of external costs must . . . be a pivotal aim of environmental policy." What does he mean by this? Do you agree? What problems arise in implementing this principle? What can be done to improve its implementation?
4. Explain Jacoby's model of the "Dynamic Relationships Between Public Values, Governmental Regulations, and Corporate Resource Allocations." Evaluate the significance of this model in (a) explaining the roles of business and government in dealing with the pollution problems and (b) determining how we may improve our system to deal more effectively with the pollution problems.

# Problems in cleansing the ohio river

## michael k. drapkin and thomas l. ehrich

**Michael K. Drapkin and Thomas L. Ehrich, staff reporters for *The Wall Street Journal*, explain the major types of political and economic problems that are involved in dealing with the pollution of the Ohio River.**

The sanitary engineers who assess the water of the Ohio River for drinking purposes use a vivid jargon. Sometimes they describe the water's taste and odor as "cucumber." Sometimes it's "medicinal." And all too often it's "pigpen."

That the Ohio River should sometimes smell like a pigpen discourages conservationists laboring to clean up America's polluted rivers. During the past 20 years, the Ohio has been the target of the broadest cleanup effort ever directed at a U.S. river—an effort many experts regard as a model for attacking pollution on other major streams. It has involved eight states, the Federal Government, hundreds of municipalities and thousands of private concerns. The cost to date has been close to $1 billion.

The effort has achieved some success. Most experts agree that the Ohio is indeed cleaner today than at any time since the 1930s. But the amount of filth that still pours into the 981-mile-long Ohio—once known to French explorers as La Belle Riviere—appalls pollution fighters.

## BLUISH-BLACK GOO

For example: At Midland, Pa., pipes from a Crucible Steel Corp. titanium plant spew a bright green, poisonous waste fluid into the river. At Steubenville, Ohio, iron oxide from steel company blast furnaces stains the river a reddish brown. Just below Wheeling, W.Va., an Ashland Oil Co. plant pours a bluish-black goo down a bank into the water. Upstream at Aliquippa, Pa., oil discharged from a Jones & Laughlin Steel Corp. plant leaves iridescent splotches that flash green and blue as they float lazily away with the current.

Private industry is by no means the only offender. In some spots along the Ohio, a powerful stench of raw sewage wafts across the

Michael K. Drapkin and Thomas L. Ehrich, "The Dirty Ohio," *Wall Street Journal*, March 17, 1969, p. 1 ff. Reprinted by permission.

water, the product of communities that dump their untreated sewage in the river.   Three hundred communities on the Ohio and its tributaries have no sewage plants.

Even larger cities that have sewage treatment plants often don't process their sewage adequately.   At Pittsburgh, a $100 million plant built in the late 1950s removes lumps of raw sewage, tin cans and other debris from the area's sewer water before it reaches the river.   But the 150 million gallons of water that pass through the plant and into the Ohio daily still carry a heavy load of acid, chemicals, oil, grease and brine.

One reason the cleanup of the Ohio is taking so long is that it was an enormous technical task to begin with.   Industrialization—and pollution—of the Ohio have been under way for nearly 200 years.   The Ohio River Basin, draining an area larger than Germany and the Netherlands combined, is rich with raw materials for the making of iron, steel and chemicals.   Three-fourths of known U.S. coal reserves underlie the basin, and its forests provide a quarter of the nation's hardwood.   The broad, placid river itself provides water, transportation and a means of waste removal for industry and cities.   Today the 10-state basin has a population of 24 million, supported by 38,000 industrial plants.

## FROM PITTSBURGH TO CAIRO

The Ohio is formed at the juncture of the Allegheny and Monongahela Rivers at Pittsburgh.   It flows in wide loops through the hills of Western Pennsylvania, down the border between Ohio and West Virginia, along the Kentucky-Indiana line and past the southern tip of Illinois to empty into the Mississippi at Cairo, Ill.   Into the Ohio flow a dozen major rivers, several of which are themselves centers of industrialization—including the Allegheny, Monongahela and Beaver in Pennsylvania; the Kanawha in West Virginia; the Miami, Scioto and Muskingum in Ohio; the Big Sandy in Kentucky; and the Wabash in Indiana.

Over the years, private industry and government alike have tended to regard the Ohio and its tributaries not as something to conserve but as something to use—and a major use is waste disposal.   In fact, the main function of most early sewage systems in the basin was to "get the waste into the rivers as fast as possible," says Richard A. Vanderhoof, Cincinnati-based regional director of the Interior Department's Water Pollution Control Agency.

By the end of World War II, the Ohio was almost a dead stream, so laden with pollutants that its waters were unfit for swimming, recreational boating or even many industrial uses.   Fish life was practically wiped out.   Though many communities continued to use Ohio River water for municipal water systems, extensive purification treatment was required.

## FORMIDABLE POLITICAL OBSTACLES

Yet the technical problems of cleaning up the river weren't insurmountable. The most formidable obstacles were political and economic—and it is these problems that largely remain unsolved today. The difficulties they have posed for those trying to clean up the Ohio are much like those facing conservationists trying to clean up any interstate river.

The effort to clean up the Ohio was organized in 1948 under the Ohio River Valley Water Sanitation Commission (ORSANCO), formed by a compact among eight of the 10 basin states. ORSANCO's job was to draw up antipollution standards and then to encourage government and industry throughout the basin to implement them.

ORSANCO's technical skill has been widely acknowledged. It pioneered in analysis of pollutants and their effects. In fact, criteria for water quality control drawn up by ORSANCO were incorporated into the Federal Water Quality Control Act of 1965.

But ORSANCO lacks enforcement strength. Until the Federal antipollution law was passed, ORSANCO had to rely on state laws to control offenders. Even now, it is reluctant to demand legal action because it depends heavily on the political support of state governments —which, in turn, often are more interested in encouraging industry than in regulating it. As a result, some critics say, ORSANCO has sometimes failed to point a finger at offenders and use its influence to see that they are whipped into line.

"You can't clean up the Ohio River by putting out slick paper brochures or using engaging semantics," says Murray Stein, enforcement chief of the Federal Water Pollution Control Agency. "The people of the Ohio Basin have done a lot of talking, but if you want a clean river, you have to have a rigid timetable" for improvement.

ORSANCO officials contend, however, that enforcement isn't their job. They argue that their role is to educate polluters, as well as the public, with the hope that pressures for cleanup efforts will result. ORSANCO has persuaded most industries and communities along the Ohio to take at least some steps toward complying with the commission's standards. But in the absence of stern enforcement measures, most haven't come close to meeting them.

Even with the new enforcement powers of the Federal law, authorities are finding it hard to curb polluters. Current Federal and state requirements call for polluters to make specific improvements by 1972 or 1973, but some skeptics doubt that the schedule will be met. Federal officials calculate the remaining cost of cleaning up the Ohio Basin at $2 billion—a staggering outlay over a relatively brief period.

A major obstacle is the insistence by many of the polluters that the Federal Government bear the lion's share of the cost. While the Government has become increasingly involved in antipollution work, the Vietnam war and other problems have left little Federal money for pollution control.

## CORPORATE RELUCTANCE

Industrial concerns, noting that municipalities usually get at least some Federal help with pollution control, are reluctant to shoulder the entire burden themselves. As a result, many companies take only those steps that are forced upon them. "We installed a lot of (pollution) abatement equipment at our Aliquippa plant, but we didn't do it until the Federal and state people raised their standards," admits Earl Young, manager of technical services for Jones & Laughlin Steel.

One company that has won praise from pollution fighters for its voluntary efforts is National Steel Corp. When it added a giant new steelmaking shop to its plant at Weirton, W.Va., in 1967, National installed extensive water pollution control equipment that is said to make its waste water cleaner than that of most cities. After the equipment was installed, a huge sludge mass—two inches thick and 2,500 feet long—slowly disappeared from alongside the plant. The sludge had built up from oil discharged by the plant before the new equipment was installed.

But National complains about paying its own way. George Angevine, vice president, says that the Government has paid about 21% of the cost of municipal sewage treatment facilities during the past 20 years. "It hasn't paid for any of industry's efforts," he says. "We should get tax credits for pollution control."

Steel men figure that roughly 10% of the cost of a modern $1 billion steelmaking facility goes for water pollution control—not to mention the cost of equipment for controlling air pollution. Moreover, it costs as much as 35% more to equip an old plant with water pollution control gear than it does to build the equipment into a new plant.

Many companies say they would rather close some old plants than meet the high costs of pollution control. "If I know I am going to phase out a plant in three years, I've got to think twice about putting millions into controlling pollution," says a steel company executive.

PPG Industries Inc. says meeting the state of Ohio's limits on discharge of calcium chloride into the Tuscarawas River, an Ohio River tributary, would force PPG to close its Barberton, Ohio, soda ash plant. This is the second largest chemical plant in the state.

A PPG spokesman says the company has the technical means to solve the pollution problem, but to do so would mean either spending too much money or reducing soda ash output to a level below the break-even point. Some 2,600 workers would be laid off if the plant, built in 1899, should close.

Some companies, of course, may be bluffing when they threaten to close plants rather than meet pollution control standards. But Government officials are reluctant to push them too hard. "It's easy to say, 'Clean up, Mac,' but we're not in the business of putting people out of work," says the Interior Department's Mr. Vanderhoof.

In some instances, antipollution rules are said to have scared away companies planning to build plants in the Ohio Basin. A few years ago Union Carbide Corp. decided against building a second chemical plant at South Charleston, W.Va., where it already had one facility, and built instead in Louisiana. Ed Henry, chief of the West Virginia Water Resources Department, says antipollution requirements were the reason. The company doesn't deny that the requirements were considered, but it contends that other factors, such as access to raw materials, played a larger role in the decision.

State governments are keenly aware of the economic importance of industry in the Ohio Basin, and they have been notably reluctant to enforce antipollution measures that would discourage companies. "Every state has a department of commerce that is striving for all the industry it can get, and each state also has a department of health that worries about such things as pollution," says Mr. Vanderhoof. "It depends on which is the strongest—and so far the health departments haven't been strong enough."

Federal authorities tick off a list of companies that, for whatever reason, continue to be major polluters of the Ohio or its tributaries. The list includes Wheeling-Pittsburgh Steel Corp., Allied Chemical Co., Koppers Co., U.S. Steel Corp., Copperweld Steel Co., Textron Inc., American Chain & Cable Co. and Union Carbide.

The companies acknowledge that they are contributing to pollution, but some contend the pollution levels aren't as high as Federal authorities say. Moreover, the companies all say they are working, often on state-approved timetables, to clean it up. American Chain & Cable says its pollution problem already has improved substantially with the closing of one operation at its plant on the Monongahela River and adds that it is now setting out to clean up remaining "minor" problems. "We used to be a gross violator," a spokesman says.

## AN INVISIBLE POISON

Much of the waste dumped into the rivers consists of such highly visible compounds as oil or colored chemicals, but pollution fighters say much pollution is invisible.  For instance, Union Carbide dumps phenol, a caustic and poisonous—but invisible—chemical, into the water at its Riverside, Ohio, plant.  The Federal Water Pollution Control Agency says the concentration of phenol downstream from the plant is "about 40 times" the acceptable level.  (A company spokesman says, however, that Ohio state standards permit the plant to continue dumping phenol until 1975.)

One of the most troublesome types of industrial pollution is acid drainage from coal mines.  Sulphuric acid is formed when air and water act chemically upon rock in mines.  The acid is carried by water drainage to streams that eventually flow into the Ohio or its tributaries.  It leaves a dark yellow or brown stain on river banks and rocks, kills fish and often forces industrial plants to treat their water with softeners and chlorine before they can use it in manufacturing.  The acid also corrodes barges and water intake equipment of both industrial and municipal water systems.

While coal companies are credited generally with doing a good job of controlling drainage from active mines, they are criticized by pollution fighters for having failed to find practical ways to stop acid drainage from the thousands of abandoned mines in the Ohio basin.  Often the cost of removing acid from an abandoned mine's drainage is more than the mine was worth when it was active.  An official of Pennsylvania's Sanitary Water Board estimates the cost of cleaning up acid drainage in Western Pennsylvania alone at about $400 million over the next decade.

The effects of acid pollution are most evident in the Monongahela River, which flows through the coal fields of West Virginia before emptying into the Ohio.  Mr. Vanderhoof calls the Monongahela an "open cesspool."  At Pittsburgh, where the Allegheny and the Ohio are often ice-covered in midwinter, the Monongahela remains completely free of ice, largely because of the acid.

Cleaning up municipal sewage is no easy task either.  Though most cities installed basic, or primary, treatment facilities like Pittsburgh's during the 1950s, few have the secondary treatment plants that pollution fighters say are now necessary for a thorough job of pollutant removal.  Cincinnati, Louisville, Evansville, Indianapolis, Dayton and Charleston all discharge sewage into the Ohio or its tributaries—and all lack secondary plants.  "A large city with only primary treatment is worse than many small towns with no treatment at all," complains one Federal official.

But communities are faced with rising costs and voter resistance to tax hikes or bond issues. Thus, they are reluctant to move without Federal help.

The jockeying for Federal funds has delayed some facilities for years. Several years ago, Wellsburg, W.Va., a town of 5,000, was offered a Federal grant of $346,650, then about 30% of the cost of a sewage treatment plant. But town fathers rejected the offer, saying they needed a 50% grant. Since then the estimated cost of a plant has risen to $1.8 million from $1.2 million, and Wellsburg now wants at least $900,000 from the Government. The $346,650 offer is still open—and Wellsburg, lacking even a primary treatment plant, continues to dump raw sewage into the Ohio.

Some communities resist efforts to get them to build facilities. Pittsburgh's Allegheny County Sanitation Authority has stubbornly resisted demands that it build a secondary sewage treatment plant. The Pennsylvania Sanitary Water Board ordered it in 1965 to build such a facility, but the authority has stalled while trying to get Federal help. Despite the present plant's failure to remove many pollutants, the authority's executive director, Leon Wald, contends that a secondary plant is an unnecessary luxury whose need has been "greatly exaggerated."

**QUESTIONS**

1. Explain some of the political problems that must be resolved before much can be done to clean up a dirty river like the Ohio.
2. Explain the major economic problems that must be faced and resolved to clean up the Ohio.
3. Is it possible that the economic problem is more difficult to solve than the governmental-legislative problem?
4. What solutions do you advocate to resolve the political and economic problems?

# The dilemma in building new power plants

## chet holifield and craig hosmer

**Chet Holifield and Craig Hosmer are U. S. congressional representatives and both have been concerned with the generation of power through atomic energy. In this article they succinctly explain a major dilemma that exists between the rising demands for power and the public protests against the environmental pollution of power generating plants.**

A horror story of 1980:

The thermometer climbs to 106 deg. in Van Nuys as Southern California swelters through the 10th day of a brutal August heat wave. No relief is in sight, the weatherman says. Every air conditioner from Santa Barbara to San Diego is running at full blast.

At power stations, throughout the area, plant superintendents uneasily watch the electrical demand grow. Reserve capacity is called on the line. But it won't be enough.

Power companies broadcast an urgent message: "Turn off the air conditioners. Avoid the use of electrical appliances. Leave the lights off. Our generating equipment is approaching absolute capacity."

The public roars its protest. The accusing finger is pointed straight at the local power company.

"Don't blame us," the company president says. "We've been trying to build new generating plants for years, but every time we choose a site someone objects. They say we're spoiling the environment. We've been tied up in so many lawsuits that our construction program has been set back five years.

"All the world loves electricity, but all the world hates electrical generating plants," he moans. End of scenario.

## CRISIS EVER SHARPER

No one looks forward to this type of confrontation, least of all the electric companies. Yet every warning sign indicates this is precisely where California is headed unless immediate steps are taken to assure that suitable sites will be available on which to build the needed power facilities.

Chet Holifield and Craig Hosmer, "State Should 'Site' Power Plants," *Los Angeles Times*, November 30, 1969, Section G. Reprinted from the *Los Angeles Times*, November 30, 1969, Section G-7, by permission of the authors.

The sad truth is this: the number of potential power plant sites in California continues to shrink while the public's demand for electricity continues to climb. The state's peak demand for electricity during 1969 was 24 million kilowatts. Within 10 years it will climb to 55 million kilowatts and require more generating capacity than the entire nation did in 1950.

Potential sites to install this new capacity diminish as people and industry spread across the land. Growing public concern over environmental quality adds new difficulties to the problem. Already, new oil-fired generators have been effectively banned from the Los Angeles basin, and public resentment over existing facilities grows with each smog alert.

Nuclear power plants undoubtedly represent the electrical generating stations of the future, particularly in Southern California. Nuclear plants do not release air pollutants. They are economical, quiet, architecturally attractive and, generally, they make better neighbors than conventional plants.

Unfortunately, locating sites for nuclear plants in California is even more difficult than for ordinary plants. The historic battle over the proposed Malibu reactor is a superlative example. The San Andreas Fault and its seismic cousins place many areas in the state off-limits to nuclear reactors.

In addition, nuclear plants require proportionately more cooling water than conventional plants, making oceanfront sites almost mandatory, particularly in water-scarce Southern California. This alarms recreation and conservation groups which rightfully seek to preserve as much beach as possible.

Despite this, we are confident that nuclear reactors have a great future in California. Given time and effort, the siting problems will be solved. Economic improvement in the present crop of nuclear reactors and the advent of the highly efficient "breeder" reactors, which produce more fuel than they consume, will continue to keep California a low power-cost region.

But to realize this bright future, a program is needed now to assure timely availability of adequate plant sites. The problem is more complex than just locating sufficient land. The herculean task poses these questions:

Where are we going to build the 45 million kilowatts of capacity which will be needed over the next 10 years?

Can we meet this load growth and still assure protection of the environment, particularly preservation of our beaches?

Can both objectives be met while simultaneously keeping the cost of electricity down?

It is apparent that the plant-by-plant approach typifying utility planning today will not suffice in the future. No longer can electric companies build anywhere it suits them. Today they can expect vigorous public opposition to their construction plants, almost regardless of where a plant is to be built.

As a consequence, assuring future availability of electric power in California demands long-range, statewide planning and site acquisition. Power plant siting is becoming critical nationwide, but California's population growth, soaring land values, seismicity, atmospheric conditions and water shortage make our need even more obvious and more urgent.

Our awareness of this need for a long-term policy approach to power plant siting has caused us to propose to Gov. Reagan:

> Creation of a Power Plant Siting Authority capable of assuring that the need for sites is fulfilled without undue deterioration of the environment.
>
> Development of several large land areas in the state called Power Parks upon which future plants would be isolated.

The authority would inventory currently available power plant sites, estimate the needs for several decades ahead and assess the deficit. Under suitable ground rules, taking into consideration both the need for power and the need for environmental preservation, it would identify areas suitable for power development.

The authority's charter should give it power to tax and issue public obligations, as well as the right of condemnation, plus quasi-judicial powers to resolve conflicts involving land-use priorities. Acting either directly, or by coordinating and assisting public and private utilities, the authority would spearhead the purchase and development of power parks.

It might be possible and desirable to go outside the state for part of the land, in which case interstate or regional compacts could work to the advantage of both California and her neighbors.

This plan will take large areas of the state's invaluable scenic and recreational resources out from under the threat of power development. At the same time it will assure setting aside sufficient land, at today's prices, to meet the electrical load growth of the future.

The clustering of several generating plants on a single large site will allow new economics of scale to be achieved. For example, a remote area economically unsuitable for a single plant might become attractive for several plants. Specifically, we have in mind locations away from the beaches. It may be economical to run ocean cooling water conduits a few miles inland to a multiple plant location, but not to a single plant.

Another critical area of activity for the proposed authority would be an intensive research and development program on advanced siting techniques needed after the power parks are filled. Possibilities include man-made islands for power and desalting plants, floating power islands or ocean-bottom siting.

## TRANSMISSION FACTOR

Should progress with extra-high voltage transmission technology make possible very long line transmission, then the radius of search for suitable sites will be extended significantly from metropolitan load centers. The matter of cooperative arrangements with other states will become more attractive.

To recover its costs, the authority would levy pro-rata charges on all of the state's utilities to assure that no single utility, be it publicly or privately owned, could pre-empt the cheap and easy sites to the disadvantage of other utilities and their customers. In this way, all would share the advantages of the prime sites and the minor disadvantages of the others.

These are obviously bold ideas. We believe them worthy of study and discussion. The initial reactions of the governor and certain key members of the Legislature have been favorable. The utilities may find merit in them as the problems they face become better defined.

We have pointed out that we are receptive to other ideas, other approaches—but we feel that the concept of long-range site planning is so urgent in California that we must begin somewhere, and begin soon.

In many ways California's future power needs are similar in magnitude to the water needs we faced in the 1920's. The courage and foresight of the Metropolitan Water District and the Statewide Water Plan solved the area's water problems for decades. The demand for electricity requires no less vision if the growth of the state and the welfare of its citizens are to be ensured.

## QUESTIONS

1. If such a horror does take place as described in this article, who is to blame? the public utilities? the governments involved? the people?
2. Do you have a government-business planning problem in your community such as the one in the article?
3. Why is it so difficult to plan ahead in such situations?

4. Do you think the authority suggested is the best way to assure the necessary planning and action?
5. Do you have any suggestions to improve government-business planning in areas such as the one in the article?
6. How far do you think joint government-business planning should go in the case of public utilities?

# Business and the Urban Crisis

**8**

# The pros of black capitalism

## richard n. farmer

Richard N. Farmer is Chairman of the Department of International Business Administration, Indiana University. In this article he succinctly concludes that black capitalism has merit but that it will not make much of a dent in the solution of urban problems.

Some observers of the American scene take a gloomy view of the future of black capitalism. In their judgment, there is not much hope in this concept as a cure for urban ills, given all the problems associated with developing new entrepreneurs among our Negro population. Basically, their arguments are well-founded; it is highly unlikely that any black capitalism program, however developed and financed, will ever make much of a dent in our overwhelming urban problems. Those who expect that a few billion dollars poured into this area will transform the ghetto are likely to be disillusioned.

However, black capitalism should not be written off as a total failure. If one considers the modest gains that might be made by a realistic approach, it is possible that some support for such a program would pay big dividends—although not in the short run. There is no magic here, nor even a faint hope that the results will revitalize the inner city. But a modest effort, built on a realistic set of assumptions, could have positive impact. These conclusions are based on a program now in operation at Indiana University, which sends students to consult with black small businessmen in Indianapolis, and on data developed in Indianapolis and Gary by survey work in the black business community.

## PRESENT MISCONCEPTIONS

The types of programs envisioned by government planners for black business are unlikely to work for much the same reasons that so many foreign aid programs are relatively unsuccessful. The wrong model has been applied to the problem, and, as a result, all the wrong variables are dealt with. The really important variables rarely get tackled in a systematic manner. Federal programs tend to have several erroneous characteristics.

*They are far too ambitious.* Work with small businessmen has

Reprinted with the permission of the publisher from BUSINESS HORIZONS, Volume 13, February 1970, pp. 37–40.

driven home to us the real difficulty of moving rapidly toward business improvements. It is not uncommon for a team of rather sophisticated M.B.A. consultants to spend a hundred man-days working with a small businessman and succeed in raising his net profits by only 10 percent. Moving from perhaps $3,000 in net income this year to $3,300 next year represents an improvement, but such gains are not likely to shake the world. These gains are also diminished by an economic consideration. The consultants this year are likely to be highly paid business consultants, staff men, and junior managers next year. If they are worth $100 per day then, they may be worth at least $50 per day now. Students willingly give their time, but providing perhaps $5,000 of free consulting for a $300 gain suggests the economic impracticality of such large-scale projects.

To expect a marginal small businessman (black or white) to move from two employees and $20,000 in sales this year to perhaps a hundred employees and $1 million in sales next year is totally unrealistic. Booms and Ward mentioned some of the major reasons, . . . but did not note that smaller businessmen have great difficulty in making such a managerial leap; typically, they just do not know enough to do the job.

*The programs raise all the wrong hopes.* The expectations are strikingly similar to those related to aid programs in poor countries. Miracles seem about to happen: incomes will jump and everybody will have well-paying jobs. But they do not happen. Hopes are destroyed as reality slowly sinks in, and big-ticket programs are wrecked along with more modest workable ones.

*The programs assume that the key to the problem is a shortage of capital.* This is totally wrong. The real problem is the shortage of skill, ability, and the kinds of behavioral characteristics that would make a successful large capitalist. We have never been unable to obtain a reasonable loan from a variety of public and private sources if the small firm is sound and deserving. Clearly, there has been discrimination in the past, but now, if anything, there appears to be "reverse" discrimination. We have obtained loans for rather shaky and unbankable types of black operations, which, if white-owned, would probably be denied capital by lending agencies.

The real problem is that so few small businessmen are able to use capital wisely. Most of them are good technicians; this is how they got into business in the first place. But they tend to be bad managers. Their books (if any) are in poor shape; planning is often absent completely; and control systems leak like sieves. Money loaned to such entrepreneurs would be quickly lost.

As already noted, training men to utilize capital efficiently is a labor-intensive, time-consuming process. The labor required is exactly that in most short supply—namely, highly trained business consultants and managers.

## BLACK BUSINESS THE RIGHT WAY

It is possible to build a modest program for black entrepreneurship that might pay some long-term dividends, as well as complement more realistic efforts in other sectors.  Such a plan would have four major characteristics.

*It would be modest.*  Perhaps a few hundred million dollars spent correctly is about all that could be absorbed in the entire United States. This more modest approach, incidentally, might also achieve one very real objective: to keep the fast buck boys out of the game.  Whenever government money is being doled out in big chunks, the possibilities of con jobs in the program are very real.

One major reason for not needing a great deal of money is that if we can figure out how to produce a group of good potential black entrepreneurs, the normal small business capital markets can easily handle their needs (mainly through banks and S.B.A.'s).  People with sound businesses and good plans can find capital.

*It would be focussed largely on practical business training for existing and potential small businessmen.*  Our own Indianapolis work suggests that existing small firms, those who are thinking of starting firms, and those who get wind of training programs all want help. These are far more than any set of existing or potential trained human resources can handle at present.  We do not have the trained manpower to handle more than existing or potential businessmen.

Clients, if they should ever be needed, are not hard to generate.  Already a whole set of institutions exists that can cooperate by passing the word, screening potential firms, and finding existing firms in trouble.  The Urban League, C.A.P., the National Alliance of Businessmen, and many others are ready to do the job.

*The program would utilize largely the existing pool of trained, high skill manpower available for such training.*  There is only one of these: students in schools of business.  Many of these young people are willing to help out with smaller firms if asked, often for small fees or none at all.

Anyone who starts a big aid program for small struggling firms by hiring existing manpower to train such people is going to be disillusioned.  The right kinds of people can easily find good jobs elsewhere, and they already have.  What is available are students, and they tend to be overtrained for the job at hand.  Quite a few B-schools have had small programs of this sort (Indiana, Stanford, Harvard, and Columbia, to name a few), and their experiences should be looked at closely.   If these young people can not do the job, it is unlikely to be done at all.

*The program should zero in on the innumerable entry controls prevalent in many businesses.*   Personal entry controls fill a good-sized book just to list; firm entry controls are particularly vicious in motor freight and passenger transportation, where late arrivals are excluded from any activity.   If you were not in the game in 1926 or 1935, you are forever excluded.

If we are serious about black capitalism, or, for that matter, capitalism in general, it is about time that we started to act like it.   It is time for the successful manager to stop complaining pompously that young men just do not want to get into business for themselves any more; he should realize that two-thirds of the feasible alternatives are partially or totally blocked from entry.   We could start 400 small taxi firms in Indianapolis alone next year if the entry control law were changed. None of these would become a gold mine, but they would provide reasonable living for a lot of people now unemployed or underemployed. In addition, these firms would do a better job for consumers than the present system; service would improve and would cost less.

It is highly unlikely that anything of this sort will happen.   We preach the virtues of free enterprise, we encourage blacks and others to enter business, and then we make quite sure that all our upper middle-class subsidies are preserved and protected, even if in the process some of the more interesting possibilities are ruined.   No wonder blacks question our real motives.   To put it bluntly, we are quite cynical, and a lot of the talk about helping blacks is a fraud. They know it too.

Modest programs, even if successful, are not likely to change the world.   What they may do is to contribute toward the economic development of some of the poorer segments of our population.   With some luck, a few of the more capable black capitalists will grow enough, become efficient enough, and perhaps even brave enough to become capitalists—not black capitalists.   The real business opportunities are out in the mainstream, not in some decaying ghetto.   But a shrewd black businessman, who has done his homework and struggled for years against overwhelming odds, might make it.   He should not be surrendered so casually.   What he needs is knowledge and confidence, not cash.   A program of the sort suggested above might do this for a few outstanding men.

And the rest?   Not much will happen.   A few small firms might become a bit better, and their increased efficiency may help both them and their clients.   A man netting $3,000 a year, after a lot of work and worry by students, may get up to netting $5,000 a year.   The only ones who will really care will be his consultants and his own family.   But such gains, in a part of America where any gain is extremely hard to come by, could in the end represent something worthwhile.

Another argument in favor of black capitalism has little to do with blacks, but may in the end be most important of all. I encourage my white and black students to work with small, marginal black firms in the ghetto. I have no trouble finding volunteers; we pay nothing, yet plenty of young men are willing to go. As one might expect in a volunteer program run and managed by students, we end up with the truly marginal and submarginal small firms. Modestly successful black-owned firms have their own professional sources of support. One outcome of this program is that an immature, white middle-class student will grow up in about five weeks while he works with his firm. The client may be a submarginal, one-man retail operation with a negative net worth, but, for the first time in his life, the student finds out what it is like to do a man's work in a world which he never really knew existed.

Such young men will go on to big corporations as junior managers and staff men, and they take with them an experience that will make them a bit different forevermore in their business careers. This sort of consulting work creates in most of the young people working with it a sensitivity to social problems that they otherwise might never have developed.

Of course, and as usual, this is one more black man's subsidy to the white man. But in the end, it may end up being worthwhile. The submarginal client becomes marginal, which is no big deal for the world but is important to the client. The student grows up and discovers that what he has been learning is not-at all well known, even in business circles. And, perhaps most important of all, we whites have had an opportunity to conduct a relevant dialogue with our hard-working black counterparts in business. In a world of racial tension, this alone may make black capitalism worthwhile.

**QUESTIONS**

1. Do you agree or disagree with Farmer's proposals for a program aimed at encouraging the development and growth of black capitalism in America? Why or why not?
2. What do you consider to be the advantages and/or disadvantages of black capitalism programs? Specify and justify your beliefs.
3. What has business done to support black capitalism?
4. What should be the role of the business community and government in the development and implementation of black capitalism programs?

# A hidden issue in minority employment

## richard a. goodman

Richard A. Goodman is Assistant Professor of Business Administration, University of California at Los Angeles. In this article he points to the problem of differing values and objectives of minorities and the companies in which they work, and he discusses methods to produce a reasonably satisfactory relationship.

There has been considerable foot-dragging on the part of corporations with relation to the employment of minority members. Part of this foot-dragging is "economic"; minority members are unskilled and educationally disadvantaged, and therefore a training program is required to make productive employees. Such a training program is often considered economically unfeasible vis-à-vis an adequate return on investment. Part of this foot-dragging is prejudice, to varying degrees and at many levels in the organizational hierarchy, against the minority groups. Part of this foot-dragging is the unconscious recognition that even the white members of the organization cannot effectively influence the operational value system of the organization. That is, organizations do not effectively deal with value conflict among their white members, and the appreciation of this unarticulated phenomenon tends to engender a go-slow attitude when considering the employment of personnel who might not "fit."

While not intending to negate the issues of "economics" or prejudice, I will explore the hidden issue of low tolerance for value conflict. This issue is raised clearly by the recent work of William McKelvey who states:

> In recent years the conflict between [personal] . . . objectives . . . and the goals of large . . . organizations has been the subject of an increasing number of books and articles. This conflict, which may conceivably arise in any kind of an organization, is one where expectations, aspirations, and values of an employee are different from those of the organization.

There is a growing appreciation, illustrated by various organizational theorists, that the value systems inherent in organizations and in individuals are not sufficiently similar to allow the assumption of commonality.

Chris Argyris articulated this when he described the tendency of organizations to inhibit the maturing process of their members. That is, organizations tended to restrict independence, to limit alternate behavior patterns, to demand a relatively short time perspective, and to discourage the development of a deep interest pattern.

Similarly, Robert Dubin, in an early study of the "central life interests" of workers, tended to find that they did not view the work situation as a place to get their satisfactions. He continues by noting that organizational devices to encourage commitment to organizational objectives normally have been based on the assumption that the working time of an employee is one of his central life interests. Within the limit of Dubin's study, however, this is not true. Small wonder that progress toward stronger organizational commitment has been slow.

## NONCONFORMIST EMPLOYEES

The preceding discussion suggests that the incidence of value conflict between employee and organization is likely to be significant. It then becomes interesting to speculate on what behavior ensues from a value conflict situation. This raises the issue which served as a focus in the McKelvey study: "What happens when [employees] begin to see that the organization they are working for is not fulfilling their . . . expectations?"

Although McKelvey used a framework which allowed several typical behaviors, his study identified a predominant form. This form he called "active, cynic" or "insurgent." His findings are thus stated:

> These results suggest that scientists and engineers who perceive that their professional expectations are not being fulfilled by the organization are most likely to feel that they have little control over their career advancement (cynicism). They are quite likely to choose not to change their own values and expectations to fit well with those of the organization (non-passivity).

The employee who is behaving in the active, cynic style can be characterized as one who is working for a change in the organizational system. He continues to believe that his criticisms will actually affect the alteration of that system. This continual belief in the eventual ability to accomplish change and the behavior which often follows from such a belief leads to a further major finding of McKelvey. This style (active, cynic) is "the style least likely to be coupled with high eligibility for promotion." The low eligibility for promotion tends to ensure that people in the upper echelons of an organization have relatively similar value systems.

This work of McKelvey and that of authors such as William H. Whyte, Jr., and Melville Dalton seem to support the conclusion that sameness in values is an attribute treasured by organizations. Further, their work suggests that value sameness is more prevalent the higher one looks in the organizational hierarchy. The end result of this sort of behavior is to disenfranchise people who have different value systems and who do not conform. American industry does not seem to have the organizational abilities to tolerate value conflicts, and it is this hidden issue which seems most likely to contribute to turbulent progress in the minority employment programs of various organizations.

One of the clear trends in the question of minority problems is the fact that the Negro and, to some lesser extent, the Mexican-American are becoming more and more insistent upon a satisfactory role in United States society. A satisfactory role means being actually represented in the society and thereby contributing to the fashioning of the future of this society. It explicitly requires the ability of the minority group to influence the operational value system of the society. The ability to influence is a complex and troublesome concept when considered on a societal level, but when transformed to an organizational level this ability and its corollary, the achievement of a satisfactory role, appear possible.

At the organizational level the complexity associated with assuring a satisfactory role for minority members is greatly reduced. Here the question of a satisfactory role continues to require that the minority groups have the ability to influence, but in this case it is the operational value system of the organization that is influenced.

Turning to the specific problem of minority employment, an initial axiomatic statement would be as follows: as the influx of minority group employees grows in number, more and more members of the organization will have value systems which are at variance with that of the organization. It then follows that unless an organization can devise some process of adapting to this value conflict and making it "constructive value conflict," the influx of minority members will simply lead to frustration and turmoil.

The issue raised is not one that has an easy solution. Only limited guidance is available from the literature on organizational behavior.

The most prominent recommendation for an adaptive device which potentially allows for constructive value conflict comes from Rensis Likert. His recommendation of a "linking pin" organizational form is will known. (See Figure 1.)

The essence of his recommendation is that decision making should be done by the entire group of men, with the man who "supervises" serving as a linking pin to the next level of the organization. The essential assumption of Likert's proposal is that each man in any specific triangle is equally influential. An organization which operates under this recommendation has great potential for handling value conflict.

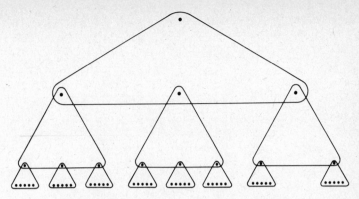

FIGURE 1    The Linking Pin Organization. Adapted from Rensis
Likert, *New Patterns in Management* (New York: McGraw-Hill, 1966)

But it does not necessarily avoid the issue of promotions being given
to the men whose values match those of the organization.  It seems,
therefore, that while Likert's proposal has the potential for handling
value conflict it does not protect an organization from value-oriented
promotion practices.  Parenthetically, it does seem that task conflict
can be handled well by this device, regardless of the value conflict
problem.

Another model of organizational behavior which has potentiality for
handling value conflict is that of Richard Cyert and James March.
They describe organizations as a set of "viable coalitions."  The coalitions are formed by various forms of negotiating and are relatively
stable over time.  A coalition mapping of an organization can be seen
in Figure 2.  The coalitions tend to determine organizational objectives
which are forged from the value systems of the coalition participants
by the negotiation process.  The basic ingredient necessary for this
conceptualization to be operational in the minority area is the provision
of a source of bargaining power for the minority groups.  To more fully
allow for effective value conflict the minority participants must have
some measure of power.  To date, most of this power has resided
external to the firm in the hands of various civil rights groups.

For a considerable period of time, the major influx of minority group
employees will be seen in the lower echelons of the organization.  David
Mechanic has described how occupants of an organization's lower
echelons can exert power and influence.  His definition of sources of
power include access to people, information, and instrumentalities.

The power of participants who control access to people can be
exemplified by the secretary who screens calls and callers for her boss
or the machine shop supervisor who does or does not allow you to
speak directly with the men working on your project.  Control of

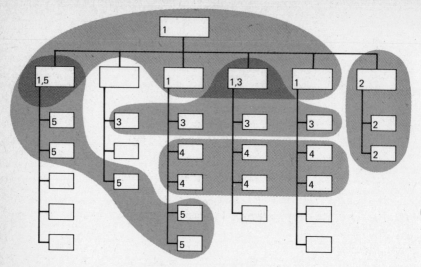

FIGURE 2    Coalition Mapping of an Organization

access to information concerns a wide variety of actions, including whether or not to report an impending schedule variance and whom to inform in advance about organization switches. Examples of control over access to instrumentalities are the "actual" assignment of priorities on computer runs, illustration work, or the use of company special facilities. To a large extent, the initial positioning of newly hired minority members will not even give them access to these sources of power. As such, even this coalition concept will not encourage the desired effective value conflict since there is little power available to the lower participants.

## A POWER ROLE

The logical conclusion to this discussion is simply to provide some source of power to new entrants to the organization. This would then set the stage for a mode of value conflict which would provide most organizational participants with a role in defining the operational value system. But it does not provide for a constructive value conflict situation. It only provides for value conflict per se. It can go either way.

The situation must be leavened with a dose of "winning while losing." Dubin has described a situation which encourages conflict without destroying conflict resolution capabilities. The essence of his discussion is that an organization must create conditions that encourage participants to:

1. Strongly present their views on a given situation.
2. Not affect the decision.
3. Come back the next time equally willing to present their views.

This continues to allow a decision-making body to understand the full implications of a decision, both functional and dysfunctional.

With this in mind, my concluding recommendation is as follows: Consider carefully the areas of an organization within which lower participants have relevant contributions to make. Within those areas, encourage participative decision making under conditions which provide a winning-while-losing atmosphere. In such a situation a constructive conflict of values might be worked out and, at the same time, provide an ever-increasing satisfactory role for minority participants. It is important to note that such a recommendation is only an enabling condition for the development of constructive value conflict. It is not a final answer. The final solution to these problems will continue to be elusive for many years to come.

## QUESTIONS

1. According to Goodman, "as the influx of minority group employees grows in number, more and more members of the organization will have value systems which are at variance with that of the organization." Do you believe American industry has the organizational abilities to tolerate such value conflicts? Why or why not? Be specific.
2. Evaluate and analyze Likert's recommendations for an adaptive device—the "linking pin" organizational form—that allows for constructive value conflict.
3. Compare and contrast Likert's model of organizational behavior for handling value conflicts with that of Cyert and March.
4. Do you agree or disagree with Goodman's conclusions?

# Vicious circles in slum housing

### ronald a. buel

**Ronald A. Buel, staff reporter for *The Wall Street Journal*, describes a series of vicious circles that can trap slum dwellers and perpetuate deteriorating housing.**

Lela McDaniel couldn't get anybody to fix the leaky toilet in her home in this city's West Oakland ghetto. Allan F. McCoy can't get a loan to build houses there. And West Oakland's streets have no curbs.

These situations are related by more than locale. Persons familiar with the community say they illustrate how the policies of absentee landlords, white-owned lending institutions and the city government interlock—with or without conscious intent—in a series of vicious circles that trap most of Oakland's black residents in a decaying slum.

Some efforts to reverse the decay are under way. But the job is immense, as is obvious to anyone strolling through the "flatlands" that stretch for several miles from downtown Oakland along San Francisco Bay. The streets are lined almost entirely with single-family houses, about half owner-occupied and half rental units. The Oakland Planning Commission classes 64% of all the houses as "dilapidated" or "deteriorating."

. . .

To a visitor, that estimate seems conservative. Just about every house seems in obvious need of repairs and refurbishing. But some stand out as particularly bad because of their collapsing porches and boarded-up windows. When they are checked in city property records, they invariably turn out to be owned by absentee landlords.

Mrs. McDaniel, 64, rented one such house with her three granddaughters. She says a repairman came to fix the leaky toilet last spring, "but he didn't have enough wire with him so he went away"—and hadn't come back when she moved out last November. Some critics, of course, suggest that tenants' lack of initiative in keeping up properties on their own is one reason for the deterioration.

The now-vacant house and 27 others in the ghetto are owned by Southern Pacific Railroad. Enrico La Barbera, the city's chief housing inspector, calls them "collectively, the worst housing in all Oakland." And Negro leaders are after the city to condemn the houses and order them torn down if Southern Pacific can't or won't fix them up.

A Southern Pacific spokesman, however, says, "We can only afford to

Ronald A. Buel, "Creating a Slum," *Wall Street Journal*, January 30, 1969, pp. 1, 13. Reprinted with permission of *Wall Street Journal*.

make the most urgent of repairs." He explains that the houses rent for $35 to $55 a month, and that's not enough to cover the taxes. The agent who manages the railroad's houses adds that the Southern Pacific spent a total of $779 on maintenance and repairs for the 31 ghetto houses it owned in 1967.

. . .

The city, for its part, is reluctant to order the houses torn down; it fears that their tenants then will have nowhere to live. The likelihood that new buildings would be put up to replace the houses is remote. Only seven new one-family houses have been built in the ghetto in the last eight years.

Allan McCoy, a Negro general contractor, indicates one problem. A while ago, he says, he planned to build in West Oakland three "real attractive (rental) town houses so I could bring better tenants to the area." But, he says, banks and savings and loan associations wouldn't lend the $30,000 he needed to start construction.

Lending institutions with branches near the ghetto (no bank or S&L has a branch inside West Oakland) confirm that this was no isolated incident. They are reluctant to make any sort of real-estate, construction or home-repair loans there. "We've made fewer than a half-dozen real-estate loans in West Oakland in the past few years," says Harold Osborne, regional loan vice president of American Savings & Loan Association.

There are obviously many factors behind the area's decay, and some would place high on the list the economic backwardness of residents, whether from inertia or from lack of training. But other observers stress that many of the causes of the deterioration lie elsewhere. And, they say, an important part of the explanation for West Oakland's decline begins with the missing curbs.

Many West Oakland streets once had curbs, put up by builders who developed the area in the 1940s. But they were redwood—and, says a city engineer, "the city doesn't maintain redwood curbs," only concrete ones. So the curbs have deteriorated over the years, and few traces of them are left today.

. . .

Some results: Rain water collects in huge puddles in the winter, making the going sloppy for residents crossing the streets. The city's street-cleaning equipment doesn't work properly on blocks without curbs, so the streets remain strewn with litter and broken glass. And there are no trees in the ghetto; the city won't plant any because it fears that, with no curbs, cars would run into the trees and knock them down.

A worse result: Vicious Circle No. 1. The city charges $15 to $25 a frontage foot to put in new curbs. Most West Oaklanders can't pay that in cash.  But "when the homeowner goes to a bank for a modernization loan that might also help him pay for curbs, he discovers banks won't make modernization loans on 'unimproved' streets"—a category that includes those without curbs—says Bruce Beasley, a neighborhood leader.  Louis Boitano, regional loan supervisor for First Savings & Loan Association, explains:  "If there are no curbs and the streets are unimproved . . . we feel we're taking added risk" on a loan.

Vicious Circle No. 2 quickly follows.  Without modernization loans, many owner-occupied houses run down eventually.  Absentee landlords, Negro residents charge, then feel under no compulsion to spend money to repair their rental houses in the neighborhood.  And leaders say the decay of the rental houses increases their reluctance to make modernization loans.  "If half the houses in an area aren't owner-occupied and suffer deferred maintenance, you don't have much stability in the area," comments Mr. Osborne of American Savings & Loan.

Eventually, some houses may deteriorate so much that the city orders them torn down.  Though Oakland is reluctant to condemn Southern Pacific's present houses, it has condemned 243 ghetto houses in the last 10 years.  One result has been to dot West Oakland with vacant lots, including 86 owned by Southern Pacific.  Most are filled either with garbage dumped by ghetto residents or with abandoned cars piled up by junk dealers who rent the lots.

Another result has been Vicious Circle No. 3.  Lenders say the city has been especially quick to condemn houses that banks or S&Ls have had to foreclose because the owners couldn't repay loans, leaving the lenders with useless vacant lots on their hands.  This, say the lenders, makes them especially reluctant to make loans on any houses facing a possibility of condemnation—which, of course, are precisely the houses that loan money is most needed to fix up.

Not all West Oakland Negroes can trace these vicious circles in detail.  The role of absentee landlords, for instance, is not understood by some of their own tenants—including Mrs. McDaniel, who doesn't know her former home is owned by Southern Pacific.  She tells an inquirer that the owner is "Mr. Hall"—a local grocer who, in fact, only collects rent and does odd jobs for the railroad's real estate agent.

. . .

But there's no doubt the spiral of housing decay has contributed to a bitterness in West Oakland that race relations experts for years have expected to explode into a riot.  So far it hasn't—but community-relations men aren't certain that's reassuring.  West Oakland is a stronghold of the ultramilitant Black Panthers.

Some efforts to relieve ghetto frustrations peacefully—and to smash the vicious circles—have begun recently.  Bank of America last summer announced a program to advance up to $100 million for real-estate loans in blighted and riot-prone areas in California. The bank says it has lent about $7 million so far around the state. "This is our response to the charge that lending institutions have perpetuated a vicious circle by refusing to make loans in such areas," says a spokesman. Bank of America won't say how many, if any, loans it has made in West Oakland.

The Oakland Redevelopment Agency has designated a 75-block area that includes over a fifth of the ghetto a "rehabilitation area." Homeowners in the area are eligible for loans under a Federal program. In the past two years, 54 families have borrowed $600,000 of repair money at 3% annual interest under this program, and another 22 families have received outright grants of $1,500 each to fix up their homes. Oakland has high hopes, too, of receiving a big Federal Model Cities grant to build new housing in West Oakland.

．．．

A Federal official, however, concedes the rehabilitation-loan program made "scant progress," relative to the ghetto's needs, through 1968. And Negroes are skeptical about progress in some other fields.

Arlene Slaughter, an Oakland real estate agent, says that S&Ls, "if they have money loaned in West Oakland, are trying to find a way to get it out, not put more in." She charges that the lenders won't even finance the resale of ghetto houses—so that the ghetto homeowner unable to make repairs on his house has little chance to sell it to someone who might have the money to fix it up.

Though some West Oakland residents who live in rental housing are vague about their landlords, others focus their anger on what they feel is exploitation by absentee owners. This exploitation charge is leveled not only by militants but also by moderate civil-rights leaders. They say that landlords have reaped big profits out of decaying housing in the ghetto—an area where average family income is a bleak $4,000 a year—by charging relatively high rents while spending little on repairs or maintenance. Southern Pacific's $35-to-$55-a-month rents aren't typical of the ghetto; the average rent on a four-room house is about $100 a month.

．．．

Not all the exploiters are white, Negro leaders concede. "Some of the worst landlords are black ministers who've gotten their hands on a little loot," claims Clifford Sweet, a Negro lawyer with the Legal Aid Society. He says one client had to sleep on the floor of his apartment when he returned from a stay in a hospital because his landlord, a Negro minister, had removed all the furniture; the tenant had fallen behind in rent payments while he was sick.

Other Negroes concede that not all the white landlords are exploiters.

Many—though not all—make an exception for Valva Realty Corp., a white-owned concern that is the biggest owner of property in West Oakland and also holds mortgages on owner-occupied homes in the area.

Many ghetto residents heatedly defend Valva from exploitation charges, contending that it has made real-estate loans to West Oaklanders at reasonable rates when nobody else would. Other Negroes, however, accuse Valva of deliberately foreclosing loans on property it hears the local redevelopment agency wants to purchase, taking over the properties and selling them to the agency at a high profit.

Robert Valva, who runs the company with his brother William, concedes Valva has profited by selling properties to the redevelopment agency but denies that it makes a practice of foreclosing loans to do so. "The only case where we've foreclosed to sell to the city was one where the guy was a year and a half behind in payments," he says.

Ghetto opinion is more united in denunciation of two other big landlords: Southern Pacific and Ned R. Reed, one of the biggest individual owners of ghetto property.

* * *

Southern Pacific, Negroes charge, is in the ghetto as a speculator, buying up properties and spending little or nothing on them while waiting for their value to rise so that they can be resold at a profit. The railroad, they note, has bought its West Oakland properties over the past 10 years.

Southern Pacific denies it acquired the properties as speculations. It originally planned to convert the properties to industrial use. But it does concede West Oakland property values in general have been increasing—a point that infuriates Mr. McCoy, the contractor, and other Negroes who have been turned down for loans on the ground that ghetto real estate is a risky investment. There is reason to expect a further rise in values; for example, a new rapid-transit station and a big post office are under construction adjacent to Southern Pacific's biggest West Oakland property.

Meanwhile, says Southern Pacific, it is losing money on its West Oakland houses, partly because it tries not to be tough on tenants. (For its overall operations, the railroad reported a record profit of $107.6 million in 1968.) Southern Pacific says it has instructed its agent not to make any special effort to collect back rent and not to evict anyone—not even the several tenants the railroad claims owe as much as $300 in unpaid rent.

* * *

Mr. Reed follows different policies, as he readily admits. "In this business you've got to use ruthless tactics," says the 48-year-old father of three, who once was a Methodist missionary in India. He is now a research chemist at Merritt Junior College in Oakland and operates his real-estate business as a sideline.

That Mr. Reed's tactics have been successful is beyond question. Starting 14 years ago with investment money contributed partly by fellow Merritt professors, he has become chief owner of 50 Oakland homes and apartment buildings, many in the ghetto. He estimates the total value of the properties at $3 million and says his own share is about $1,250,000. Merritt Junior College has been a leader in the San Francisco area in admitting Negro students, and some of Mr. Reed's students and former students at the college are also tenants of his buildings.

Mr. Reed denies that he is an exploiter or even an absentee landlord. Although he now employs six helpers, he says he spends many hours a week personally doing maintenance work on his buildings, including much of the plumbing and wiring.

But Mr. Reed concedes he has "stopped maintaining" some ghetto buildings "because the tenants just destroyed them anyway." And he describes in considerable detail his procedures for promptly evicting tenants who fall behind in paying rent, attributing much of his success to these procedures.

. . .

The first three times he tried to get court orders to evict "deadbeats," says Mr. Reed, it took him two months to accomplish each eviction, and one cost him $1,000 in legal fees and tenant moving costs. "Now I've wised up," he says. He now gets an eviction order from the Oakland small claims court in 20 days, for a cost of $3—and with no interference from Legal Aid Society lawyers, who aren't permitted in small claims court.

Once armed with an eviction notice, Mr. Reed follows a procedure he describes this way: "I ask that they move and give them a few days. If they aren't out by the time I've asked, I gather all my workmen together and we go en masse to the house. I gain peaceable entry, a legal requirement, and try to negotiate about the tenant's departure. If I get static, we remove all the doors and windows and if I own the stove and refrigerator, I remove them, too."

Another tactic Mr. Reed says he has used is entering a home while a "deadbeat" is out and removing a TV or hi-fi set or sometimes all the furniture. He says "local laws give the landlord a lien right on the tenant's personal belongings if he is behind in rent." A local case has been interpreted to obliterate this lien right, however, "so now I only use this technique in fully furnished units," he says.

Can the city do anything about the decaying slum? Not as long as loan money to improve ghetto housing is so scarce, say some sources. But others say the city could improve conditions if it would make greater use of its condemnation powers. They dispute the city's contention that better housing could not be found for the displaced residents, and they say that Oakland hasn't hesitated to condemn houses needed for new freeways and the like.

The city has made some efforts to provide better housing for ghetto blacks, but Negroes regard them as fumbling at best. The city is one of the biggest owners of ghetto property; it runs four public-housing projects in West Oakland with a total of 667 apartments and also leases a number of private homes and apartments that it rents to needy blacks.

. . .

Some tenants complain that the private homes the city leases are in need of repairs, and the Oakland Legal Aid Society has filed a lawsuit on behalf of some of the tenants requesting that improvements be made.

The public-housing projects have a waiting list of over 1,200 families, largely because rent is set at a reasonable 21% of a family's income (a tenants' suit prevented an increase to 33%). But tenants already in the units are by no means entirely pleased with them.

The Chestnut Court project is "run like a Southern plantation," claims Juanita Barnes, head of a tenants' organization there. "Tenants can be and are evicted without proper cause, and Housing Authority personnel can enter apartments at any time and for any reason," she says. The authority says eviction and entering rights are necessary to maintain control of the projects and denies they are abused.

## QUESTIONS

1. It is apparent from this article that in cases where the blame cannot be easily assessed and, as a consequence, inaction ensues in the solution of an urgent problem, bad situations can become much worse. Yet a situation such as the one prevailing in Oakland will have to be corrected. Who should undertake this task? How and why? If you were in charge of solving Oakland's problems, how would you do it? Present your own plan of action and justify it.
2. What should be the role of the business community in general in helping to alleviate existing problems similar to those in Oakland and preventing others from developing?
3. Do you think the solution of problems such as those in Oakland's ghetto area should lie entirely with the government? Why or why not?

# A business "adopts" a school

## kenneth c. field

Kenneth C. Field, staff reporter for *The Wall Street Journal,* describes some of the things the Michigan Bell Telephone Company has done for a school, some of the headaches incurred, and some of the encouraging results.

There's a new "parent" involved in the affairs of Northern High School here: Michigan Bell Telephone Co.

Michigan Bell "adopted" Northern High, a largely Negro school, after the riots that wracked this city's black neighborhoods in 1967. Since then, the company has funneled equipment and personnel into the school, offering vocational education and guidance and academic help to the 1,800 students. Equally important, Northern High grads are being given an inside track for jobs with the company when they graduate.

The project has given Michigan Bell a number of headaches. Some black militants here say they regard the program as mainly a public relations gimmick; others accuse the company of "using" the school to keep itself stocked with low-level workers. Some of Michigan Bell's vocational offerings have been criticized as being beneath the intelligence of students. Regular members of Northern High's faculty grumble that a private corporation has no business "meddling" in a public school.

Nevertheless, the program is continuing. To date, it has provided telephone jobs for 75 recent Northern High grads. Its results have been encouraging enough to persuade other companies to undertake similar adoptions.

. . .

Last year Chrysler Corp. took a parental interest in Northwestern High School here. Among other things, Chrysler installed a modern $150,000 garage for training auto repairmen. Aetna Life Insurance Co. has adopted a high school in Hartford, Conn., and telephone company units in Chicago and Milwaukee have done the same in their communities. In a more sweeping move, Ford Motor Co., General Electric Co., Avco Corp. and Procter & Gamble Co. recently adopted the entire, 2,000-pupil school system of Lincoln Heights, Ohio, a nearly all-Negro suburb of Cincinnati.

---

Kenneth C. Field, "Michigan Bell Finds Headaches, Rewards in 'Adopting' School," *Wall Street Journal,* January 15, 1969, pp. 1, 17. Reprinted with permission of the *Wall Street Journal.*

Even though the Detroit riots gave the adoption project its final push, Michigan Bell officials say that they previously had been pondering ways to better prepare Negro youths for employment. "One of the things we knew needed attention was acquainting the kids with the basics of the world of work—how to look for a job, how to fill out a job application, how to go through an interview," says Edward Hodges, general employment supervisor at the company.

So along with the technical classes on aspects of phone company operations, Michigan Bell introduced courses at Northern High on how to go about finding work. Practice job interviews with company personnel men are one part of this instruction. The company asserts that this training will stand Northern High graduates in good stead whether or not they wind up working for Michigan Bell.

The firm also has tried to reinforce the instruction by bringing in some of its Negro employes as teachers. For example, a class in charm and grooming for girls is taught by a Negro woman office supervisor, and retail sales lectures have been given by a Yellow Pages advertising salesman who graduated from Northern High night school after having dropped out of high school several years before. He gets in an occasional word about the value of finishing school.

. . .

All of the 22 courses Michigan Bell is offering at Northern High are geared to the job market, and this has sparked much of the criticism aimed at the project. "Big business is fashioning the school's curriculum after its own employment needs," asserts Charles Colding, a recent Northern High grad employed as a consultant to New Detroit, a private group engaged in job, education and housing programs in the city's ghetto. "If business wants to make a contribution to our community, let it be purely monetary. As it is, they're taking over the education of blacks just to teach them how to push buttons on an assembly line."

Michigan Bell says that never has been its intention. It points out that attendance at the courses it offers at Northern High is purely voluntary and that its presence at the school hasn't been accompanied by diminished emphasis on academic programs. It adds that it has hired Northern grads for repair and computer jobs as well as for less-skilled posts.

The company has shown itself to be somewhat sensitive to criticism like Mr. Colding's, however. Last summer it branched out from vocational offerings by sponsoring remedial reading, speech and math courses at the school, paying a $5-a-day incentive to pupils who attended. Moreover, it now gives college scholarships to four Northern grads a year with no strings on future employment attached.

Vocational courses in the project also have been reexamined. One six-week class in basic electricity had to be supplemented after students ran through the assigned text in only two weeks. A class in data-processing was revised after students proved in one session that they could handle more difficult material. "Some of the programs were pegged too low for the kids—they're sharper than we gave them credit for being," says William Rice, Michigan Bell's supervisor for urban affairs.

Some Detroit Negroes are skeptical that projects such as Michigan Bell's can have any lasting impact on employment problems of ghetto residents. Such programs "never will be successful unless they are accompanied by a curriculum in all schools that will make it possible to feed students into the job market on an upgraded level," says Mrs. Carole Williams, who heads the Volunteer Placement Corps, a nonprofit group that helps find jobs for ghetto youths. She was an early and vocal critic of the project.

Nevertheless, Mrs. Williams thinks the adoption has had some value. "Anything that makes business more aware of the problems our kids face in finding a career after graduation is all to the good," she says.

Andrew Perry, a Northern High grad who landed a $98-a-week job as an equipment installer at Michigan Bell as a result of the program, goes a bit further. "I'm pretty happy with my job," he says. "It's all right with me if they did this for their own benefit."

## QUESTIONS

1. Should a private company "adopt" a school as did Michigan Bell?
2. If you think a private company can and should aid in the educational process, specify precisely what you think it can and should do.
3. If you were advising the principal of a high school and the president of a company who were about to embark on a project of "adoption," what limits would you place on the role of the private company?

# Business Ethics:
# Standards and Cases

**9**

# Is the golden rule a useful guide to business decision making?

### craig c. lundberg

Craig C. Lundberg, Associate Professor of Behavioral Science and Administration, Southern Methodist University, analyzes the applicability of an ancient rule for ethical conduct to today's business behavior.

As I have talked with business managers I have been impressed that the vast majority of these men propose the Golden Rule as the most important guide for organizational behavior. Certainly this maxim is well-known as a guide for human conduct, yet regardless of its popularity we might question its adequacy as a business policy. Let me focus this paper by contrasting two sets of reasoning:

> The Golden Rule is the best general prescription for regulating human relationships, therefore, it is a good maxim for behavior in business especially within complex modern organization settings.
>
> The Golden Rule is a guide for human relations which is very limited in its applications in modern society. It must be applied with caution or not at all in contemporary business practice.

In the pages to follow I will note how the reasoning supporting the first assertion is generally believed, but will rely on my frame of reference as a social scientist to argue in favor of the second position. To do this I will differentiate between the Golden Rule as a religious norm and as a guide to ethical fairness in exchange relationships. Then I will examine some assumptions implicit in the rule and underline aspects which are simply unclear.

## RELIGIOUS UNIVERSALITY OF THE GOLDEN RULE

While familiar the Golden Rule is stated in numerous forms. The book of Matthew, for instance, states that: "All things whatsoever ye would that men should do to you, do ye so unto them: for this is the Law and the Prophets." The medieval Biblical injunction, "Love thy neighbor as

Craig C. Lundberg, "The Golden Rule and Business Management: Quo Vadis?" *Economic and Business Bulletin*, 20 (January 1968), 36–40. Reprinted by permission of the author.

thyself" has of course been most commonly interpreted with the contemporary maxim, "Do unto others as you would like them to do unto you."

We should not assume that the Golden Rule is primarily associated with Christianity for most other religions carry some version of it. In the Talmud, for example, we find, "What is hateful to you, do not do to your fellow man. That this is the entire law; all the rest is commentary." Confucianism, too, in the Analects has, "Surely it is the maxim of loving kindness: do not unto others that you would not have them do unto you." Buddhism in the Udana-Yarga says, "Hurt not others in ways that you yourself would find hurtful." Islam joins the chorus with, "Not one of you is a believer until he desires for his brother that which he desires for himself." And in the Mahabharata the Brahman injunction says, "This is the sum of duty: do not do unto others which would cause you pain if done to you." And so we see that the Golden Rule exists throughout the major religions of mankind.

## THE RULE AS A GUIDE FOR EXCHANGES

We must at this point distinguish between the Jewish-Christian norm of brotherly love and the Golden Rule of fairness-ethics. The Biblical

> Love thy neighbor as thyself,

is a norm of Jewish-Christian brotherly love; it means love your neighbor, that is, to feel responsible for and at one with him. The Golden Rule as interpreted today is quite different. Perhaps it is no accident that the Golden Rule has become one of the most popular religious maxims of today because it can be interpreted in terms of fairness-ethics, which sounds a great deal like the religious maxims, but which in fact has quite a different meaning, namely, be fair in your exchanges with others. Contrast with the religious norm is complete for fairness-ethics means do not feel responsible and at one, but feel distant and separate; respect the rights of your neighbor, but do not love him. This differentiation between religious norm and a maxim of fairness-ethics is made so that we can focus on the latter, which is the principle or generalization in the fields of human relations as conceived by business management today.

## DISTORTIONS AND CHANGES IN MEANING

The Golden Rule is very well known in western culture; it is a fairness-ethics injunction; and it is usually accepted unquestioning. Although probably the most revered of common sense generalizations handed down by our industrial forebears, Golden Rule has not gone unthought about or completely unchallenged.  As our society has become more liberal and the value of individual work has been widened to include a value of individual differences, the Golden Rule has been revamped.  The playwright Bernard Shaw, for instance, has rewritten the Golden Rule:

> Don't do unto others as you would have them do unto you because their tastes may be different.

Even Shaw's version has been altered.  A well-known psychologist has rephrased the Golden Rule to serve as a guide for ethical conduct or as a guide for amiable relations among men:

> Do unto others as you would have them do unto you if you were they.

This last statement of the rule seems to take Shaw's point that one man's meat is another man's poison, and adds the contemporary concern we have for empathy, the usefulness of putting ourselves in another person's place so we can appreciate how he thinks and feels.

In a recent graduate course and in a recent executive development program for middle managers, I asked participants to write out the versions of the Golden Rule known to them.  The response was overwhelming and reflects and shows how far the Golden Rule has pervaded the mainstream of our business culture, everything from "an eye for an eye, a tooth for a tooth" to "every girl has a father"; from "You pat my back, I'll pat yours but you pat me first" to "drive carefully, the life you save may be your own"; from "The only way to have a friend is to be one" to "owe no man anything."  Variations are reported implicit in our everyday petitions for help, such as "Share the United way" or "Give blood, the gift of life"; and we find variations in advertising such as one card manufacturer who asks that you give his card to show you care enough to send the very best, and of course there are even business philosophies such as the Murray D. Lincoln's "Intelligent selfishness."

We often hear people talk about the imperatives of life, and of course the Golden Rule is often promoted in just that way.  It was the German-Scottish philosopher Immanuel Kant who conceived of the categorical imperative, the unconditional command of nature.  It, too, sounds much like the Golden Rule:

> Act so that the principle of your action could be made a universal law.

When men act on the Golden Rule as if it were such an imperative, . . . then we can expect confusion and perhaps even injustice to occur.

## ON APPLYING THE GOLDEN RULE

We see that from a religious origin strained through the web and woof of an industrial society the Golden Rule has come to reside in humor, in philosophy, and common sense, in fact nearly all arenas of contemporary life. The question still remains, however, is it a useful imperative? Can we take it as a generalized principle of, or guide for, human relationships? Let us now examine a few simple situations which, while hypothetical, could very well exist, and as we look at them let us ask ourselves about the utility of applying the Golden Rule in each case.

Picture a janitor and the president of a major corporation approaching the lobby doors of the corporation's downtown headquarters building. The two men approach the doors simultaneously. Who will open the door for whom and with what effects on the men?

Consider the marketing vice president of a major American business firm promptly arriving at the stated time for an appointment with an executive of potentially the largest purchaser of his product in Venezuela. After an hour and a half of waiting the v.p. actively considers leaving.

Consider the personnel manager of a local company picking up his telephone to hear his counterpart in a competitor's firm asking if he would provide a summer job for the other man's high school age son.

Picture a computer expert who is new to a business deciding not to include certain critical information in his first report to his superior because he thinks it might jeopardize the existence of his function in the firm.

In the hypothetical examples above the parties have represented different organizational statuses, different cultures, different personal needs and capabilities for action, and different constraints on their behavior. In each example a literal application of the Golden Rule would be rather difficult for most reasonable people—they would feel the pressures of expectations and no doubt worry about the consequences to their responses to these situations. Perhaps these examples force us to wonder as to the universal application of the rule, and perhaps to question the assumption on which it is based. Let us now turn to this latter aspect.

## ASSUMPTIONS BEHIND THE GOLDEN RULE

One assumption in the Golden Rule is that the "others" in an exchange situation are in fact capable of reciprocating the behavior. We quickly remember that persons are not equal in terms of abilities, at least adults, and clearly are not equally capable in terms of the organizational power they command. You might go on with this assumption and ask whether the "others" are in fact motivated to reciprocate, that is, whether they would want to return similar behaviors if it were possible too. A second assumption would be that either party to an exchange really understands the consequences to the behavior—how, in fact, will the others really feel and think. This is of course contingent on their having similar goals or aims, and in most cases this seems extremely unlikely. A third major assumption is that the Golden Rule assumes that other rules are not being violated whether they be formal, explicit rules or other implicit perhaps informal ones, such as custom. Take the privilege and duty which come with certain statuses in our society, perhaps illustrated in the first example above. Today, too, we have a widespread understanding that business practice should not include reciprocity in regard to purchasing, for example, and this may in certain instances conflict with the Golden Rule injunction. A fourth assumption has to do with the assumed similarity of preference or taste of the parties to the Golden Rule. One could confuse or sadden, hurt, or disadvantage another who did not have somewhat similar preferences or tastes, that is, values and interests like ours. Cross cultural examples often make this point clearly.

Let us now examine the Golden Rule in terms of its clarity. Unless it is specific and explicit it becomes a maxim hard to follow. We might begin by asking about the unit of action. Are the actions implied in the rule a person or persons, groups or some larger social? Are you and the others in the Golden Rule to be seen as representatives of various social units or as independent citizens or persons in their own right, or does it make a difference? Of course the word "do" in the Golden Rule can mean many things too, and as usually interpreted all behaviors are included. Another thing which is not too clear has to do with the adequacy of resources. In most human situations there is a scarcity of resources. A major unclear aspect of the Golden Rule has to do with the amount and/or frequency of the exchange. Most people read the Golden Rule as implying some kind of equality. It would seem in our discussion of assumptions above that people are not equally capable or motivated to enter into an equal kind of exchange. In fact, we know from the new field of equity theory that the equality of exchange is almost never really expected. The act implied in the Golden Rule is of course conditioned by perception of the parties, and we know from the research in psychology that emotional and situational factors among others, can alter and distort what is perceived to be done to oneself, this seemingly inviting considerable creative distortion and error. And of course the Golden Rule is not very clear as to how one measures the consequences which arise by using it. Do we look at both mental and physical consequences, how does the time dimension come in, and so on?

## EVALUATION OF THE GOLDEN RULE

We have seen that the Golden Rule, at least as a maxim of fairness-ethics, is extremely popular, and widely applied in our industrial society. By means of some hypothetical illustrations and by examining more directly the assumption behind and the lack of clarity in the Golden Rule we have also been able to offer some comment on the adequacy of this rule as a general principle of organizational behavior. I believe that we have demonstrated that the Golden Rule cannot be taken as a categorical imperative, that in fact one would have to be extremely careful in applying it in business and other human affairs. I do not want to appear as relegating all common sense knowledge to the dustbin for in fact the scientific study of human relations is able to confirm a lot of the tried and true folklore and rules of thumb. It is crucial, however, to know when injunctions from the past are no longer applicable or to be able to identify the conditions when they do not apply. Such has been our intent in examining the Golden Rule's validity for contemporary business management.

## QUESTIONS

1. What is your own interpretation of the meaning of the Golden Rule? Trace the historical development of this rule as a guide for organizational behavior.
2. Critically analyze and evaluate the major assumptions behind the Golden Rule.
3. Can a businessman apply the Golden Rule to his decisions? Explain your position.

# Is business bluffing ethical?

### albert z. carr

**Albert Z. Carr, a former consultant to businesses and now a full-time writer, says in this controversial article that the ethics of business are not those of society but rather those of the poker game.**

A respected businessman with whom I discussed the theme of this article remarked with some heat, "You mean to say you're going to encourage men to bluff? Why, bluffing is nothing more than a form of lying! You're advising them to lie!"

I agreed that the basis of private morality is a respect for truth and that the closer a businessman comes to the truth, the more he deserves respect. At the same time, I suggested that most bluffing in business might be regarded simply as game strategy—much like bluffing in poker, which does not reflect on the morality of the bluffer.

I quoted Henry Taylor, the British statesman who pointed out that "falsehood ceases to be falsehood when it is understood on all sides that the truth is not expected to be spoken"—an exact description of bluffing in poker, diplomacy, and business. I cited the analogy of the criminal court, where the criminal is not expected to tell the truth when he pleads "not guilty." Everyone from the judge down takes it for granted that the job of the defendant's attorney is to get his client off, not to reveal the truth; and this is considered ethical practice. I mentioned Representative Omar Burleson, the Democrat from Texas, who was quoted as saying, in regard to the ethics of Congress, "Ethics is a barrel of worms"—a pungent summing up of the problem of deciding who is ethical in politics.

I reminded my friend that millions of businessmen feel constrained every day to say *yes* to their bosses when they secretly believe *no* and that this is generally accepted as permissible strategy when the alternative might be the loss of a job. The essential point, I said, is that the ethics of business are game ethics, different from the ethics of religion.

He remained unconvinced. Referring to the company of which he is president, he declared: "Maybe that's good enough for some businessmen, but I can tell you that we pride ourselves on our ethics. In 30 years not one customer has ever questioned my word or asked to check our figures. We're loyal to our customers and fair to our suppliers. I

Albert Z. Carr, "Is Business Bluffing Ethical?" *Harvard Business Review*, 40 (January–February 1968). © 1968 by the President and Fellows of Harvard College; all rights reserved.

regard my handshake on a deal as a contract. I've never entered into price-fixing schemes with my competitors. I've never allowed my salesmen to spread injurious rumors about other companies. Our union contract is the best in our industry. And, if I do say so myself, our ethical standards are of the highest!"

He really was saying, without realizing it, that he was living up to the ethical standards of the business game—which are a far cry from those of private life. Like a gentlemanly poker player, he did not play in cahoots with others at the table, try to smear their reputations, or hold back chips he owed them.

But this same fine man, at that very time, was allowing one of his products to be advertised in a way that made it sound a great deal better than it actually was. Another item in his product line was notorious among dealers for its "built-in obsolescence." He was holding back from the market a much-improved product because he did not want it to interfere with sales of the inferior item it would have replaced. He had joined with certain of his competitors in hiring a lobbyist to push a state legislature, by methods that he preferred not to know too much about, into amending a bill then being enacted.

In his view these things had nothing to do with ethics; they were merely normal business practice. He himself undoubtedly avoided outright falsehoods—never lied in so many words. But the entire organization that he ruled was deeply involved in numerous strategies of deception.

## PRESSURE TO DECEIVE

Most executives from time to time are almost compelled, in the interests of their companies or themselves, to practice some form of deception when negotiating with customers, dealers, labor unions, government officials, or even other departments of their companies. By conscious misstatements, concealment of pertinent facts, or exaggeration—in short, by bluffing—they seek to persuade others to agree with them. I think it is fair to say that if the individual executive refuses to bluff from time to time—if he feels obligated to tell the truth, the whole truth, and nothing but the truth—he is ignoring opportunities permitted under the rules and is at a heavy disadvantage in his business dealings.

But here and there a businessman is unable to reconcile himself to the bluff in which he plays a part. His conscience, perhaps spurred by religious idealism, troubles him. He feels guilty; he may develop an ulcer or a nervous tic. Before any executive can make profitable use of the strategy of the bluff, he needs to make sure that in bluffing he will not lose self-respect or become emotionally disturbed.  If he is to reconcile personal integrity and high standards of honesty with the practical requirements of business, he must feel that his bluffs are ethically justified.  The justification rests on the fact that business, as practiced by individuals as well as by corporations, has the impersonal character of a game—a game that demands both special strategy and an understanding of its special ethics.

The game is played at all levels of corporate life, from the highest to the lowest.  At the very instant that a man decides to enter business, he may be forced into a game situation, as is shown by the recent experience of a Cornell honor graduate who applied for a job with a large company:

> This applicant was given a psychological test which included the statement, "Of the following magazines, check any that you have read either regularly or from time to time, and double-check those which interest you most.  *Reader's Digest, Time, Fortune, Saturday Evening Post, The New Republic, Life, Look, Ramparts, Newsweek, Business Week, U.S. News & World Report, The Nation, Playboy, Esquire, Harper's, Sports Illustrated.*"
>
> His tastes in reading were broad, and at one time or another he had read almost all of these magazines.  He was a subscriber to *The New Republic,* an enthusiast for *Ramparts,* and an avid student of the pictures in *Playboy.*  He was not sure whether his interest in *Playboy* would be held against him, but he had a shrewd suspicion that if he confessed to an interest in *Ramparts* and *The New Republic,* he would be thought a liberal, a radical, or at least an intellectual, and his chances of getting the job, which he needed, would greatly diminish.  He therefore checked five of the more conservative magazines.  Apparently it was a sound decision, for he got the job.
>
> He had made a game player's decision, consistent with business ethics.

A similar case is that of a magazine space salesman who, owing to a merger, suddenly found himself out of a job:

> This man was 58, and, in spite of a good record, his chance of getting a job elsewhere in a business where youth is favored in hiring practice was not good.  He was a vigorous, healthy man, and only a considerable amount of gray in his hair suggested his age.  Before beginning his job search he touched up his hair with a black dye to confine the gray to his temples.  He knew that the truth about his age might well come out in time, but he calculated that he could deal with that situation when it arose.  He and his wife decided that he could easily pass for 45, and he so stated his age on his résumé.

This was a lie; yet within the accepted rules of the business game, no moral culpability attaches to it.

## THE POKER ANALOGY

We can learn a good deal about the nature of business by comparing it with poker. While both have a large element of chance, in the long run the winner is the man who plays with steady skill. In both games ultimate victory requires intimate knowledge of the rules, insight into the psychology of the other players, a bold front, a considerable amount of self-discipline, and the ability to respond swiftly and effectively to opportunities provided by chance.

No one expects poker to be played on the ethical principles preached in churches. In poker it is right and proper to bluff a friend out of the rewards of being dealt a good hand. A player feels no more than a slight twinge of sympathy, if that, when—with nothing better than a single ace in his hand—he strips a heavy loser, who holds a pair, of the rest of his chips. It was up to the other fellow to protect himself. In the words of an excellent poker player, former President Harry Truman, "If you can't stand the heat, stay out of the kitchen." If one shows mercy to a loser in poker, it is a personal gesture, divorced from the rules of the game.

Poker has its special ethics, and here I am not referring to rules against cheating. The man who keeps an ace up his sleeve or who marks the cards is more than unethical; he is a crook, and can be punished as such—kicked out of the game or, in the Old West, shot.

In contrast to the cheat, the unethical poker player is one who, while abiding by the letter of the rules, finds ways to put the other players at an unfair disadvantage. Perhaps he unnerves them with loud talk. Or he tries to get them drunk. Or he plays in cahoots with someone else at the table. Ethical poker players frown on such tactics.

Poker's own brand of ethics is different from the ethical ideals of civilized human relationships. The game calls for distrust of the other fellow. It ignores the claim of friendship. Cunning deception and concealment of one's strength and intentions, not kindness and openheartedness, are vital in poker. No one thinks any the worse of poker on that account. And no one should think any the worse of the game of business because its standards of right and wrong differ from the prevailing traditions of morality in our society.

## DISCARD THE GOLDEN RULE

This view of business is especially worrisome to people without much business experience. A minister of my acquaintance once protested that business cannot possibly function in our society unless it is based on the Judeo-Christian system of ethics.  He told me:

> I know some businessmen have supplied call girls to customers, but there are always a few rotten apples in every barrel.  That doesn't mean the rest of the fruit isn't sound.  Surely the vast majority of businessmen are ethical.  I myself am acquainted with many who adhere to strict codes of ethics based fundamentally on religious teachings.  They contribute to good causes.  They partici- pate in community activities.  They cooperate with other com- panies to improve working conditions in their industries.  Certainly they are not indifferent to ethics.

That most businessmen are not indifferent to ethics in their private lives, everyone will agree.  My point is that in their office lives they cease to be private citizens; they become game players who must be guided by a somewhat different set of ethical standards.

The point was forcefully made to me by a Midwestern executive who has given a good deal of thought to the question:

> So long as a businessman complies with the laws of the land and avoids telling malicious lies, he's ethical.  If the law as written gives a man a wide-open chance to make a killing, he'd been a fool not to take advantage of it.  If he doesn't, somebody else will.  There's no obligation on him to stop and consider who is going to get hurt.  If the law says he can do it, that's all the justification he needs.  There's nothing unethical about that.  It's just plain business sense.

This executive (call him Robbins) took the stand that even industrial espionage, which is frowned on by some businessmen, ought not to be considered unethical.  He recalled a recent meeting of the National Industrial Conference Board where an authority on marketing made a speech in which he deplored the employment of spies by business or- ganizations.  More and more companies, he pointed out, find it cheaper to penetrate the secrets of competitors with concealed cameras and microphones or by bribing employees than to set up costly research and design departments of their own.  A whole branch of the electron- ics industry has grown up with this trend, he continued, providing equipment to make industrial espionage easier.

Disturbing?  The marketing expert found it so.  But when it came to a remedy, he could only appeal to "respect for the golden rule."  Robbins thought this a confession of defeat, believing that the golden rule, for all its value as an ideal for society, is simply not feasible as a guide for business.  A good part of the time the businessman is try- ing to do unto others as he hopes others will *not* do unto him.  Robbins continued:

Espionage of one kind or another has become so common in business that it's like taking a drink during Prohibition—it's not considered sinful. And we don't even have Prohibition where espionage is concerned; the law is very tolerant in this area. There's no more shame for a business that uses secret agents than there is for a nation. Bear in mind that there already is at least one large corporation—you can buy its stock over the counter—that makes millions by providing counterespionage service to industrial firms. Espionage in business is not an ethical problem; it's an established technique of business competition.

### "We Don't Make the Laws"

Wherever we turn in business, we can perceive the sharp distinction between its ethical standards and those of the churches. Newspapers abound with sensational stories growing out of this distinction:

We read one day that Senator Philip A. Hart of Michigan has attacked food processors for deceptive packaging of numerous products.

The next day there is a Congressional to-do over Ralph Nader's book, *Unsafe At Any Speed,* which demonstrates that automobile companies for years have neglected the safety of car-owning families.

Then another Senator, Lee Metcalf of Montana, and journalist Vic Reinemer show in their book, *Overcharge,* the methods by which utility companies elude regulating government bodies to extract unduly large payments from users of electricity.

These are merely dramatic instances of a prevailing condition; there is hardly a major industry at which a similar attack could not be aimed. Critics of business regard such behavior as unethical, but the companies concerned know that they are merely playing the business game.

Among the most respected of our business institutions are the insurance companies. A group of insurance executives meeting recently in New England was startled when their guest speaker, social critic Daniel Patrick Moynihan, roundly berated them for "unethical" practices. They had been guilty, Moynihan alleged, of using outdated actuarial tables to obtain unfairly high premiums. They habitually delayed the hearings of lawsuits against them in order to tire out the plaintiffs and win cheap settlements. In their employment policies they used ingenious devices to discriminate against certain minority groups.

It was difficult for the audience to deny the validity of these charges. But these men were business game players. Their reaction to Moynihan's attack was much the same as that of the automobile manufacturers to Nader, of the utilities to Senator Metcalf, and of the food processors to Senator Hart.  If the laws governing their businesses change, or if public opinion becomes clamorous, they will make the necessary adjustments.  But morally they have in their view done nothing wrong.  As long as they comply with the letter of the law, they are within their rights to operate their businesses as they see fit.

The small business is in the same position as the great corporation in this respect.  For example:

> In 1967 a key manufacturer was accused of providing master keys for automobiles to mail-order customers, although it was obvious that some of the purchasers might be automobile thieves.  His defense was plain and straightforward.  If there was nothing in the law to prevent him from selling his keys to anyone who ordered them, it was not up to him to inquire as to his customers' motives.  Why was it any worse, he insisted, for him to sell car keys by mail, than for mail-order houses to sell guns that might be used for murder?  Until the law was changed, the key manufacturer could regard himself as being just as ethical as any other businessman by the rules of the business game.

Violations of the ethical ideals of society are common in business, but they are not necessarily violations of business principles.  Each year the Federal Trade Commission orders hundreds of companies, many of them of the first magnitude, to "cease and desist" from practices which, judged by ordinary standards, are of questionable morality but which are stoutly defended by the companies concerned.

In one case, a firm manufacturing a well-known mouthwash was accused of using a cheap form of alcohol possibly deleterious to health.  The company's chief executive, after testifying in Washington, made this comment privately:

> We broke no law.  We're in a highly competitive industry.  If we're going to stay in business, we have to look for profit wherever the law permits.  We don't make the laws.  We obey them.  Then why do we have to put up with this "holier than thou" talk about ethics?  It's sheer hypocrisy.  We're not in business to promote ethics.  Look at the cigarette companies, for God's sake!  If the ethics aren't embodied in the laws by the men who made them, you can't expect businessmen to fill the lack.  Why, a sudden submission to Christian ethics by businessmen would bring about the greatest economic upheaval in history!

It may be noted that the government failed to prove its case against him.

### Cast Illusions Aside

Talk about ethics by businessmen is often a thin decorative coating over the hard realities of the game:

Once I listened to a speech by a young executive who pointed to a new industry code as proof that his company and its competitors were deeply aware of their responsibilities to society. It was a code of ethics, he said. The industry was going to police itself, to dissuade constituent companies from wrongdoing. His eyes shone with conviction and enthusiasm.

The same day there was a meeting in a hotel room where the industry's top executives met with the "czar" who was to administer the new code, a man of high repute. No one who was present could doubt their common attitude. In their eyes the code was designed primarily to forestall a move by the federal government to impose stern restrictions on the industry. They felt that the code would hamper them a good deal less than new federal laws would. It was, in other words, conceived as a protection for the industry, not for the public.

The young executive accepted the surface explanation of the code; these leaders, all experienced game players, did not deceive themselves for a moment about its purpose.

The illusion that business can afford to be guided by ethics as conceived in private life is often fostered by speeches and articles containing such phrases as, "It pays to be ethical," or, "Sound ethics is good business." Actually this is not an ethical position at all; it is a self-serving calculation in disguise. The speaker is really saying that in the long run a company can make more money if it does not antagonize competitors, suppliers, employees, and customers by squeezing them too hard. He is saying that oversharp policies reduce ultimate gains. That is true, but it has nothing to do with ethics. The underlying attitude is much like that in the familiar story of the shopkeeper who finds an extra $20 bill in the cash register, debates with himself the ethical problem—should he tell his partner?—and finally decides to share the money because the gesture will give him an edge over the s.o.b. the next time they quarrel.

I think it is fair to sum up the prevailing attitude of businessmen on ethics as follows:

We live in what is probably the most competitive of the world's civilized societies. Our customs encourage a high degree of aggression in the individual's striving for success. Business is our main area of competition, and it has been ritualized into a game of strategy. The basic rules of the game have been set by the government, which attempts to detect and punish business frauds. But as long as a company does not transgress the rules of the game set by law, it has the legal right to shape its strategy without reference to anything but its profits. If it takes a long-term view of its profits, it will preserve amicable relations, so far as possible, with those with whom it deals. A wise businessman will not seek advantage to the point where he generates dangerous hostility among employees, competitors, customers, government, or the public at large. But decisions in this area are, in the final test, decisions of strategy, not of ethics.

## THE INDIVIDUAL AND THE GAME

An individual within a company often finds it difficult to adjust to the requirements of the business game. He tries to preserve his private ethical standards in situations that call for game strategy. When he is obliged to carry out company policies that challenge his conception of himself as an ethical man, he suffers.

It disturbs him when he is ordered, for instance, to deny a raise to a man who deserves it, to fire an employee of long standing, to prepare advertising that he believes to be misleading, to conceal facts that he feels customers are entitled to know, to cheapen the quality of materials used in the manufacture of an established product, to sell as new a product that he knows to be rebuilt, to exaggerate the curative powers of a medicinal preparation, or to coerce dealers.

There are some fortunate executives who, by the nature of their work and circumstances, never have to face problems of this kind. But in one form or another the ethical dilemma is felt sooner or later by most businessmen. Possibly the dilemma is most painful not when the company forces the action on the executive but when he originates it himself—that is, when he has taken or is contemplating a step which is in his own interest but which runs counter to his early moral conditioning. To illustrate:

> The manager of an export department, eager to show rising sales, is pressed by a big customer to provide invoices which, while containing no overt falsehood that would violate a U.S. law, are so worded that the customer may be able to evade certain taxes in his homeland.
> A company president finds that an aging executive, within a few years of retirement and his pension, is not as productive as formerly. Should he be kept on?
> The produce manager of a supermarket debates with himself whether to get rid of a lot of half-rotten tomatoes by including one, with its good side exposed, in every tomato six-pack.
> An accountant discovers that he has taken an improper deduction on his company's tax return and fears the consequences if he calls the matter to the president's attention, though he himself has done nothing illegal. Perhaps if he says nothing, no one will notice the error.
> A chief executive officer is asked by his directors to comment on a

rumor that he owns stock in another company with which he has placed large orders. He could deny it, for the stock is in the name of his son-in-law and he has earlier formally instructed his son-in-law to sell the holding.

Temptations of this kind constantly arise in business. If an executive allows himself to be torn between a decision based on business considerations and one based on his private ethical code, he exposes himself to a grave psychological strain.

This is not to say that sound business strategy necessarily runs counter to ethical ideals. They may frequently coincide; and when they do, everyone is gratified. But the major tests of every move in business, as in all games of strategy, are legality and profit. A man who intends to be a winner in the business game must have a game player's attitude.

The business strategist's decisions must be as impersonal as those of a surgeon performing an operation—concentrating on objective and technique, and subordinating personal feelings. If the chief executive admits that his son-in-law owns the stock, it is because he stands to lose more if the fact comes out later than if he states it boldly and at once. If the supermarket manager orders the rotten tomatoes to be discarded, he does so to avoid an increase in consumer complaints and a loss of good will. The company president decides not to fire the elderly executive in the belief that the negative reaction of other employees would in the long run cost the company more than it would lose in keeping him and paying his pension.

All sensible businessmen prefer to be truthful, but they seldom feel inclined to tell the *whole* truth. In the business game truth-telling usually has to be kept within narrow limits if trouble is to be avoided. The point was neatly made a long time ago (in 1888) by one of John D. Rockefeller's associates, Paul Babcock, to Standard Oil Company executives who were about to testify before a government investigating committee: "Parry every question with answers which, while perfectly truthful, are evasive of *bottom* facts." This was, is, and probably always will be regarded as wise and permissible business strategy.

### For Office Use Only

An executive's family life can easily be dislocated if he fails to make a sharp distinction between the ethical systems of the home and the office—or if his wife does not grasp that distinction. Many a businessman who has remarked to his wife, "I had to let Jones go today" or "I had to admit to the boss that Jim has been goofing off lately," has been met with an indignant protest. "How could you do a thing like that?

You know Jones is over 50 and will have a lot of trouble getting another job." Or, "You did that to Jim? With his wife ill and all the worry she's been having with the kids?"

If the executive insists that he had no choice because the profits of the company and his own security were involved, he may see a certain cool and ominous reappraisal in his wife's eyes. Many wives are not prepared to accept the fact that business operates with a special code of ethics. An illuminating illustration of this comes from a Southern sales executive who related a conversation he had had with his wife at a time when a hotly contested political campaign was being waged in their state:

I made the mistake of telling her that I had had lunch with Colby, who gives me about half my business. Colby mentioned that his company had a stake in the election. Then he said, 'By the way, I'm treasurer of the citizens' committee for Lang. I'm collecting contributions. Can I count on you for a hundred dollars?

Well, there I was. I was opposed to Lang, but I knew Colby. If he withdrew his business I could be in a bad spot. So I just smiled and wrote out a check then and there. He thanked me, and we started to talk about his next order. Maybe he thought I shared his political views. If so, I wasn't going to lose any sleep over it.

I should have had sense enough not to tell Mary about it. She hit the ceiling. She said she was disappointed in me. She said I hadn't acted like a man, that I should have stood up to Colby.

I said, "Look, it was an either-or situation. I had to do it or risk losing the business."

She came back at me with, "I don't believe it. You could have been honest with him. You could have said that you didn't feel you ought to contribute to a campaign for a man you weren't going to vote for. I'm sure he would have understood."

I said, "Mary, you're a wonderful woman, but you're way off the track. Do you know what would have happened if I had said that? Colby would have smiled and said, 'Oh, I didn't realize. Forget it.' But in his eyes from that moment I would be an oddball, maybe a bit of a radical. He would have listened to me talk about his order and would have promised to give it consideration. After that I wouldn't hear from him for a week. Then I would telephone and learn from his secretary that he wasn't yet ready to place the order. And in about a month I would hear through the grapevine that he was giving his business to another company. A month after that I'd be out of a job."

She was silent for a while. Then she said, "Tom, something is wrong with business when a man is forced to choose between his family's security and his moral obligation to himself. It's easy for me to say you should have stood up to him—but if you had, you might have felt you were betraying me and the kids. I'm sorry that you did it, Tom, but I can't blame you. Something is wrong with business!"

This wife saw the problem in terms of moral obligation as conceived in private life; her husband saw it as a matter of game strategy. As a player in a weak position, he felt that he could not afford to indulge an ethical sentiment that might have cost him his seat at the table.

### Playing to Win

Some men might challenge the Colbys of business—might accept serious setbacks to their business careers rather than risk a feeling of moral cowardice. They merit our respect—but as private individuals, not businessmen. When the skillful player of the business game is compelled to submit to unfair pressure, he does not castigate himself for moral weakness. Instead, he strives to put himself into a strong position where he can defend himself against such pressures in the future without loss.

If a man plans to take a seat in the business game, he owes it to himself to master the principles by which the game is played, including its special ethical outlook. He can then hardly fail to recognize that an occasional bluff may well be justified in terms of the game's ethics and warranted in terms of economic necessity. Once he clears his mind on this point, he is in a good position to match his strategy against that of the other players. He can then determine objectively whether a bluff in a given situation has a good chance of succeeding and can decide when and how to bluff, without a feeling of ethical transgression.

To be a winner, a man must play to win. This does not mean that he must be ruthless, cruel, harsh, or treacherous. On the contrary, the better his reputation for integrity, honesty, and decency, the better his chances of victory will be in the long run. But from time to time every businessman, like every poker player, is offered a choice between certain loss or bluffing within the legal rules of the game. If he is not resigned to losing, if he wants to rise in his company and industry, then in such a crisis he will bluff—and bluff hard.

Every now and then one meets a successful businessman who has conveniently forgotten the small or large deceptions that he practiced on his way to fortune. "God gave me my money," old John D. Rockefeller once piously told a Sunday school class. It would be a rare tycoon in our time who would risk the horse laugh with which such a remark would be greeted.

In the last third of the twentieth century even children are aware that if a man has become prosperous in business, he has sometimes departed from the strict truth in order to overcome obstacles or has practiced the more subtle deceptions of the half-truth or the misleading omission. Whatever the form of the bluff, it is an integral part of the game, and the executive who does not master its techniques is not likely to accumulate much money or power.

## QUESTIONS

1. Henry Taylor has pointed out that "falsehood ceases to be falsehood when it is understood on all sides that the truth is not expected to be spoken." Critically analyze and evaluate this statement, and present your own views on this subject.
2. Carr believes that "the ethics of business are game ethics, different from the ethics of religion." What is he trying to say? Do you agree? Why or why not?
3. Where and how can one draw the line between ethics and normal business practices? Justify and illustrate.
4. Do you believe that we can learn a great deal about the nature of business by comparing it with poker? How and why?
5. Do you agree or disagree with Carr's views on the subject of business ethics? Why or why not? What are your own feelings on this subject? (See readers' comments on Carr's article in "Showdown on 'Business Bluffing.'" *Harvard Business Review,* 40 (May–June 1968), 162–170.)

# Standards for business conduct

# business ethics advisory council

The Business Ethics Advisory Council, organized by the U.S. Department of Commerce, prepared the following set of questions, which, it was hoped, businessmen would ponder and answer in such a fashion as to improve the ethical levels of business conduct.

## A STATEMENT ON BUSINESS ETHICS AND A CALL FOR ACTION

The ethical standards of American businessmen, like those of the American people, are founded upon our religious heritage and our traditions of social, political, and economic freedom. They impose upon each man high obligations in his dealings with his fellowmen, and make all men stewards of the common good. Immutable, well-understood guides to performance generally are effective, but new ethical problems are created constantly by the ever-increasing complexity of society. In business, as in every other activity, therefore, men must continually seek to identify new and appropriate standards.

Over the years, American businessmen in the main have continually endeavored to demonstrate their responsiveness to their ethical obligations in our free society. They have themselves initiated and welcomed from others calls for the improvement of their ethical performance, regarding each as a challenge to establish and meet ever higher ethical goals. In consequence, the ethical standards that should guide business enterprise in this country have steadily risen over the years, and this has had a profound influence on the performance of the business community.

As the ethical standards and conduct of American private enterprise have improved, so also has there developed a public demand for proper performance and a keen sensitivity to lapses from those standards. The full realization by the business community of its future opportunities and, indeed, the maintenance of public confidence require a continuing pursuit of the highest standards of ethical conduct.

Attainment of this objective is not without difficulty. Business enterprises, large and small, have relationships in many directions—with

U. S. Department of Commerce, Business Ethics Advisory Council, *A Statement on Business Ethics and a Call for Action* (Washington: Government Printing Office, 1962).

stockholders and other owners, employees, customers, suppliers, government, and the public in general. The traditional emphasis on freedom, competition, and progress in our economic system often brings the varying interests of these groups into conflict, so that many difficult and complex ethical problems can arise in any enterprise. While all relationships of an enterprise to these groups are regulated in some degree by law, compliance with law can only provide a minimum standard of conduct. Beyond legal obligations, the policies and actions of businessmen must be based upon a regard for the proper claims of all affected groups.

Moreover, in many business situations the decision that must be made is not the simple choice between absolute right and absolute wrong. The decisions of business frequently must be made in highly complex and ever-changing circumstances, and at times involve either adhering to earlier standards or developing new ones. Such decisions affect profoundly not only the business enterprise, but our society as a whole. Indeed, the responsible position of American business—both large and small—obligates each participant to lead rather than follow.

A weighty responsibility therefore rests upon all those who manage business enterprises, as well as upon all others who influence the environment in which business operates. In the final analysis, however, the primary moral duty to establish high ethical standards and adequate procedures for their enforcement in each enterprise must rest with its policymaking body—its board of directors and its top management.

We, therefore, now propose that current efforts be expanded and intensified and that new efforts now be undertaken by the American business community to hasten its attainment of those high ethical standards that derive from our heritage and traditions. We urge all enterprises, business groups, and associations to accept responsibility —each for itself and in its own most appropriate way—to develop methods and programs for encouraging and sustaining these efforts on a continuous basis. We believe in this goal, we accept it, and we encourage all to pursue its attainment.

## SOME QUESTIONS FOR BUSINESSMEN

The following questions are designed to facilitate the examination by American businessmen of their ethical standards and performance. They are intended to illustrate the kinds of questions that must be identified and considered by each business enterprise if it is to achieve compliance with those high ethical standards that derive from our heritage and traditions.  Every reader will think of others.  No single list can possibly encompass all of the demands for ethical judgments that must be met by men in business.

### 1.  General Understanding

Do we have in our organization current, well-considered statements of the ethical principles that should guide our officers and employees in specific situations that arise in our business activities, both domestic and foreign?  Do we revise these statements periodically to cover new situations and changing laws and social patterns?

Have those statements been the fruit of discussion in which all members of policy-determining management have had an opportunity to participate?

Have we given to our officers and employees at all levels sufficient motivation to search out ethical factors in business problems and apply high ethical standards in their solution?  What have we done to eliminate opposing pressures?

Have we provided officers and employees with an easily accessible means of obtaining counsel on and resolution of ethical problems that may arise in their activities?  Do they use it?

Do we know whether our officers and employees apply in their daily activities the ethical standards we have promulgated?  Do we reward those who do so and penalize those who do not?

### 2.  Compliance with Law

Having in mind the complexities and ever-changing patterns of modern law and government regulation:

What are we doing to make sure that our officers and employees are informed about and comply with laws and regulations affecting their activities?

Have we made clear that it is our policy to obey even those laws which we may think unwise and seek to have changed?

Do we have adequate internal checks on our compliance with law?

Have we established a simple and readily available procedure for our officers and employees to seek legal guidance in their activities?  Do they use it?

### 3.  Conflicts of Interest

Do we have a current, well-considered statement of policy regarding potential conflict of interest problems of our directors, officers and employees?  If so, does it cover conflicts which may arise in connection with such activities as: transactions with or involving our company;

acquiring interests in or performing services for our customers, distributors, suppliers and competitors; buying and selling our company's securities; or the personal undertaking of what might be called company opportunities?

What mechanism do we have for enabling our directors, officers and employees to make ethical judgments when conflicts of interest do arise?

Do we require regular reports, or do we leave it to our directors, officers and employees to disclose such activities voluntarily?

### 4. Entertainment, Gifts, and Expenses

Have we defined our company policy on accepting and making expenditures for gifts and entertainment? Are the criteria as to occasion and amount clearly stated or are they left merely to the judgment of the officer or employee?

Do we disseminate information about our company policy to the organizations with which we deal?

Do we require adequate reports of both the giving and receiving of gifts and entertainment; are they supported in sufficient detail; are they subject to review by appropriate authority; and could the payment or receipt be justified to our stockholders, the government, and the public?

### 5. Customers and Suppliers

Have we taken appropriate steps to keep our advertising and sales representations truthful and fair? Are these steps effective?

How often do we review our advertising, literature, labels, and packaging? Do they give our customers a fair understanding of the true quality, quantity, price and function of our products? Does our service as well as our product measure up to our basic obligations and our representations?

Do we fairly make good on flaws and defects? Is this a matter of stated policy? Do we know that our employees, distributors, dealers and agents follow it?

Do we avoid favoritism and discrimination and otherwise treat our customers and suppliers fairly and equitably in all of our dealings with them?

### 6. Social Responsibilities

Every business enterprise has manifold responsibilities to the society of which it is a part. The prime legal and social obligation of the managers of a business is to operate it for the long-term profit of its owners. Concurrent social responsibilities pertain to a company's treatment of its past, present and prospective employees and to its various relationships with customers, suppliers, government, the community and the public at large. These responsibilities may often be, or appear to be, in conflict, and at times a management's recognition of its broad responsibilities may affect the amount of an enterprise's immediate profits and the means of attaining them.

The problems that businessmen must solve in this area are often exceedingly perplexing. One may begin his reflections on this subject by asking—

Have we reviewed our company policies in the light of our responsibilities to society? Are our employees aware of the interaction between our business policies and our social responsibilities?

Do we have a clearly understood concept of our obligation to assess our responsibilities to stockholders, employees, customers, suppliers, our community and the public?

Do we recognize and impress upon all our officers and employees the fact that our free enterprise system and our individual business enterprises can thrive and grow only to the extent that they contribute to the welfare of our country and its people?

## QUESTIONS

1. Critically analyze and evaluate the council's proposals concerning the ethical conduct of American business. What are the basic weaknesses of such proposals, and how would you improve them?

2. Do you think that the ethical standards and conduct of American private enterprise have improved recently? How has this come about? Elaborate.

3. Present your own plan of action ensuring a greater degree of ethical behavior and conduct by the country's business community.

4. Do you think advisory bodies such as the Business Ethics Advisory Council are capable of improving the level of ethical conduct in business? Why or why not?

5. Compare the level of ethics between large and small companies, business and the federal government, a large company and a local government, and a small business and lawyers.

# Chapter 9 Cases in Business Ethics

# Willard Atkinson *

Willard Atkinson has been with the Tiller Container Corporation for 40 years and is now in charge of production for a very large division. When Atkinson first worked for the company, he was quite capable of dealing with the problems of production that he encountered. Atkinson has not bothered to keep abreast of new production techniques and, since he was successful in getting two bright young MBAs who not only are highly competent in production techniques but excellent general managers as well, has tended to delegate more and more of his responsibilities to these men. There is little, if any, doubt that he could not manage the affairs of his department without the talents of these young men. The men have made it known that they may leave unless brighter opportunities are opened for them, and the management knows they would be extremely difficult to replace. About the only place they would fit in the company would be in Atkinson's job.

Atkinson is now 60 years of age. The voluntary retirement age of the company is 65, and the mandatory retirement age is 70. Atkinson has made it known that because he is in good health, he intends to stay until mandatory retirement. The president is thinking seriously of asking him to take early retirement in order to save one of the two young men on his staff whose talents are sorely needed in the company. Early retirement now will give Atkinson 40 percent of his salary, whereas voluntary retirement at 65 will give him 50 percent.

## QUESTIONS

1. Do you think Atkinson is behaving ethically?
2. If the president of the Tiller Container Corporation forces Atkinson to take early retirement, do you think he is acting ethically?
3. If you were one of the younger men, what would you do?

---

* See Arthur L. Svenson, "An Augean Stable—The Case of Management Featherbeds," *California Management Review,* 4 (Summer 1963), 17–22.

# Crisis at XYZ

National Electronics Company, the parent of many subsidiaries, was embarrassed by having to report substantially lower earnings than had been previously announced to the public. Shortly afterward, the news media reported for XYZ Company, one of National's subsidiaries, a new president and a new vice-president of finance (replacing the former controller). John Smith, president of XYZ, and George Logan, controller, had been withholding information from the parent company about the poor financial condition of XYZ.

Smith had made a decision to go after two large contracts. Smith's managers disagreed with his optimistic estimate of the probabilities of getting them, but he persisted and became more and more committed financially. Finally XYZ failed to get the contracts, and the poor financial position of the company had to be made known to headquarters. Had XYZ won the contracts, Smith would have been a hero. As it turned out, he "resigned," and his resignation was accepted.

One director of National said that out-and-out fraud was involved, while another thought this was a situation directly attributable to the pressures on men like Smith to make profits. In such instances men like Smith tend to take the optimistic view.

A major question that arose was why a number of top managers at XYZ, who had close affiliations with men at National, did not go above Smith and make the situation known? Investigation showed that loyalty to Smith was high, and as a result, they accepted his position.

## QUESTIONS

1. Was there a violation of common standards of ethics? *
2. Who was to blame for the fiasco?
3. What would you have done had you been the controller?

---

* For a detailed discussion, see John J. Fendrock, "Crisis in Conscience at Quasar," *Harvard Business Review*, 46 (March–April 1968), 112–120, and John J. Fendrock, "Sequel to Quasar Stellar," *Harvard Business Review*, 46 (September–October 1968), 14–48.

# William Robertson

William Robertson, a senior vice-president of the Chicago Steel Corporation, wrote an article for a national magazine deploring the fact that his company, together with other corporations in the Chicago area, had not done enough to avoid polluting Lake Michigan and, furthermore, ought to take the lead in really getting everyone involved to clean up the lake. He laid out a program costing hundreds of millions of dollars.

Some of the customers of the corporation became annoyed at this blast because they felt the net result would be demands by the government to undertake costly antipollution programs that they could not afford. The more disgruntled customers actually canceled orders.

The top management of the corporation felt that Robertson had gone much too far. They felt they had done much to avoid polluting the lake and that this publicity denigrated what they had done and promised not only to get them involved in very costly programs, but to embroil the company in all sorts of political and social battles in which the corporation should not become engaged. As a result, the chairman and chief executive officer asked Robertson never again to comment publicly without clearing his statement in advance with him.

Robertson resigned, saying that he refused to give up his responsibilities as a citizen. This action was considered too drastic by the top management, who suggested that he manage for a year or so a new plant in France, which the corporation had recently acquired under the leadership of Robertson, and which Robertson often expressed a deep interest in running for a few years. Robertson refused, saying that his conscience would not permit him to evade the issue in this fashion.

Robertson's friends viewed the matter in different ways. One executive said, "I have devoted my life to this corporation and its well-being is a matter of major significance to me. If I have to give up a few things to support the company that is a small price to pay. My compensation is high and covers many things I may not like." Another said, "As long as Bill works for the company it seems to me he ought to accept the company position and not stick a knife in its back." Another took a more philosophical position, saying, "No one has forced Bill to take his job. But, so long as he has the job he cannot, as a major officer of the company, separate himself from it. He enjoys free speech under the Constitution, but the Constitution does not protect his job. The company has a right to defend itself from public statements of its officers if it wishes to do so."

**QUESTIONS**

1. To what extent should a corporation protect its image or ask an executive to follow a prescribed company position on a public issue, if an individual feels he is deprived of a right to speak out as he sees fit?

2. How far should a corporation be permitted to go in protecting its position by depriving an individual of his investment in his job when he speaks out contrary to company policy?

# Lester Hogan

On August 9, 1968, Dr. C. Lester Hogan resigned as the vice-president and general manager of the Semiconductor Division of Motorola, Inc., in Phoenix, to become president of a major competitor, Fairchild Camera & Instrument Corporation of Mountain View, California. As a former professor of physics, Dr. Hogan combined his technical skills with managerial capability to lift his Motorola Division from low levels to a leader in the field. When he resigned, seven top managers representing the entire senior management of Motorola's Semiconductor Division left to join him. Shortly thereafter, 15 additional professional personnel followed him to Mountain View.

Although there apparently had been some dissatisfaction with Motorola, it was thought that Dr. Hogan would remain, in light of a recent salary increase from $80,000 to $90,000 and an option on 10,000 shares of Motorola stock (later reduced to 9,000 to satisfy objections from other executives). He had accumulated about $250,000 from previous options but had problems in financing his recently tendered options. Fairchild offered him a salary of $120,000 a year, an interest-free personal loan from Sherman Fairchild, chairman of the board of Fairchild, amounting to $5,400,000 to permit Dr. Hogan to exercise an option for 90,000 shares of Fairchild stock at $60 a share for three years after the date of employment. By October 1968 the stock had risen to $80. He also was given an additional 10,000 shares of restricted stock at $10 a share.

Motorola filed a suit charging "unfair competition" and asked for any profits that Dr. Hogan and the seven senior managers might make from stock options and salary. Fairchild filed a countersuit accusing Motorola of pirating personnel from Fairchild. Motorola, said Fairchild, does not come into court with clean hands. Furthermore, Motorola's suit would prevent an employee from changing employers and constitute involuntary servitude. Executive mobility is a fact of life today.

Businessmen were sharply divided about whether Dr. Hogan's move was ethical. "I think it's reprehensible," said one manager. "Stealing key employees is getting business the cheap way." Another industrialist said, "I don't want to pass moral judgment, but an officer of a company has responsibility to shareholders, for example, and also he should set an example of professionalism to the technical community."

On the other hand, the chief of another company said, "In considering how long Hogan had worked for Motorola (10 years), his ability to pull these other executives out indicates an insufficient incentive in Motorola."

Another top executive agreed in saying, "If there is insufficient challenge and opportunity to grow with the company, naturally they will go with him if they can." Others said, "It is not wrong. This is a free society." But another said, "This sort of thing has happened in the past, but not anywhere near this magnitude. At some point, a rational mark is passed. That mark, for my money, has been overstepped in this case."

Hogan, in an interview, said, "After all, slavery was abolished 100 years ago. I think I have a choice." But he suggested he had some doubts about the move in saying, "A man has obligations to many things—to his company, to himself and his family, to his country. Is this move right or wrong? Is this ethical or unethical? I don't know. I know this: I have obligations also to people I've known through life, who've helped me become a success. One has to weigh this, too. I weighed all obligations, honestly and sincerely."

Hogan asserted there was no issue of a transfer of trade secrets, since Fairchild's technological excellence is very great. "It's silly to talk about bringing trade secrets to Fairchild," he said. "Fairchild has been the technological leader in this industry for ten years. Losing a trade secret to Fairchild is a kind of a joke."

So far as the move of people is concerned, Hogan insisted that all of the personnel he hired came to him, not the other way around. Furthermore, Motorola was still in a strong position.*

## QUESTIONS

1. Does a top manager have the right to transfer to a major competitor and take his most important executives with him?
2. Is it likely that a move such as this will result in revealing trade secrets?
3. Even though the court may decide in Hogan's and Fairchild's favor, is this an ethical move?

---

* Abstracted from Arelo Sederberg, "The Hogan 'Raid': What Is Executive Piracy?" *Los Angeles Times*, Section I, Sunday, October 6, 1968; and "The Fight That Fairchild Won," *Business Week*, October 5, 1968, pp. 106–115.

# Short incidents in business ethics

# john w. clark

John W. Clark, S. J., who prepared the following cases, gave the questionnaire to business executives. The results, which appear in his book *Religion and the Moral Standards of American Businessmen*, might be interesting to students who complete the questionnaire.

## QUESTIONNAIRE

1. Instructions: Please check the alternative which best expresses your ethical judgment of the following cases:

   A. Recently a number of high-ranking executives of several electrical companies were convicted and sentenced to jail for conspiring to fix the prices of heavy electrical-equipment products. Their defense counsel argued that while their action was technically illegal, they sought to rationalize a chaotic pricing situation. What is your evaluation of the action of these executives?

   | | |
   |---|---|
   | approve | 1 |
   | somewhat approve | 2 |
   | somewhat disapprove | 3 |
   | disapprove | 4 |

   B. John Saxor is the Pacific Coast Sales Representative of Ajax Tool Company. He has been instructed by his superior, Mr. Bruce Maynard, Vice-President of Sales, to adopt a sales policy Saxor considers unethical. Mr. Maynard and Saxor have discussed the policy at length, and it is apparent Maynard thinks the policy is quite ethical. He orders Saxor to follow the policy, and Saxor reluctantly does so. What is your opinion of Saxor's action?

   | | |
   |---|---|
   | approve | 1 |
   | somewhat approve | 2 |
   | somewhat disapprove | 3 |
   | disapprove | 4 |

From John W. Clark, S. J., *Religion and the Moral Standards of American Businessmen* (Cincinnati, Ohio: South-Western Publishing Company, 1966), Appendix A, pp. 178–191. Reprinted by permission.

C.  Lawrence Stone, a member of the Board of Directors of Scott
    Electronics Corporation, has just learned that the company
    is about to announce a 2-for-1 stock split and an increase of
    dividends.  Stone personally is on the brink of bankruptcy.
    A quick gain of a few thousand dollars can save him from
    economic and social ruin.  He decides to take advantage of
    this information concerning the stock split by purchasing
    stock now to sell in a few days at a profit.

    |  |  |
    |---|---|
    | approve | 1 |
    | somewhat approve | 2 |
    | somewhat disapprove | 3 |
    | disapprove | 4 |

D.  James Sherman sells used cars for Harrison Auto Company.
    Although he feels that the cars he sells are reasonably priced
    for the market, in his sales talk he is forced to match the ex-
    travagant claims and tactics of his competitors.  The com-
    pany engages in such practices as setting back speedometers,
    superficially hiding major defects, and putting pressure on
    prospects to close a deal on their first visit.  Sherman knows
    that the company could not survive without such practices;
    yet he personally feels repugnance toward them.  Neverthe-
    less he follows these practices.

    |  |  |
    |---|---|
    | approve | 1 |
    | somewhat approve | 2 |
    | somewhat disapprove | 3 |
    | disapprove | 4 |

E.  The Reed Engineering Company faces a very competitive
    situation in bidding for a contract to construct a new store
    for a large discount chain.  Inasmuch as the company is ser-
    iously in need of the work, A. Wallis Jennings, one of the part-
    ners in the company, suggests that Reed submit a bid which
    will certainly be low, and then make its margin on the use of
    inferior materials.  Jennings is certain this can be done with-
    out arousing the suspicion of building inspectors.  Jennings
    argues that any company which is awarded the contract will
    have to do that since the bidding will be so competitive.  Mr.
    Elwood Reed, senior partner in the company, agrees that it
    will be necessary to do this.  He observes that it is not an in-
    frequent practice anyway.

    |  |  |
    |---|---|
    | approve | 1 |
    | somewhat approve | 2 |

|                     |   |
|---------------------|---|
| somewhat disapprove | 3 |
| disapprove          | 4 |

F.  Brian George is a salesman for Sweet Soap Company. With commissions, his salary usually comes to about $12,000 per year. George usually supplements this to the extent of about $600 per year by charging certain unauthorized personal expenses against his expense account. He feels that this is a common practice in his company; and if everybody else is doing it, he doesn't see why he shouldn't do it also.

|                     |   |
|---------------------|---|
| approve             | 1 |
| somewhat approve    | 2 |
| somewhat disapprove | 3 |
| disapprove          | 4 |

G.  Wallace Brown, Treasurer of Lloyd Enterprises, is about to retire and contemplates recommending one of his two assistants for promotion to Treasurer. Brown is sure that his recommendation will be accepted, but he also knows that the assistant not recommended will find his promotion opportunities seriously limited. One of the assistants, William Grimes, seems to him the most qualified for the new assignment, but the other assistant, John Leonard, is the nephew of the president of Lloyd's biggest customer. Though Brown hates to do it, he recommends Leonard for the job because he feels his relationship with his uncle will help Lloyd's.

|                     |   |
|---------------------|---|
| approve             | 1 |
| somewhat approve    | 2 |
| somewhat disapprove | 3 |
| disapprove          | 4 |

H.  Mr. Irving Kraft, editor of the Diamond City *Daily News* is troubled. He has just received a visit from Mr. Raymond Cramer, a public relations executive with the Aztec Department Store. Aztec is a big advertiser in the *Daily News*, and its continued purchase of advertising space is very important to the paper. Recently the department store sold a large quantity of electrical appliances which proved defective and refused to exchange the merchandise for better quality appliances. The *Daily News* at the present time is running a series of articles on local business firms. Mr. Cramer wants to be sure that a story on the Aztec Department Store will contain no mention of this unfortunate occurrence. Mr. Kraft is troubled; but in order not to offend this important advertiser, he agrees not to mention the sale of the defective appliances.

| | |
|---|---|
| approve | 1 |
| somewhat approve | 2 |
| somewhat disapprove | 3 |
| disapprove | 4 |

I. Robert Schall and Company, Public Accountants, have been called in to audit the books of the Lakewood Trucking Company in anticipation of a public sale of stock. In the course of the audit Mr. Schall discovers an item that leaves him puzzled: a $20,000 advertising expense paid to the Chicago Advertising Company. This was a one-payment expense three years ago, and no further business has been done with the Chicago firm. When questioned by Mr. Schall, Mr. Clarence Wallen, President of the trucking company, readily admits this money was used as a bribe to pay a union official. "It was a question of paying up or going out of business," Mr. Wallen explains. Since the company has now been unionized by a reputable union, Mr. Wallen sees no possibility of this situation recurring. He asks Mr. Schall to make no mention of this in his Auditor's Report. Since the firm seems soundly managed in every other respect, Mr. Schall agrees to Mr. Wallen's request.

| | |
|---|---|
| approve | 1 |
| somewhat approve | 2 |
| somewhat disapprove | 3 |
| disapprove | 4 |

J. Howard Piser, President of Piser Fashions Co., has heard rumors that a competitor, Sunset Fashions, is coming out with a new line of spring styles which in all likelihood will sweep the market. Piser cannot afford to wait until the new styles come out, so he hires Robert Bishop, plant supervisor of Sunset. Although Mr. Bishop is not a designer, in his capacity of plant supervisor he has become thoroughly familiar with the new Sunset line. It is understood that Mr. Bishop will make known to his new employer the full details of the new Sunset styles.

| | |
|---|---|
| approve | 1 |
| somewhat approve | 2 |
| somewhat disapprove | 3 |
| disapprove | 4 |

K.  Richard Cobb is a salesman for Lester and Braddock, stock-brokers.  He has been instructed to recommend to his cus-tomers some Central Electric Power Co. bonds, as the broker-age firm is carrying a heavy inventory in these bonds at the present time.  Cobb does not feel the bonds are a good invest-ment under present circumstances; and he is reluctant to recommend them.  However, after some thought, he decides to follow the company directive and recommend the bonds.

| | |
|---|---|
| approve | 1 |
| somewhat approve | 2 |
| somewhat disapprove | 3 |
| disapprove | 4 |

L.  Recently "Big Steel" has been criticized for not using every means at its disposal to ease racial tensions in Birmingham. In particular, it was contended that U. S. Steel should exert pressure for integration by letting banks and suppliers know that it would give more business to those who favored better opportunities for Negroes.  At a news conference, Chairman of the Board of U. S. Steel, Roger M. Blough, rejected such proposals and observed that corporation officials who are citizens in a community "can exercise what small influence they may have as citizens.  But for a corporation to attempt to exert any kind of economic compulsion to achieve a par-ticular end in the social area seems to be quite beyond what a corporation should do."

| | |
|---|---|
| approve | 1 |
| somewhat approve | 2 |
| somewhat disapprove | 3 |
| disapprove | 4 |

M.  Jenkins Manufacturing Company is faced with the necessity of closing down one of its two Los Angeles plants.  This will necessitate laying off about 100 employees.  Another 100 em-ployees will be transferred to the other plant in the same area. Though the company is not unionized, generous allowances have been set aside for separation pay.  The problem which Mr. Howard Jenkins, company president, faces is whether to discharge older and more highly paid workers who have been with the company for a number of years, or the younger and less highly paid workers who have less seniority.  The indus-try is a competitive one; and Mr. Jenkins is concerned about his company's ability to compete, so he decides to discharge the older employees.

approve                    1
somewhat approve           2
somewhat disapprove        3
disapprove                 4

**N.** The Dodd Textile Company makes shirts in a large western city. Because of the severity of competition, the company is forced to hire employees from immigrant and other under-privileged groups which accept substandard wages. Recently union officials have accused such plants as this as maintaining "sweat-shop conditions." Lesley Smith, the owner, admits conditions are not ideal and that employees can hardly make sufficient wages for a minimum living standard; but, he says, he is at least providing some employment for people who would otherwise probably be unemployed. Further, he feels he's entitled to his own profits which he would not receive if he raised wages.

approve                    1
somewhat approve           2
somewhat disapprove        3
disapprove                 4

**O.** The St. Clair Importing Company, a U. S. firm, wholly owns a Canadian subsidiary, the Montclair Importing Company. Montclair has been offered the opportunity to merchandise a number of products manufactured in Red China. The Chinese price of these products is so attractive that the Canadian firm estimates it will be able to increase substantially the usual markup and still sell the products at a retail price below Canadian prices. The U. S. firm has contacted the U. S. State Department; and while it would be illegal and against public policy for the American firm to market the products in the U. S., there is no prohibition for the Canadian subsidiary to sell them in Canada. The firm decides to complete negotiations and distribute the products through its Canadian subsidiary.

approve                    1
somewhat approve           2
somewhat disapprove        3
disapprove                 4

**P.** The Wiley Electric Company has a program to help colleges in the U. S. It agrees to match the contribution of any of its employees to colleges of their choice. Recently objection has been made to this policy on the grounds that it is distributing stockholder funds without their consent. The company has responded to this objection by pointing out that by such a policy it is fulfilling its community obligations.

| | |
|---|---|
| approve | 1 |
| somewhat approve | 2 |
| somewhat disapprove | 3 |
| disapprove | 4 |

Q. Dean Joseph Maynard of Redwood University has approached Mr. Robert Schall of Robert Schall and Company, Public Accountants, and has requested him to take a small number of foreign students as accounting apprentices for the summer months. These men are graduate accounting students who lack any contact with practical business conditions in the U. S. After consulting his staff, Mr. Schall concludes that bringing such inexperienced men into the firm for such a short length of time will be a burden to the company's operation. He refuses the Dean's request but offers to speak to the students at the University.

| | |
|---|---|
| approve | 1 |
| somewhat approve | 2 |
| somewhat disapprove | 3 |
| disapprove | 4 |

R. Harry Ruckus, Vice-President of Westerly Chemical Company, feels that sending expensive Christmas gifts to customers compromises their position as buyers, and thus is a form of bribery. Yet he knows that this is a common practice among his competitors and that sales are likely to be adversely affected by failure to conform to the traditional practice. He decides to send the gifts.

| | |
|---|---|
| approve | 1 |
| somewhat approve | 2 |
| somewhat disapprove | 3 |
| disapprove | 4 |

S. The Kauffman Construction Company has just submitted a bid on a new city hall for Diamond City. Two days ago Mr. William Henderson, Assistant to the Mayor of Diamond City, visited the office of Mr. Karl Kauffman and hinted that his company would be awarded the bid if Mr. Kauffman was willing to contribute $10,000 to the Mayor's campaign for reelection. Kauffman needed this contract badly to keep his con-

struction crews organized and working through the next few
months, so he agreed to make the campaign contribution
from the company funds.

|                       |   |
|-----------------------|---|
| approve               | 1 |
| somewhat approve      | 2 |
| somewhat disapprove   | 3 |
| disapprove            | 4 |

T. Western Petroleum, Inc., has a large refinery located in the
suburbs of a large California city. The company has for
years burned the waste products at this plant as the most
efficient means of waste disposal. Though there is an ordi-
nance against burning rubbish in the area, the company was
easily able to get an exemption for refinery operations. The
burning of waste petroleum products does cause soot and
odor to spread through neighboring housing tracts. Mr. Dud-
ley Johnson, Vice-President of Production, suggests that the
company install a filter which will reduce considerably the
amount of impurities released by the disposal system.
Though the cost of this filter is substantial and will noticeably
reduce net income for several years, the company goes ahead
with its installation.

|                       |   |
|-----------------------|---|
| approve               | 1 |
| somewhat approve      | 2 |
| somewhat disapprove   | 3 |
| disapprove            | 4 |

U. Walter Preston, purchasing agent for Comfort Furniture Company, asks his friend William Nelson to become his partner
in the establishment of a new firm. Preston suggests that
they start a small trucking company to haul furniture from
Comfort's suppliers to the company's main warehouse in
Philadelphia. Preston, in his capacity as purchasing agent,
will direct Comfort's suppliers to send their orders via the
new freight firm. Prices of the new firm will be competitive,
but the certainty of a steady flow of freight will make the firm
quite profitable. Nelson is to manage the trucking company
while Preston stays with Comfort Furniture. Nelson wonders
if such an arrangement is ethical, but finally agrees to the
formation of the new firm.

|                       |   |
|-----------------------|---|
| approve               | 1 |
| somewhat approve      | 2 |
| somewhat disapprove   | 3 |
| disapprove            | 4 |

V.  The Board of Directors of the Boldt Manufacturing Company has decided to close down its Eastbrook plant in four months. The plant employs 200 workers in a Michigan town of 30,000. At a recent Board meeting, Paul Belcher, company Treasurer, has urged that the employees not be informed of this decision until the actual day of their dismissal. If this is not done, he argues, absenteeism and productivity declines will seriously hamper output. Henry Roscoe, Personnel Director, feels that the employees should be given some advance notice in order to plan necessary adjustments, even at the cost of absenteeism and productivity declines. Nevertheless, Roscoe is overruled, and the company keeps the plant shutdown a secret.

|                     |   |
|---------------------|---|
| approve             | 1 |
| somewhat approve    | 2 |
| somewhat disapprove | 3 |
| disapprove          | 4 |

W.  Brown Motor Company has been producing automobiles in Detroit for over twenty years. Though corporate responsibilities are heavy, Mr. James Wilhelm, President, has always spent some company-paid time in community activities and has encouraged his subordinates to do likewise. He recently summed up his philosophy on this subject in the following way: "It is no longer just enough to build a better mousetrap. Good industrial citizenship consists mainly in becoming a part of the community and cultivating genuinely friendly relationships with the people who live in it. A company can become too exclusively profit-oriented."

|                     |   |
|---------------------|---|
| approve             | 1 |
| somewhat approve    | 2 |
| somewhat disapprove | 3 |
| disapprove          | 4 |

X.  Big Productions, Inc., produces a weekly TV program which stresses violence and brutality among juvenile gangs in the slum area of a large but unnamed American city. The program is very popular and receives high Nielsen ratings, but several community leaders have publicly criticized the program as contributing to juvenile delinquency. The company has argued that its function is to make and market a popular product, not to attempt to upgrade the moral values of society.

|                     |   |
|---------------------|---|
| approve             | 1 |
| somewhat approve    | 2 |

somewhat  disapprove      3
disapprove      4

Y.   In 1946, at the close of World War II, the major auto companies found themselves in a "sellers' market," that is, for
some months after postwar production was resumed, the demand for new cars exceeded the supply. Instead of selling
the new cars for the high price the market would bear, the
auto manufacturers rather set their prices considerably lower
and aimed for a traditional pattern of gross margin on sales
even though this meant less profit than was possible under
the circumstances. What is your opinion of this decision of
the auto manufacturers?

approve      1
somewhat approve      2
somewhat  disapprove      3
disapprove      4

Z.   King Development Company has just purchased 1,000 acres
of Arizona desert. The land, although in an undeveloped
area, is only a few miles off the main highway between
Phoenix and Tucson. The tract has been named "Desert
Estates" and has been divided into 1-acre parcels. The company intends to sell these parcels by mail at $449 per acre. A
well has been sunk on one parcel to prove the availability of
water, and the development company also plans to bring
electrical service to the site at its own expense. While advertisements will not be fraudulent, they will stress the
potential appreciation of property values in Desert Estates.

approve      1
somewhat approve      2
somewhat  disapprove      3
disapprove      4

2.   Rank (1–5) the following as qualities you would like to find in
your associates:

_____leadership
_____hard work
_____ability to get along with others
_____thrift
_____technical knowhow

3.   Rank (1–5) the following as qualities you would like to find in your
associates:

_____sensitivity to others
_____honesty
_____dedication to the organization
_____breadth of interests
_____judgment

4. Rank (1–5) the following qualities according to their importance for business success:

_____hard work
_____family and social connections
_____ability to get along with others
_____dedication to the organization
_____honesty

5. Which of the following men would you prefer to work with?

   a. Harry White: "I think that if a man joins a reputable company and then remains sensitive and responsive to the ethical values of his colleagues, he won't stray far from the ethical ideal."

   b. Bob Easton: "I have some strong ethical commitments I've formulated through the years, and I'll resign before I compromise these principles."

   |         |   |
   |---------|---|
   | White   | 1 |
   | Easton  | 2 |

6. Rank (1–6) the following according to their importance in influencing ethical conduct in business generally.

_____family training
_____conduct of superiors
_____conduct of peers
_____school and university training
_____religious training
_____practices in industry

7. What is the one unethical practice in your industry you would most like to see eliminated?

8. List some other practices in your industry you consider unethical:

9. Below are listed some suggestions which have been proposed for the improvement of business ethics. What is your opinion of these suggestions?

|  | Approve | Somewhat Approve | Somewhat Disapprove | Disapprove |
|---|---|---|---|---|
| a. Develop some widely accepted general principles of business ethics. | | | | |
| b. Introduce courses in Business Ethics in business schools. | | | | |
| c. Introduce industry codes of ethical practices. | | | | |
| d. Legislate stronger governmental regulation of business. | | | | |
| e. Encourage a more active participation of religious leaders in developing general ethical norms for business. | | | | |

10. What suggestions would you make as effective means of improving business ethics?

.  .  .

# The Supersonic Transport: Fly or Ground?

# 10

Editor's Note: In 1961 the Congress, at the request of the Federal Aviation Agency (FAA), appropriated $11 million for a feasibility study of the supersonic transport (SST). In the next year the idea was pushed ahead with the announcement that a British-French consortium was going to build a supersonic transport called Concorde. Then Pan American World Airways ordered six Concordes in 1963. President Kennedy shortly thereafter announced a design competition for American aircraft makers and a commitment that the federal government would give financial support for the research and development of the airplane. Opposition developed in the Congress, but the project went ahead, and in 1966 the FAA announced that the Boeing Aircraft Corporation had won over the Lockheed Aircraft Corporation.

The government agreed to pay 90 percent of the estimated development cost of $1 billion for two prototypes and 75 percent of any overrun up to an additional $100 million. The government would receive, in turn, royalty payments on all airplanes sold beginning with the 101st.

It calculated its investment would be returned when the 300th plane was sold. The prototype flight was to take place early in 1973, and if everything proceeded on schedule, production would begin soon thereafter with the first deliveries to airlines to be made in early 1978.

In December 1970 President Nixon asked the Congress for an additional $290 million for fiscal 1971. The request passed the House but was defeated in the Senate after bitter debate. The Senate authorized expenditures through March 31, 1971, after which there were no appropriations. The President returned to the Congress early in 1971 with a request for $134 million to continue the SST program through to the end of the current fiscal year. The House voted against this appropriation. In a 51–46 vote on March 24, 1971, the Senate rejected the request, and the program, therefore, ended on March 31, 1971.

The SST issue may well arise again in the future. If the specific case of the SST does not arise, the issues associated with it will appear in a different form, hence the debate will have relevancy for a long time.

# The case for the supersonic transport

## harvey ardman

**Harvey Ardman, Science and Technology Editor for the Research Institute of America, here sets forth the case for the SST by answering the major objections against it and setting forth the main points of the proponents.**

The development of an American supersonic transport airplane, to carry commercial passengers between continents three times as fast as current jets, has been a controversial subject for quite a few years now.

Government funds as well as private funds are needed to help bear the enormous cost of development, so the creation of an American SST is in the area of public debate, and it has been debated to a fare-thee-well.

A host of objections to the SST has been raised. They include:

The great cost of development.

The need to divert government funds, instead, to poverty programs and other social purposes.

The lack of any apparent need for such air speed at such cost when it can take nearly as long to get to and from the airports as it takes to fly the Atlantic right now.

The sonic booms that such planes would make, to the annoyance or worse of people and things below.

Supposed danger of radiation damage to passengers who'd fly as high as the SST's would fly.

Pollution of the upper air by jet exhausts with possibly direful effects on world climate.

Possible destruction of the high ozone layer which helps keep damaging ultra-violet rays from reaching the earth.

Anybody who has been reading the papers or listening to radio or TV knows that these discouraging objections have received the most attention in the public debate. They have gotten the headlines, the prime spots in news broadcasts and the blasts of some of the politicians. In the recent elections some candidates of both parties included anti-SST platforms in their campaigning. Alarmed conservation and anti-pollution groups have issued these objections to the SST broadside.

Harvey Ardman, "The Case for the Supersonic Transport," *The American Legion Magazine*, 89 (December 1970), 4–8, 44–47. Copyright 1970, *The American Legion Magazine*. Reprinted by permission.

The public is entitled to hear and weigh these points.  The SST is a public question, and these are not the kind of objections that should be swept under the rug.

The public is equally entitled to hear the answers to them and the reasons why an American SST is wanted, if we are really supposed to reach great decisions through the expressed will of an informed public.

Inexpert propagandists have been fantastically wrong in their treatment of scientific developments in the past.  So wrong have they been that in a recent release the Nat'l Aeronautic Ass'n—which is *for* the SST—had a bit of fun with the media's habit of giving the bigger play to SST objections.  The NAA dug up an Oct. 9, 1903, *New York Times* editorial that appeared after Professor Langley's Flying Machine had crashed into the Potomac on Oct. 7 of that year.

Langley's attempt to fly was a "ridiculous fiasco," said the *Times* then.  It went on to say that it would take "from one million to ten million years" to evolve a machine that would really fly, *if* we could eliminate "the existing relation between weight and strength in inorganic materials."  Birds are organic and can fly, machines were inorganic and cannot, it explained.  We'd be better advised, it said, to devote our efforts to more profitable things.

Langley's plane crashed in the Potomac again on Dec. 8, 1903.  Two days later the *Times* of those days was back scolding him.  The unsolvable problem of flight, it patiently explained to Langley, was that because there is always a weakest part to any mechanical device, extra strength must be built in to provide a safety factor.  "To allow it in an aeroplane," Langley was advised, "would be to weight it so that it would be too heavy for its purpose."

As a lesson in newspaper science, let it be noted that Langley's plane was later proved flyable, and that when the above editorial appeared on Dec. 10 the *Times* had just seven days left for the life of its explanation of why man would not fly until at least the year 1001903 A.D.  On Dec. 17, 1903, Orville Wright took off, flew and landed a heavier-than-air machine under its own power at Kitty Hawk, N.C.

Digging up such editorials is good clean fun, of course.  It doesn't prove anything one way or the other about the SST.  But it does make a valid point.  When we get tailor-made opinion on the scientific impossibility of coping with problems, we are well advised to hark to the experts as well as the amateurs, and we are entitled to a fair shake in getting our hands on what the experts say.

Some of the objections to the SST are deadly serious, and not to be taken lightly.  Which doesn't mean that nothing can be done about them.  Some of them are pure nonsense.  Others are irrelevant.  Meanwhile, the main reason why the aviation industry and the U.S. Department of Transportation want the SST has been reported with so little emphasis—among all that has been said—that if you know what it is you're a rare bird. Do you know why those who want it want it?

The SST certainly is *not* being promoted to make sonic booms, pollute the air, change the climate, waste money or irradiate passengers.

The latter is among the objections in the nonsense category. Radiation from space is a little more at the 65,000-foot elevations that SST's would normally fly than it is at the 35,000-foot levels of our present commercial jets. At 65,000 feet, radiation generally is almost as great as it is at ground level in New York City. New York has higher than normal ground level radiation for reasons nobody yet comprehends. Normal radiation at 65,000 feet is not as great as it is in some long-inhabited areas of South America.

There are periods when solar flares intensify the radiation in the upper atmosphere. These flares are monitored and even predicted from earth. All an SST pilot need do would be to react as you do when you see a red traffic light. He'd stop. That is, stop flying at 65,000 feet and come down to a lower level—in fact he'd be ordered to.

There is a world of experience in dealing with this. Military planes have been flying with men aboard at these altitudes and higher for close to a generation now. Our U-2 pilots logged thousands of hours at 75,000 to 80,000 feet without any radiation problem. The radiation factor is not an argument against our producing SST's, but only a warning to observe precautions that are already timeworn.

Solar flares aside, there is less radiation exposure for passengers flying the Atlantic in an SST than in one of our current commercial jets. Time is a factor of radiation exposure. A passenger on a two-and-a-half-hour SST flight from New York to London at 65,000 feet will, under normal conditions, absorb less radiation than he does today making a six-and-three-quarter-hour flight at 35,000 feet. The much shorter time of exposure more than offsets the slightly higher radiation level.

If concern about radiation is to be taken seriously, we must scrap the present planes as fast as possible and get cracking with high speed SST's so that passengers need not spend so much time at high elevations. Fortunately, the radiation in either case is usually negligible. It is easily avoidable when it is not negligible. Which is why I have labeled this as a nonsense objection against producing American SST's.

At the other extreme, the sonic boom question isn't nonsense at all. A plane flying faster than sound (and the SST's would hit top speeds not quite three times the speed of sound) makes a boom that makes a bang on land and sea below. There is no known way to prevent a plane that's flying faster than sound from making a sonic boom.

The designers, planners and proponents of the SST have been more aware of this than anyone else. The boom is a bug they can't lick entirely.

If we get our own SST's they will have to be, and will be, tightly regulated when it comes to making booms.  The regulations of SST flight proposed by the Department of Transportation are tougher than those imposed on supersonic military planes.  So when it comes to the booms that you might hear from SST's, you can say they will be scarcer and weaker than whatever booms you have been hearing from military planes.  In fact, you can expect none unless you're at sea.  This does not overcome the objection, and nothing can overcome objections to booms if there are to be booms.

SST's will be forbidden to fly at boom speeds over land in U.S. territory, and other countries have their own rules.  Planes are not being sought for strictly land routes, but only for transoceanic flight.  When and if they fly from, say, Chicago to London, they will still have a speed of advantage during the land portion of the flight of 200 to 250 mph over current commercial planes without making booms on the ground.

They will be forbidden to make booms until they are out to sea. Most of their supersonic speed will be at around 65,000 feet over water. They will not dive and maneuver like military planes.  Dives and low-level flight produce the window-breaking, dynamite-like booms that have been experienced from military planes.

It is no kindness to ships at sea to make any booms.  What kind of booms will ships hear?  Sonic booms are measured in pounds per square foot (*psf*) in excess of the existing air pressure.  A *psf* of 120 is a helluva boom.  It doesn't directly injure people but nothing else good can be said about it.  The plaster-cracking, window-shattering boom can have a *psf* as low as 10 to 20.  A diving or low-level fighter plane can produce one easily.

The SST in its level flight at its prescribed altitude will make booms of from 1.5 to 2.2 *psf* on the water below.  This is like a thunderclap from maybe half a mile away—not distant, not right on top of you.  It exerts the same *psf* that hits the ears of a Volkswagen driver when he swings his car door shut.  At one point in its climb to cruising altitude the SST will make a boom of 3.5 *psf*.  This is like a nearer thunderclap. Ships are surely going to hear these thunderclaps caused by SST's when they hit their transoceanic speeds.  It's nothing to cheer about, but neither does it seem to have been a problem of great dimension so far.  For many years military planes have been flying all the oceans at Mach 2 (scientific jargon for twice the speed of sound) without creating a maritime problem.

But let's not kiss off sonic booms.  Who wants them even if SST's won't make bad ones at sea and none over land?  The problem here is a different one.  We won't escape booms from supersonic transports by preventing the United States from developing SST's.  Britain, France and Russia are making SST's. They've flown theirs while all we have is a dummy.

U.S. and European airlines have already reserved 74 SST's from pending British and French production. Foreign-make SST's are going to be flying the oceans, and making booms over them, whether we develop our own SST's or not. If we keep American firms from making SST's we will lose the business and still get the booms. The boom question, then, is a question of regulation, and not a reason to keep us out of the SST business.

Here we get to the real reason why our aviation experts in and out of the industry want to keep going full speed on SST development.

It is purely economic.

The livelihoods of the Americans whose jobs and income depend on our aerospace industry require us to be ahead of the world in supersonic commercial jet plane design, manufacture, performance and sales in the years ahead. We cannot match the low cost of cheap labor abroad, and we live or die in business competition with the rest of the world by keeping ahead or not keeping ahead in performance.

The SST is the next generation of passenger planes. While we debate whether there should or should not be SST's, our aviation industry is already seriously behind the time schedule of foreign competitors in developing a marketable SST for the world's airlines.

We have more than a million people directly employed in the aerospace industry. We have a total of more than four million whose incomes are directly identifiable with aerospace production and sales, when we include subcontractors and suppliers who are not themselves directly a part of aerospace.

From now through the 1980's the health of the industry will depend largely on whether or not we make and sell the lion's share of the coming generation of SST passenger planes.

According to present plans, the joint British-French SST, the Concorde, will be ready for scheduled flights between 1972 and 1974. The Boeing SST, by contrast, is well behind that. It can't enter commercial service until 1978, even if it suffers no further delay.

The drawing-board Boeing is far superior to the already-flown Concorde. No airline would prefer a Concorde to a Boeing if it were offered a choice of two proven planes that meet the present specifications of each, though a Concorde would cost less. The major world airlines might sit out the four-to-six-year time difference for most of their SST purchases if they could be assured that the Boeing would be available about on target.

The Boeing's superiority is based on an American technology that cannot yet be duplicated abroad. It would cruise about 430 mph faster than the Concorde with more than twice as many passengers.

What the airlines want is more speed while carrying more passengers.

It isn't that they are concerned about saving each passenger four hours or so in crossing the Atlantic. Probably not one passenger in ten could do much with the time saved, though few would choose a seven-hour flight if a two-and-a-half-hour one were available. What interests the airlines is that a single plane could carry far more people in any given time.

A 298-passenger Boeing SST, designed to cruise at 1,780 mph, could make 27 N.Y.-London round trips in the flying time that the new Boeing 747 needs to make ten round trips at its 595 mph cruising speed. Scheduling, turnaround and on-ground factors may not allow full use of this advantage, but the first Boeing SST will probably be twice as productive in passenger haul as a 747, and later ones as much as 2½ times as productive.

Of course, this kind of SST performance represents vast operating savings for the airlines. None of them want to fly many slower planes and crews, and support terminal facilities for them, to do what a few SST's might be doing for their competitors.

This kind of performance could also do something more for passengers than save them a few hours. The economical performance of SST's would hold their air fares down. If we stay with the present planes, airline efficiency will hit a plateau. Thereafter, transoceanic air fares must rise with inflation. The better economic performance of SST's will hold fares down. For most passengers, the dollar savings in fares will probably mean more in the future than the hours saved on each trip.

The present Concorde, designed to carry 128 passengers at 1,350 mph cruising speeds, is so superior to the jets now flying that, without a Boeing SST, the world's airlines would go for Concordes, as their 74 existing orders for Concordes attest.

But it's so inferior to the Boeing's planned performance that the Concorde couldn't stand the competition of an assured Boeing SST.

Rumors keep pouring out of Europe that the Concorde will be abandoned, whether we produce a Boeing SST or not.

Rumors about multi-million-dollar projects often have multi-million-dollar motives behind them. Every fresh rumor that the Concorde will never go into full production is heralded here as proof that we don't need the Boeing SST after all, and it promotes delay in Boeing SST development. Every delay of the Boeing SST gives the Concorde's makers more time to sell the first models and more time to work on improvements that might make it more competitive with the Boeing. The British Concorde is probably quietly in production now.

Some of our own responsible people outside of the aerospace industry have taken all of this lightly. It is deadly serious (a) to the Concorde makers abroad who are proceeding with the ship in Britain and France behind the façade of rumor, and (b) to everyone whose bread and butter comes from airplane production in the United States.

The widespread public and political campaigns against the SST here are fostering near panic in our aerospace industry. The whole industry is hurting today, even though (thanks to its past technological superiority) it has previously suffered far less from foreign competition than most of our other major industries.

U.S. aerospace is now seriously depressed for a variety of reasons which may not change for the better soon, and it looks to the SST to give it the lift it needs.

Our plane-making industry was on the rise until recently. In 1968 we hit an all-time peak of 1,418,000 people directly employed in aerospace. Well over 4 million more benefited directly from subcontracting and supply orders placed with other industries. Throughout the 60's, U.S. aerospace throve (1) on its near-monopoly of free-world civilian plane sales; (2) on its space contracts for NASA; (3) on its manufacture of U.S. Air Force, Navy and Marine Corps planes and; (4) on its sales of military planes abroad.

In civilian plane sales alone we have provided very nearly all the planes flown by U.S. airlines, while 84% of all jets flown by commercial airlines in the free world today are American made.

In June of 1970, those directly employed were down to 1,160,000. Some 258,000 jobs had disappeared in a little over a year. Cities like Seattle, Los Angeles, Wichita, Dallas and Fort Worth suddenly suffered widespread unemployment.

By next March, the outlook is that another 174,000 jobs in the industry will have disappeared. With each job that goes, roughly three people in subcontracting and supply firms lose work due to the disappearance of aerospace orders.

The industry had been doing better than ever in the sale of civilian planes here and abroad until just recently, when, unfortunately, it needed to do better yet.

We sold $3.2 billion worth of commercial planes in 1966—with about $1 billion in sales overseas. In 1969, we hit a high of $5.6 billion, with almost $2 billion in foreign sales.

Since then a series of blows has struck the industry.

Commercial plane orders of current jets slipped off because of internal crises in the airlines.

Our government cut back both its military and its space-program orders.

National policy dictated that we not sell military planes to aggressive small countries abroad. The French moved into that market. With assured sales left them by our moving out of the picture, they have now produced a better small fighter for small nations' purposes.

Today, South American countries no longer buy any U.S. combat planes. They get them chiefly from France.

Readers may applaud or condemn these losses of military and space orders, as they choose. For our aerospace industry they mean that the bread and butter of millions of Americans must depend more than ever on holding and enlarging the commercial plane market.

But in the commercial field we have been losing ground in the foreign airlines markets even when we get the business. The trouble is that jets that fly slower than sound are beginning to respond to the law of diminishing economic returns for us. Even when we bring out a better subsonic jet, there's less of it that's brand new. More of it can be made abroad by firms that have caught up with the American technology that first developed today's basic models.

What has been happening is that when McDonnell-Douglas gets a contract to provide planes for Canada, Canada stipulates that she'll make the wings and tail. When Lockheed signs an order to supply planes for British airlines, Britain stipulates that she'll install Rolls-Royce engines in them—and so on. In short, there's less work for the U.S. plane-makers even when they get foreign orders.

The same thing applies to replacement parts of existing models, which are a good part of the business. As fast as they can, other industrial countries learn to make their own parts for older model planes that they buy from us.

Even if nobody makes an SST, this will only get worse. If the whole world freezes commercial plane performance at about the level of the present 595 mph Boeing 747, it will only be a matter of time before other countries, with cheaper labor, will provide equivalent planes cheaper for their airlines *and ours.* All they need is time to catch up with American know-how, if the march of our know-how is willfully arrested.

They are catching up fast. This October a consortium of European nations was reported to be dealing with Britain for trade favors, in return for which they'd stop buying General Electric jet engines in favor of all British engines on their airlines.

They'll not only catch up, but they'll get ahead of us too, if we willfully check our own progress and they don't.

The first pilot model Concorde flew in March 1969. It broke the sound barrier that October. This Oct. 10, a Concorde hit 1,320 mph in level course flight.

The Russian TU-144 made its maiden flight on Dec. 31, 1968. It broke the sound barrier in June 1969 and hit 1,336 mph last May. The Soviets expect the first one to be carrying 120 passengers at a top speed of 1,550 mph in 1972. There's good evidence that Russia is bidding for world markets in a big way.

The 298-passenger, 1,780 mph Boeing exists only in the form of a full-scale mock-up in the huge workrooms of the Boeing Seattle plant. If that's where it stops we will be in the industry-wide position that Henry Ford was in when he stuck to his Model T into the late 1920's after his competitors had passed him by in making good, low-priced cars. Henry had to close shop and start all over, and Ford hasn't regained its one-time lead over General Motors since. When the first Concorde flies an ocean with paying passengers, our new 747 will become a Model T of intercontinental flight.

The catastrophe that awaits us if we pull a Model T performance in plane-making will go far beyond the total depression of our aircraft industry.

That industry has been pulling more than its weight in holding up our balance of trade with other nations and in checking the disastrous flow of American dollars abroad.

Let's not review the ground we've lost to foreign competition in the auto, the movie, the camera and the huge electronics industries—as well as steel, textiles and many others—both at home and abroad. In 1970, the details read like a funeral dirge.

Plane-making has been perhaps the brightest spot in this whole picture. Consider that if our $5.6 billion trade in commercial plane sales in 1969 had gone to foreign firms the United States would have lost another $11.2 billion in both trade balance and dollar flow—from $5.6 billion in to $5.6 billion out. The best present estimates of what we'll lose as a nation in trade balance and outward dollar flow, if the Concorde flies and the Boeing doesn't, run as high as $50 billion between 1978 and 1990.

Had enough? These are the reasons why those who want the Boeing SST want it, and to say more about why would belabor the point.

We Americans can only live at our living standard if we keep ahead in technology, and constantly offer the rest of the world better products than it can make.

That's what we bet on when we joined the other nations in a series of long-term agreements to do away with protective tariffs. The other nations bet that they could manufacture existing products cheaper than we could. And they can. We bet that we could make what they couldn't. And we can if we will.

When we could make electronics products that they couldn't, we owned the world electronics market. But given a few years for them to study our products, we could no longer rule the mass electronics market. By 1972, inroads made chiefly by Japan and West Germany will see us with an unfavorable balance of trade in electronic products.

The Boeing SST may be late on the scene, compared to the Concorde; but if it moves on schedule it will rule the roost for years.

Britain and France built their huge investment in the Concorde around an aluminum technology.  They designed it for about the top speed that an aluminum fuselage can endure, due to the heat of air friction.

That speed is about 1,350 mph for safe cruising and up to 1,550 mph for short bursts only, under favorable conditions.  The Soviets went the whole limit and gave their TU-144 a capability of 1,550 mph.  It will hardly ever do that, because it cannot safely do it for long.

In both cases these foreign planes went right to the limit of the known technology, which is probably why their makers dared challenge the American giant.  And of course they worked out all their systems, design and power plants for the speeds they had in mind.

But if we were slower, one reason was that we were developing a titanium technology for fuselages and structure that can stand far greater air-friction heat.  We have the technology today.  We have used it in two military models.  Nobody else has it in such shape as to project mass airplane production on a titanium fuselage base.

Some day it will be copied, if anyone dares sink all that capital in another attempt to get ahead of us.  All of our SST basic research and development has moved ahead with an over-1700 mph plane in mind, and a technological ceiling of above 2,000 mph.

Boeing got the official nod as the chief plane designer and producer.

GE has been developing the powerful engines.  Various work and research has been parceled out from time to time to such firms as Aerojet General, Avco, Fairchild Hiller, LTV Aerospace, Northrop, North American Rockwell, Rohr, Garrett, Goodyear, Uniroyal, Bendix, Hamilton Standard, Litton Industries and Sperry.  Others will enter the field in time.  McDonnell-Douglas ought to be one such, as it rates high in titanium technology.


If this is a formidable array of lobbyists for the SST (and it is) it is also an array of those who employ the bulk of the millions whose livelihood depends on American plane production and sales.  The technology they are working on would virtually force the Concorde to start over.

It is interesting to note the objection made to the SST to the effect that the large sums of government money needed to help underwrite the development are needed instead for poverty programs.

It is estimated that it will take a little over $1.6 billion to make and test our prototype Boeing SST.  Boeing and GE (the major contractors) would put up about $300 million between them, the airlines would put up about $60 million and the government would advance close to $1.3 billion.  Still more will be needed to get full production under way.

About $1 billion has already been spent, and of course Congress doesn't switch money from plane production to poverty programs. It treats them separately.

More to the point was an article in the *Harvard Business Review* by the mayor of St. Louis a year or so ago, discussing St. Louis' terrible poverty problems. McDonnell-Douglas, a major St. Louis employer and a major U.S. plane-maker, was held up as a fine example of an industry which restyled its jobs and its production methods in order to employ more unskilled labor in St. Louis. One need only walk among the laid off workers in the many U.S. cities that are hurt by the aerospace cutbacks to get it from them that what hurts aerospace makes poverty grow.

"The SST will make and save full production jobs in the late 1970's and the 1980's," says William Magruder, former test pilot and Lockheed executive who now heads up the Department of Transportation's special SST division. "Our present poverty situation is aggravated because somebody failed to look ahead in the 1950's and 1960's. The SST looks ahead to jobs in the 1980's, and if we'll do more of that in industry today we'll have less poverty then."

The SST is still moving ahead in Seattle and elsewhere today, and employing thousands of workers who'll lose their jobs if Congress turns thumbs down on continued SST development.

The basic SST contracts between Boeing, GE and the government provide that the government will get its development investment back with the sale of the 300th Boeing SST. If 500 are sold—as expected— the government will directly profit $1.1 billion from its investment. Somebody has guesstimated that employment on the SST, if it goes ahead full steam, will net between $6 and $7 billion in income taxes. How they do this arithmetic I don't know, but anyone would agree that the tax revenues from the billions of aerospace income from SST's would be plenty.

One SST will cost an airline about $52 million at 1978 prices, compared to $24 million for a Boeing 747 today and more in 1978. Sale of 500 SST's would involve a gross initial cost of $26 billion to the airlines.* Overseas routes for 500 in the 1980's have already been projected, which explains how the sponsors hit on the 500 figure.

Since commercial flight began, plane owners have consistently recaptured the cost of a new plane in five to six years.

The role of the airlines is ambiguous. As businesses, they'd rather use and wear out their present equipment than invest immediately in a new generation of passenger planes. If the world's airlines were one cartel, they'd probably quietly agree among themselves not to use any SST's for a long time, and let the aerospace industry worry about its own problems.

---

* For simplicity, we pretend that the airlines buy the planes themselves. Actually, they are sometimes financed by pools of large investors and rented to the airlines.

But the facts of life are that our antitrust laws forbid any such conspiracy here, while the foreign airlines hope to get the transoceanic business with Concordes if they can.

Conceding that a good SST would be the superior competitive plane, our airlines don't dare stay with 747's once BOAC, Air France, *et al.*, or their own American rivals, are offering 1,350 mph flights over the seas. You *can* stick with the Model T, but only if your competitors don't go you one better.

So our overseas airlines are going along on both sides of the SST fence, while worrying chiefly that they haven't yet paid for their 747's. They are reserving Concordes in order to be able to compete as soon as European lines are flying them, and reserving and investing in Boeing's too. Ten airlines have put up $60 million for Boeing development, which may be credited to future purchases. Twenty-six of them have deposited $22.4 million as down payments to reserve 122 Boeing SST's when and if they are produced on schedule.

In official expressions, recognizing the facts of life, airline presidents have said they are for the Boeing SST and want to be sure it's a good one.

This about sums up the factual situation that foreign competition makes SST's a dead certainty, and our debate is really about whether we should willfully deprive ourselves of the business. It's the story of the small fighter plane all over again. We didn't prevent little nations from buying combat planes when we refused to sell them, we just sent the business to France.

This does not dispose of various objections dealing with air pollution, noise pollution, and various claimed damaging effects in the upper atmosphere—from destroying the ozone shield to altering the climate.

These objections have a high emotional content, and some of them a fear content. It is extremely difficult to find a factual basis for them except for some truths that are out of proportion to their conclusions. Several of them are of this sort: "Arsenic is poison. There is arsenic in sea water. So sea water will give you arsenic poisoning." It will not, because the volume of water you'd have to drink would kill you first.

Predictions that SST's would alter the climate claim that the moisture left in vapor trails at 65,000 feet would remain there and accumulate a cloud level over the earth in time. There are no known facts to support such a prediction. SST's can hardly ever produce vapor trails when cruising at 65,000 feet. One severe thunderstorm can deposit as much water in the stratosphere as 400 SST's flying four transoceanic flights, and there have been up to 6,000 thunderstorms a day for untold millions of years.

By the same token, there is no basis in known fact for the allegation that water deposited at high altitudes by SST's could destroy the ozone layer, which acts as a shield to keep out damaging ultra-violet rays from the sun.  Again, the insignificance of SST water contributions to the total vastness of the atmosphere allows no such prediction.  The problem has been carefully studied.  In the absence of any evidence supporting such allegations the studies continue, however, since the subject is not a trivial one even if the supporting evidence for the charges is lacking.

Since amateurs are sounding off on these subjects every day, the public is at least entitled to access to the following expert opinion released by the Department of Transportation:

"Two scientific groups—The National Research Council of the National Academy of Sciences, and the Office of Meteorological Research —have studied the situation and report that there will be no appreciable disturbance of the earth's normal atmospheric balance by a fleet of SST's making 1,600 flights per day."

How about ordinary pollution by smoke, hydrocarbons and other exhaust pollutants?  Jet engines don't pollute as much as internal combustion engines.  The latest jet engines have smokeless burners that reduce emissions for ground operations by 70% for smoke particles and by 45% for smog ingredients.  The SST's will have better pollution control equipment, since the latest in pollution-control design will be engineered into them from the start.

A Boeing SST fully loaded, going at top speed, will be the polluting equivalent of three cars doing 60 mph.  If the maximum of 500 planned Boeings were all flying at once, they'd pollute the world's atmosphere about as much as the next 1,500 cars to pass on your nearest thruway, and far less than the more numerous slower planes they'd replace.

Present Boeing design suggests that one Boeing SST will make a little more sideline noise on runways and takeoff than a 707 or 747.  Boeing engineers are betting that with eight years to work on it their intensive research into noise control will make the SST as "quiet" as (i.e.: no more noisy than) any other jetliner.  But the present design is noisier.

SST's should relieve airport and airways congestion.  They'll fly far above the presently-used air lanes, and, like the 747, permit more passengers to be moved on fewer flights.  Such haul capacity may become absolutely necessary the way public air travel keeps growing.

But both the pros and cons of these sidelight issues are not part of the essential case for the SST.  The economic meaning of the big ships to 4 million Americans and our total economy is the big case for the SST.

# The case against the SST

## charles h. percy

**Senator Charles H. Percy lays out the case against the SST in the following statement, which he presented during the SST debates in the Senate in December 1970.**

MR. PERCY. Mr. President, today I wish to address myself to various aspects of the Government's role in financing the development of the supersonic transport.

First, however, I suggest putting the SST into historical perspective. When the House Committee on Science and Astronautics considered the SST back in 1960, and recommended its development, our national attitude toward technological progress was very different from what it is now. In 1960 we were only 3 years past sputnik, and all over the country we had been working to make science a priority concern. Largely in reaction to the Soviets having put a satellite in orbit, we agonizingly reexamined our schools to find out why children were not growing up to be more scientifically literate. We developed new science courses for the schools, and we put more money into college-level science research. We accelerated the space program, and established the man on the moon goal, which we recently attained.

In the early sixties we glorified the entire range of technological achievements typified by the space program. It was not surprising that the SST was given the go-ahead, because it was regarded as another potentially elegant American technological achievement—in the same class with satellites and moon rockets. When President Kennedy in 1963 asked the Congress to approve the project, he said that the SST would "demonstrate the technological accomplishments which can be achieved under a democratic, free enterprise system," and that the SST would "advance the frontiers of technical knowledge."

At that time these goals seemed reasonable. By 1970, however, we have accomplished great technological feats and reaped appropriate credit. In comparison with putting men on the moon, the SST is small potatoes, and everybody knows it. For several years the U.S. Air Force has had in routine operation, a fleet of supersonic—mach 3—SR-71

U. S., Cong., Senate, *Congressional Record*, 91st Cong., 2nd sess., December 2, 1970, Vol. 116, pp. 19176–19182.

reconnaissance aircraft which fly higher and faster than the designs of the SST. But we are still grappling with an SST program. Although much money has been spent on the program, we now have an advantage in our decision making, because much more is known about the type of aircraft that will result from the program, about its environmental effects and its economic prospects. We are also not making decisions in the emotional, science-at-any-cost atmosphere of the early 1960's. We are trying to weigh the costs of the SST, in dollars and in environmental degradation, against the benefits claimed for the program. It would be well, therefore, for us to focus on some of the financial implications of the SST development program.

## THE FEDERAL ROLE IN FINANCING DEVELOPMENT

In the SST program the Government has undertaken to finance the development of a private civil aircraft, which is to be sold in a competitive open market. How well does the program stand up to the criteria of private capitalism? Ordinarily, a business concern looks for a market, and then builds the product to fill that demand. The free enterprise system has a built-in system of incentives that keep the entrepreneur aware, every step of the way, of the risks he is taking, and in the most realistic terms, aware of the market outlook for his product. If he has a product that looks like a poor seller, he will have difficulty raising the capital to produce it, because a commitment to a poor or risky product denies investors the chance to invest in a more certain and more profitable one. He commits his limited resources to a product whose success he can reasonably predict, not one whose success depends on a chain of tenuous assumptions and involves unduly high risks.

In the case of the SST, the Government assumed both roles—entrepreneur and investor. As William Magruder, director of SST development, has stated in hearings before the Appropriations Committee, the Government initiated the project and took it to the corporations on a contract basis. The project thus became a sure thing for the companies that are building the SST; they do not have to worry about the risk, or about the alternatives to which they could apply their time and money. If they do what they agreed to do under the contract, they get paid. However, there are no performance guarantees. Thus, for the life of the prototype program, the contractors need not concern themselves about the market for their product. They have a guaranteed market, consisting of the Government. They chip in 10 percent of the costs, and the Government pays the rest.

## LACK OF INCENTIVES FOR SUCCESS

Because of this, the usual incentives that make a business venture constantly adjust itself to the market outlook are absent. This accounts for what appears to be a lack of concern with the SST engine, which Aviation Economist George Eads termed "a marginal performer." Lack of the market incentive makes it possible for SST proponents to promise noise-reduction devices, because they can ignore the outcome Dr. Eads cited—that the engines "cannot bear the weight or thrust penalties that would be imposed in order to conform to any reasonable noise standards." Engines large enough to produce the required take-off thrust and support noise suppressors would penalize the aircraft unacceptably in payload and range.

This is only one symptom of the general problem—that a Government R. & D. program is not a trustworthy place to build an airplane that has to survive the market test. Our history with military aircraft bears this out. As long as the military purpose of a plane was more important than its costs, Government R. & D. worked fairly well. But only one American military plane had even modest success in commercial aviation—the Boeing Stratocruiser. The rest could not compete because the high costs made them unfeasible for commercial service. For instance, Lockheed went to the expense of having the C-141 cargo aircraft certificated by the FAA for commercial service, but none has been sold for that purpose. Other aircraft developed for commercial service, such as the DC-6 and the Boeing 707, had military predecessors. But Government-funded development has not been a source of viable commercial planes.

I would like to interject here that I have discussed the matter with officials of the Department of Defense, and various officials in the Air Force and the other services to see whether or not there is any military need for the SST. If it is commercially feasible for us to fly passengers or cargo at that rate of speed, the military, certainly, which never holds back on its requirements or needs, might have a comparable use. There is simply no possibility that the military will underwrite a penny of this cost. There is no military use. They cannot afford the low ratio of payload to high cost to move men and materials any place in the world to wage war or for the purposes of defense.

I maintain if it is not worth it to the Pentagon, it is hardly feasible to the commercial airlines which now have an 80 percent debt ratio and can hardly afford purchases of the 747 much less the SST.

We are not talking only about the costs of development. We are talking about the cost of underwriting preproduction and produc-

tion.  The deeper we get into this quicksand, the more difficult it will
be to extract ourselves.

. . .

## UNCRITICAL MANAGEMENT

Can we substitute a careful Government watchdog function for these
market incentives?  Apparently not, to judge from the vigor with
which the Department of Transportation has assumed the advocate's
role in the SST matter.  Ordinarily, we might expect the Department to
carefully scrutinize this program.  Instead, we find that the scrutiny is
mainly concentrated on responses to those aspects of the SST that have
become public issues.  The fact that the SST was going to be so noisy
that airport operators might ban it somehow escaped the attention of
the Department of Transportation until a few weeks ago, when it decided the subject needed further study and announced a multimillion-
dollar research program.

Another symptom of the preference for advocacy rather than critical
analysis was the 1966 feasibility study of the SST program, done by the
Federal Aviation Administration.  The frequently cited prediction that
500 SST's could be sold comes from that report, and it was based on
the assumption by the FAA that passengers value the time saved on an
SST flight at one and a half times their earnings per hour.  When the
Institute for Defense Analysis studied the SST market for the FAA and
offered a prediction that, at $40 million apiece, only 366 SST's would
be sold by 1990, the FAA was not satisfied.

. . .

MR. COOK.  Mr. President, . . .  Some people have tried to convince
me to vote for the SST on the theory that the Government is going to
get its money back.  I think we are being very foolish if we think the
U.S. Government is going to get a return on its money on a project that
private bankers and financial lending institutions believe is a money
loser.

MR. PROXMIRE.  Mr. President, if the Senator will permit me to comment on that, because that is an excellent point, I overlooked in my
response to the Senator from Illinois, the fact that there can be overruns, and big ones.  We get overruns any time we get into big technology problems.  This is not a question of using simple metals.  There
is involved in this U.S. SST a brand new metal, brushed titanium honey-
comb, an exotic metal, not used before.  So when we get into these
new materials, overruns are common.

The Government, as the Senator from Kentucky has pointed out, has
not a chance to get its money back.

MR. PERCY.   Mr. President, may I respond to both of my colleagues on that particular point?   I took it on myself to speak on the Concorde program not only in this country, but in England, to the best experts I could find.

Mr. Magruder has the responsibility of selling this program to the Congress and to the country for the administration.   He came to my office and I said:

> I would like to offer this proposition to you.   Let us forget all the environmental factors for a moment—factors which I do not think we can forget except in theory—and get down to dollars and cents.   Let us assume I would be willing to put in a piece of legislation to make the airlines and the aircraft manufacturers and everyone else absolutely whole on this project.   I would be willing to sponsor legislation that would free them from any obligation to pay the Government back a penny of the money it has already spent.   In fact, I would not only free the airlines of the $700 million obligation for funds the Government has already put in, but another $100 million in addition.   I would be willing to sweeten the pot and put in another $100 million so that the airlines would have $1 billion even if you get the Government out of this program, so we can make a rational decision on the basis of whether or not it is economical to go ahead with the SST project and whether the economic opportunities are such as to make it worth while, even if you have to pull it out of landing at Los Angeles and New York.

On the basis of this proposition, I asked Mr. Magruder:

> Would the aircraft companies and banks pick up the remaining balance of $300 million, freeing them to put up their own money for the purpose of developing an economically viable project?

I have already gone to some banks and airlines and suggested this.

Mr. Magruder reported back that he had contacted investment companies and there was absolutely no interest expressed on the part of any banking or investment firm, regardless of how large a consortium might be involved, in putting one single penny of private interest money into this project, even with the incentive that they would be free from obligation to pay this money back.

I simply ask now, if the airlines and the manufacturers and the banks will not finance it, why then stick the customer—the taxpayer—with these enormous costs in order that a businessman might save a couple of hours, two or three times a year, when he flies to London, especially when that same businessman often cannot in less than 3 hours commuting time get from his home to work and back every single working day of the week?

Now, to me, that just does not make any sense whatsoever but a lot of things in Government do not make sense.   What we are trying to do is make sense out of these programs on the Senate floor through a rational analysis of prospects for payback for the country, for the tax-payers, and for the public generally—not for a very small specific group who might stand to benefit somewhat by the SST.

. . .

MR. COOK.   Mr. President, I would like to add one more thing, if I may. Let us suppose the Federal Government does realize a small return on its money.   Are we going to figure into this project the costs that the Federal Government is going to have to pay to develop local airports along the east coast and west coast of the United States in preparation for this aircraft?   Are we going to have to pay local communities for the sound abatement equipment that will be necessary, if we can convince them to adapt their local facilities for the utilization of these aircraft?   If we are going to have to pay for those things—and obviously we are—should not these costs also be included in the total amount that the Federal Government must expend on this questionable project?   Or will these other development costs come before the Senate in another appropriation bill?

In order to determine whether the project is profitable, I think we must look at the whole ledger.   If we are going to look at it like a business proposition in order to determine what amount of money will be returned, then we must take into account all the airport modifications that will have to be made.

There is one other question that should be raised.   Were any Federal funds of any kind put into the 747 program?   I think the answer is no. They knew it was an economically viable aircraft, and thus the free-enterprise system put its money and talents into it.   They did not ask for a dime of public money.

. . .

MR. GOLDWATER. . . . Again I ask my friend from Illinois, what is different about building an airplane from what this Government has been building, ever since it became a government, for transportation?

MR. PERCY.   I shall be happy to reply.   If I may quote from a well-known book, "The Conscience of a Conservative," there is a growing tendency on the part of the Federal Government to get into more and more and more fields, and we do have to start drawing the line.

I would certainly say we ought to draw the line where it makes no sense whatsoever, on any basis, to go into a program—particularly when that program stands to benefit only the top 1 or 2 percent of the population.   That ought to be a clear-cut case where we can draw the line.   If a proposal is merely going to benefit either the high-income people who can afford to go around the world, or businessmen who have expense accounts and can afford to get to London or wherever they are going regardless of cost, then I think we ought to draw the line there, and tell them that they ought to have what commercial aviation can provide to them.

But when the Federal Government goes into and subsidizes such programs, and leaves the low-income people in my city of Chicago, for example, without adequate transportation because a transit system is going broke with a $25-million loss this year, and increases every year or two in rates for mass transit force the low-income people completely out of access to mass transit, I would say the priorities are entirely out of line and we ought to try to find a way to help the lower income people, rather than cater to a very small fringe group at the top.

And as I ask, even for that group, what sense does it make to try to save them a few hours at such a cost? I have just come from a trip that took me all over Africa and Europe, and I could not figure out at all where the SST would have benefited me on the long flights I took, from Helsinki to Addis Ababa in Ethiopia, and Nigeria, and all the way up to London. What time could I have saved? They could not have made those flights nonstop, because their range is so short. They could not have gone over land areas; they would have had to go out to sea. I do not know whether the city of London would have even let the plane land.

With that kind of rationale facing me, I cannot possibly see why the Federal Government or the Federal Treasury should invest in such a program. It really astounds me that an outspoken and articulate conservative could argue that as long as the Federal Government is in all these other things, why not let them get into this other element?

Let them get into everything, then. I just cannot see the sense of it.

MR. GOLDWATER. If the Senator will yield further, it makes sense to me, for one good reason. I do not say that the airlines need this airplane today or tomorrow.

MR. PERCY. If they had it, it would break them.

MR. GOLDWATER. Maybe not even in 1980. But some day, some airline in this country, in answer to competition which will develop overseas, will ask somebody for an SST, and we will not have it.

The only industry in which this country leads the world is the aircraft industry. The Senator wonders why a conservative like myself would see sense to this proposition. I see a return on it. I do not see returns from some of the investments we have made, in canals and highways, and so on; but I think in this case, whether we are talking about the supersonic transport or what, the fallout will be of tremendous value to this country, just as from the $28 billion we have spent on space. The fallout from this program, I am sure, will be, as I have stated before, more than $28 billion within the next 5 years.

Either we are going to have this airplane or someone else is going to have it. I imagine the same arguments were made when Henry

Ford started to make automobiles. I imagine the same arguments were made about the subways, and about trolley cars. Here we are looking at something the world is going to have, whether we vote for it in the Senate or not. The world someday will have SST. Not today, not tomorrow, but it is coming, just as sure as we stand here arguing about it.

I understand thoroughly the Senator's objection to this. I respect it. I know that he has tremendous background in the fields that can give him the answers to this. But I have to say that I think we are going to make a tremendous mistake, and I think everyone in this Chamber will live to regret having denied this country continued leadership in the one industry in which we still retain leadership.

. . .

MR. PERCY. . . . Mr. President, now, in the few minutes remaining to me, I should like to complete my prepared remarks, picking up where I mentioned that the Institute for Defense Analysis studied the SST market for the FAA and offered a prediction that, at $40 million apiece, only 366 SST's would be sold by 1990, a prediction which left the FAA unsatisfied. The FAA threw out the passenger preference function the consultants had used in their calculations—a figure indicating that passengers value travel time at the same dollar value as their earnings per hour. FAA asked the airlines for their estimate of this function, and the airlines responded with a rough estimate that passengers valued travel time at twice their earnings per hour. The FAA's report states:

> It is evident from comments received from the airlines that the consultants' estimate is probably based on inadequate data.

The FAA then split the differences, and, using a figure of 1.5, came up with the optimistic assumption that 500 SST's could be sold. A later detailed study showed, however, that business travelers value their air travel time at 0.4 times the hourly family income, and that pleasure travelers value theirs at zero. Since approximately 30 percent of transatlantic air travel is pleasure travel, this throws more serious doubt on the 500-plane market.

The same undemanding attitude of the Department of Transportation is shown by the fact that the prototypes we are being asked to buy are not really very much like the production models already designed. For example, the prototype would be 57 tons lighter in weight than the production specifications and would have many parts made of aluminum, instead of the titanium to be used in production models. As a result, the test flights will not be indicative of the true operating characteristics that will make or break the SST as a commercial airplane.

. . .

Mr. President, with the trouble the airlines are having in financing the airplanes they have in a highly commercial viable market, how are we ever going to finance the operations?

## NEED FOR GOVERNMENT CAPITAL

The only justification cited by SST proponents for massive Federal appropriations is the lack of private capital.  Mr. Magruder testified in hearings before the Appropriations Committee that—

> The size of the financial burden exceeds the capabilities of any single or joint private U.S. industrial aerospace concern.

This is true enough.  But in a venture of this magnitude a business concern never relies on its own capital:  It borrows the money.  So it is immaterial whether the aircraft companies have the money.  Funds are available to underwrite good business ventures.  The automobile industry, for example, is able every year to get the $500 million needed to finance its model changes.

. . .

Mr. President, the real reason for this reliance on Government capital may be found in the 1966 feasibility report, which concluded:

> The financial requirements of the program are many times as large as any past commercial aircraft development, and are beyond the financial capability of private industry and the normal credit channels, especially for a program characterized by such high risk.

I think it is clearly the high risk, which DOT did not mention in its testimony this year, that is at the heart of the matter.  If the SST were as sure an investment as the DOT witnesses would like us to believe, then private capital would be available.

Since there are many risks involved, many known disadvantages and limited benefits to be gained, the Government should take its money elsewhere, to some of the programs which unquestionably are needed now.

## PRODUCTION FINANCING

Quite aside from the development phase of the SST program, it is not clear that private investors will finance the production phase, which is where the repayment of Government funds is supposed to begin.  If private financing does not materialize, the Government would have a choice between dropping the program and forgetting the more than

$1.7 billion spent on development, or spending more money to get production under way.

The intention of DOT is clear enough—to secure private capital for production. However, Mr. Magruder testified on August 27 that no financing plan will be available until June 30, 1972. That, of course, is of little help to us in making a decision in the fall of 1970. The witness did not volunteer that the due date of the required financing plan has been slipped repeatedly by the Government from the original contract date of mid-1968.

The 1966 feasibility report, which was so certain of success on other aspects of the SST, expressed some uncertainty on production financing. "The engine manufacturer," the study concluded, "could develop the necessary financial support." But the airplane manufacturer—Boeing—was another story. Even then Boeing was at work on the financial plan, which is now not to be available until 1972. After surveying the possible sources of financing, the feasibility report concluded:

> In any event, one solution, which would cover all or any part of this financing deficiency, is feasible: The Government could act as a guarantor of the funds required.

I serve as a member of the Subcommittee on Economy in Government of the Joint Economic Committee. In May 1970 we convened hearings on Federal transportation expenditures. One of the witnesses was the Under Secretary of Transportation, James Beggs. Asked by Chairman Proxmire whether the Government would get involved in the production financing, Mr. Beggs replied:

> Mr. Chairman, I am on record, as I think Mr. Yates stated, in the Appropriations Committee with the statement that while I was of the opinion that private financing would be available, if it were not at that time and if felt that we had a successful SST program on our hands—that is, a successful transport after the prototype testing—and it required some government guaranteed loans, then I would think that we would so recommend.

And how much would that cost? The minimum estimate is in the FAA feasibility report, which cited a financing requirement of $1.064 billion for Boeing's part of the operation. Mr. Beggs told the subcommittee $1 billion would be needed. Other witnesses thought $5 to $7 billion would be involved.

One airline executive said that if 500 planes need to be produced to break even on the project, then an estimated investment of $50 million in each plane would require $20 to $25 billion total financing by an industry that already has an 80 percent debt to total capital ratio. His summation of the prospects: "Impossible."

And let us remember recent history.  After financing both development and production of the VC-10 and Super VC-10, Great Britain exported only seven of the airplanes—two to Ghana Airways and five to East Africa Airways.  When you start bypassing the built-in incentives of the market economy, you have to expect trouble in getting into the market.

## ENVIRONMENTAL COSTS

In addition to the economic costs, we must consider the substantial environmental costs of the SST program, which do not enter the economic calculations directly.

The noise produced by the SST on takeoff would add to the problems of the already beleaguered airport operators, and inflict major new annoyances and health hazards on families near airports.

Lawrence Moss, an engineer who spoke on behalf of the Sierra Club before the Appropriations Committee, said that at an airport having 100 SST takeoffs per day, the noise exposure index would exceed 30 as far as 9 miles away from the airport.  More recently, Mr. Moss has published calculations and maps showing very large areas of New York, San Francisco, Los Angeles, Seattle, Boston, Honolulu, and Anchorage with noise exposure index above 30, as a consequence of the estimated number of SST operations from those cities.  The Department of Transportation recommends that for noise exposure greater than 30, "new, single-dwelling construction should generally be avoided.".  Schools, hospitals, churches, theaters, and auditoriums are stated to be incompatible with this noise level.

These figures are independent of the "sideline noise" and "community noise" figures that have been in dispute.  The President's Council on Environmental Quality also told the Subcommittee on Economy in Government that the noise problem was serious and had not yet been solved.  DOT, to be sure, belatedly launched a study and appointed an advisory board on noise, but it is clearly far from overcoming the problem.

The sonic boom has not yet been adequately dealt with by the Department of Transportation.  It has proposed a Federal aviation regulation to ban civil aircraft sonic booms, except for those necessary for aircraft development.  But it has failed to respond to the Senate Appropriations Committee's year-old request for draft legislation to ban the sonic boom.  This can only lend credence to fears that if the SST were to enter commercial service, the FAA would alter the regulation to permit overland supersonic flights.

Testimony by the Council on Environmental Quality raised the possibility of climatic change as a result of high-altitude exhaust emissions by a fleet of SST's.  This possibility was later substantiated by a MIT study of critical environmental problems.  Recently, Myron Tribus, Assistant Secretary of Commerce and head of an advisory committee to the Office of Supersonic Transport Development, attempted to allay concern about such an outcome.  However, his statement failed to address the basic finding of the MIT group—that stratospheric smog, consisting of both gases and particles, would be created that would raise the stratosphere's temperature by 6 to 7 degrees.  The MIT group, comprising some of our Nation's leading scientists in this field, did not know what the surface effect might be.  Yet, the SST prototype program cannot and need not help us on this point, because scientists can test the atmospheric hypotheses using balloons, high-altitude U-2 aircraft and military supersonics.  I think we should know the effects on the atmosphere before we commit ourselves further.

A further environmental problem concerns the excessive fuel consumption of the SST—according to one account, twice the fuel per passenger-mile of a 747.  At a time when fuel is being depleted very rapidly, it would be ill advised to initiate a mode of transportation that will waste fuel at this rate.

## STOP FUNDING THE SST

The environmental and economic implications of the SST program add up to one conclusion:  It is time to stop Federal funding of the SST.

We have so many social and environmental programs that are underfunded that I do not think we can justify, to ourselves or to the American people, further expenditures on the SST program.  At best, the SST will not produce the benefits claimed for it.  At worst, it will require a commitment of $3 billion or $4 billion more in tax dollars needed elsewhere, and result in environmental degradation and the waste of natural resources.  I strongly urge that the SST program be terminated.

Before closing, I should like to bring to the attention of my colleagues a thoughtful memorandum on the SST program prepared by James H. Douglas, who was Secretary of the Air Force and Deputy Secretary of Defense in the Eisenhower administration. . . .

### Funding the Supersonic Transport Prototypes
### James H. Douglas

Congress is presently faced with the Administration's recommendation to appropriate $290 million to continue the SST program, including the construction of two supersonic transport prototypes by Boeing.

Today one reads in the press and hears on television that we must go ahead with building the Boeing SST prototype as:

1. Not to do so will result in our losing preeminence in building advanced aircraft;
2. Not to do so will result in the airlines of the world buying the British-French Concorde or the Russian airplane which is similar to the Concorde; and
3. Not to do so will result in loss of our export market in air transport aircraft and a serious adverse effect on our balance of payments.

It seems to be assumed that if we are willing to spend the money a satisfactory supersonic transport will be built, and that if we do not push ahead with Boeing the airlines of the world will be flying the Concorde. The natural enthusiasm of air frame and engine contractors and subcontractors, associations of commerce, and many members of Congress for a program bound up with national prestige seems to obscure several basic considerations:

1. It is generally agreed that the sonic boom of supersonic transports now planned or being flown will require a prohibition against their flying across the continental United States or other inhabited areas at supersonic speeds.
2. The Concorde and the Russian SST require the use of afterburner for takeoff, and this raises the noise level on takeoff far above anything tolerated at present and well above an acceptable level. It seems probable that FAA and airport authorities may not permit these aircraft to use our airports unless their noise problem is solved, and solution of this problem is not just around the corner.
3. The international and domestic airlines are staggering under the burden of acquiring and operating a new generation of immense jet aircraft. The economic problems of this task should preclude any early production of an American SST for the limited use that is presently foreseen for such an aircraft. Industry needs and economics, and not Government promotion, should determine when to undertake construction of SST prototypes.

. . .

Chicago doesn't do too badly on [the] map, but what it doesn't show is the noise of SST's landing or taking off. The takeoff noise is said to equal that of about 10 of today's jets, all roaring at once.

Both Los Angeles and New York are saying they won't even let the SST's land at their airports. Chicago should do the same about O'Hare. SST traffic in and out of O'Hare would make the present jet traffic sound like mosquitoes buzzing.

. . .

# Stopping the SST is a grave mistake

## richard m. nixon

**President Richard M. Nixon commented as follows on the action taken by the Senate in December 1970 to withhold funding for the SST.**

The action of the U.S. Senate in disapproving the SST is a devastating mistake both because of its immediate impact and because it will have profound long-range consequences for this country. I urge both Houses of Congress to reverse this action.

Because of our transition from a wartime to a peacetime economy we are experiencing substantial unemployment in the aerospace industry. The Senate's action means the loss of at least 150,000 jobs in that and other industries.

Another immediate impact results from waste. The SST prototype phase is now 50 percent complete. Halting work now—and destroying a development effort well on its way to completion—would be a waste of nearly $700 million of our national resources. It would be like stopping the construction of a house when it was time to put in the doors. There is another aspect to this waste: It would cost nearly $278 million in contract terminations under the present law to simply close down this project—only slightly less than the $290 million being sought at this time to continue the program.

Most important, taking a longer range view, halting the SST now could well be a mortal blow to our aerospace industry for years to come. The research and development and the accomplishments of this industry have been major factors in giving the United States a superior position in the field of technology. We must not abandon this national advantage now.

Beyond the effects on the aerospace industry, the SST program will have an extremely important impact on our whole economy. It will have a deep effect on our balance of payments and on the tax revenues coming into our treasury.

I am well aware of the many concerns that have been voiced about the possible effects Supersonic transports might have on the environment. I want to reassure the Congress that the two prototype aircraft will in no way affect the environment. As for possible later effects, we have an extensive research project under way to insure against damage. Further progress on the part of the U.S. in the SST field will give this

---

Statement released by the White House, December 6, 1970.

country a much stronger voice with regard to any long range effects on the environment than if we permit other nations to take over the entire field. And this they will surely do if we retire from this project now. The SST is an airplane that will be built and flown. This issue is simply which nation will build them.

Throughout the history of aviation, the United States has been first in this field. If the action of the Senate is not reversed, our country will be relegated to second place in an area of technological capability vital to our economy and of profound importance in the future.

I believe that the Senate's unfortunate action can be and should be corrected.

# Chapter 14 Questions

1. Is the SST economically justified? Are there factors for and against the building of this airplane that equal if not outweigh the economic considerations in a decision to build it? Explain what these other factors are and how you weigh them.
2. If you were advising the President of the United States, would you recommend that the SST program be supported by the government? Explain your position.
3. In your judgment, will the Boeing Company have a monopoly in this case? If your answer is affirmative, then explain whether you think the government is justified in permitting it.
4. Assuming that this public-private enterprise is acceptable, explain precisely how you would recommend that the government and industry share the cost of development and what the profit-sharing formula should be. Defend your position.
5. What are the similarities and differences between the government-industry SST program and the Apollo program?
6. Do you think that programs such as these might set a pattern for the resolution of some of our major social problems that involve huge engineering problems? Explain your position.
7. Can you think of any government-industry ventures of the past, aside from the two referred to above? Can you think of any circumstances in the future that would justify this sort of government-industry mixed venture? Assuming that there will be such mixed ventures in the future, lay out a plan that will assure that the best, rather than the worst, features of government and private industry will be predominant.
8. Do you believe that the data presented on both sides of this case illustrate the fact that on major issues equally dedicated and prestigious experts find themselves on opposite sides. Why is this? What problems does this create for the decision maker? for the general public?

# The Affluent, the Post-Industrial, and the Great Society

**11**

# Galbraith's "affluent society"

### paul t. homan

**Paul T. Homan had a long and distinguished career as an economist. This review, written toward the end of his life, is a cogent analysis of J. Kenneth Galbraith's book *The Affluent Society* (Boston: Houghton Mifflin, 1958), which has had a continuing popularity as a critical view of our socioeconomic system.**

In the present century, the only English-speaking economists to achieve much of either fame or notoriety beyond professional circles have been Veblen and Keynes. This did not happen because they were foremost in their scientific contributions to knowledge. It happened for two reasons: first, because they brought fresh thinking peculiarly applicable to the social and economic problems of their times and, second, because they possessed a peculiar combination of shock-producing originality of mind and rhetorical persuasiveness. Nor was their impact accidental or fortuitous. They deliberately directed their great intellectual powers to influencing their generation, first through their professional colleagues and then through both direct and indirect transmission to a wider public. A few lesser economists have attempted somewhat similar missions with indifferent success, but generally speaking, it is not a role to which economists aspire, being content to pursue their scientific work and on occasions to serve as technical consultants in matters of economic policy.

It would be an exaggeration to say that J. K. Galbraith has now entered this exclusive company on equal terms. But with his widely-read book, *The Affluent Society*, he may be said to have entered the environs and to be, as yet lightly, knocking at the door. At the least, he possesses some of the superficial stigmata of the society. He has taken a leaf out of Keynes' method in the *General Theory*. Keynes started off by profaning one of the sacred altars of economic doctrine and, having thus startled his audience into alert attention, proceeded to unfold a persuasive argument. Galbraith has also taken a leaf out of Veblen. Veblen was a satirist, and used caricature to compel attention to neglected aspects of reality. In the field of social commentary it is a valid, not to say an indispensable, method. It is certainly true that we all entertain conventional attitudes toward the life around us;

Paul T. Homan, "Galbraith's 'Affluent Society.'" © 1959 by The Regents of the University of California. Reprinted from CALIFORNIA MANAGEMENT REVIEW, Vol. 1, Spring 1959, pp. 97–111, by permission of The Regents.

and it is important that from time to time we be shocked into recognizing the shortcomings of these attitudes in relation to the seething world of social reality.

This is where Galbraith's service mainly lies, in exposing the inadequacy of much conventional thinking and in opening up neglected facets of familiar facts. In doing so, he is deliberately "destructive." His attitude is that constructive improvement in our social arrangements is impossible until people have seen "the comfortable and the accepted" in new perspectives. They have to be shocked out of complacency. So he provides a shocker. ". . . an essay such as this," he says, "is far more important for what it destroys—or to speak more accurately, for the destruction which it crystallizes, since the ultimate enemy of myth is circumstance—than for what it creates" (p. 182). He does, indeed, go on to some constructive proposals, but these, though worth attention, are hardly more than marginal to the range of problems he has presented.

Since it was his intention to write a controversial book, he cannot have been disappointed in the result. He may, nevertheless, have been surprised, not merely at the intensity of the opinions ranging from rage to adulation, but more particularly at the distortions to which his ideas have been subjected. From reading the reviews, one could hardly imagine they all referred to the same book. In private discussion, it is clear that Galbraith is receiving the treatment reserved for all writers of controversial best-sellers—that of having what are supposed to be his ideas bandied about by people who have never read the book.

"Galbraith," like "Keynes," seems destined to become a naughty word in some circles and a holy word in other circles, with a range of meanings in between. His book might be considered a sort of economic *Lolita*.

Even those who have read the book are able to find, not merely many things to argue about, but many meanings. Thus, in the First National City Bank *Monthly Letter* (January 1959) one reads that "Professor Galbraith . . . says Americans are too well off." As I read the book, he says they are not as well off as they have the means to be. It all depends on what you mean by "well off." Again, a fellow economist, Colin Clark, writing in the *National Review* (October 11, 1958) says: ". . . it is much better, Professor Galbraith teaches, to have the economy run by powerful cartels and monopolies in the European style, protected by high tariffs." I cannot myself find anything which justifies this dictum. "The conclusion to which this book leads," Clark further finds, is a "new class," "ominously reminiscent of Orwell's 1984," "the custodians, virtually the sole custodians, of culture." So far as I can discover, Galbraith is looking for ways to recruit a growing proportion of the population to the ranks of those who really enjoy their work and leisure.

The unfavorable comments are not confined to those with conservative attitudes. For example, Leon Keyserling, a colleague of Galbraith on the Advisory Committee on Economic Policy of the Democratic Advisory Council, writing in *The New Republic* (October 27, 1958), challenges Galbraith's central thesis right down the middle. And many professional economists adopt a posture of slightly sneering deprecation.

The fact is that Galbraith "asks for" this kind of treatment. He asks for it in three ways. In the first place, he charges that practically all attitudes toward economic policy—whether liberal or conservative, lay or professional—reflect various forms of "conventional wisdom" which is out of touch with the realities of contemporary economic life. He therefore arouses opposition in as many quarters as possible. In the second place, he pursues his critical argument with a not too gentle irony, supported by a witty turn of thought and a gift for the telling phrase. People do not like this sort of treatment. In the third place, he covers complicated questions with extreme brevity, which, together with his placing of emphasis, opens the way to misinterpretation.

Galbraith organizes his argument around "a modern paradox": "why it is that as production has increased in modern times concern for production seems also to have increased" (p. 120). He has spent over a hundred pages leading up to this statement of the paradox; one hundred and sixty pages later he hopes that he has destroyed "the thralldom of a myth—the myth that production, by its overpowering importance and its ineluctable difficulty, is the central problem of our lives" (p. 280). Thereafter, for the final seventy pages, he explores "new goals."

In the first of these three divisions, he explains the preoccupation with production by reference to earlier economic circumstances and patterns of economic thought. In the second, he examines the weaknesses in our administration of productive resources, establishes the relative unimportance of much that is produced, and states his views on some unsolved problems which continue to harass the American economic society. In the third, he goes a short distance toward proposing remedies.

While the central argument is essentially rather simple, it is not easy to summarize the whole range of Galbraith's thinking. The reason is that his mind flows out in eddies and excursions in a series of interesting, witty, and sometimes brilliant commentaries on aspects of American life and thought. Much of the interest of the book, and no doubt most of its popularity, are to be found in these excursions. But they cannot be conveyed with brevity. I shall therefore attempt to summarize only his sober central argument.

The best way to organize this summary is to start in the middle and work in both directions. The focal point is that much of what we now produce is of secondary importance and could be dispensed with without serious discomfort or sacrifice of well-being, except as it is related to competitive standards of consumption. He establishes this thesis by three lines of argument. The first is a casual look around, pointing to the frivolous elements in our objects of consumption. The second is that the wants which these things satisfy are not spontaneous with the consuming public, but are themselves produced by the selling arts. Production leads to consumer desires, and not *vice versa*. The third is based upon the economic principle of diminishing utility—that as additional goods become available they satisfy decreasingly urgent wants.

This third point leads into a rather technical examination of the economists' theory of consumer behavior. While diminishing utility may be accepted as operative at any given time, an economist can reasonably argue that it does not hold for comparing the urgency of wants in one period of time with that of another. Increases of income may open up whole new areas of consumption possibility and the marginal strength of desire in these new circumstances may be no less, or even greater, than in the earlier situation. Conceding some force to this idea on technical grounds, Galbraith nevertheless is ironically critical of economists for not looking behind these new wants to their business and sociological sources. By taking wants for granted as data, and by defining the economic function as that of satisfying wants to the fullest degree possible from available resources, the economists give their tacit blessing to all production in purely quantitative terms, disregarding the artificial character of the want structure and applying no qualitative tests. In this behavior, economists are, he judges, victims of the ethos of our times, to which they bring the support of outdated ideas.

From this central thesis, we turn back to the origins of the contemporary over-emphasis on production as such. Galbraith has led up to his thesis by a skillful *résumé* of past economic thought bearing on the subject. For Ricardo, a century and a half ago, the economic prospects of most of the human race were dim. Nature was niggardly; and the propensity of the population to increase tended to cancel out any gains. Such improvement as was possible depended upon improvements in productive capacity and methods. The best way to ensure this was to give the fullest play to the incentive of self-interest. Business enterprise and competitive organization were, he thought, the best ways to maximize the production which would alleviate the general poverty. Maximum personal liberty, a good thing in itself, joined with economic expediency to comprise a system of economic morality.

Private enterprise and competitive organization, however, introduced three disturbing elements into the system. The first was great inequality of fortune. The pushing and ingenious innovators could amass fortunes to be enjoyed in the midst of pervading poverty; this led to moral uneasiness about the system; and reform movements to mitigate the situation reflected sharp conflicts of economic interest. Those who enjoyed the blessings were at pains to justify the system in every possible way, including the appeal to the laws of God and nature.

The second disturbing element was economic insecurity. Competition was no respecter of individual fortunes. Firms and individuals were made or broken according to the rules of the market. This led to persistent efforts at all levels of the system to achieve some degree of economic security. The third disturbing element was the fact of severe periodic depressions, generally regarded as a normal but self-correcting feature of the system. This phase of his account Galbraith summarizes as follows: "To the lingering fear that poverty might be normal, the increasing conviction that inequality was inevitable and the sense of individual insecurity which was inherent in the competitive model, the orthodox view of the business cycle added a much more general sense of disquiet" (p. 46).

American potentialities, and the optimism they engendered, somewhat softened this gloomy outlook. But thought was divided. On one side was a line of reformers ultimately crystallized in Veblen, who felt that a satisfactory destiny for the common run of mankind would require drastic departure from the structure of capitalism. On the other side, at the favored top of the structure, Social Darwinism provided a new rationale for the system. The central doctrine was that life is a struggle for the survival of the fittest, and the free market was the arena for this struggle. Struggle for survival being nature's law, the cruelties and tragedies inherent in the system were turned into the unavoidable details of racial evolution, in which poverty would be ended by weeding out the unfit. If this doctrine could be used as a pleasant rationalization of inequality and the great new fortunes, it also received some support from the oldest of American traditions: that anyone worth his salt could make his way in the world.

But Social Darwinism was not a doctrine acceptable to the mass of the people living under the new industrial conditions generated by technological change. The political forces of democracy could be used to change institutions and to soften the struggle. Moreover, it was difficult to use Social Darwinism to rationalize the position of the rising great corporations, as distinct from captains of industry.

Nevertheless, as a sort of residue, Social Darwinism brought into the "age of affluence" a presumption that poverty, insecurity and inequality were inherent in the life of economic society, even the most favored. In addition, it strengthened the mystique of the market which, if no longer the protector of the vigor of the race, was the final refuge of the liberty of the individual. It thus created impalpable barriers to "social measures designed to rescue the individual from the privation or to protect him from the hazards of economic life" (p. 63). At the same time, the subtly pervasive ideas of Marx suggested the continuance of great economic ills.

"Up to twenty or twenty-five years ago," Galbraith summarizes, ". . . the broad impact of economic ideas . . . could not but leave a man with a sense of the depth, pervasiveness, and burden of the economic problem and, on the whole, with the improbability of a happy outcome" (p. 75). The depression of the nineteen thirties accentuated the old economic problems. "These—productivity, inequality, and insecurity—were the ancient preoccupations of economics. They were never more its preoccupations than in the nineteen thirties as the subject stood in a great valley facing, all unknowingly, a mountainous rise in well-being" (p. 7).

This rising tide of opulence, Galbraith goes on to argue, has greatly changed the essential character of our economic problems. In the first place, it has largely hushed the old complaints against inequality and reform proposals based on redistribution. Something has been done in this direction through the graduated income tax, while full employment and upward wage pressures have leveled income from below. At bottom, the retreat of inequality as an issue is attributable to the general rise in economic well-being. The wealthy have become less important, less visible, and less subject to envy; and there is little inclination to question the functional role of some inequality as an incentive to enterprise and as a source of capital. Increased production has become the alternative to redistribution—"the great solvent of the tensions associated with inequality" (p. 95).

Similarly, the insecurity created by competition has become a dwindling preoccupation. All groups hounded by such insecurity have had an incentive to diminish it, and their efforts by and large have been fairly successful. The great corporations, he says, have achieved a considerable power to protect their market position and no longer suffer from serious competitive hazards. Other groups—unions, farmers, the aged, the unemployed, and professional and business groups—have had their insecurity much diminished by government action or their own collective action. In addition, the great generalized source of insecurity, business depressions, are no longer regarded as inevitable. It has become a principal goal of public policy to stabilize the economy at a level where something close to full employment is maintained.  Assuming that this effort will be moderately successful, economic insecurity, if not finished business, will at least have given way to problems of a lower order of urgency.

The conclusion stares one in the face: "Thus the effort to enhance economic security becomes the driving force behind production" (p. 119).  This brings us back to where we started in this section—the "modern paradox . . . that as production has increased in modern times concern for production seems also to have increased."  The reason for the concern is no longer that a mere quantitative increase in the things produced is of much importance to consumers as a means of banishing poverty.  Production is, however, of the utmost importance as a means to maintain continuity of livelihood.  Maintaining a high level of employment presents serious problems.  At the same time, since it is not the things-in-themselves that are important, new economic vistas open up.  At the margins of production, attention can be turned from mere quantitative output to the qualitative character of what is to be produced.  To these problems and these vistas Galbraith devotes the remainder of his book.

In leading up to this point Galbraith has accomplished an intellectual *tour de force* by compressing into so small a space an account of the economic ideas and circumstances which generated American attitudes toward production.  One can quibble at details—at the distortions compelled by brevity, at omissions, at degrees of emphasis.  But in the large the account is a valid one, skillfully rendered.  At the same time he has done something very different, and more arguable.  He has infiltrated a very personal interpretation of what has happened to the American economy.  Increasing security and increasing productivity have, he finds, gone hand in hand.  This gives him a sympathetic attitude toward almost all efforts to eliminate insecurity—whether by private groups or by public action, from great corporations through union strength and farm programs to social security measures.  He does not necessarily approve the various stratagems of self-interested groups, but he downgrades the possible damage they may do.  At the base of his thinking is a thoroughgoing dissent from the view, popular in the policy writing of many economists, that the economy should be kept as near the competitive model as possible.  This posture, it might be thought, should gain him the approval of all sorts of vested interest.  But most of this latent support he throws away in the course of the argument which I shall summarize in the next section.

He has also downgraded the issue of inequality which has been so close to the heart of many reform movements.  It is no doubt true, as he says, that a generally rising level of economic well-being has diverted attention from inequality as a popular issue.  But there are latent aspects which persist even in an opulent society. In the thinking of many people, a nearer approach to equality is a necessary condition of the "good society" to which they aspire. These more distant reaches of social philosophy do not enter into Galbraith's field of vision. He thereby dissociates himself from reform movements of any broad character.

Galbraith's central argument was summarized at the beginning of the preceding section to the general effect that much production is mis-directed into frivolous channels, precariously supported by an artifi-cially induced consumer demand, while socially more important goals are being neglected. We must now see how this argument is elabo-rated and the problems of social action into which it leads.

"Our peacetime concern for production," Galbraith says, "is selective and traditional" (p. 132). This divides into two points. The first is that improvements in the methods of production are neglected in fields where they could produce striking results. We take for granted that the innovations and investments which actually take place are the most useful ones. But they are largely concentrated in strong firms in particular industries which can afford the necessary research and experimentation; "there is no special concern about the industry that does no research and makes little technological progress" (p. 129), for example, coal-mining. Investments in education which could yield great productive results are neglected. These and other unexploited opportunities for increasing production are adduced as evidence that, in spite of protestations to the contrary, our society really regards production as a problem of relatively low urgency: ". . . at any given time," he asserts, "both our total output and its rate of increase are only a small part of what it might be, perhaps only a minor fraction" (p. 132).

The other and, for Galbraith, much more fundamental point is that, "In the general view it is privately produced production that is im-portant, and that nearly alone" (p. 133). "At best public services are a necessary evil; at worst they are a malign tendency" (p. 133). That the importance attached to private production is inordinate is, he thinks, demonstrated by the obvious unimportance of much that is produced. Yet much of the "conventional wisdom" is devoted to justifying the actual flow of goods. Here the economists' theory of consumer de-mand does yeoman service. Nothing, however, so clearly exposes the marginal unimportance of production as the fact that the very wants it satisfies have themselves to be manufactured. The ball is kept roll-ing by the ancient trait of emulation and the requirements of social prestige. We are trapped into a grinding pursuit of larger income to satisfy purely conventional desires. The increasing affluence of our society provides no escape.  But "Among the many models of the good society no one has urged the squirrel wheel" (p. 159).

Galbraith identifies the American business community as the great vested interest in maintaining the myth of the importance of production.  This interest is not solely pecuniary; it is also a matter of prestige.  Beginning with the depression years, the dominating place of businessmen in the prestige ratings faded before the encroachments of government and of the "liberals" whose ideas defined the enhanced role of government.  The liberals, however, have forfeited their own position.  The depression called for public action to raise the level of production and employment; but when that emergency was over, liberals failed to invent any other program and were left with no creed except that of an expanding economy.  This simply places them in a subordinate role to the business community which is responsible for production.  Since businessmen have to a large degree accepted the role of government as an important regulator of the general level of economic activity, the liberals can contribute only marginal comment as to potentialities for expansion.

Another point where Galbraith finds the emphasis upon production to be misplaced is in its relation to national defense.  He sets out to destroy "the myth that military power is a function of economic output" (p. 178).  For a war like World War II, and even for a limited war like Korea, a strong addiction to consumer goods limited the speed and extent of transference of resources to military purposes.  For future wars, or even for the strategy of deterrence, "the question is not the size of the economy but how much can be diverted to public purposes" (p. 178).  "It is not gross output but usable military output which counts" (p. 166).  Reviewing the political history on this point, and the attitudes of Secretaries of the Treasury and Defense as to what we could "afford" for defense, Galbraith concludes that the conventional emphasis on high consumption acts as a positive obstacle to an adequate program of national defense.

In one respect, Galbraith proceeds, production is as important as it ever was—for reasons of economic security.  Productive activity must go on as a source of income, and must expand to absorb an expanding labor force.  For serving this function, however, the present structure of production is precarious.  The reason for this is that, in addition to creating the wants to be satisfied, the business community also creates the means of payment with which to satisfy them.  Expanding production is matched by an expanding volume of consumer debt.  The arts of persuasion are extended to persuading people to commit their future incomes to present consumption.  Expansion of production comes to depend upon expanded debt.  Increased spending comes when it is least needed, in prosperous times, and adds to inflationary pressures.

Any slow-down in debt creation creates unemployment. "Drastic and spiraling liquidation" of this credit is always within the range of possibility, adding an additional hazard to the latent volatility of business credit and spending for investment purposes.

The processes of consumer demand creation and its financing thus constitute one of the central problems of an affluent society. Another is the tendency to chronic or recurrent inflation.

The principal element of interest in Galbraith's treatment of the inflation problem is his argument that reliance on monetary policy as an anti-inflation device is an "evasion." He starts from the assumption that over a substantial part of the industrial system, marked by oligopoly, price increases are not closely tied to capacity operation or to rising demand. For a variety of reasons of policy, managements do not set prices to maximize short-run profits, and firms therefore typically have "a reserve of unliquidated gains from unmade price advances" (p. 217). Wage demands by unions commonly provide the occasion for price increases, giving rise to the wage-price spiral. This spiral is not really a "cost-push" phenomenon, but part of the strategy of business in determining when to raise prices and increase profits. Higher living costs and higher profits then provide the incentives to unions to generate another wage increase. "The wage, price, profit spiral originates in the part of the economy where firms with a strong (or oligopolistic) market position bargain with strong unions" (p. 220).

With this source of inflation, monetary policy makes only a secondary contact and is ineffective. Moreover, monetary policy is in conflict with the machinery of consumer want creation and financing and is unlikely to make much effective contact with them. Also, if effectively applied, monetary policy would collide with the investment process which supports economic growth. Investment spending is "the most mercurial dominion of economic activity"; any effort to reach price inflation by this route runs the danger of precipitating a depression.

For these and other reasons, monetary policy is likely to be either ineffective or so dangerous that it will be too sparingly used to reach the sources of inflation. The place where monetary policy can be effective is upon competitive industries such as agriculture. But this is not where the inflationary pressures originate.

Galbraith is also rather skeptical of the other conventional instrument for fighting inflation, fiscal policy. It would ordinarily require increased taxes and budget surpluses, hard to engineer politically. To be effective, moreover, it would have to cut back general market demand so far as to create substantial unemployment and the rate of economic growth which would support full employment.

Thus we arrive at an impasse. Price stability under present market conditions requires a substantial margin of unemployment. But "We are impelled by present attitudes and goals to seek to operate the economy at capacity where . . . inflation must be regarded not as an abnormal but as a normal prospect" (pp. 248–49). Thus, inflation stands out as a second unsolved problem of the affluent society. This problem might be brought under control by a limited use of direct price and wage controls at critical points of inflationary pressure, in conjunction with discreet use of monetary and fiscal policies. The "conventional wisdom," however, has only horror for this blasphemous idea.

The third and last problem to which Galbraith turns his attention is what to produce. This one lies close to his heart and arises directly out of his earlier ironical *exposé* of the frivolous uses to which we put much of our productive resources. He proposes "a satisfactory relationship between the supply of privately produced goods and services and those of the state" (p. 255) to which he gives the name of "social balance." He provides a long and impressive list of useful public services which might be had at the cost only of foregoing unimportant, silly or meretricious objects of consumption.

There arises, of course, the shadow of the sovereign consumer. The usual view is that consumers can have what they want, and can take as much of their real income in public services as they collectively decide. On this point Galbraith makes a telling rebuttal. The cards are stacked. All the arts of persuasion are on one side. In addition, the whole heritage of prejudice turns the support of public services into a "burden." Further, any extension of the public service raises the question of who is to pay, and tends to break "the truce on inequality." Inflation, moreover, undermines the attractiveness of public employment. The problems of social balance are most severe at the state and local level where the revenue problems are most difficult. In these impeding circumstances, even "To suggest that we canvass our public wants to see where happiness can be improved by more and better services has a sharply radical tone. . . . By contrast the man who devises a nostrum for a nonexistent need and then successfully promotes both remains one of nature's noblemen" (p. 269).

What to do? Galbraith does not go very far in pursuit of this question. His main purpose has been, as he says, "to destroy." Or, more accurately, to subject people to "a major wrench" in their attitudes. Once the thralldom of mere quantitative production is broken, there must be a "concern for new goals." If "efficiency" in the production of trivialities becomes less important, we shall have to review our society in new terms self-consciously directed to promoting "the good life"— the terms of "compassion, individual happiness and well-being, the minimization of community and other social tensions" (p. 289). In the business world, "the relation of the modern corporation to the people who comprise it—their chance for dignity, individuality, and full development of personality—may be at least as important as efficiency" (p. 288). What is ultimately at stake is a system of social morality. In a world of poverty, some case could be made for a system of morality which imposed rules of economic efficiency, however cruel to individuals. In an opulent world, some other rules are necessary. Opulence must be made to further other goals—those which will cultivate the essential worth and dignity of man.

This is the broad message. Meantime, as he has shown, there are immediate, concrete problems. Toward the solution of these he throws out a few suggested lines of advance.

Inflation he finds intolerable as "the implacable enemy of social balance," but at the same time practically certain to persist under conditions of full employment. If price stability requires unemployment, people must still live. To alleviate the burden of unemployment, he proposes that unemployment compensation should be on a sliding scale, going higher as the level of unemployment increases. One merit of this is, he finds, that "no particular group of people is singled out for misfortune when demand falls below full employment levels" (p. 303). The other merit is that the more sustained level of consumer demand would itself limit the deviation from full employment levels. The plan would "make tolerable the unemployment which is associated with price stability" (p. 305). If a maximum employment policy is followed, curbing inflation will, he thinks, require the use of direct price and wage controls on a limited scale. He does not advocate it, but at the same time is not terrified by the prospect.

The second proposal is a plan for financing an expanded program of public services at the state and local level, the "large ready-made needs for schools, hospitals, slum-clearance and urban development, sanitation, parks, playgrounds, police, and a thousand other things" (p. 308). To smooth the way toward a better social balance, Galbraith sees the need for "a system of taxation which automatically makes a pro rata share of increasing income available to public authority for public purposes" (p. 311). Since so much of the problem of adequate public services is at the state and local level (and given the existing federal income tax structure), a much expanded use of the sales tax is proposed on consumer goods and services. He makes a reasoned defense of this proposal against the conventional liberal objections to sales taxes.

In a third sphere, proposals are made to cope with the remnants of poverty which linger on even in an affluent society. This poverty Galbraith classifies as mainly (1) "case poverty" associated with deficiencies in the qualities of individuals, and (2) "insular poverty" associated with special environmental situations and with factors producing occupational and regional immobility. The first principle is to maintain a social minimum income for decency and comfort.  The second is to take whatever other steps are required to prevent poverty from being self-perpetuating in families and districts.  Around this principle cluster a whole group of possible measures—slum clearance, housing, emigration from rural slums, but in particular educational and other services which will enable individuals to take advantage of the opportunities afforded by the general opulence of society.

The fourth direction for policy does not so easily reduce itself to specific proposals.  It centers around a general goal of making the working life more pleasant and satisfying.  What Galbraith calls the "New Class" is that large and rapidly expanding group whose work is inherently interesting and not just a job to be done, and whose educational opportunities give them access to superior cultural activities. He proposes a public policy of deliberately promoting the enlargement of this "class" to the ultimate end of getting as many as possible of the whole population into a happy state of pleasure in their work and richness in their cultural life.  The idea is merely sketched in—with such brevity that it gives no real clue to what processes of sociological change would be involved.  The "class" orientation given to the discussion is unfortunate since it opens the way to a snobbish interpretation of what I judge to be Galbraith's unsnobbish intent.

The book ends on the note of the capacities of our economic society to promote (1) "happiness," (2) survival in the military sense, and (3) aid to other parts of the world in their efforts to escape from poverty.  In none of these directions does he find that the contemporary emphasis upon increase of consumer goods will aid in the solution of the most urgent social problems of our times.

As the preceding summary will have demonstrated, Galbraith's argument explores a wide territory.  At the center lies the thesis concerning the relative marginal unimportance of the consumer goods with which our structure of production presents us.  To guard this thesis, he has set up barricades to all quarters of the compass; or in perhaps a better metaphor, he has sent out commando raiding squads in all directions. He is not simply guarding the thesis from attack; he is out to divide, disconcert and disorganize its enemies.

But the thesis itself is purely instrumental.  The destructive attack upon the "conventional wisdom" is only a preliminary to a constructive approach to lines of improvement.  These lines imply a substantial expansion in the public sector of the economy.  Galbraith's conviction is that, if people can only be made to *see* what they are sacrificing by clinging to modes of thought and action imposed by tradition and vested interest, they will then have a basis for choice between the greater and the lesser good.

In carrying out his design, Galbraith intrudes his attention into almost every important topic of economic policy discussion, and many minor ones; and also on occasion into even broader sociological territory. The discussion ranges from social philosophy in the broadest sense to the minutiae of interest rates, from national security to slums, from business prejudices to the refinements of economic theory. In whatever direction, the usual purpose is to lay the ghost of some idea or practice or policy.

One consequence of this wide-flung discourse is that each topic is compressed into narrow compass. Brevity prevents "well-balanced" discussion of anything. The sharply stated opinions, without qualification, at times carry an air of arrogance. There are more blacks and whites, and fewer shades of gray, than a more judicious mind might think to be called for. Practically every point in the book takes up a controversial subject—that is why it is there. There is something for almost everyone to disagree with, and something to agree with. In these circumstances, it is quite impossible, in a brief article, to present critical commentary over the range of topics he takes up. An adequate critique would require a book at least as long as the original. I shall, therefore, in conclusion present only a few brief notes.

1. The main importance of the book lies, not in its detailed points, but in the message which is conveyed by its totality. The message is that, when a free society has banished the poverty which has through endless time been the plague of mankind, it must shake off the obsession for maximizing the production of whatever consumer goods the market brings forth. It must reconsider its goals. It must think about the ways in which, upon a firm economic base, man's life can be made more satisfying and spiritually richer, about how the higher aspirations and potentialities of man can be more nearly fulfilled. What is involved is not a problem of maximization in any strictly economic sense, but a whole social philosophy.

On this front Galbraith occupies the strongest possible position. He is right, too, in thinking that progress in this direction requires that people be jolted out of conventional habits of thought. In this respect, he is unduly modest about the role of fresh thinking. "Ideas," he says, "are inherently conservative. They yield not to the attack of other ideas but to the massive onslaught of circumstances with which they cannot contend" (p. 20). This is to denigrate his own services and those of others like him. Changing circumstances generate a welter of ideas, some of which will prevail. There is a necessary battle of ideas. There is no certainty that "good" ideas will prevail. But unless one thinks they have a chance, there would be no point in attempting to formulate them except as a special form of egoism.

The philosophy that Galbraith entertains has a content much deeper than the strictly economic. It is of a piece with much current thinking among social philosophers and among a number of other social scientists. At the center of it stands a strong sense of the dignity of man and a conviction that any satisfactory destiny depends upon the sense of human dignity and the quality of "loving-kindness." Galbraith is an economist, and expresses the philosophy in some of its economic aspects. Even though unimpressed by all the more technical points in his economic analysis, one could still applaud his vigorous espousal of this philosophy.

Galbraith would not, I think, object to being credited with this philosophy. But he would probably insist in being judged, not solely on his philosophy, but on the merits of his narrower economic arguments. To these I must then briefly turn.

2. His central thesis, that a substantial portion of our productive resources are devoted to frivolous uses, is hardly open to argument. There is a margin for transference to other uses or a margin for slacking off, if people can be convinced of the superior qualitative advantages of the alternatives. Galbraith is somewhat haphazard in parading these alternatives, and, by spending so much space satirizing consumption, opens himself to the charge of saying that we have "too much." But this is not his point. We merely have too much of the wrong things.

We are foregoing qualitatively superior services. We are providing inadequate social minima for the unfortunate. We are skimping on the right kind of educational and cultural opportunities. We let conventional consumption requirements impair our thinking and weaken our policy on national defense. We let it also deter us from doing what is both wise and humane in assisting other peoples to improve their economic condition. Less "efficiency" in production or more leisure are simply two among many possible alternatives. But the argument as a whole does not mean that production is unimportant as such; or that technological progress and growth are of no account.

The general argument being accepted, there is nevertheless a range of topics which he neglects, but which cannot be conjured away. For example, Galbraith appears to justify the "truce on inequality" which opulence and rising standards of living have brought. This raises two points. The first is that, though most people have escaped real poverty, a substantial portion fall short of what they can reasonably aspire to in an opulent society. The second is that, so long as great inequality continues to exist, the inescapable emulative stresses are certain to make larger income a primary object of desire. If those at the bottom can only move upward by a total raising of the structure of inequality, then *to them* increased production is bound to seem extremely important. The inequality problem stays with us in much more complicated ways than I can take up here.

Another difficulty is that a substantial transfer of income into public sources, as Galbraith proposes, will not of itself solve the problem of "frivolity" in consumption. He never attempts to quantify such a transfer. But let us assume a transfer of 10 per cent, of disposable personal income, or say $30 billion, an amount which would increase as national income increases. Even if by democratic processes such a transfer were approved, there is no assurance that it would be at the expense of the frivolities which Galbraith deplores. There is nothing in his line of thought that would inhibit the continued use of the arts of persuasion. Nor has he any substitute for the use of these arts as the condition of business survival. The problem is rooted in much more stubborn sociological and business conditions than he takes time to explore. Not only a thoroughgoing shift in popular attitudes, but also a drastic modification of business organization and practice would be required. On how to make headway on this front, Galbraith provides no lead.

3. Turning to a more technical point, I have no question that Galbraith's criticism of the way some economists apply the theory of consumer choice is well-taken. The theory serves a perfectly legitimate role in relation to the role of "economic sovereignty" in competitive markets. But economists play a game of hide-and-seek with it. As "scientists," they allege, it is no part of their function to go behind the rationale of individual choices. At the same time, they tend to get the theory entangled in a lopsided philosophy of liberty and a welter of "welfare propositions." These serve not only to distort the nature of problems of public policy involving collective action; they also obscure, or even deny, the necessity of qualitative thinking in the field of consumption. Galbraith is well-advised to spotlight this potent enemy to his whole line of approach.

4. The corollary to Galbraith's central thesis is, of course, an expanded public role in providing services. To my mind, his argument on this point is persuasive so far as it goes. But the subject is not free both of debating points and of real difficulties. In the first place, it can be shown that public expenditures have been rising at a faster rate than national income. This is not an important point in itself, since it does not isolate the rise in defense costs, and ignores the relative merits of the alternative uses of resources. In the second place, the question of the effect of higher taxes on business incentives arises. Galbraith tries to outflank this one by his sales tax proposal. But his principal reason for this proposal appears to be to keep the sleeping dog of inequality asleep. As I have suggested earlier, this is not a dog

that will stay asleep. So the incentive question is brought back into the picture for more discussion than Galbraith gives it and more than I can attempt here.

Another type of question centers on the capacity of actual political processes to produce satisfactory results. Colin Clark, apart from his ideas on taxation, opposes the proposals on the grounds of the incompetence and corruption of public officials. More important is the power of all sorts of pressure groups to divert funds from the public treasury in their own behalf. Galbraith does not face this question squarely. So far as he deals with such activity, he interprets it as part of the general effort to eliminate insecurity. Since he is "for" security, he creates the impression of something like blanket endorsement of such efforts. He rather summarily sidesteps any effort to apply either economic or moral tests. This is a pity, because I think the difficulty is not in his basic thinking, but in his treatment.

Expansion of the public economy involves a political process, and not all aspects of this process are going to be pretty. A good deal of nonsense is talked about pressure groups in a sort of blanket condemnation. Such groups are in fact a primary means by which proposals for the public agenda originate—good, bad, and indifferent. Proposals have to be sorted out. Galbraith neglects this side of the problem, and tends to assume an outcome acceptable to his critical judgment. To support important expansion of the public economy requires a certain optimism concerning the potentialities of the democratic process. In Galbraith's defense, it may be said that, in the absence of such hopefulness, there would be little point in even inquiring how we might climb onto a higher trajectory of well-being, where well-being takes on new qualitative meanings.

The fact that Galbraith never qualifies his proposals takes some of the edge off them. He does not even suggest at what point of distribution of resources between private and public uses we might begin to consider the "social balance" satisfactory. J. M. Clark and many other economists, sociologists, and political scientists have pointed out why and where modern urban and industrial conditions require increase in the public services. Galbraith's argument suggests that such increase can be had for the mere sacrifice of what in any case is useless, meaningless, or worse. But how far this switchover could defensibly be carried he fails to consider. Whether he is far out in the front of the vanguard, or a fairly conservative member of the forward-looking ranks, one has no way of judging.

5. The least satisfactory part of Galbraith's argument is his discussion of the problem of inflation. Here he deeply concurs in the "conventional wisdom" that inflation is a "bad thing." He supports the opinion, widely held in "reactionary" circles, that it can be curbed only

by maintaining a substantial margin of unemployment. His only originality here is a plan for looking after the unemployed more generously.

At a more technical level stands his adverse view of the possible effectiveness of monetary and fiscal policies. He is, I think, trapped into under-estimating them by his desire to highlight his views on the degree to which inflation may originate in other quarters than easy credit and excessive money demand. His analysis of the wage-price-profit spiral is thought-provoking and, within proper limits, no doubt valid. But it has to be located within, and not substituted for, a much broader examination of the sources of inflation.

Every economist is, of course, aware of the difficulties of making full employment and price stability run in double harness. It may not even be possible, and Galbraith is correct in pointing out (what are economic commonplaces) the economic dangers in using monetary and fiscal policy to the point of full effectiveness, and the accompanying political inhibitions. He is also correct in pointing out that they have discriminatory effects upon different segments of the economy. But it is hardly to be doubted that they are still useful instruments which, wisely used, will relieve the burden to be placed on other methods of control. I do not think that Galbraith would disagree. He has, however, so placed his emphasis as to invite another interpretation.

The impression is hard to shake off that there is some ambiguity, if not actual inconsistency, in the argument. Or perhaps it is only obscurity. As I understand him, Galbraith reads monetary policy out on the grounds (1) that it does not effectively reach the persistent sources of inflation, (2) that it is highly discriminatory among sectors of the economy, and (3) that if effectively used, it presents great dangers in the most mercurial area, that of business investment. As to fiscal policy, if I understand him correctly, it is the proper agency through which to create the precautionary amount of unemployment needed to prevent inflation, but even here he underlines the dangers in the investment sphere. He is skeptical of its effective use because of political opposition deriving both from the business community and from the labor community which backs a full employment policy. It is this skepticism which leads him on to consider the possible necessity of selective price and wage control.

The analysis is sketchy, and makes no strong impression on the mind except in a negative way, as to the barriers to effective use of monetary and fiscal policies. There is no full-blown presentation of the sources of inflation, nor any review of the best professional thinking on the subject. The sharpest policy issue of all is completely passed over—the view that a minor degree of controlled inflation with full employment is the lesser evil among all the available alternatives. Even when assuming that full employment will be the over-riding principle of policy, he turns to direct price and wage control without balancing it against controlled inflation. It is not a pleasant pair of alternatives from which to choose, but there can be reasonable difference of opinion about which is the lesser evil, if such a choice has actually to be made.

For the serious shortcomings of the inflation analysis, Galbraith might plead a partially valid defense of unavoidable brevity. It has provided him a context within which to put a few of his pet ideas on consumer credit, price-wage relations, monetary policy and the pressure of political forces. Perhaps that was all it was intended to do. It has, however, the appearance of attempting to do more. That is where it falls short.

6. The way in which an economist deals with the subject of inflation always discloses something of his "vision" of the future structural and operational characteristics of the economic system, something indeed of his economic philosophy. At that level, some of the issues are nicely joined by Neil Jacoby's article [*California Management Review*, Vol. 1 (Spring 1959)]. Jacoby, like Galbraith, finds formidable obstacles to the effective application of monetary and fiscal policy, arising out of inflexible prices and the characteristics of market structure. As a remedy, he seems to look to a restoration of competitive conditions sufficiently far-reaching that flexible prices and mobile resources will respond more readily to monetary and fiscal measures. If this remedy is not forthcoming, then Jacoby, like Galbraith and others, will have to begin looking for other remedies supplementary to monetary and fiscal policy.

Galbraith, by contrast, not only disbelieves in any such intense reactivation of competitive forces, but considers it positively undesirable. Not that he puts competition right out of the picture as a useful regulating influence; but his sympathy for efforts to achieve economic security, joined with his prior principle of "countervailing power," causes him to place the central problems of economic policy in the context of well-established economic power positions. The state thereby necessarily becomes involved in lines of action which would be irrelevant under conditions of thoroughgoing competitive organization.

These contrasting visions, or philosophies, present probably the most fundamental cleavage in contemporary economic opinion. Many people try to patrol both sides of the street, or sit on the fence. It is not necessary for anyone to choose an extreme position on either wing; but in due course the major alignment must fall in one direction or the other. For myself, I think the alignment within which Galbraith defines his position more likely to predominate, and therefore to furnish the environment within which the ongoing processes of social adjustment must be accomplished.

These notes will suggest that *The Affluent Society* is not a book which anyone will swallow whole. It contains interpretations of fact which are subject to reasonable differences of interpretation. It presents opinions upon which reasonable men may disagree. The technical economic analysis is at some points less than adequate. But these are secondary defects in a book which is not merely interesting and stimulating, but in a sense pathbreaking. There was a period earlier in this century when Social Economics was the arena of active discussion in both its meanings—as critical commentary on economic institutions and ideas, and as constructive thinking on the means of social improvement. These realms of intellectual discourse have fallen into a state of extreme neglect. J. M. Clark almost single-handed among outstanding economists has kept the tradition alive. Galbraith moves in as the strongest recent recruit to the revival of this excellent tradition.

In the sphere which it enters, *The Affluent Society* is only a preliminary exercise. It is, as he says, primarily an exercise in destructive thought. Much intellectual travail will be required to formulate goals and policies suitable to the changing circumstances of American life, and much political travail to give them effect. It takes an act of faith to believe that the human race, or its American membership, may successfully engage in constructive thought and intelligent collective action in its own best behalf.

## QUESTIONS

1. Galbraith organizes his argument around a "modern paradox": Why is it "that as production has increased in modern times concern for production seems also to have increased"? Critically analyze and evaluate this statement to explain what you think Galbraith means and what significance he attaches to it.
2. Explain the central themes of Galbraith's book and Homan's evaluation of them.
3. What, according to Galbraith, are the major unresolved problems of our affluent society? How does he suggest solving them?
4. Do you think Galbraith's book is an important one? Explain your position.

# Galbraith's "the new industrial state"

neil h. jacoby

Neil H. Jacoby presents the main theses of Galbraith's book *The New Industrial State* (Boston: Houghton Mifflin, 1967) and his critical evaluation of them.

The reader is promised much in Professor Galbraith's new book. Jacket copy asserts that it offers "a single comprehensive view of modern economic life and the changes that are shaping it," that "it breaks radically new ground for the initiated," and that "it will be the talk of this year and the subject of solid study for years to come." In his Introduction, Galbraith confides that his book opens the door to the whole room of which his *Affluent Society* afforded a mere peep through the window. Awed by these fulsome claims, the reader naturally opens this treatise in the spirit with which he would approach a first reading of the Book of Revelations.

Unfortunately, the show does not live up to its advance billing. Much in the book that is true is not new. Much of what is new is either half-true or misleading. And there is a good deal that is simply unimportant. However, Galbraith's sprightly style and penchant for coining new phrases to describe familiar ideas will no doubt endow the book with both influence and profitability.

## GALBRAITH'S VIEWS

What is Galbraith's vision of the new industrial state? His essential views can, without serious distortion, be stated briefly in the following propositions:

1. As a result of technological and social changes, the United States economy is now dominated and its character determined by 500 to 600 large industrial corporations which jointly account for about half of all national production.

2. Unlike the "entrepreneurial corporation" of an earlier age, the **modern "mature corporation" is managed by professional bureaucrats** with little or no ownership interest. This management staff (Galbraith

Neil H. Jacoby, "Professor Galbraith's *The New Industrial State.*" © 1968 by The Regents of the University of California. Reprinted from CALIFORNIA MANAGEMENT REVIEW, Vol. 10, Spring 1968, pp. 91–94, by permission of The Regents.

calls it the "technostructure") wields the powers of corporate decision. It makes corporate policies by committee action, and leadership functions are mainly ceremonial. Neither stockholders nor the board of directors exert meaningful influence, the former being ignorant and scattered and the latter being controlled by the management.

3. The **goal of corporate management is rapid growth** of the firm's sales at an acceptable rate of profit, rather than a maximum rate of return on investment, because efforts to maximize profits would carry high risks and threaten management's control. Managements are motivated primarily by a desire for identification and an opportunity to adapt corporate goals to their own purposes, not by pecuniary rewards.

4. **The essential function of management is planning,** or control of the environment, which frees corporate bureaucracies from the vagaries of capital markets, changes in consumer demand, and other external forces that might interfere with the maintenance of an adequate level of earnings. Planning has replaced the market as the basic guide of corporate action. Managements control prices and sales of their products by advertising and sales promotion. The "accepted sequence" of a flow of instruction from consumers to markets to producers has been replaced by a "revised sequence" of control of consumers by producers through planning.

5. **Government intervenes to aid in the realization of corporate purposes** in a number of ways. It attempts to maintain an adequate level of demand for business products and services. It meets corporate needs for new technological knowledge by maintaining a high level of military expenditures. (The concept of the Cold War provides a necessary official "image" to support this spending.) It controls prices and wages through the "guideposts," because market competition can no longer be counted upon to provide the stability of price levels that the corporation needs. Indeed, **the goals of the mature corporation and of the state have become identical,** and managements of corporations heavily engaged in defense production are mere extensions of the federal bureaucracy.

6. **The intellectual community** (Galbraith calls it the "educational and scientific estate") **has replaced the financial community as the group of highest prestige in American society.** Corporate managements are dependent upon it for trained manpower and new ideas. It is the guardian of those social values, such as esthetics, humanities, health, and recreation, that the industrial corporation ignores or resists because they do not directly serve its purposes.

7. Industrial societies, whether of the American or Soviet types, will continue to converge in their operating policies, replacing the market by planning. Ultimately, **private enterprises will disappear; mature**

**corporations will become socialized** and will form part of the larger administrative apparatus of the state.

## IS HE RIGHT?

One general impression conveyed by this book is that the large industrial corporation now dominates not only the economy but also the polity and society of the United States. It has made all social institutions subservient to its purposes—government, labor unions, financial institutions, consumers, even the educational system! It has attained a near-monopoly of social purposes. The United States Chamber of Commerce and the National Association of Manufacturers might as well disband!

Another general thrust of the treatise is that large industrial corporations have subverted the competitive market economy. They have sent the United States down the road to socialism and an economy indistinguishable in its main features from that of the Soviet Union.

This broad-gauged attack on the accepted basic character of the American economy is in the tradition of Veblen's *The Theory of Business Enterprise*, written some fifty years ago. A probing review of its main theses indicates that its vision of the character and destination of the United States economy is no less distorted and misleading than that of its predecessor. Taken individually or collectively, Galbraith's major propositions simply do not present an accurate description of the contemporary structure and operation of the American business system or of its future evolution.

In the first place, it is unscientific to describe the character of the United States economy in terms of 500 to 600 large corporations, which, according to the United States Department of Labor, account for **under thirty per cent of the total employment** in the economy and no more than thirty per cent of its production. It can be argued that the real "cutting edge" of the economy, its vital forces of growth and change, are found among the millions of other enterprises that collectively produce more than two-thirds of the nation's output. They do much of the experimenting and innovating that later finds its way into the large firms through mergers, hiring, or licensing. Most of these enterprises are managed by men with strong ownership interest who are profit maximizers and have strong pecuniary incentives. Collectively, they define the character of the United States economy as clearly—if not more so—than the corporate giants. Any scientific description of the "industrial state" would necessarily have to treat the anatomy and physiology of this two-thirds of the business community as thoroughly as the other third.

Galbraith's view of the management process in the large corporation is a caricature of the truth. The big firm is not the tool of its management committees with an innocuous board of directors and faceless and powerless stockholders. To be sure, in a complex environment, the knowledge of many specialists must be brought to bear upon corporate decisions, and committees play their part. Yet, the large decisions upon which the enterprise's long-term future hang are in the end made by its board of directors, acting on the advice of the chief executive officer. All students of management agree that committees are not efficient decision-making bodies. The quality of executive leadership is all-important, as any member of a corporate board that has lost its chief executive soon recognizes. The Sewell Averys and Tom Girdlers of a past generation find their counterparts in the Charles Thorntons (Litton Industries), James Lings (Ling-Temco-Vought), and James McDonnells (McDonnell-Douglas) of today—to mention only a few members of the billion-dollar-a-year corporate club who cannot be described as "ceremonial heads."

Galbraith also appears unaware of the important consequences of the institutionalization of common stock ownership since World War II. Managers of investment companies, pension trusts, and insurance companies have become highly sophisticated and vocal stockholders of large corporations. Their good opinions are sedulously cultivated by corporate officers, lest their corporate equities be unloaded on the market, with depressing consequences on prices, and the firm become a candidate for a take-over bid by the management of a more aggressive firm. The fact that most disenchanted stockholders sell their stock, like refugees from beyond the Iron Curtain who "vote with their feet," does not mean that this action is without influence on corporate management. A company whose stock is out of favor and depressed is unable to negotiate on favorable terms for additional funds or mergers involving exchange of securities, so that this avenue of corporate growth is closed to it. Why, indeed, do presidents of big companies spend so much time communicating with societies of security analysts, if they can afford to ignore their stockholders?

Although all students of management theory will agree that corporate planning has become a crucial function, Galbraith mistakes the true function and nature of the planning process. **Planning has not replaced the market** as a guide to corporate action. Rather, the estimated courses of the markets in which the firm buys and sells are taken into account in making plans; corporate plans are revised periodically in the light of changing signals given by these markets. The degree of control that even the largest corporation can exert over the price and sales volume of its products by means of advertising and other sales promotional activities is very slight compared to the power of the market. Every sizable company can point to a "boneyard" of new products that failed despite sincere and powerful promotional efforts. **Planning attempts to reduce risk of loss by better measurement of market forces.**

I was recently told the experience of one of the nation's largest food companies in introducing a new "snack" product. It designed the product explicitly to meet presumed growth in this segment of the food market, after exhaustive market research and testing of a number of alternatives. Its tests having affirmative results, the company made large investments in production machinery and brought out the product on the national market, supported by extensive advertising. When asked how it priced the product, the response was that it set the same price of $0.39 per package as competitive snacks, on the ground that it had to meet competition! In short, here was a new and differentiated product, introduced to the market with a full panoply of sales promotional gimmicks, for which the market provided the pricing guide. There was no "revised sequence" of instruction in this case: the "accepted sequence" of instruction from consumers to the market to the producer was sedulously followed. All that sales promotional activities could do was to enhance the consumer response that market research showed to be latent. Galbraith's news about the demise of the market is, to say the least, grossly exaggerated!

Galbraith is also confused when he likens the corporate planning of American enterprises to those of Soviet enterprises. The plans of the Soviet enterprise accept as data the prices for its raw materials, labor, and products that are fixed by the central planners. The plans of American enterprises are, as noted above, predicated on market-determined prices. Because market prices change more frequently than official prices, in response to consumers' preferences, the plans of American corporations are necessarily more flexible and subject to more frequent revision. Galbraith thus propagates a serious error when he tells the reader: "U.S. and Soviet industry both work within a framework of controlled prices" (p. 191).

Galbraith's view that the typical large corporation seeks to "satisfize" rather than maximize the rate of profit on investment will find both support and dissent among students of corporation finance. Here is an area requiring more research before judgments can be confidently expressed. The notion that corporate executives and staff members work primarily for other motives than pecuniary gain is also dubious. In my experience as a corporate director, I have been impressed by the frequency with which employee compensation and stock option matters come up for consideration. The typical corporation manager seems to have a lively and sustained interest in his financial rewards. The burgeoning industry of "executive placement" firms in the United

States also offers testimony to the continued superior influence of the dollar over organizational loyalties.

Galbraith presents the military expenditure programs of the United States Department of Defense as a clever plot of American corporate managers to provide adequate demand for corporate products and a supply of government-financed technology. The Cold War is merely "official imagery" to justify expenditures necessary to serve the needs of the industrial system. Of course, these are not new ideas. Communist propagandists have been saying these things for years. Those who take a more sober view of nuclear proliferation in a politically unstable world will shake their heads in disbelief. In the tense days of the Cuban missile crisis of 1961, perhaps even Galbraith would concede that United States "official imagery" had produced the military power to force the Soviet Union to remove its nuclear guns from our head!

No doubt officers of the United States Chamber of Commerce, the National Association of Manufacturers, and the AFL-CIO will read with astonishment that wage price "guideposts" are necessary to prevent inflation in an economy from which effective competition has disappeared. After the well-documented failure of the guideposts in the United States and the failure of "incomes" policies in the western European countries to deal with the problem of price inflation, it is incredible that Galbraith should describe the guideposts as the greatest economic innovation since Keynes' theory of full employment demand! It is now increasingly recognized that the only fundamental solution to the problem of creeping cost inflation lies in strengthening the forces of competition throughout the economy. An important element of this program, of course, must be withdrawal of the federal government from its numerous price-fixing and price-supporting activities.

Finally, Galbraith's forecast of the demise of private enterprise, like his vision of the attrition of the market, must provoke incredulity among observers of world economic trends. The evidence is overwhelming, in both market-oriented and centrally planned economies, that governments are finding that broad delegations of authority to enterprise managers are essential to operating efficiency. They are also finding that the guidance provided enterprises by market-determined prices is more accurate and results in less waste than by centrally planned prices. There are more instances of denationalization of government enterprise than of nationalization of privately owned enterprises. In short, the evidence is that private ownership, market pricing, and competition are playing enlarging roles in the world's economic life, rather than diminishing roles—on both sides of the Iron Curtain!

## CONCLUSIONS

It is clear that this wordy 412-page book does not provide "a single comprehensive view of modern economic life and of the changes that are shaping it." It provides a distorted description of the structure and operation of one segment of the United States economy. Galbraith accepted responsibility for carrying out an infinitely difficult task; it would have been becoming if he had acknowledged the many ramifications of the subject, pointed to the tentative nature of many of his observations, and identified issues requiring further investigation before judgments could be expressed. Indeed, **publication of a book purveying so much error and so lacking in scientific scholarship points to the need for much more intensive research into United States business policies.** One of the great foundations could well spend some money in establishing a center for the study of corporate policy in a university strong in business administration and economics.

## QUESTIONS

1. Summarize Galbraith's vision of the new industrial state. What does Jacoby say about this vision?
2. Jacoby claims that Galbraith's book does not provide "a single comprehensive view of modern economic life and of the changes that are shaping it." Is he really justified in attacking Galbraith on this issue?
3. Do you think that Galbraith exaggerates or is really ignorant of such matters as the managerial process in large corporations, the extent to which corporations can really influence consumers, and the real nature of corporate planning processes? Explain your position.

# The great society                    lyndon b. johnson

Lyndon B. Johnson, former President of the United States, described his vision of the future in the following well-known commencement address.  He did many things to help achieve the Great Society, but the Vietnamese war massively diverted attention from his efforts.

President Hatcher, Governor Romney, Ladies and Gentlemen:

I have come today from the turmoil of your capital to the tranquility of your campus to speak about the future of your country.

The purpose of protecting the life of our nation and preserving the liberty of our citizens is to pursue the happiness of our people.

Our success in that pursuit is the test of our success as a nation.

For a century we labored to settle and subdue a continent.  For half a century, we called upon unbounded invention and untiring industry to create an order of plenty for all our people.

The challenge of the next half century is whether we have the wisdom to use that wealth to enrich and elevate our national life—and to advance the quality of American civilization.

Your imagination, your initiative, your indignation will determine whether we build a society where progress is the servant of our needs, or a society where old values and new visions are buried under unbridled growth.

For in your time we have the opportunity to move not only toward the rich society and the powerful society, but upward to the Great Society.

The Great Society rests on abundance and liberty for all.  It demands an end to poverty and racial injustice—to which we are totally committed in our time.  But that is just the beginning.

The Great Society is a place where every child can find knowledge to enrich his mind and enlarge his talents.  It is a place where leisure is a welcome chance to build and reflect, not a feared cause of boredom and restlessness.  It is a place where the city of man serves not only the needs of the body and the demands of commerce, but the desire for beauty and the hunger for community.

It is a place where man can renew contact with nature.  It is a place which honors creation for its own sake, and for what it adds to the understanding of the race.  It is a place where men are more

Address at the One Hundred Twentieth Commencement of The University of Michigan, May 22, 1964.

concerned with the quality of their goals than the quantity of their goods.

But, most of all, the Great Society is not a safe harbor, a resting place, a final objective, a finished work. It is a challenge constantly renewed, beckoning us toward a destiny where the meaning of our lives matches the marvelous products of our labor.

I want to talk to you today about three places where we can begin to build the Great Society—in our cities, in our countryside and in our classrooms.

Many of you will live to see the day, fifty years from now, where there will be 400 million Americans; four-fifths of them in urban areas. In the remainder of this century urban populations will double, city land will double, and we will have to build homes, highways and facilities equal to all those built since this country was settled.

In the next forty years we must rebuild the entire urban United States.

Aristotle said: "Men come together in cities in order to live, but they remain together in order to live the good life." It is harder and harder to live the good life in American cities.

The catalogue of ills is long: There is the decay of the centers and the despoiling of the suburbs. There is not enough housing for our people or transportation for our traffic. Open land is vanishing and old landmarks are violated.

Worst of all, expansion is eroding the precious and time honored values of community with neighbors and communion with nature.

The loss of these values breeds loneliness and boredom and indifference.

Our society will never be great until our cities are great. Today the frontier of imagination and innovation is inside those cities, not beyond their borders.

New experiments are already going on. It will be the task of your generation to make the American city a place where future generations will come, not only to live, but to live the good life.

A second place where we begin to build the Great Society is in our countryside. We have always prided ourselves on being not only America the strong and America the free, but America the beautiful. Today that beauty is in danger.

The water we drink, the food we eat, the very air we breathe, are threatened with pollution. Our parks are overcrowded, and our seashore overburdened. Green fields and dense forests are disappearing.

A few years ago we were concerned about the Ugly American. Today we must act to prevent an Ugly America. For once the battle is lost, once our natural splendor is destroyed, it can never be recaptured.

And once man can no longer walk with beauty or wonder at nature his spirit will wither and his sustenance be wasted.

A third place to build the Great Society is in the classrooms of America. There your children's life will be helped.

Our Society will not be great until every young mind is set free to scan the farthest reaches of thought and imagination.

We are still far from that goal.

Today 8 million adult Americans—more than the entire population of Michigan—have not finished five years of school. Nearly twenty million have not finished eight years of school. Nearly 54 million—more than one quarter of America—have not finished high school.

Each year more than 100,000 high school graduates, with proved ability, do not enter college because they cannot afford it.

And if we cannot educate today's youth, what will we do in 1970 when elementary school enrollment will be five million greater than 1960. High school enrollment will rise by five million. College enrollment will increase by more than three million.

In many places classrooms are overcrowded and curricula are outdated. Most of our qualified teachers are underpaid, and many of our paid teachers are unqualified.

We must give every child a place to sit and a teacher to learn from. Poverty must not be a bar to learning, and learning must offer an escape from poverty.

But more classrooms, and more teachers are not enough. We must seek an educational system which grows in excellence as it grows in size.

This means better training for our teachers. It means preparing youth to enjoy their hours of leisure as well as their hours of labor. It means exploring new techniques of teaching, to find new ways to stimulate the love of learning and the capacity for creation.

These are three of the central issues of the Great Society. While our government has many programs directed at those issues, I do not pretend we have the full answer to these problems.

But I do promise this.

We are going to assemble the best thought and broadest knowledge from all over the world to find those answers. I intend to establish working groups to prepare a series of conferences and meetings—on the cities, on natural beauty, on the quality of education, and on other emerging challenges.

From these studies, we will begin to set our course toward the Great Society.

The solution to these problems does not rest on a massive program in Washington, nor can it rely solely on the strained resources of local authority. They require us to create new concepts of cooperation—

a creative federalism—between the national capitol and the leaders of local communities.

Woodrow Wilson once wrote: "Every man sent out from his university should be a man of his nation as well as a man of his time."

Within your lifetime powerful forces, already loosed, will take us toward a way of life beyond the realm of our experience, almost beyond the bounds of our imagination.

For better or worse, your generation has been appointed by history to deal with those problems and lead America toward a new age.

You have the chance never before afforded to any people in any age. You can help build a society where the demands of morality, and the needs of the spirit, can be realized in the life of the nation.

Will you join in the battle to give every citizen the full equality which God enjoins and the law requires—whatever his belief, or race, or the color of his skin?

Will you join in the battle to give every citizen an escape from the crushing weight of poverty?

Will you join in the battle to make it possible for all nations to live in enduring peace—as neighbors and not as mortal enemies?

Will you join in the battle to build the Great Society—to prove that our material progress is only the foundation on which we build a richer life of mind and spirit?

There are those that say this battle cannot be done; that we are condemned to a soulless wealth. I do not agree. We have the power to shape the civilization we want. But we need your will—your labor —your hearts—if we are to build that kind of society.

Those who came to this land sought to build more than a new country. They sought a new world. I have come here to your campus to say that you can make their vision our reality. Let us from this moment begin our work so that in the future men will look back and say: It was then, after a long and weary way, that man turned the exploits of his genius to the enrichment of his life.

## QUESTIONS

1. Do you think that a "Great Society" like that envisioned by President Johnson can be developed in this country? Why or why not? Be specific.
2. Would you consider this country today as being a "Great Society" relative to other societies in this world, past and present? Illustrate your position.

# Should the Government Guarantee a $250,000,000 Loan to Lockheed?

# 12

Editor's Note: In terms of sales of $2.5 billion in 1970, Lockheed was in that year the nation's largest aerospace contractor. The company has built a long line of successful aerospace products, including the Polaris and Poseidon missiles, the Agena space rocket, antisubmarine aircraft, Navy ships, electronic equipment, the C-5A cargo transport, and many other major pieces of equipment. Beginning in mid-1969 the company had a series of shattering blows involving contract cancellations and disagreement over contract costs, the net impact of which was a pre-tax loss for the company of about $500 million. The company wanted to take the issues to court, particularly that of the C-5A, but the Department of Defense in early 1971 forced the company to accept the losses or forgo other defense contracts. One result, of course, was to create a severe cash drain. Net earnings fell from a profit of $44.5 million in 1968 to a loss of $32.6 million in 1969 and $86.3 million in 1970. The company's stockholders' equity dropped from $371 million in 1968 to $235 million in 1970.

In February 1971 Rolls Royce Ltd. of England announced bankruptcy because of cost and schedule overruns associated with the production of the RB-211 engine designed for the Lockheed L-1011 TriStar air bus. When the contract for the RB-211 was signed in 1968, it was hailed as a master stroke for Lockheed because it got a quiet engine some 300 pounds lighter than other comparable engines; it helped the United States in its balance-of-payments problem because a British consortium was set up to purchase 50 Lockheed TriStars as a part of the "package deal"; the British received a major stimulus to continue their technical capability in the aerospace field; and the British economy was expected to gain by this contract, which potentially would bring in $2 billion and create some 20,000 jobs. Although the British government was not a party to the contract between Lockheed and Rolls Royce, it agreed to contribute 70 percent, or $110 million, of the estimated research and development costs of the engine.

Unfortunately, the British ran into technical problems with the engine. The fan blades were to be made of Hyfil, a composite material of carbon fibers bonded with epoxy resins, to reduce engine weight. It was discovered that rain and hail eroded the tips of these blades. This problem was corrected by inserting metal laminations, which, however, created stress at the roots of the blades, and it was further found that ingestion of large birds in the engines broke the blades. Rolls then had to turn to titanium, a new technology.

In the meantime, delivery schedules were set back some six months, and the costs of the engine leaped from the contract price of $840,000 to over $1,100,000. This additional cost, plus heavy penalties for contract schedule delay, was, for the 555 engines under contract, a far greater financial burden than the company could bear. The British government refused to subsidize the engine further, and the company went into bankruptcy.

The British government created a new nationalized company, Rolls-Royce (1971) Ltd., to carry on negotiations with Lockheed. Upon the negotiation of a higher engine price ($1,020,000 per engine) and more Practical delivery schedules, the British government agreed to pay for further development costs of the engine. (In June 1971 the government had agreed to support $310 million of the costs.) Lockheed was able to hold its 178 firm orders, and the U.S. banks agreed to go along with the new arrangements. But a question arose as to new financing of $250 million needed by Lockheed. At the same time, the British government, wanting to make sure that Lockheed would not collapse and leave it holding a depreciated asset, asked for a U.S. government guaranty that Lockheed would survive. The banks, who had not originated the guaranty idea, quickly asked for a guaranty for the requested loan, and Lockheed was forced to go to the government for it. The British government put a deadline of August 8, 1971, for the U.S. government's assurance that Lockheed would stay in business and be able to buy the first 555 engines to be produced by Rolls Royce. In early August 1971 the Senate by a one-vote margin approved a bill that was identical with that passed shortly before by the House and thus guaranteed the loan. The bill established an emergency loan guarantee board to be headed by the Secretary of the Treasury and having as members the Chairman of the Federal Reserve Board and the Chairman of the Securities and Exchange Commission. The board was given authority to guarantee loans up to $250 million, after finding, among other things, that the guaranty "is needed to enable the borrower to continue to furnish goods or services and failure to meet this need would adversely and seriously affect the economy of or employment in the nation or any region thereof." Although the bill does not specifically name Lockheed, there was no question about the fact that this company was to be the sole beneficiary of the passage of the bill. (For further details see U.S., Cong., Senate, *Hearings Before the Senate Banking, Housing and Urban Affairs Committee on S. 1891*, 92nd Cong., 2nd sess., June 1971.)

# The case for the l-1011 lockheed transport loan guarantee

## john b. connally

Secretary of the Treasury John B. Connally presented the government's case to support a $250,000,000 loan guaranty in the following statement, which he made before the Senate Banking, Housing and Urban Affairs Committee.

Mr. Chairman and members of this distinguished Committee:

I appreciate the willingness of this Committee to schedule prompt hearings on S. 1891, the Administration's request for authority to guarantee loans to the Lockheed Aircraft Corp. in an amount up to $250 million. Right at the start, let me make clear that no one would be happier than I if there were some way to provide the financing necessary to keep this company in business without involving Federal Government guarantees. But I am persuaded that is not the case.

The choice before us, therefore, is whether or not to take the calculated risk that $250 million of additional funds, provided under government guarantee, will be sufficient to finance Lockheed over the period of peak borrowing requirements in the next couple of years associated with its heaviest investment in the L-1011 program. After weighing the possibility of loss of taxpayers' money against the certainty of loss, both of employment and scrapped investment if Lockheed goes into bankruptcy, I am convinced our choice must be to act, and to act quickly, to provide the guarantee authority.

Let me begin by outlining the reasoning that brought me to this conclusion.

Foremost in my mind is the imperative need to protect and foster the rising confidence that will gradually restore the jobs and growth lost in recent months. There is no need to recount in detail for this Committee the chain of events which led to the current economic slack—massive increases in Federal spending, without adequate tax increases, in the late 1960's . . . as a result, an economy captured by inflation and inflationary expectations . . . and, finally, the firm application of strict fiscal and monetary policies to restrain the boom and restore stability.

The costs of these necessary restraints have been high—the human cost in terms of unemployment; the material cost in terms of lost out-

S. 1891, June 7, 1971.

put. And these costs have been even greater—at the same time that overall activity was being restrained, large amounts of resources were withdrawn from the defense and space industries, resources which could not be immediately utilized elsewhere.

The opposite of confidence is fear. Restoration of confidence means, in effect, the elimination of fear. And just at this time, with the economy moving ahead and unemployment topping out, the failure of the nation's largest defense contractor—with 72,000 employees earning $830 million a year, 35,000 suppliers, and $2½ billion in annual sales—would, beyond any shadow of doubt, generate deep-seated fears.

Workers throughout the aerospace industry—not just those thrown out of work by the bankruptcy—would face heightened competition for their own jobs, and they would be afraid.

Stockholders throughout American industry—not just those in Lockheed—might well question the future values of their own investments. The result would be market repercussions that could severely dampen and perhaps even thwart the business recovery.

Consequently, Mr. Chairman, the basic motivation for our recommendation is not simply a concern for a particular company or a particular industry—although we seem prone to forget the tremendous contributions made by the defense and aerospace industries to our security and progress. Rather, the primary motivation is a deep concern for the well-being of the American people.

Let me now turn to the specific consequences of the loss of the amounts already invested in the Lockheed L-1011, the company's widebody air bus. At this point in time, only a few months from the date Lockheed had expected to begin delivering planes to the airlines, its investment (and that of its subcontractors) amounts to about $1.3 billion. Only a small fraction of this investment could be salvaged if the L-1011 were dropped at this stage. In fact, the company estimates that more than $1 billion of this investment would have only scrap value in such circumstances.

Underlying this investment in physical inventories is a financial commitment that would have to be largely written off. Apart from the net equity of Lockheed's 55,000 shareholders, which now amounts to about $235 million, subcontractors are estimated to have invested $350 million in the program, a consortium of 24 banks has loans outstanding to the company of $400 million, airlines have made prepayments amounting to about $240 million, and debenture holders have claims of another $135 million.

Now it's very hard to predict each and every consequence which would attend a Lockheed failure. But one thing is certain, the L-1011 would be dead. The stockholders almost certainly would see the value of their shares wiped out. Among the company's suppliers, most, probably, would be able to survive, but perhaps others would not.

Similarly, the airline purchasers of the L-1011 could ill afford to lose the sums they have deposited with Lockheed as prepayments. These deposits, for example, amount to $90 million for TWA, $68 million for Eastern, and $36 million for Delta. At a time when most airlines are beset by rising costs, shrinking revenues, and severe operating losses, this added burden should not lightly be thrust upon them.

The banks, with loans secured by collateral, would obviously suffer less than unsecured creditors.

Another loser from a Lockheed bankruptcy would be the Federal Government itself. With respect to military procurement, for example, it is simply not practical to assume that Lockheed could go into bankruptcy without adversely affecting the cost of performing under existing contracts. This would result, if for no other reason, from the fact that a trustee could well find it impossible to carry out such contracts if to do so would require new capital, or would result in losses to the company's other creditors. Even if bankruptcy did not result in higher costs, it would inevitably result in substantial delays on military procurement under the rigid procedures required in reorganization. Conversely, of course, a bankrupt Lockheed would hardly be in a strong position to bid on new defense contracts, particularly those involving any substantial outlay of investment funds.

In addition, the Treasury would suffer tax losses. Just as the Government is a partner in business profits, it is a partner in business losses. Lockheed's creditors could take some solace in deducting their losses on their tax forms. Any estimate of the exact cost to the Government of these tax losses would be speculation, but it is hard to imagine that the net tax loss on $1 billion of written off investments wouldn't exceed substantially the $250 million guarantee.

So far, I have been describing the potential losses from a Lockheed bankruptcy in terms of dollars and cents. But there is an even more important consequence of the L-1011's demise, namely the unemployment it creates. Prior to the Rolls Royce bankruptcy, there were some 17,800 workers employed by Lockheed on the L-1011 program. Since February, nearly 8,000 have been temporarily laid off. The remaining 10,000 will lose their jobs as well if the L-1011 program is scrapped.

Similarly, Lockheed's suppliers, who were estimated to have been employing some 16,000 people in 32 states directly on L-1011 work in January have had to reduce their work forces to only about 6,500 at present because of the curtailment of work following the Rolls Royce bankruptcy.

Moreover, though it is more difficult to estimate, it is evident that for every employee directly laid off, others in communities where their income was counted on will also suffer. It is estimated that counting this indirect impact, a total of 60,000 employees will end up without jobs if the L-1011 is shut down. Even on a direct basis, the cost is heavy, as the reductions that have already taken place show.

The cost of this added unemployment has to be measured in terms of the impact on particular geographic areas where unemployment is already well above the national average, and on the aerospace industry that has already suffered a disproportionate reduction in employment as a result of (1) the winding down of military orders, (2) cutbacks in the space program, and (3) the cancellation of the SST.

As Assistant Secretary Weidenbaum testified before the Subcommittee on Production and Stabilization of this Committee three weeks ago, from a peak of over 1.4 million jobs in 1967, total aerospace employment declined to less than 1.1 million jobs at the end of last year and has been projected to be down to 943,000 by the end of this year. This would represent a cumulative decline of about one-third in four years. Moreover, of the major metropolitan areas with substantial unemployment, at least six are in this category primarily because of aerospace unemployment.

At a time when the Government is spending $1–1½ billion annually on job training programs, it would be ironic to withhold authority for guarantees—guarantees we believe will be costless—that could preserve the jobs of fully trained aerospace workers. In this connection, I've heard it said that the people laid off by Lockheed could just commute a few miles further and pick up a job with, say, McDonnell-Douglas. But if I have any sense of how such a transfer might take place, it would involve considerable delays at the least, and would never be the smooth operation some people imply. For example, I find it hard to imagine that the nearly 3,000 employees of AVCO in Nashville, Tennessee, where the L-1011 wings are made, would have an easy time moving to Canada, where the wings for the DC-10 are manufactured.

If there are strong reasons for taking action to prevent the collapse of Lockheed and its L-1011 program, how can we be sure that the action proposed—guarantee authority for up to $250 million of additional loans—will do the job. The answer is that we can't be absolutely sure, but I firmly believe on the basis of the evidence available to us that it is enough. I have reviewed the data prepared by Lockheed, and . . . a chart [follows] which summarizes the borrowing requirements as presently projected.

As you can see from that chart [Figure 1], the company forecasts peak borrowing needs of $650 million in late 1972. By that time, it is expected that additional airline prepayments—above and beyond those initially agreed to—will have provided about $100 million of the needed financing. The banks will continue their $400 million of financing,

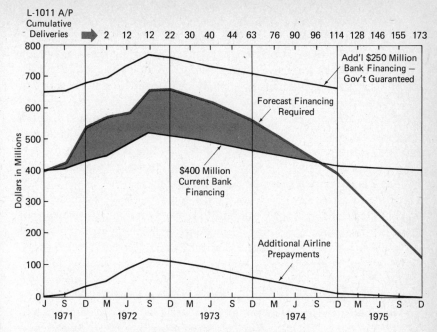

FIGURE 1    Financing Plan and Borrowing Requirements

and in addition will provide $150 million under government guarantee. The chart also shows that funds under guarantee will have been completely repaid by the end of 1974, at which time just over 100 planes will have been delivered.

Now forecasts are just that—forecasts. Moreover, I am well aware that Lockheed's controversies with the Department of Defense raise questions as to its forecasting ability. I believe, however, Lockheed has made every effort to prepare in connection with its L-1011 program what is a fair and accurate picture of what they expect to take place in the next five years. Critical to any forecast, however, are the premises upon which it is based and I think we should all take specific note of the major ones. Essentially, they involve (1) the actual number of L-1011's that are sold; (2) the ability to keep production costs in line with current estimates; and (3) the ability to generate new defense business.

With respect to the first of these points, Lockheed has firm orders for 103 L-1011 aircraft, and options for 75 more. They estimate the market for the basic wide-body air bus to be 775 planes by 1980.

I want to make it clear that I will not use the authority to guarantee loans unless and until all the major purchasers have signed firm new contracts renewing their original commitments.

While I am on this point, I would like to be sure the Committee understands that I am not talking about break-even points in terms of sales. It should not be of major concern to the Government in connection with this proposal whether Lockheed makes a profit on the 220 aircraft in their five year forecast. As a matter of fact, they won't. But they will generate enough cash from sales well short of that point to pay off the loans guaranteed by the Government, and that's really what counts. And of primary importance to the workers involved, the corporation would have more than a fighting chance— indeed, a good chance—to regain its overall financial health and remain a going concern. The Government also has a big stake here, for Lockheed is the nation's largest defense contractor.

So far as cost control is concerned, I can give the Committee some idea of the exposure. The total L-1011 program for 220 planes, not including propulsion systems, represents estimated direct costs of $3,300 million. Of this amount, some $800 million has already been incurred, and the company's estimating procedures on this amount have held up well.

Finally, with respect to new military orders, I would like to point out that Lockheed is forecasting that sales to the U. S. Government will decline from $2.7 billion in 1971 to $1.4 billion in 1973, with levels of about $1.5 billion projected for 1974 and 1975. Nevertheless, despite this sharp decline it is still true that some 50–60 percent of sales to the U. S. Government in 1974 and 1975 represents new business that may or may not materialize.

I have checked with the Department of Defense on this matter, and I understand they feel that while Lockheed's estimates on anticipated defense business are much more realistic than at times in the past, they still may be on the high side, possibly by as much as 30 percent in the last years of the forecast (1974–75). I should mention at the same time that reduced sales to the military do not affect cash flows to anything like the same extent. For example, I asked Lockheed to recalculate the impact on cash of reduced sales to the Government on new orders of 10 percent in 1973, 20 percent in 1974 and 30 percent in 1975, plus a 5 percent reduction in follow-on sales in each of these years. The total cumulative reduction in cash—the amount available to repay government guaranteed loans—by the year 1975, taking account of reduced taxes on lower profits, was only $20 million.

Apart from the essential assumptions underlying Lockheed's projections of cash needs, there is the question of the internal consistency of the projections themselves. In this connection, the Department of Transportation is satisfied that the financial program as outlined in Lockheed's projections is internally consistent with the assumptions made by Lockheed. Arthur Young, the company's auditor, likewise believes that the forecast has been compiled to appropriately reflect the stated assumptions and the estimates.  Also the major banks on the basis of their review believe Lockheed's estimates to be reasonable.

But what if these projections turn out to be wrong and the company's fortunes deteriorate?  What protection is there for the taxpayers' money?

I think it is reasonable to assume that in the event of bankruptcy the taxpayers' money will be fully protected.  The present bill provides that in case of bankruptcy the amount of loan guaranteed by the Government shall be secured by a prior lien on all of the company's assets and by the top priority in bankruptcy.  In submitting this legislation to Congress, we felt that under the circumstances the Government should have this superior status.

I realize the legislation as written would amend the Bankruptcy Act, and technical and legal arguments may be offered as to why the Government should not come ahead of all other previously secured creditors.  However, even if the Congress should eliminate or amend the section in the bill giving the Government this priority (Section 6), I have taken steps to protect fully the Government's interest.

I have entered into a memorandum of understanding with Lockheed and the banks which provides that the bank loan to Lockheed—the existing $400 million loan plus any additional loans up to $250 million —will be secured by a single collateral pool.  This pool will include all of the collateral the banks have to secure the $400 million they have advanced to Lockheed plus such other property as I shall approve.  In case of bankruptcy, the collateral will be used first to satisfy the portion of the bank loan guaranteed by the Government. In my opinion, Lockheed has sufficient assets to secure fully the $250 million that may be guaranteed by the Government.

I think it should also be pointed out that Lockheed has approximately $10 million of secured debentures presently outstanding.  The banks have agreed to see to it that in the event of bankruptcy these claims are satisfied so that they will not endanger the Government's security.  In short, the Government's claim will be paid off first from whatever assets there are in the collateral pool at the time of bankruptcy.

At this point, let me summarize the case as I see it.  For want of a relatively small amount of additional financing, it is almost certain that in the absence of Federal guarantees the L-1011 program would be terminated and the company forced into bankruptcy.  The whole of the sizeable investment in the L-1011 would be lost.  The costs of such a failure in terms of lost jobs, scrapped inventories, financial hardships, and undermined confidence would be very great.  I believe there is a good chance that these adverse consequences can be avoided if the Congress is prepared to authorize guarantees in an amount of

$250 million to finance Lockheed over its period of peak cash needs in the next couple of years.

The risks to the taxpayer are very small indeed.

Current projections indicate that all government guaranteed money will have been repaid by the end of 1974 after delivery of just over 100 aircraft, which is less than current firm orders.

The guaranteed funds will be used on a last in—first out basis.

And in the event of bankruptcy, the Government will have first lien on all Lockheed assets pledged under the Bank Loan Agreement.

I fully recognize that there are members of this Committee, and members of the Congress generally, who do not share the Administration's view that the costs of failure to act far outweigh the risks of providing guarantees.  I think it would be useful therefore to review some of the questions that have been raised concerning this matter, and try to provide the answers as I see them.

Perhaps the most frequently voiced concern is that the Government, by acting to help Lockheed Aircraft Corporation in its present difficulties, is setting an undesirable precedent for similar intervention by the Government in the future.  There are several things that should be said in response to this point.

In one sense, of course, credit assistance by the Federal Government is nothing new at all.  One can cite many examples of ways in which the Congress has authorized credit assistance to various sectors of the economy.  Housing is the most obvious.  According to the President's budget, Federally guaranteed mortgage loans at the end of the coming fiscal year are expected to exceed $140 billion.  In addition, the budget projects another $10 billion of outstanding Federal guarantees for low-rent public housing and an additional $3.8 billion for community development loans.

Housing is by no means the only area.  The Reconstruction Finance Corporation played a major financing role in this nation for almost two decades.  Small Business Administration loans and guarantees are expected to reach almost $4 billion within the next year.  Loans plus guarantees by the Export-Import Bank are projected to exceed $9 billion.

Also worth mentioning are the billions of dollars in banks and savings and loan deposits insured by the Federal Government, plus the recently enacted legislation establishing the Securities Investor Protection Corporation.

And, with reference to the Lockheed legislation in particular, the V-Loan program has provided many guarantees, through the Federal Reserve banks, to American corporations.

This list is not exhaustive.  But it demonstrates that Federal credit assistance to the private sector is by no means without precedent.

Just as there are those who argue that assistance to Lockheed would set an undesirable precedent, there are those who equally strongly argue that any such assistance should not be made available to Lockheed alone, but potentially, at least, similar assistance ought to be available to other categories of borrowers. Indeed, the Committee has before it a number of bills other than that submitted by the Administration which would expand the frame of reference and in greater or lesser degree further institutionalize the provision of Federal credit assistance.

Frankly, I question whether the time available permits adequate consideration of these other bills. Time is of the essence. Workers have already been laid off, and only a resumption of the L-1011 program will permit them to be rehired. Lockheed and its subcontractors are continuing to expend resources on the L-1011 program to keep it going and in the earnest hope that Congress will provide the guarantee authority needed to see it through. If this is not to be the case, everyone needs to know it soon, so that the eventual losses will not be aggravated, but rather minimized. For these reasons, I urge that the Committee focus its attention on S. 1891.

A different sort of concern has been expressed by some other members of Congress, namely, that if the United States Government is to become involved in a guarantee for Lockheed, one of the stipulations should be that the engines be produced in this country rather than by Rolls Royce.

I can well understand this sentiment. In fact, no one has been more outspoken than I on the need to improve our productivity and general economic performance in this country if we are to compete successfully in a changed world. But our efforts in this respect must be directed toward opening foreign markets more fully to our products, and insisting that other countries share more equitably the burdens of defense. We cannot hope to solve our domestic problems of employment and increased output by forbidding other nations to compete in our market.

In this particular case, I believe any attempt to force domestically produced engines on Lockheed and its airline customers would be self-defeating. As you know, following the Rolls Royce bankruptcy, Lockheed seriously examined the possibility of substituting either General Electric or Pratt and Whitney engines in its L-1011. After considering all of the technical and financial factors involved, the company decided to stay with the original engines.

In principle, I question whether the government should now try to reverse that decision. In practice, Lockheed found that the substitution of domestic engines would involve additional costs of more than $100 million. Part of these extra costs reflected additional delays of six months or more for adaptation of the existing air frames to the new engine configuration.

Finally, those who would have us eliminate Rolls Royce from the competition by government decree overlook the fact that the success of the L-1011 program depends in a major way on additional sales abroad. With the Rolls Royce engine, such sales are more likely to be forthcoming. In this connection, we should not lose sight of the fact that 35 percent of the market for wide-body jets of the L-1011 type is expected by Lockheed to represent foreign sales. And for all wide-body aircraft, they estimate 50 percent sales to non-U. S. carriers.

Apart from the understandable though inadvisable desire to see U. S. Government aid contingent on the use of U. S. produced engines, there are those who argue that this whole operation represents little more than a bailout of Rolls Royce. Now it is perfectly true that if the L-1011 is consigned to the scrap heap for want of additional financing, the British investment in the Rolls Royce engine will likewise have been largely wasted.

But that is quite a different matter from alleging a U. S. subsidy of Rolls Royce. On the contrary, the U. S. Government is putting up no money at all in the first instance, even for Lockheed. None of the funds provided under U. S. Government guarantee will be used other than by Lockheed. In contrast, the British Government is prepared to spend whatever additional funds are necessary to bring the RB-211 engine up to certification at 42 thousand pounds thrust on a hot day. In addition the British Government intends to make up any difference between the readjusted sales price on the 555 engines presently on order, and the costs of producing those engines. Finally, the British Government has confirmed its guarantee of spares throughout the life of the engines. These commitments represent a substantial additional investment of funds by the British Government in the program.

# The lockheed bail-out: A threat to free enterprise

## william proxmire

Senator William Proxmire presented the case against the government's guaranteeing a loan to Lockheed in the following speech, which he made before the National Federation of Independent Business, May 18, 1971.

I am delighted to have the opportunity to address the National Federation of Independent Business. Despite the trend towards industrial concentration, small business firms have been the source of much of our technical and economic progress. Your organization has been an articulate and convincing spokesman for the small businessman. It has done an excellent job in representing the needs of small business to government officials in Washington.

Today, I want to speak to you about a grave threat to our system of free competitive enterprise. I am referring to the Administration's proposal to bail out the Lockheed Aircraft Corporation with a $250 million Federal loan guarantee. If this proposal is approved by the Congress, it could mark the beginning of a new era of increased governmental control over business and industry. It is indeed ironic that such a proposal would come from a supposedly conservative Administration.

The nation's top business leaders are universally opposed to the Lockheed bail-out and rightfully so. I believe the proposed loan guarantee is unfair to all efficiently managed business firms—both large and small.

For nearly two hundred years, our economic system has been founded on the principle of free and open competition. We have sought to maximize competition in order to provide the best product to the public at the lowest possible price. In so doing, the free market system has exerted a harsh but useful discipline on business enterprise. Efficient and well managed firms are rewarded with higher profits and sales. Inefficient and poorly managed firms are penalized —the ultimate penalty being bankruptcy and receivership.

The freedom to fail may at times appear to be an overly painful solution—particularly to the firm going out of business. But business failures serve a higher public purpose. They are the means by which

Senator William Proxmire, "The Lockheed Bail-Out: A Threat to Free Enterprise," Speech Before the National Federation of Independent Business, Washington, D. C., May 18, 1971.

our economy discards obsolete or inefficient ways of doing business. In this way, the overall efficiency of our economy is improved. Business failures are not tragic events to be prevented—they are the sign of a healthy and productive economy. The freedom to fail is in no small way responsible for our unsurpassed record of economic achievement. Without the freedom to fail, our economy would still be producing buggy whips and kerosene lamps.

The principles which have made our economy grow and prosper would be seriously compromised by the Lockheed loan guarantee. Instead of penalizing inefficiency and mismanagement, we would be rewarding it. Instead of retiring inept executives, we would be perpetuating them in their jobs. Instead of holding men accountable for their mistakes, we would bail them out.

Despite the size of the aid being sought, Lockheed has been strangely reluctant to open its books to the public. For example, I tried repeatedly to obtain a cash flow statement from the company. This is a statement which any prudent banker would insist upon before making a loan. Company officials have refused to make such a statement available to the Congress.

The reason given for the loan guarantee is to permit continued production of the L-1011 Tristar air bus. Bankers are said to be reluctant to finance the project on their own given the uncertain commercial feasibility of the plane. For example, Lockheed has orders for only 178 planes whereas most industry experts put the break-even point at around 250. If the L-1011 is a commercial flop, where will Lockheed get the money to repay the $250 million in guaranteed loans? If the project fails it is the Federal taxpayer who will foot the bill.

In other words, the Administration is asking Congress to risk $250 million of the taxpayers' money to guarantee a loan which the nation's top bankers feel is too risky to make on their own. If the project is commercially sound, why won't Lockheed's bankers finance it? A group of 24 of the country's largest banks have already loaned Lockheed $400 million on the L-1011 project. I would think these bankers would be more than willing to loan an additional $250 million to protect their original investment if there was a reasonable prospect of repayment. If there is not a reasonable prospect of repayment, why should the Federal taxpayer be called upon to take the risk?

There is some evidence that it is not the banks who are insisting upon the Federal guarantee but rather the British government. British officials say they will not loan Rolls Royce the money needed to complete production on the engines for the L-1011 unless the U. S. government guarantees bank loans to Lockheed. Even if U. S. bankers are willing to make unguaranteed loans to Lockheed the British government would not be satisfied.

It is interesting to examine the reasoning implicit in the British position. The British government naturally doesn't want to put more money into Rolls Royce without assurances that there will be a market for the engines. If Lockheed fails, there is no market. The probability that Lockheed will fail is not reduced by a guaranteed loan as opposed to an unguaranteed loan. A loan guarantee does not insure the success of the project—it merely guarantees the banks against loss. Why, then, is the British government so insistent that the U. S. government guarantee the loan? The answer must be that they assume the U. S. government will not permit the company to fail if $250 million of taxpayer funds are at risk. In other words, the British assume that the U. S. government will bail out Lockheed with additional guaranteed loans or with additional defense contracts or with more favorable terms on existing contracts such as the C-5A in order to protect the $250 million guarantee. That is why they want the U. S. loan guarantee and are not satisfied with unguaranteed loans.

The British drove a hard bargain and U. S. negotiators knuckled under despite the fact that our side had a better hand. For example, the General Electric Corporation has offered to supply engines for the L-1011 air frame at a price which would not increase the overall cost of the plane compared to the price with the Rolls Royce engine. Moreover, the G.E. engine would be built to the original contract specifications rather than to the lower specifications proposed by Rolls Royce and the British government. Even more important, U. S. jobs would have increased by about 10,000 and our balance of payments would have been bolstered. A U. S. engine would also involve more subcontracts to U. S. business firms, thus strengthening our economy.

If the U. S. government had said no to the British, Lockheed would have been forced to renegotiate its engine contract with a U. S. supplier such as G.E. or Pratt and Whitney. U. S. banks would no longer have had the British government as an ally in pressing for a Federal guarantee. Assuming a reasonable prospect of repayment, I am convinced that U. S. bankers would then have agreed to make additional loans to Lockheed without a Federal guarantee in order to protect their original investment. Under these circumstances, everyone would benefit except the British. The Administration's bill, therefore, is really a bail-out of Rolls Royce and the British government at the expense of the United States. Once again our government has been done in by the British.

But what if the bankers would not put up the money. The Administration argues that this would force Lockheed into bankruptcy and throw the 24,000 men on the L-1011 project out of work. A Federal loan guarantee would keep the L-1011 project alive and preserve the 24,000 jobs according to the Administration's argument.

Under what circumstances would the banks agree to jeopardize their existing $400 million investment by permitting Lockheed to declare bankruptcy?  Only if the bankers were convinced there was no reasonable prospect of getting their money back would they refuse to loan an additional $250 million to Lockheed for the L-1011 project.  If the L-1011 is that poor a risk a Federal loan guarantee will not save the 24,000 jobs—it will only postpone the ultimate day of reckoning while losing the taxpayers' $250 million.  If the L-1011 cannot compete in the market place, it is better to cut our losses now rather than throwing the public's money down the Lockheed rathole.

Actually, the concern over jobs is misplaced.  Even if Lockheed cancelled the L-1011 project, the slack would be taken up by its competitors—most probably McDonnell-Douglas, producer of the DC-10.  The McDonnell-Douglas plant in Long Beach is only 30 miles from the Lockheed plant in Burbank.  While there would be transition problems, most if not all of the discharged workers could ultimately find reemployment with McDonnell-Douglas.  Moreover, at least 10,000 new jobs would be created if McDonnell-Douglas replaced Lockheed since the DC-10 uses the American built G.E. engines rather than the Rolls Royce engine.

There is no way the United States can come out ahead under the Lockheed bail-out.  Moreover, there is much to be lost.

The most obvious loss is the taxpayers' $250 million if the L-1011 project fails.  The loss may be direct and obvious if the loan is in default.  However, the loss is more likely to be indirect and hidden and it could substantially exceed the $250 million.  The Administration would probably try to avoid the embarrassment of a formal default by bailing out Lockheed in other ways.  They might award them noncompetitive defense contracts.  Or they might relax the terms on existing contracts.  Either way will cost the taxpayer money.  The loss could exceed $250 million since the Administration might be willing to pay more in hidden subsidies in order to avoid the public embarrassment of a loan default.

Secondly, the proposed guarantee sets a dangerous precedent for our economy.  It tells the business community "don't worry about efficiency.  Uncle Sam will pick up the tab if you are in danger of failing, provided you are big enough."  There is already talk about broadening the legislation to cover additional large companies who find themselves in financial difficulties.  The availability of Federal guarantees removes the incentive for sound management.  The long term damage to the efficiency of the economy can be enormous.

Third, the proposed guarantee is unfair to Lockheed competitors who must now compete against the Federal government as well as Lockheed.  Moreover, the Federal government is now likely to favor

Lockheed over other contractors in order to protect the guarantee. Since 80% of defense procurement is not awarded through competitive bidding, the opportunities for favoritism are abundant. Well managed firms will find themselves losing out on contracts to Lockheed even though the well managed firms submit lower bids.

Fourth, the proposed guarantee is grossly unfair to small business. It applies only to large firms and not to small firms. It sets a precedent that big firms cannot be allowed to fail but little ones can. If Lockheed can get a Federal guarantee to keep from going broke, why shouldn't the same aid be extended to all firms, large and small?

In 1970, there were 10,700 business failures not counting railroads, financial institutions, and many one-man proprietorships. Almost all of the 10,700 were small—98% had liabilities under $1 million. The total liabilities of the 10,700 failing firms were $1.9 billion, considerably larger than Lockheed's total liabilities of $1.3 billion at the beginning of 1970.

The failure of the 10,700 small firms in 1970 involves a greater impact on the economy than the failure of Lockheed. Total liabilities are nearly 50% greater than Lockheed's. Moreover, many of the small firms were liquidated, whereas most of Lockheed's business would continue under court appointed trustees. Even the Administration admits that Lockheed's defense contracts would continue under bankruptcy. Only the Tristar would be cut back. About $1 billion of Lockheed's total liabilities are connected with the L-1011. Thus the failure of the 10,700 firms with liabilities of $1.9 billion had nearly twice the impact on the economy that a Lockheed failure would have.

If a Lockheed failure is so disastrous, why not prevent all business failures? It is unfair to single out one firm for immortality simply because it is large.

Fifth, if the proposed guarantee sets a precedent for bailing out other large corporations, the trend towards industrial concentration will be increased. Big business will be protected from failure whereas small business will not. What is really proposed is socialism for big business and free enterprise for small business. The inevitable result is that big business will grow even faster at the expense of small business. More and more resources will be concentrated in the hands of fewer and fewer firms.

Sixth, governmental bail-outs of large companies inevitably increase Federal control over business. If large companies run to Washington every time they are in financial trouble, the Federal government will soon dominate business decision making. I can think of no quicker road to state socialism.

Seventh, government bail-outs distort the allocation of resources in our economy. They concentrate resources in poorly managed firms when these resources should be shifted to better managed firms. The discipline of the market system is frustrated.

The word bankruptcy is a frightening word. It conjures up an image of total extinction. Those who say we cannot permit Lockheed to fail imply that all of its work will suddenly stop and all its employees will be thrown out of their jobs.

Actually, bankruptcy is nowhere near as harsh. All of the defense work of Lockheed—over 80% of its business—would continue. Admiral Rickover testified to this effect and it was confirmed by Secretary Connally.

When a large firm such as Penn-Central goes bankrupt, the firm is not liquidated—it is reorganized. The old management is kicked out and new management is appointed by the court. In the case of Penn-Central, this has had a beneficial effect on the company. The trains are still running and they even found the missing box cars which had been so cleverly hidden.

The only unemployment resulting from the Penn-Central bankruptcy has been on the part of top management. I can think of no greater benefit to the long term prosperity of Lockheed than to change its management. Here is an executive team that managed to lose nearly $500 million on four major government contracts all at the same time. Here is a management that ran up a $2 billion cost over-run on the C-5A which still does not meet Air Force requirements. Here is a management that lost $60 million on its last commercial aircraft, the Lockheed Electra. Here is a management which produced the F-104 fighter which the U. S. Air Force declines to use and which has been grounded by the German government, the primary purchaser. Here is a management which hitched its latest commercial venture—the L-1011—to a failing British company.

Are these disasters bad luck or bad management? When so many things go wrong, I submit that the management is to blame. We are now being asked to reward this managerial incompetence with a $250 million loan guarantee. I hope that the Congress will give a resounding no to this unwise venture.

# Chapter 12 Questions

1. What are the major issues that are central in any decision to make the loan guaranty?
2. Draw up a cost/benefit analysis concerning the major issues. (Aside from points presented in Secretary Connally's remarks, it may be noted that Lockheed still owes the government $100 million on the C-5A settlement, which would be lost to the government if the company went bankrupt.)
3. Argue the case for and against this loan guaranty as a threat to the free enterprise system.
4. If you were in the U.S. Congress, how would you vote? Defend your position.

# The Military-Industrial Complex

# The need for a strong defense establishment

### richard m. nixon

**President Richard M. Nixon makes a strong plea for the military establishment to be capable of defending the nation in a hostile world.**

You are entering the military service of your country when the nation's potential adversaries abroad have never been stronger and when your critics at home have never been more numerous.

It is open season on the armed forces. Military programs are ridiculed as needless if not deliberate waste. The military profession is derided in some of the so-called best circles of America. Patriotism is considered by some to be a backward fetish of the uneducated and unsophisticated. Nationalism is hailed and applauded as a panacea for the ills of every nation—except the United States of America.

This paradox of military power is a symptom of something far deeper that is stirring in our body politic. It goes beyond the dissent about the war in Vietnam. It goes behind the fear of the "military industrial complex."

The underlying questions are really these:

What is America's role in the world? What are the responsibilities of a great nation toward protecting freedom beyond its shores? Can we ever be left in peace if we do not actively assume the burden of keeping the peace?

When great questions are posed, fundamental differences of opinion come into focus. It serves no purpose to gloss over these differences, or to try to pretend that they are mere matters of degree.

Because there is one school of thought that holds that the road to understanding with the Soviet Union and Communist China lies through a downgrading of our own alliances and what amounts to a unilateral reduction of our own arms—in order to demonstrate our "good faith."

They believe that we can be conciliatory and accommodating only if we do not have the strength to be otherwise. They believe America will be able to deal with the possibility of peace only when we are unable to cope with the threat of war.

Those who think that way have grown weary of the weight of free world leadership that fell upon us in the wake of World War II. They

---

From remarks of the President at Commencement Exercises at the Air Force Academy, Colorado Springs, June 4, 1969.

**363**

argue that we, the United States, are as much responsible for the tensions in the world as the adversary we face.

They assert that the United States is blocking the road to peace by maintaining its military strength at home and its defenses abroad.  If we would only reduce our forces, they contend, tensions would disappear and the chances for peace would brighten.

America's powerful military presence on the world scene, they believe, makes peace abroad improbable and peace at home impossible.

Now we should never underestimate the appeal of the isolationist school of thought.  Their slogans are simplistic and powerful: "Charity begins at home.  Let's first solve our problems at home and then we can deal with the problems of the world."

This simple formula touches a responsive chord with many an overburdened taxpayer.  It would be easy, easy for the President of the United States to buy some popularity by going along with the new isolationists.  But I submit to you that it would be disastrous for our nation and the world.

I hold a totally different view of the world, and I come to a different conclusion about the direction America must take.

Imagine for a moment, if you will, what would happen to this world if America were to become a dropout in assuming the responsibility for defending peace and freedom in the world.  As every world leader knows, and as even the most outspoken critics of America would admit, the rest of the world would live in terror.

Because if America were to turn its back on the world, there would be peace that would settle over this planet, but it would be the kind of peace that suffocated freedom in Czechoslovakia.

The danger to us has changed, but it has not vanished.  We must revitalize our alliances, not abandon them.

We must rule out unilateral disarmament, because in the real world it wouldn't work.  If we pursue arms control as an end in itself, we will not achieve our end.  The adversaries in the world are not in conflict because they are armed.  They are armed because they are in conflict, and have not yet learned peaceful ways to resolve their conflicting national interests.

The aggressors of this world are not going to give the United States a period of grace in which to put our domestic house in order—just as the crises within our society cannot be put on a back burner until we resolve the problem of Vietnam.

The most successful solutions that we can possibly imagine for our domestic programs will be meaningless if we are not around to enjoy them.  Nor can we conduct a successful peace policy abroad if our society is at war with itself at home.

There is no advancement for Americans at home in a retreat from the problems of the world. I say that America has a vital national interest in world stability, and no other nation can uphold that interest for us.

We stand at a crossroad in our history. We shall reaffirm our destiny for greatness or we shall choose instead to withdraw into ourselves. The choice will affect far more than our foreign policy; it will determine the quality of our lives.

A nation needs many qualities, but it needs faith and confidence above all. Skeptics do not build societies; the idealists are the builders. Only societies that believe in themselves can rise to their challenges. Let us not, then, post a false choice between meeting our responsibilities abroad and meeting the needs of our people at home. We shall meet both or we shall meet neither.

That is why my disagreement with the skeptics and the isolationists is fundamental. They have lost the vision indispensable to great leadership. They observe the problems that confront us; they measure our resources and then they despair. When the first vessels set out from Europe for the new world these men would have weighed the risks and they would have stayed behind. When the colonists on the Eastern seaboard started across the Appalachians to the unknown reaches of the Ohio Valley, these men would have counted the costs and they would have stayed behind.

Our current exploration of space makes the point vividly: Here is testimony to man's vision and to man's courage. The journey of the astronauts is more than a technical achievement; it is a reaching-out of the human spirit. It lifts our sights; it demonstrates that magnificent conceptions can be made real.

They inspire us and at the same time they teach us true humility. What could bring home to us more the limitations of the human scale than the hauntingly beautiful picture of our earth seen from the moon?

When the first man stands on the moon next month every American will stand taller because of what he has done, and we should be proud of this magnificent achievement.

We will know then that every man achieves his own greatness by reaching out beyond himself, and so it is with nations. When a nation believes in itself—as Athenians did in their golden age, as Italians did in the Renaissance—that nation can perform miracles. Only when a nation means something to itself can it mean something to others.

That is why I believe a resurgence of American idealism can bring about a modern miracle—and that modern miracle is a world order of peace and justice.

I know that every member of this graduating class is, in that sense, an idealist.

However, I must warn you that in the years to come you may hear your commitment to the American responsibility in the world derided as a form of militarism.　It is important that you recognize that straw-man issue for what it is, the outward sign of a desire by some to turn America inward and to have America turn away from greatness.　I am not speaking about those responsible critics who reveal waste and in-efficiency in our defense establishment, who demand clear answers on procurement policies, who want to make sure new weapons systems will truly add to our defense.　On the contrary, you should be in the vanguard of that movement.　Nor do I speak of those with sharp eyes and sharp pencils who are examining our post-Vietnam planning with other pressing national priorities in mind.　I count myself as one of those.

But as your Commander-in-Chief, I want to relay to you as future officers in our armed forces some of my thoughts on some of these great issues of national moment.

I worked closely with President Eisenhower for eight years.　I know what he meant when he said ". . . we must guard against the acquisi-tion of unwarranted influence, whether sought or unsought, by the mili-tary industrial complex."

Many people conveniently forget that he followed that warning with another:　"We must also be alert to the equal and opposite danger that public policy could itself become the captive of a scientific-technologi-cal elite."

We sometimes forget that in that same Farewell Address, President Eisenhower spoke of the need for national security.　He said: "A vital element in keeping the peace is our military establishment.　Our arms must be mighty, ready for instant action, so that no potential aggressor may be tempted to risk his own destruction."

I say to you, my fellow Americans, let us never forget those wise words of one of America's greatest leaders.

The American defense establishment should never be a sacred cow, but on the other hand, the American military should never be any-body's scapegoat.

America's wealth is enormous, but it is not limitless.　Every dollar available in the Federal Government has been taken from the American people in taxes.　A responsible government has a duty to be prudent when it spends the people's money.　There is no more justification for wasting money on unnecessary military hardware than there is for wasting it on unwarranted social programs.

There can be no question that we should not spend unnecessarily for defense.　But we must also not confuse our priorities.

The question, I submit, in defense spending is a very simple one: "How much is necessary?"　The President of the United States is the man charged with making that judgment.　After a complete review of our foreign and defense policies I have submitted requests to the Congress for military appropriations—some of these are admittedly controversial. These requests represent the minimum I believe essential for the United States to meet its current and long-range obligations to itself and to the free world. I have asked only for those programs and those expenditures that I believe are necessary to guarantee the security of this country and to honor our obligations. I will bear the responsibility for those judgments. I do not consider my recommendations infallible. But if I have made a mistake, I pray that it is on the side of too much and not too little. If we do too much it will cost us our money. If we do too little, it may cost us our lives.

Mistakes in military policy today can be irretrievable. Time lost in this age of science can never be regained. America had months to prepare and to catch up in order to wage World War I. We had months and even years in order to catch up so we could play a role in winning World War II. When a war can be decided in twenty minutes, the nation that is behind will have no time to catch up.

I say: Let America never fall behind in maintaining the defenses necessary for the strength of this nation.

I have no choice in my decisions but to come down on the side of security because history has dealt harshly with those nations who have taken the other course.

So, in that spirit, to the members of this graduating class, let me offer this credo for the defenders of our nation:

I believe that we must balance our need for survival as a nation with our need for survival as a people. Americans, soldiers and civilians, must remember that defense is not an end in itself—it is a way of holding fast to the deepest values known to civilized men.

I believe that our defense establishment will remain the servants of our national policy of bringing about peace in the world and that those in any way connected with the military must scrupulously avoid even the appearance of becoming the master of that policy.

I believe that every man in uniform is a citizen first and a serviceman second, and that we must resist any attempt to isolate or separate the defenders from the defended. So you can see that in this regard, those who agitate for the removal of the ROTC from college campuses contribute to an unwanted militarism.

I believe that the basis for decisions on defense spending must be "what do we do, what do we need for our security" and not "what will this mean for business and employment." The Defense Department must never be considered as a modern WPA. There are far better ways for government to help insure a sound prosperity and high employment.

I feel that moderation has a moral significance only in those who have another choice. The weak can only plead; magnanimity and restraint gain moral meaning coming from the strong.

I believe that defense decisions must be made on the hard realities of the offensive capabilities of our potential adversaries, and not on the fervent hopes about their intentions. With Thomas Jefferson, we can prefer "the flatteries of hope" to the gloom of despair, but we cannot survive in the real world if we plan our defense in a dream world.

I believe we must take risks for peace—but calculated risks, not foolish risks. We shall not trade our defenses for a disarming smile or charming words. We are prepared for new initiatives in the control of arms in the context of other specific moves to reduce tensions around the world.

I believe that America is not going to become a Garrison State, or a Welfare State, or a Police State—simply because the American people will defend our values from those forces external or internal that would challenge or erode them.

And I believe this above all: That this nation shall continue to be a source of world leadership, a source of freedom's strength, in creating a just world order that will bring an end to war.

# The pentagon vs. free enterprise

## william proxmire

Senator William Proxmire, a severe critic of the military-industrial complex, complains in the following article that the military-industrial complex has acquired too much influence and as a result gets more budget allocation than it should. Furthermore, he elaborates on what he considers to be inefficiencies in the spending of defense money.

The military-industrial complex has a great and pervasive influence on the life of the United States. Everyone agrees on that. But whether its influence is unwarranted or unhealthy is, of course, the question that has provoked heated national debate. The size and influence of the complex have given rise to legitimate concern, because of the military's tendency to identify national security with ever-larger arsenals, and because of its growing and heretofore unchallenged claim on the natural and human resources needed to combat the country's domestic ills. Compounding this concern is the documented evidence that the military and defense industries are guilty of inefficient and otherwise questionable business practices—particularly in the area of procurement—that not only are wasteful but stifle the principle of open competition that is basic to our free enterprise system.

Military and military-related spending now totals more than $80-billion annually and consumes a tenth of the Gross National Product. Because the defense budget has not been as thoroughly scrutinized and debated as budgets for civilian programs, and because of past experience with national security costs greatly exceeding initial estimates, the allocation of these funds is of primary importance. The defense budget should not be allowed to just "grow," but should be subject to the same control as the rest of the budget.

In the past, only one-tenth of the total staff of the Bureau of the Budget has been assigned to review the military budget. In all fairness, Robert Mayo, the present director of the bureau, has testified that in the future military expenditures will be subject to the same scrutiny as are civilian programs. This review is absolutely essential, and I hope that it will be accomplished. My own investigations and those of Congress's Joint Economic Committee reveal that approximately $10-billion could be cut without diminishing national security in the least, and the Subcommittee on Economy in Government in its report *The*

Senator William Proxmire, "The Pentagon Vs. Free Enterprise," *Saturday Review*, January 31, 1970, pp. 14–17. Copyright 1970 Saturday Review, Inc.

*Military Budget and National Economic Priorities* has formally recommended that such a cut be made.

In fiscal year 1969, $42-billion was awarded in contracts for defense procurement, making it the largest single item in the military budget (about 25 per cent of the total federal budget), and most important, therefore, to those concerned with rising military costs.  Procurement includes defense contracts and all purchases or rentals of supplies, equipment, and services.  Procurement is often referred to as the life-blood of defense contractors.

The most efficient and economical way to approach procurement is through competitive bidding; the Congress has repeatedly and consistently directed the Department of Defense to buy competitively. The Pentagon, however, increasingly resorts to practices that reduce competition, and relies more and more heavily on negotiated procurement.  Formally advertised competitive military contract dollar awards dropped from 13.4 per cent in fiscal year 1967 to 11 per cent in fiscal year 1969.  Single source procurement increased to 57.9 per cent.  Last year, about 90 per cent of the Pentagon's and 98 per cent of NASA's contract awards were negotiated under "exceptions"—too often broad and vague exceptions.

The Defense Department, of course, defends negotiated procurement as being comparable to competitive bidding, but only competitive procurement can really give the desired emphasis to dollar cost.  Negotiation on nonprice elements cannot completely or successfully substitute for price competition.  Experts who have appeared before the Subcommittee on Economy in Government have indicated that procurement costs in the absence of competition can be from 25 per cent to 50 per cent higher than they would have been had competition been present.

Negotiated arrangements can also lend themselves to repeated dealings with certain favored and trusted suppliers.  If desired, there are practically effortless ways to get around the regulations requiring competitive bidding.  As a part of these regulations, the 1962 Truth-in-Negotiations Act was designed to protect the taxpayer in the absence of true competition, but if a procurement officer determines that competition is adequate or that a standard catalogue price is in effect, the act does not apply.  It is also possible to waive the requirements (again under the Truth-in-Negotiations Act) for a contractor to supply cost data.  Defense firms, fully aware of the existence of these loopholes, may refuse to supply the cost data even at the risk of loss of a sale. This amounts to a gamble that the government needs their product enough to waive the requirements eventually and proceed with the purchase.

When a firm has actually won a contract to do the research on a major weapons system, it occupies a favored position and is more likely to be chosen to do the work on actual production of the system. In the jargon of defense spending, this is known as being "locked into" a contract. The knowledge gained during the research phase undoubtedly provides a competitive advantage in subsequent negotiations—an advantage that usually means the production contract.

Another way for the firm to improve its position over the life of the contract is commonly referred to as "buy in, get well later." Once a contractor has won the contract, if his costs increase or he cannot meet the agreed delivery date, the government will "get him well" by meeting the higher price or accepting later delivery.

Gordon W. Rule, a civilian procurement officer with responsibility for the F-111, the attack plane whose production has been cut back drastically because of mechanical problems and soaring costs, has told the subcommittee, "No matter how poor the quality, how late the product, and how high the cost, they [the defense contractors] know nothing will happen to them." Thus, the contractors attach the greatest importance to submitting low estimates in order to win the contract even if they suspect at the time that costs will have to be raised later.

Prices and costs can be easily increased during production through the numerous change orders issued (which can potentially number in the thousands on a major system). Referred to as "contract nourishment," these change orders can be initiated by either the government or the supplier, and are not adequately controlled or audited—a point I will elaborate on in my discussion of defense firm accounting practices.

The Subcommittee on Economy in Government has again recommended (in its report of last May) that the Defense Department make greater use of competitive bidding in order to eliminate these problems. If necessary, further legislation should be enacted to make the submission of cost and pricing data mandatory under the Truth-in-Negotiations Act for all contracts awarded other than through formally advertised price competition procedures, and in all sole-source procurements whether or not formally advertised.

Under the conditions just outlined, it does not take much imagination to see how defense suppliers might come to occupy a secure position. Indeed, some companies do almost all of their business with the Department of Defense. In fiscal year 1968, the 100 largest defense contractors were awarded 67.4 per cent of total defense contracts, the highest percentage since 1965. The largest firms hold "entrenched" positions: eighty-four of the firms on the list of 100 largest firms in 1968 had also been on the list in 1967; eighteen of those on the list of the largest twenty-five were on this list in both 1967 and 1968. The five firms doing over $1-billion worth of business with the government in 1967 maintained this volume in the subsequent year.

In spite of their key positions with respect to defense procurement, some of these large firms, such as Lockheed, Boeing, General Dynamics, North American Rockwell, and Litton Industries, refused to appear when invited to testify at recent hearings of the Subcommittee on Economy in Government. To say the least, it appears curious that they would not want to present their views, unless of course they have nothing to add.

In addition to repeated dealings with these same firms, the involvement or relationship between the Pentagon and its suppliers is reinforced by the common practice of interchanging personnel. Many retired officers leave their procurement responsibilities to take positions with the very firms with which they have been negotiating. At present, more than 2,100 retired officers of the rank of colonel or higher are holding jobs with firms doing defense work. The ten companies employing the largest number of them had 1,065 on their payrolls, an average of 106, three times the average number employed in 1959.

The Subcommittee on Economy in Government, recognizing this conflict-of-interest potential, recommended that the Government Accounting Office compile a defense-industrial personnel exchange directory—a kind of catalogue of the officials who have moved from the Pentagon to defense industries or vice versa. My amendment to the military authorization act calls for yearly Pentagon disclosure of the names of all retired military procurement officers, all those of the rank of major or higher, and all former civilian personnel who occupied high positions (GS-13 or above) in the Department of Defense who go to work for the big contractors. It also calls for annual disclosures of the names of former defense contractor employees who now occupy high positions in the Department of Defense.

What this lack of competitive procedure and poor business practices means to the government and taxpayers is higher bills to pay for inefficiencies and waste. The higher costs simply do not buy more security. The extensive and pervasive economic inefficiency and waste in military procurement have been well documented by the investigations of the Subcommittee on Economy in Government, by other committees of the House and Senate, and by the General Accounting Office.

Assistant Secretary of the Air Force Robert H. Charles testified that "the procurement of our major weapons systems has in the past been characterized by enormous cost overruns—several hundred per cent—and by technical performance that did not come up to promise." He attributed a substantial portion of the waste to cost reimbursement type contracts, and to the absence of price competition.

Richard A. Stubbing, a defense analyst at the Bureau of the Budget, in a study of the performance of complex weapons systems, concluded: "The low overall performance of electronics in major weapons systems developed and produced in the last decade should give pause to even the most outspoken advocates of military-hardware programs."

It has been repeatedly pointed out that the greatest cost overruns occur in negotiated contracts. Even in the absence of overruns, however, evidence has been presented that prices are being negotiated at too high a level from the beginning. Further, a retired Air Force officer, Col. A. W. Buesking, a former director of management systems control in the Office of the Assistant Secretary of Defense, summarized a study he had conducted by saying that control systems essential to prevent excessive costs did not exist.

The cost overruns on the C-5A cargo plane (recently grounded with a wing crack) are the most shocking example of the defense industry's inefficiency and mismanagement. The total cost overrun in the C-5A program has been revealed to be as much as $2-billion. The program originally called for 120 C-5A planes to cost the government $3.4-billion, but because of cost overruns, mainly experienced in the performance of the Lockheed C-5A contract, actual costs will total $5.3-billion. Last November the Air Force finally conceded that the cost increases made at least part of the program too expensive to continue, and it announced it would buy only eighty-one of the planes.

Still another example is a more than $200-million overrun on the Mark II Avionics program—the radars, computers, and inertial equipment for the F-111. The original contract price was $143-million, and former Secretary Charles has revealed that the actual costs may go as high as $360-million. On the Mark XVII program, the reentry system for the Minuteman, the original contract price was $36.4-million, but the actual costs had reached $70.2-million at the time the contract was ended.

In December 1969, the General Accounting Office reported that the costs of fifty-seven major weapons systems had increased by $21-billion. However, this figure is seriously understated, in my judgment, because of the inadequacies of the Pentagon's cost-information system. GAO found that the Pentagon still does not maintain a central inventory of the major weapons systems that would show their costs and other information.

The cost to the government and taxpayers is further increased, because the government encourages inefficiency. Let me elaborate on this incredible statement. The Department of Defense supplies both fixed and working capital to many contractors. DOD often owns the plant in which the contractor will work. Too frequently the amount of property owned by the government exceeds that of the defense company. Further, a disproportionate amount of this government equipment is held by the larger contractors.

In fiscal year 1968, the amount of industrial plant equipment costing over $1,000 that was used by the defense suppliers totaled $2.7-billion—a $100-million increase over the $2.6-billion of 1967.

The Pentagon supplies working capital by making "progress payments" that can reimburse contractors for as much as 100 per cent of incurred costs. Incurred cost reimbursement payments might be a better name, however, since progress payments have no correlation to the amount of work actually completed. Under these circumstances money advanced as progress payments really amounts to a kind of no-interest government loan that inflates contractors' profits. Given this "free" working capital, a contractor is in a position to bid low for other government work or to finance commercial work. It is possible for a contractor to incur costs equal to 75 per cent of the original contract price while completing only 50 per cent or less of the job. Not only is the Department of Defense providing a negative incentive for a firm to use its own working capital, but at the same time it is developing a financial stake in the contractor.

In the C-5A case, Lockheed received progress payments of $1.52-billion on reported incurred costs of $1.57-billion, as of May 30, 1969. In addition, the contract is being performed in a government-owned plant. The plant and the government-owned machinery employed at the plant have an original acquisition cost of $113.8-million.

Yet another instance of these most unusual business practices is the government's policy with regard to patent rights. It permits contractors to obtain exclusive patent rights, free of charge, on inventions produced in the performance of their contracts. Admiral Rickover and Murray Weidenbaum (now Assistant Secretary of the Treasury) both contend that this practice further reduces competition because it gives the "ins" a competitive advantage over the "outs." Legislative action should be taken to establish uniform guidelines for all federal agencies on the use of patents obtained for inventions made under government contract.

Admiral Rickover also testified that $2-billion of excessive costs results from the absence of uniform accounting standards alone. It is difficult to accurately determine costs and profits. "In one case," reported Admiral Rickover, "the Navy allowed a shipbuilder to charge salaries and other pay directly on government contracts, while similar costs on commercial contracts were charged as overhead and allocated to both government and commercial work. The government was thus paying directly for work done on commercial contracts. The Navy had accepted these costing methods because, it said, the contractor's system conformed to generally accepted accounting principles. In this particular case the GAO eventually found that the government had been overcharged by more than $5-million."

To quote Admiral Rickover further on the problems of accounting standards, "Thus, contractors can use change orders as a basis for repricing these contracts. They have almost unlimited freedom in pricing change orders, because their accounting system will never show the cost of the work. The government can never really evaluate the amounts claimed, or check up to see if it paid too much."

The Subcommittee on Economy in Government has recommended that the Department of Defense require contractors to maintain books and records on firm-fixed-price contracts showing the costs of manufacturing all components in accordance with uniform accounting standards.

Not only should there be tighter control on cost records, but something must be done in the area of profits. The Department of Defense cannot accurately state what profits are in defense procurement. First, it defines profits as a percentage of costs, and does not report profits as a return on investment. Second, the Department of Defense does not obtain complete information about profits on firm-fixed-price contracts. Third, without uniform accounting standards, it is difficult, if not impossible, to discover the costs and profits in defense production unless months are spent to reconstruct contractors' books.

Many witnesses have told the subcommittee that profits in defense are higher than nondefense profits. Murray Weidenbaum found in his study "that between 1962 and 1965 a sample of large defense contractors earned 17.5 per cent net profit (measured as a return on investment), while companies of similar size doing business in the commercial market earned 10.6 per cent."

Profits should also be considered both as a percentage of costs and as a return on investment. Since the Department of Defense supplies fixed and working capital in many cases, defense contractors would show an enormously high return on investment if it were computed.

Another recommendation of the subcommittee is that the GAO study the feasibility of incorporating into its review of contractors the should-cost method of estimating costs on the basis of industrial engineering and financial management principles. In this way, cost estimates could be freed from being based on original estimates that may be inflated.

Finally, we can point to a relation between defense spending and inflation. Both the Korean war period and the Vietnam era have been accompanied by price increases; this suggests that defense expenditures have made significant contributions to inflationary pressures. The consequent reduced value of savings and fixed income assets during periods of inflation and the 10 per cent income tax surcharge are certainly taxpayer burdens as much as the high cost of the defense budget.

High interest rates may eventually stop the inflation, but they hurt the homeowner, the aged, the consumer, and the small businessman in the process. A more intelligent way to curb the price spiral would be to cut defense costs.

The record is clear. Our priorities as a nation need to be restructured, and the place to start is with the bloated defense budget. Only when Congress is again in control of the entire budget can we make progress on the domestic front.

# How to get rid of a complex

## william r. wilson

**William R. Wilson, Vice-President of Public Relations at the Lockheed Aircraft Corporation, defends the military-industrial complex in the following speech.**

The military-industrial complex is a subject I have been interested in for a long time. In fact, I sounded like a prophet of gloom in our company a few years ago when I first began to call attention to the early attacks on the complex. I predicted they would grow into a massive issue. It's no satisfaction to be proved right. I feel a little like Cassandra, the Greek prophetess, whose predictions, accurate though they were, were fated never to be believed.

In any case, I have been watching the attack gain momentum. I have been impressed with the vigor with which it has been pursued. And I have been dismayed by the distortions on which it has flourished.

So I'd like to congratulate the NAM on its effort to present a more analytical and more objective view of the problem.

Of course, I am a member of the industry side of the military-industrial complex, so I suppose I'm not entirely objective myself. But I don't intend to be a blind apologist for the complex. I admit to my own biases as a member of a company that has borne much of the brunt of the attack. I also admit to certain imperfections in the system—there are, for example, some contracting methods that have given us at Lockheed a great deal of trouble and exposed us to a high degree of risk, and we're not entirely happy with them. And I am sure it is easy to find other faults with the system, just as it is possible to find fault with any system in which human beings are involved.

But I keep remembering one thing. The military-industrial complex has played a large part—and I think a determining part—in keeping our country and the world free from a major war during the past 25 or 30 years. This is nothing to be taken lightly. Whatever its faults, a system that has achieved this deserves much better treatment than it has been getting. So, first let's review the history and nature of the attacks upon the military-industrial complex, particularly as they have affected public opinion, and try to suggest what they are leading up to.

William R. Wilson, "How to Get Rid of a Complex," *Dateline*, May 1970, pp. 4–6. Reprinted by permission of the author.

## ATTACKS

Of course, these attacks have come from many different directions. And they have been made by many different groups with apparent motives ranging from the most idealistic to the most dubious. Some of them have been aimed at reducing the complex, some at reforming it, others at getting rid of it.

Let's assume for the moment you wanted to get rid of the military-industrial complex. How would you go about it? You might well try some of the things its attackers have done.

First, you could attack it just because it is big. We Americans tend to suspect anything big—big government, big corporations, big unions. Maybe we long for the good old days when things were smaller. Or maybe we just like the underdog instead of the big guys.

The early attacks on the complex stressed this point. You remember we were told to guard against its undue influence because it was so large. People like former Science Advisor Jerome Wiesner warned us about this. They were afraid that checks and balances in the system —things like civilian control, Congressional reviews of programs and appropriations and the existence of other competing groups might someday not prove adequate. Later attacks, like those of John Galbraith, alleged that indeed these checks and balances were not enough. The complex was already so big that it couldn't be checked.

Or, again, you might attack the complex on the ground that it is wasteful and inefficient. You do this in various ways. You pick out programs that were started and then stopped—like the manned orbiting laboratory. Or you pick out weapon systems that never reached full expectations—systems like the F-111. Or you pick out systems we have never had occasion to use—missiles like Minuteman or Polaris. We have even been told that the Polaris was a waste of money because we have never used it!

Or you could try another tack. You could concentrate on cost over-runs. You could argue that because a program costs more than its original estimate, it proved bad management, waste and inefficiency on the part of the contractor or laxity on the part of the customer. You don't have to be too careful with your figures on this because you're dealing in a very complex and confusing area. You don't have to be too careful with your logic because you have a magic word—"cost overrun"—and of course everybody assumes this means the taxpayer is getting gypped—even if he is getting a bargain.

We at Lockheed have a lot of very bloody experience in counteracting this argument. Our C-5A Galaxy has almost become a synonym for cost overrun. The amount of overrun was vastly exaggerated in the press, the reasons were seldom adequately explained, and everyone was left with the impression that all the overrun represented waste and that the excess costs were somehow being pocketed by us. The fact is, of course, that we're making no money at all on the program and still have a chance of losing some. Nevertheless, the Air Force will receive an outstanding aircraft that will meet all its specifications.

Allied to this charge of waste is another you could use—profiteering. Because defense contractors are large companies, because the programs they're working on are so big, because the costs tend to grow, it follows naturally that defense companies must be making piles of money. Never mind that all the studies show their earnings are low and getting lower. They must be making it somehow!

And if you want still another line of attack, you can somehow imply collusion or wrongdoing. You can say contracts are specially written for certain companies—as indeed it was said of us on the C-5A. You can refer to repricing clauses as "golden handshakes." Or you can point to industry's employment of retired military officers as evidence of some kind of underhanded skulduggery.

All of these attacks have been made. They all add up to a powerful thrust against the industry. I don't discount their effect on the public mind or on Congress. The evidence is all around us. There is little doubt they have weakened our defense posture.

But still and all, these charges are not the perfect answer to getting rid of the complex. For one thing, the attacks can be answered and answered effectively, even though it is an uphill battle to dislodge entrenched public opinion. We at Lockheed have, I think, answered some of them effectively before Congressional committees investigating C-5A cost growth. Others have answered other charges.

And, where the system can be shown to be at fault, it can be changed. Greater emphasis can be given to civilian controls, more information can be given Congress, contracting procedures can be improved.

All this may change the complex somewhat. It may weaken it. It may even improve it. But it will not really get rid of it. If you want to get rid of it, you cannot simply attack it on the edges. You have to attack it at the center.


## RECOMMENDATIONS

Attacking it at the center involves attacking the need for its existence. You have to ask the question, "Do we really need a military-industrial complex—a strong team effort between military and defense industry to provide for the defense of the United States and whatever commitments or obligations we have abroad?"

This question is basic.  If we admit the need, then we accept the complex, and the argument becomes one of how it should operate— how it should function.  But if we attack the need, then we attack the complex at the root.

So if you're planning on getting rid of the military-industrial complex, ultimately you ought to plan on getting around to asking this question of whether we need it at all.

Are there people asking it?  Indeed there are.  Perhaps they think that now, with the complex softened and made vulnerable by all the peripheral attacks, the time is right to launch the heavy artillery. Perhaps this is what some of them intended all along.  But now they have come out in the open.  They are asking whether we really need a military-industrial establishment.  And their answer is an emphatic "no."

I have just read a recent book by Richard J. Barnet, co-director of the Institute for Policy Studies, entitled *The Economy of Death*.  The Institute for Policy Studies describes itself as an educational institution and is supported by contributions from foundations, universities and individuals.  For several years it has been holding conferences for members of Congress and their staffs, largely to enlighten them on the evils of defense.

The book is a frank proposal for dismantling the military-industrial complex, complete with detailed instructions on how to do it.  Its basic proposition is that we don't need the complex and, even more than that, its existence endangers our national security, hampers our efforts toward disarmament, and directs our national efforts and resources toward the path of death rather than the path of life.

And there is more in Mr. Barnet's book—much about nuclear overkill, about what the author considers the bloated size of our General Purpose Forces, the folly of maintaining the capacity to fight three wars, the uselessness of trying to police the world by combating revolutions in other lands, and the hopelessness—indeed the dangers— involved in pursuing technological developments in weapons either for offense or defense.

And of course there is nothing exactly new in all of this.  We have heard many of these opinions and arguments before in various places. What is so devastating is that here they are all brought together in one place to make a case for breaking up the military-industrial complex.

And what is new, so far as I know, is that Mr. Barnet goes on to tell us just how to do this.  What is his prescription?

First, he tells us what you *don't* do.  You don't nationalize the defense industry by turning it into a government arsenal, as Mr. Galbraith has suggested.  This does not solve the problem of concentration of power.  The Pentagon's ability to control a major share of the nation's industrial power is the real problem, he says. It can only be solved, he tells us, by shrinking the Pentagon to manageable size and destroying its industrial base.

So what does Mr. Barnet suggest? What he says is that we should radically reduce the flow of funds to defense. He recommends this be done by an aroused public opinion, led by activist groups composed of students, scientists, businessmen who are not Pentagon suppliers, and a fourth group—most powerful of all—members of Congress. There are suggestions for strengthening the hand of Congress and limiting the power of the Department of Defense.

Another thing he recommends is to work on the defense companies directly, turning them into hybrid public-private corporations. Then, he maintains, we should establish a National Conversion Commission to retrain and relocate people released from defense industries. He suggests subsidizing other, more peaceful projects on which some of these people may be used. And he then proposes that we reconstitute American society and redistribute wealth and power.

Now—while we are doing all this—we presumably disclaim all responsibilities for preserving peace in the rest of the planet. We point our magic wand at the Middle East, at the Communist turmoil in Southeast Asia, at the strife of nationalism versus communism throughout Africa and Latin America. We command world turmoil to stop while we dismantle the administrative, technical, and industrial structure that now shields us.

This is essentially a modern day call for isolationism—a retreat from foreign commitments made by all administrations since World War II, commitments that people like Churchill have described as a guarantee of world order and progress.

I believe this book is a prescription for disaster, partisan in its approach and extreme in its proposals. But in a strange, backhanded way, it does a service to the debate on the complex. It raises a fundamental issue—not the faults of the complex but the need for it.

## THE REAL TARGET

In many ways the military-industrial complex is the wrong target. What we are really talking about is foreign policy and defense policy. Let me quote from C. W. Borklund, editor of *Government Executive Magazine*, on this:

> The procedure is that the nation, i.e. Congress, determines foreign policy. That and the related threat estimates produce strategy which, in theory, it approves. That, in turn, decides force structures on which even the Constitution says Congress shall have the

ultimate say. And finally, last in line, force structures direct what and how many weapon systems will be bought. As a footnote, so the theory goes, Congress has, or assumes it has, a right to audit how efficiently Defense buys the weapon systems.

Mr. Borklund goes on to say that Congress spends a good deal of time worrying over the footnote and not enough time on the major questions upon which the footnote depends. If you indeed want to get rid of the military-industrial complex or reduce it significantly, the way to do it is to alter foreign policy, reassess national security needs, alter strategies, reduce force structures. The size of the military-industrial complex will be reduced in the process.

But there is no point in whittling the complex down to a size that does not fit our foreign policies and our responsibilities overseas. It is like giving a man a job to do and then not giving him the tools to do it. The result is that the job won't get done, or only part of it will get done. What current critics would do is to define the task by the tools allotted to do it.

I submit that this is an extremely foolish way to determine our task in the foreign and defense arenas. I would hate to see national policy decided by complaints over the number of retired admirals and generals employed in defense industries or even by the size of the defense establishment. If it is large now, it is because it has a large job to do. The way to make it smaller is to give it a smaller job. And the way to get rid of it completely is to give it no job at all.

Few people would go so far as this last. But there appear to be many who would like to see the job reduced and have hit upon attacking the complex as the way to reduce it. I do not believe they are right in their goal. Even if they are, it is a national tragedy to seek to accomplish it in this way.

## COMPLEX INFLUENCE

I am sure the Congressional debate—and I would hope the public debate—should be moved out of the military-industrial complex arena and into the arena of national goals—priorities, to use an "in" word— where it belongs. To those who say the massive influence of the military-industrial complex is an effective roadblock to a reordering of national goals, the obvious retort is "nonsense." Events of the last few years—budget cutbacks, program cancellations, Congressional inquiries, press and TV publicity—have all demonstrated that the power of the military-industrial complex is largely a myth.

The checks and balances in the system are strong and growing stronger. Since 1961, Congress has extended its power to review major programs and research and development before authorizing funding. Civilian control in the Department of Defense was greatly expanded under former Secretary McNamara to the point where many programs supported by Congress and the Joint Chiefs of Staff were not initiated. And cancellations and cutbacks today are almost wholesale.

In the arena of public opinion the military-industrial complex is pitifully weak.

It is often jolted by a critical press, who know that the big headlines come from the occasional mistake, not the continuing good performance.

It gets short shrift from the taxpayer, who only knows that a lot of his dollars are going in to support it and who can't see what good it's doing.

It gets nothing but scorn from the New Left activists, many of whom want to overthrow the whole society anyway and some of whom are latter-day Marxists whose aim is to weaken all free societies.

It gets little help from the general public, who regard it as big, burdensome, and necessarily wasteful, but who do not understand it.

And industry has a hard time defending itself. We at Lockheed have found this true in our own case. Our C-5A cost growth was exaggerated and perfectly good reasons for the growth were left unexplained. Yet when we tried to explain them, we were faced with the chore of explaining what must surely be one of the most complex contracts in the world. And what resulted was that we had reasoned and factual explanations on one side against emotional and oversimplified arguments on the other.

The real danger to our nation may well be not that the military-industrial complex is too strong but that it is too weak. It is very vulnerable to attack—and the attack can have grave and perhaps unwanted consequences. It is to me an extremely disturbing thought that the nation's future role on the world's stage and our future role on the world's stage and our future capacity to defend ourselves and others may be determined, not where it should be, in the highest councils of government, but by undermining the military-industrial team that has supported that role and maintained that capacity. This is a cart-before-the-horse approach.

If the attacks against the military-industrial complex succeed, the attackers—many of them—will have bought something more than they bargained for. They will have bought a new foreign and defense policy. Perhaps they will have bought a different kind of America.

The military-industrial complex is a false issue, and I am glad to see the real issue come to light, even in such wrong-headed ways as those proposed by the New Left. As long as this false issue is with us, we on the side of the complex must do our best to speak to it. Even as we do so, we run the risk of being accused of speaking from self-interest in defending particular programs or particular aspects of our operations.

What, then, can we in industry do?

We should, of course, continue to defend ourselves as well as we can against specific charges. More important, we can point out the real issues whenever we can and try to move the public debate into this broader arena. We can encourage objective studies by responsible bodies like that of the President's Blue Ribbon committee and the new Holifield Procurement Commission.

Most important of all, we can continue to do the best job we can in developing the military systems our nation requests. In the long run, effective public relations is based on effective performance. The defense industry has been performing effectively—and this truth is our great strength. We must continue to keep this truth bright and shining in the days to come.

# How to loosen the military-industrial relationship

## murray l. weidenbaum

**Murray L. Weidenbaum, formerly Professor of Economics, Washington University, and currently Assistant Secretary for Economic Policy, U. S. Treasury Department, has long been a scholarly observer of the military-industrial complex. In this speech he presents some of the economic facts of life about the complex and describes a number of policies he believes would improve the situation.**

Military spending has continued at a high level for almost two decades and shows no likelihood of significant reduction in the foreseeable future. The technological race continues among the major industrial powers and international tensions appear to worsen soon after hopeful signs of peace appear. Thus defense activities have become a substantial and more-or-less normal factor in the planning of both public agencies and private business firms.

Under such circumstances, public policy toward the conduct of the military establishment and its relations with the private sector—much of which was developed for a wartime or temporary environment—may need to be carefully reviewed in the light of the long-term nature of the high level of military outlays. In his oft-quoted farewell address, former President Eisenhower noted that the United States has "been compelled to create a permanent armaments industry of vast proportions," and that "this conjunction of an immense military establishment and a large arms industry is new in the American experience." He also warned "against the acquisition of unwarranted influence, whether sought or unsought, by the military-industrial complex."

Unfortunately, much of the attention to General Eisenhower's warning was generated by those interested in dismantling our military establishment, ignoring an earlier point in his address that the military is a "vital element in keeping the peace. . . ."

A review of the long-term relationship between the defense establishment and the rest of the economy, indeed with the rest of society, needs to be undertaken in the light of the dual concerns raised by

Speech presented to the Fourteenth Annual Institute of World Affairs, Washington State University, Pullman, Washington, March 21, 1969. Murray L. Weidenbaum, "The Military-Industrial Complex: An Economic Analysis," *Vital Speeches of the Day*, XXXV (June 15, 1969), 523–528.

General Eisenhower—promoting the national security and maintaining the strength and vitality of private enterprise.

Rather than presenting the customary lambasting of the military-industrial complex, I would like to address some of the fundamental questions, as I see them, that result from the close, continuing relationship between the military establishment and the major supplying industries.

> How can private industries be utilized for the design and production of weapon systems without converting them into unimaginative government arsenals?
>
> How can the military establishment sponsor and fund most of the new product developments undertaken by these companies without assuming the role of the entrepreneur, which is so basic to the private economy?
>
> How can the government protect the taxpayer in its dealings with defense contractors without taking on their internal decision-making functions?
>
> How can specialized capabilities be developed by a hard core of military supplies without eliminating effective competition for military business?
>
> How can the concentration of defense business in a relatively few regions (and their close dependence on it) be reduced without sacrificing efficiency and effectiveness?

In the remarks that follow, I hope to accomplish two objectives: (1) to explain the complex and often subtle nature of the relationship between the military and the private sector and (2) to indicate the specific kinds of changes in public policy that will help answer the questions that I raised and thus reduce the likelihood of any military-industrial complex hurting our society or economy.

As the armed services have come to depend on new systems and equipment of a highly scientific content, they have grown to depend less and less on their own laboratories and arsenals to design and produce the materials they use.  Increasingly, the research, development, and production of military weapon systems are being performed in the private sector via government contracts with large industrial corporations.

Were the governmental purchases similar to those of the private sector, this might not be a noteworthy development.  However, so much of these procurement funds is devoted to exotic items for which there are no established private markets—missiles, space vehicles, nuclear-powered aircraft carriers, tanks and long-range bombers.

As a result, the companies serving this specialized government market develop capabilities different than those required for successful operation in traditional commercial markets. There is a feedback here. As these companies become less effective in competing for private business and more adept at obtaining public contracts, they become heavily dependent on the government customer. Conversely, the Department of Defense maintains little capability to produce the equipment that it needs. Hence, it has come to rely almost entirely on these government-oriented corporations. Both parties—private and public—become "locked in" to a mutual or symbiotic relationship where they depend on each other.

A "demonstration" effect in other parts of the public sector is now taking place. Civilian government agencies that require large-scale technological development and production efforts are also turning to the government-oriented corporations. In most cases to date, these are the same corporations as those which dominate the military market and the products that they produce are similar. The two largest examples are space systems for NASA—an outgrowth of military ICBM programs—and the development of supersonic transport aircraft (SST) under the sponsorship of the Department of Transportation—an extension of military aircraft developments. On a smaller scale, the major defense contractors have become involved in applying advanced technology to education, health, crime control, environment pollution, and other civil public sector programs.

It is not hard to work up considerable enthusiasm for the nation's attaining some civilian return on its massive investment in military technology through this type of undertaking. However, we now have several decades of experience with the use of the government-oriented corporation in military programs, and an assessment reveals some serious side-effects. These unintended impacts of the government-industry relationship appear worthy of some analysis, particularly prior to any wholesale utilization of the government-industry relationship in the civilian segments of the public sector.

Let me therefore examine the nature of the government-oriented corporation as it has developed in carrying out military and closely related programs such as the exploration of outer space.

The great bulk of military procurements is not made in circumstances where a great number of firms present sealed bids offering to sell fairly standard commercial stock items at fixed prices. If this idyllic situation were to prevail, it is most unlikely that the phenomenon of the government-oriented corporation would have arisen at all. Rather the typical military procurement involves acquiring a highly-engineered system designed and produced to the government's own specifications and for which there are no established private markets.

An analysis of the composition of the firms supplying these military markets lends important insights into the nature of the government-oriented corporation. Because these high technology markets are so completely subject to the changing needs of the governmental cus-tomer, relationships between buyers and sellers differ from those typical in the commercial sector of the economy. By the selection of contractors, the government can control entry and exit, can greatly affect the growth of the firms involved, and can impose its way of doing business on the companies participating.

The bulk of these defense contracts are let as a result of negotiation with a group of suppliers chosen by the military buyers. These gov-ernmental buyers normally request proposals from the firms that they consider to be in a position to undertake the magnitude of research, development, and production required. However keen the competi-tion among the prospective suppliers may become, it will relate pri-marily to their technological capability and not simply to price.

Major portions of the work contracted for are performed by corpora-tions oriented to public requirements rather than to market demands. These government-oriented corporations or companies are fairly au-tonomous divisions of large, diversified corporations whose dominant customers are the defense and space agencies of the Federal Govern-ment. The close, continuing relationship between the government and these corporations is more than regulation by Federal agencies or selling in markets where the government is a major determinant of price, as in the case of public utilities, agriculture, or mining. Rather, here is the case of the intertwining of the public and private sectors so that it is difficult to identify when specific entrepreneurial or manage-ment functions in a given company are being performed primarily by government agents and when they are being carried on by private individuals on business payrolls.

A relatively limited number of companies receive the bulk of the defense contracts. In the fiscal year 1967, the 100 companies obtain-ing the largest dollar volume of military prime contracts accounted for two-thirds of the Department of Defense total.

Who are the government-oriented corporations? An analysis of the size of the top 100 defense contractors provides another dimension to the structure of these government markets. The giants of American industry do not dominate, contrary to much of the writing on the so-called military-industrial complex. Rather, the medium-size corpora-tions receive the largest share of the orders for high technology govern-ment products. The corporations with assets of $1 billion or over received only 17 percent of the defense contracts in 1965. This group includes General Motors, Ford, Standard Oil of New Jersey, RCA, Uniroyal, Eastman Kodak, Firestone Tire and Rubber, and Interna-tional Harvester. In contrast, the companies with assets in the $250 million to $1 billion range received 39 percent of the contracts, the largest share of any group. Typical firms in this category are the aerospace and electronics manufacturers—Boeing, Hughes Aircraft, Lockheed, and North American Rockwell. These certainly are not pygmies among business firms in the United States; neither are they at the very top rung of American industry. As might be expected, relatively small companies did proportionally poorer; the companies with assets below $250 million accounted for only 11 percent of the total defense contracts.

Another dimension of the structure of this government market relates to the extent of dependence on government work among the major contractors. Again, the data indicate that the firms most heavily dependent on military orders—those primarily oriented to government rather than private markets—are the medium size companies rather than the giants of American industry. Of the top 100 defense contractors, for those with assets of $5 billion or over, defense contracts equaled less than 10 percent of their sales in all cases. For those firms with assets in the $1–5 billion range, defense orders equaled less than 25 percent of sales. In contrast, about one-half of the firms with assets of $100 million to $1 billion obtained defense contracts exceeding 25 percent of their sales; in the case of 10 of these firms— AVCO, Collins Radio, General Dynamics, L-T-V, Lockheed, Martin-Marietta, McDonnell, Newport News Shipbuilding, Northrop and Raytheon—these government orders exceeded half of their sales volume. These are clearly the "government-oriented corporations."

Also the majority of the smaller firms, those with assets under $100 million, received defense contracts exceeding 50 percent of their sales. This experience is hardly typical of the thousands of smaller businesses participating in government markets. Rather, it reflects the nature of the sample, which is limited to firms receiving the largest absolute amount of defense contracts.

During the past decade, over 80 percent of the Federal government procurement of high technology products and systems has been made through negotiated rather than sealed-bid purchasing. Clearly, the prices that the government pays for goods and services are not determined by the interplay of relatively impersonal markets.

The tendency for the military establishment to rely on a fairly limited group of suppliers for the bulk of its needs has resulted in a fairly unique government-industry relationship. In their long-term dealings with these corporations that cater primarily to specialized government markets, Federal Government agencies such as the Department of Defense and NASA gradually have taken over directly or indirectly many of the decision-making functions which are normally the prerogatives of business management.

A detailed analysis of the largest segment of these government markets, Air Force procurement, recently concluded that "A new structural relationship has been created in which the Air Force, as a buyer, makes specific management decisions about policy and detailed procedures within aerospace companies that sell defense systems to the Air Force." This development may well be the most significant long-term impact of governmental procurement expenditures on the private sector of the American economy.

In a sense, the close and continuing relationship between the Department of Defense and its major suppliers is resulting in a convergence between them, which is blurring and reducing much of the distinction between public and private activities in an important branch of the American economy. In turn, this evolving government-industry relationship is raising important questions of public policy. To what extent are the government-oriented corporations becoming public rather than private mechanisms? As we will see, this is a case where the government owns most of the means of production, and much of what the private firms produce as well as important aspects of their operations are determined by the Government. Yet, the label of "socialism" does not seem to fit too comfortably.

This governmental assumption of, or active participation in, private business decision-making takes three major forms: virtually determining the choice of products the defense firm produces, strongly influencing the source of capital funds that it uses, and closely supervising its internal operations. It needs to be kept in mind, of course, that this government involvement in private industry arises mainly in the case of the "government-oriented" corporations which operate primarily in the unique and large-scale markets for military weapon systems, space systems, atomic energy development, and related high technology purchasing by the government. It hardly characterizes the procurement of standard conventional items by government agencies through fixed-price contracts awarded via sealed-bid competition.

By awarding massive contracts for research and development ($10 billion in the fiscal year 1966) the Department of Defense and NASA have come to strongly influence or determine which new products their essentially common group of contractors will design and produce. The governmental customers thus directly finance the R & D efforts and assume much of the risk of success or failure. In the commercial economy, in contrast, research and development costs normally are only recovered to the extent that they result in the sale of profitable products. Hence, the decisions to embark upon a private product research and development program are made by the sellers, who bear the risk of not recovering their technological investment.

Of course, government contractors may and do sponsor and fund some of their own R & D effort.   However, the bulk of their R & D is performed under government contract.   Much if not most of the remainder is charged as allowable overhead on their government contracts, having met the approval of contract administration officials.

This is not a partisan point I am making.   Back in the Kennedy Administration, a committee of senior government officials, chaired by then Budget Bureau Director David Bell, reported to the President in 1962 that ". . . The major initiative and responsibility for promoting and financing research and development have in many important areas been shifted from private enterprise (including academic as well as business institutions) to the Federal Government."

The government also uses its vast financial resources to supply much of the plant and equipment and working capital used by its major contractors.   A survey by the Standard Research Institute of 13 of the largest military contractors, covering the years 1957 to 1961, revealed that the cost of government-supplied property exceeded gross company property reported on corporate balance sheets.   Moreover, much of the company-owned property was used by the commercially-oriented divisions of these companies, rather than by the divisions working on government contracts.

More recently, Department of Defense expenditures for additional plant and equipment to be supplied to its contractors has risen sharply, from $56 million in the fiscal year 1965 to an estimated $330 million in the fiscal year 1967.   Historically, the major expansions in government-supplied facilities have occurred during war-time periods.   Post-war reductions in such assistance have not been on a scale to offset the expansions during hot war.   Hence, the long-term trend has been for large-scale Federal supply of fixed capital to these governmentally-oriented corporations.

In addition, approximately $5 billion of outstanding "progress" payments are held by military contractors.   Some firms report that such government-supplied funds exceed their total net worth.   Military procurements regulations provide specific incentives against the use of private working capital.   As specified in the Armed Services Procurement Regulation, progress payments equal to 80 percent of the costs incurred in government contracts generally are provided without interest charge to the contractors.

However, should these companies decide to rely on private sources for working capital, their interest payments may not be charged to the contract and hence must come out of their profits.   Presumably, this arrangement results in smaller total cost to the government because of the lower interest rates paid by the U. S. Treasury on the funds that it borrows.   However, the result also is to increase the extent to which public rather than private capital finances the operations of government contractors. Hence, the financial stake that the government has in the performance of its contractors is increased further.

Perhaps the most pervasive way in which the Federal Government assumes the management decision-making functions of its contractors is through the procurement legislation and regulations governing the awarding of these contracts. For example, the military procurement regulations require private suppliers to accept on a "take it or leave it" basis many standard clauses in their contracts which give the governmental contracting and surveillance officers numerous powers over the internal operations of these companies.

These unilaterally determined grants of authority vary from matters of substance to items so minor that they border on the ludicrous. Of course, in many instances these restrictions have been imposed to prevent actual or potential abuses or even in an effort to aid the contractors.

Certainly, governmental policy makers in the area of military contracting rarely consider the cumulative and long-term impacts on company initiative and entrepreneurship. Viewed as a totality, these restrictions represent a form of government regulation of industry. This regulation is not accomplished through the traditional independent regulatory commission, subject to the Administrative Procedures Act and similar judicial-type legislation, but rather through the unilateral exercise of the government's strong market position.

The authority assumed by the governmental "customer" includes power to review and veto company decisions as to which activities to perform in-house and which to subcontract, which firms to use as subcontractors, which products to buy domestically rather than to import, what internal financial reporting systems to establish, what type of industrial engineering and planning system to utilize, what minimum as well as average wage rates to pay, how much overtime work to authorize, and so forth. Thus, when a business firm enters into a contract with the government, the quasi-public nature of the ostensibly private enterprise is given implicit recognition by requirements that the firm conduct itself similarly to a governmental agency in abiding by policies that bind such an agency.

My favorite example of the more minor matters covered in the detailed and voluminous military procurement regulations is the prescription that the safety rules followed in the offices and factories of the contractors must be consistent with the latest edition of the Corps of Engineers' safety manual.

This entire philosophy and attitude of close government review of the internal operations of its contractors is so deeply imbedded that when statements such as the following one are added to the Armed

Services Procurement Regulation they evoke no public or industry reaction:

> Although the Government does not expect to participate in every management decision, it may reserve the right to review the contractor's management efforts. . . .

Cost-plus contracting has shifted much of the risk-bearing from the industrial seller to the governmental buyer. The use of fixed price contracts by the Department of Defense has increased in recent years. However, a major share of military contracts still is on a cost reimbursement basis. So long as this remains the case, the government determines which items of cost are "allowable" as charges to the contract, and hence, to a large extent this determines or at least strongly influences which activities and which items of expenditure the company can profitably undertake (disallowed costs directly reduce company net profits).

The government-industry relationship is a dynamic one. Numerous changes are made in military procurement regulations in the course of a year. Many of these changes further extend the role of the government in the internal operations of the contractors. The following is a sample of recently promulgated regulations: In contracts for aircraft tires, tubes, and recapping, the contractor must purchase an amount of rubber from the government's stockpile equal to at least 50 percent of the value of the contract. The contractor does not actually have to use the rubber from the stockpile in filling the government contract. He can keep it for his commercial work. Similar requirements, somewhat less restrictive in their particulars, must be met by contractors who provide aluminum products, while military contractors must buy all of their jewel bearings from the government-owned Turtle Mountain Bearing Plant in Rolla, North Dakota. Of course, if such tie-in contracts were made between two private firms, they would run afoul of the anti-trust laws.

In deciding whether costs of professional and consulting services used by a contractor are an allowable charge to a military contract, the government now decides "whether the service can be performed more economically by employment rather than by contracting"—that is, whether one of its contractors should hire an outside consultant rather than a permanent employee (the government also assumes the authority to review the qualifications of the consultant).

Help-wanted advertising is no longer an allowable cost if it is in color. Advertising for employees, if it is to be an allowable cost, must be authorized in advance. Moreover, the Pentagon recently has reported that it is reviewing "what actions on the part of the government are necessary to assure that compensation paid to contractor employees performing on government contracts is reasonable." Clearly, the trend for increased governmental involvement in internal private-business decision-making appears to be a long-continuing one.

Analyzing the problem from the viewpoint of the individual defense industry executive, we find that when company managers are faced with a large mass of government regulations, they spend time filling out forms which ought better be used for actual work on the new product being built. The typical application of government regulations is designed to ensure, on the average, satisfactory performance, or, conversely, to prevent failures. However, in doing this, the government often inhibits the performance and innovation on the part of project managers. It has been repeatedly found that these tight controls result in defense industry management performing under their capability.

Recent periods of cutbacks in military spending gave rise to demands for utilizing the supposedly unique research and development and systems management capabilities of military contractors in civilian public sector activities. Indeed, the current concern over the need to respond to the racial problems in the centers of the nation's major cities has resulted in renewed pressures for putting to work the science and intellect of our major high technology corporations in the fields of education, training, mass urban transportation, urban redevelopment, and the reduction of poverty generally. Given a decline in military spending in the near future, such action may also be an effective short-term means of preventing unemployment in defense areas. However, as a matter of long-term public policy, would it be wise for the nation to expand the method of governmental operation whereby an important branch of private industry increasingly develops the characteristics and mentality of a government arsenal? At the least, the possible existence of these adverse side-effects should be recognized and taken into account in extending the utilization of the private corporation in the government's business.

The tendency for the development of a military-industrial complex can be reduced by changing governmental procurement policies and practices so as to halt the erosion of the basic entrepreneurial character of the firms that undertake large-scale developmental programs for the Federal establishment. The plea for "disengagement" made by defense contractors needs to be given greater weight, although the public interest necessitates continuing protection and concern. Some of the changes that I propose may sound quite technical, but they do attempt to get at the heart of the matter without disrupting vital government programs.

If the following policy suggestions have any common characteristic it is that they are designed to reduce the close and continuing relationship between the Pentagon and a relatively small group of industrial firms. By reducing both the governmental orientation of these companies and the military's reliance on them, the Nation might be able to achieve the objectives I stated at the outset of this paper—to reduce the geographic concentration of defense contracts, to increase competition for military business, to protect the interests of the taxpayer, and to reduce the arsenalization of the defense industry. That is quite a tall order and the following points are not offered as a definite solution but as important steps in the right direction.

One way of reducing the financial dependence of defense companies on the Federal Treasury would be to make interest on working capital an allowable cost on military contracts. Interest on indebtedness is a standard cost of doing business and should be recognized as such. Unlike the period of rapid and uncertain expansion of defense work in the early 1940's, military contracts are now an established feature of American industry. The Treasury no longer needs to serve as banker.

A second way of strengthening the private entrepreneurial character of defense firms is to streamline and reduce the variety and scope of special provisions in procurement legislation and regulations. Let these companies develop their own safety rules to discourage employees from skidding on factory floors. We seem at times to forget why in the first place we prefer to use private enterprise rather than government arsenals to develop and produce most of our weapon systems. It is not because private corporations are better than government agencies at following rules and regulations—at doing it by the numbers. It is precisely for the opposite reason. We believe that private enterprise is more creative, more imaginative, and more resourceful.

A third way of reducing the close, continuing relationship between the Federal establishment and its major suppliers is to broaden the competitive base. This could be accomplished by encouraging commercially-oriented companies to consider military work as a possible source of diversification for them. The recommendations concerning interest on working capital and streamlining procurement procedures should help to make defense work attractive for the companies that are not now interested in government work. Moreover, defense companies should be encouraged to diversify into commercial markets, as the simplest way of reducing their dependence on government agencies. It may be natural for governmental procurement officials to favor firms whose interests are not "diluted" by commercial work. However, the diversified company may also be the more efficient one in the long run. Certainly, the diversification of industry both into and out of high technology government markets would reduce the present tendency for a relatively small number of companies and some regions of the country to become primarily dependent on Federal business.

At present, much of the military subcontracts go to companies that are prime contractors on other systems. It is not infrequent that one of these companies compete[s] against [others] for the prime contract for a new weapon system and, simultaneously, its electronics division teams up with one of its competitors and its propulsion system with another. Thus to cite a hypothetical but reasonable example, Lockheed might beat out North American Rockwell and General Dynamics for a new missile contract, but assign the propulsion subcontract to North American's Rocketdyne division and the communication system to General Dynamics' Stromberg-Carlson division. Thus, the subcontracting may not necessarily broaden the array of companies participating in the defense program, but be used to "share the wealth" among the members of the club.

More attention in the award of subcontracts should be paid to small business and other industries not actively participating in the military market as primes. Some thought also should be given to reducing the competitive advantages that accrue to the major military contractors that hold on to government-owned plant and equipment for long periods of time. The simplest approach, of course, would be to curtail the practice of furnishing plant and equipment to long-term government contractors and, instead, to give them greater incentives to make their own capital investments.

Certainly, the detailed day-to-day governmental surveillance of internal company operations which is now so characteristic of the military market is a poor precedent to follow in establishing the future roles of industry and government in public sector areas, both military and civilian.

On the positive side, governmental procurement of goods and services from the private sector might well emphasize the end results desired by governmental decision-makers, rather than prescribing the detailed manner in which industry should go about designing and manufacturing the end product. In its essence, this is the difference between detailed design specifications prepared by the governmental buyer versus clear statements of performance desired by the government. The latter approach, of course, gives maximum opportunity for private initiation and inventiveness to come to bear on the problems of the public sector.

That, of course, is the basic and difficult task of using private enterprise in the performance of public functions without either converting the companies to unimaginative arsenalized operations or letting them obtain windfall profits because of the government's inability to drive hard enough and intelligent enough bargains.

The answer is neither simple nor apparent. In part, however, it does lie in governmental policy-makers and administrators constantly being aware of the need to steer that difficult middle course between governmental arsenalization of industry, on the one hand, and private interests obtaining high profits unrelated to either the investments they have made or the risks that they have borne, on the other.

The approach that I am suggesting is neither so dramatic as a slashing attack on any military-industrial complex nor so simple as mere opposition to a war machine. I do hope that these more modest suggestions are both more constructive and somewhat more likely to be adopted.

Although it will be difficult to obtain, we need to seek that subtle balance between government and business interests which would strengthen simultaneously both the national defense and the private enterprise system.

# Chapter 13 Questions

1. What does the term "military-industrial complex" really mean?
2. What do you see as the major issues that the nation must face in considering the so-called military-industrial complex?
3. Do you agree with President Nixon and William Wilson that the fundamental issue is foreign policy which in turn rests on questions of national security? In light of world realities, isn't a firm military posture necessary for national survival?
4. Does the federal government now have sufficient control over the military-industrial complex to prevent unnecessary military expenditures and control of government by industry? Explain the factual basis for your position.
5. Is a reasonably close working relationship between industry and government in the national defense sector beneficial or detrimental to society in producing quality defenses at reasonable costs? Argue both sides of this issue, and defend your conclusions.
6. Critically evaluate Weidenbaum's recommendations for reducing the close and continuing relationship between the Pentagon and industrial companies. Are his recommendations suitable to the dimensions of the problem?
7. Assuming that a reasonable defense posture is needed, what relationships between industry and government would you recommend to achieve it? Defend your position.
8. Some critics of the complex argue that the defense industry should be nationalized to eliminate the abuses they perceive in the government-industry relationship. What does nationalization mean? Be specific in identifying those existing problems that would be eliminated under nationalization. If we were to nationalize the defense industry, can you identify other evils and/or problems that might arise?

# Fiscal, Monetary, and Incomes Policy

**14**

# How to control price inflation and other economic problems

### richard m. nixon

Following is an address to the nation by President Nixon, given on June 17, 1970, entitled "On Economic Policy and Productivity." Next appears another address of the President's, given a little more than one year later on August 15, 1971, setting forth a new and rather comprehensive economic policy. The third contribution is the official Executive Order of August 15, 1971, concerning a wage, price, and rent freeze.

What we are doing here is to deal with the problems of a nation in transition from a wartime economy to a peacetime economy. Our economy must consequently make adjustments to two great changes at the same time.

One change is that defense spending is on the way down. For the first time in 20 years, the Federal Government is spending more on human-resource programs than on national defense.

This year we are spending 1.7 billion dollars less on defense than we were a year ago. In the next year, we plan to spend 5.2 billion dollars less. This is more than a redirection of resources; this is a historic reordering of our national priorities.

The cuts in defense spending mean a shift of job opportunities away from defense production to the kind of production that meets social needs. This will require adjustment by many employees and businesses.

For example, over 400,000 military and civilian employes have been released in this past year by our armed forces. In that time, cutbacks in defense spending have reduced jobs in defense plants by about 300,000. Taken together, that's almost three quarters of a million people affected by the reduction in defense spending. Now, while many of these workers have found new jobs, it is not hard to see where much of the current increase in total unemployment has come from.

Despite the difficulties of this transition, progress toward a peacetime economy is a good sign for the labor force and for the business community.

Reduction in defense spending gives us more room in the federal budget to meet human needs at home. It makes it possible to build a much more enduring prosperity in this country.

---

Address to the Nation given by the President on June 12, 1970.

With its trials and with its hopes, a peacetime economy is clearly on the way.

We have already brought home 115,000 from Vietnam. Our success in destroying enemy supply bases in Cambodia has made it possible for us to go forward with the program for withdrawal of 150,000 more men —which I announced in my speech of April 20—without jeopardizing the lives of our men who will be brought home after that.

Our scheduled withdrawal of forces from Cambodia by June 30 will be kept. Our scheduled transition from a wartime economy to a peacetime consumer economy will be kept.

While our economy adapts to the reordering of our national priorities and resources, we are undergoing a second great change. We are trying to do something that never has been done before: to avoid a recession while we bring a major inflation to an end.

This Administration took office after a long period in which the nation lived far beyond its means. In the decade of the '60s, federal deficits totaled 57 billion dollars, and the American consumer was forced to pay the piper in terms of a rising spiral of prices.

Seventeen months ago when this Administration took office, we stood at a crossroads of economic policy. There were actually four roads open to us:

One was the road of runaway inflation—to do nothing about Government spending and rising prices, to let the boom go on booming until the bubble burst. That was the road the nation was taken on in the '60s, and the people who suffer most along that road are the millions of Americans living on fixed incomes.

The road headed in the opposite direction from that one was a possible choice as well: "Let the economy go through the wringer," as some suggested, and bring on a major recession. Well, that would stop inflation abruptly, but at a cost in human terms of broken careers and broken lives that this nation must never again have to pay.

A third choice was the route of wage and price controls. That would lead to rationing, black-marketing, total federal bureaucratic domination, and it would never get at the real causes of inflation.

That left a fourth choice: to cut down the sharp rise in federal spending and to restrain the economy firmly and steadily. In that way, prices would slow their rise without too great a hardship on the workingman, the businessman and the investor.

That was the road of responsibility. That is the road we chose, and that is the road we are continuing on today.

Because we are concerned with both prices and jobs, we have put the brakes on inflation carefully and steadily.

This did not mean that inflation could end without some slowdown in the economy. But we were willing to make a trade—to sacrifice speed in ending inflation in order to keep the economic slowdown moderate.

At the outset of our fight against inflation, we pointed out that it would take time to relieve the heavy spending programs and pressures on the economy. After that beginning, it would take more time to see that those reduced pressures result in a slowdown in price rises.

Many people wonder why we are easing some of the restraints on the economy before we have seen dramatic results in slowing down the rise in the cost of living. Why, they ask, don't we keep on with all of our measures to hold down the economy until price rises stop completely?

Let me put it this way:

It is a little like trying to bring a boat into a dock. You turn down the power well before you get to the dock and let the boat coast in. Now, if you waited until you reached the dock to turn down the power, you'd soon have to buy a new dock or a new boat.

In the same way, we're heading for the dock of price stability:

We have to ease up on the power of our restraint and let our momentum carry us safely into port.

That's why our independent central banking system has seen fit to ease up on the money supply. That is why I relaxed the cutback on federally assisted construction projects, and why I have not asked for a new surtax.

These actions are not a signal that we are giving up our fight against inflation; on the contrary, they mean that there was already enough power applied to reach the dock and now we had better make sure that we don't damage the boat.

The Federal Reserve's monetary policy, which permitted no growth in the money supply at all in the second half of 1969, has now been relaxed. In the past six months, the money supply has grown at a rate of about 6 per cent a year.

The Chairman of the Federal Reserve Board has assured the nation that there will be enough money and credit to meet future needs and that the orderly expansion of the economy will not be endangered by a lack of liquidity.

Now, I'm not asking anyone to put on rose-colored glasses. We are well aware of the forces working against us.

To make sure the coming upturn in the economy will not be of the kind that brings on a new surge of inflation, we have gained control of the runaway momentum of federal spending—the spending that triggered the rise in prices in the first place.

In the three years before this Administration took office, federal spending rose an average of 15 per cent a year—the sharpest rate of increase since the Korean War. In the current fiscal year, we slashed that rate of increase in half—to 7 per cent. And in the coming year, we intend to cut that rate of increase in spending by half again.

Now, this required some hard decisions—including, as you may recall, the veto of a popular appropriations bill—but it was vital to win the battle to hold down spending so that we could ultimately hold down prices. We are winning that battle, but we cannot let up now.

I am convinced that the basic economic road we have taken is the right road, the responsible road, the road that will curb the cost of living and lead us to orderly expansion.

However, we have to face some difficult problems:

The momentum of four years of inflation was stronger than had been anticipated. The effect on unemployment is greater than we foresaw. The pace of our progress toward price stability and high employment has not been quick enough.

Now, this does not mean that we should abandon our strategy. It does mean that we must pay heed to economic developments as we move along and adjust our tactics accordingly.

While relying basically on continued moderation in general fiscal and monetary policies, I think it is necessary and timely to supplement them with several more-specific measures.

And here are the actions I am taking to speed up the fight against inflation:

First, I shall appoint a National Commission on Productivity, with representatives from business, labor, the public and Government.

In general, productivity is a measure of how well we use our resources; in particular, it means how much real value is produced by an hour of work. In the past two years, productivity has increased far less than usual.

In order to achieve price stability, healthy growth and a rising standard of living, we must find ways of restoring growth to productivity.

This Commission's task will be to point the way toward this growth in 1970 and in the years ahead. I shall direct the Commission to give first priority to the problems we face now; we must achieve a balance between costs and productivity that will lead to more-stable prices.

Productivity in the American economy depends on the effectiveness of management; the investment of capital for research, development and advanced technology, and most of all on the training and progressive spirit of 86 million working Americans.

To give its efforts the proper base of understanding, the Commission will this summer bring together leaders of business, labor, Government and the general public to meet in a special President's Conference on Productivity.

Second, I have instructed the Council of Economic Advisers to prepare a periodic Inflation Alert.

This will spotlight the significant areas of wage and price increases and objectively analyze their impact on the price level.

This Inflation Alert will call attention to outstanding cases of price or wage increases and will be made public by the Productivity Commission.

Third, I am establishing a Regulations and Purchasing Review Board within the Federal Government.

All Government actions will be reviewed to determine where federal purchasing and regulations drive up costs and prices. Our import policy will be reviewed to see how supplies can be increased to meet rising demand without losing jobs here at home.

Now, let me specifically spell out what I will do and what I will not do.

I intend to help focus the attention of business and labor on the need for increased productivity. This is the way for them to serve their own interest while they serve the public interest. This is the only way to make sure that increases in earnings are not wiped out by the rising cost of living.

This Administration, by its spending restraint, has set the example in this past year. We believe we have now earned the credentials to call for similar restraint from business and labor to slow down inflation.

Now is the time for business at every level to take price actions more consistent with a stable cost of living, and now is the time for labor to structure its wage demands to better achieve a new stability of costs.

The fight against inflation is everybody's business. If you act against the national interest, if you contribute to inflation in your price or wage demands—then you are acting against your own best interests and your customers' best interests, and that is neither good business nor good bargaining.

If businessmen and workingmen are willing to raise their sights by lowering their demands, they will help themselves by helping to hold down everybody's cost of living.

I believe there is a new social responsibility growing up in our economic system on the part of unions and corporations. Now is the time for that social concern to take the form of specific action on the wage-price front.

Now, here is what I will not do:

I will not take this nation down the road of wage and price controls, however politically expedient that may seem. Controls and rationing may seem like an easy way out, but they are really an easy way into more trouble—to the explosion that follows when you try to clamp a lid on a rising head of steam without turning down the fire under the pot.   Wage and price controls only postpone a day of reckoning, and in so doing they rob every American of a very important part of his freedom.

Nor am I starting to use controls in disguise.   By that I mean the kind of policy whereby Government makes executive pronouncements to enforce "guidelines" in an attempt to dictate specific prices and wages without authority of law.

I realize that there are some people who get satisfaction out of seeing an individual businessman or labor leader called on the carpet and browbeaten by Government officials.   But we cannot protect the value of the dollar by passing the buck.   That sort of grandstanding distracts attention from the real cause of inflation and it can be a dangerous misuse of the power of Government.

The actions I have outlined today are well within the powers of the President.   But there are other actions that the President cannot take alone.

This is not the time for the Congress to play politics with inflation by passing legislation granting the President standby powers to impose wage and price controls.   The Congress knows I will not impose controls, because they would do more harm than good.

This is the time, however, for Congress and the President to cooperate on a program specifically addressed to help the people who need help most in a period of economic transition from a wartime to a peacetime economy.

Now, here is that program:

To provide more help now to those workers who have lost jobs, I urge the Congress to pass the legislation I proposed to expand and strengthen our unemployment-insurance system.   This legislation would cover almost 5 million more people who lack this protection now, and the system would be made more responsive to changing economic conditions.

I submitted this legislation to the Congress almost a year ago.   It's time for the Congress to act.

.   .   .

To help those in need of job training, I urge the Congress to pass the Manpower Training Act which provides an automatic increase in manpower-training funds in times of high unemployment.

I submitted this proposal to the Congress 10 months ago.   It is time for the Congress to act.

I ask for full appropriation for the Office of Economic Opportunity, and I request the Congress to provide at once a supplemental budget of

50 million dollars to provide useful training and support to young people who are out of school in the summer months.

To further protect the small investor, I support the establishment of an insurance corporation with a federal backstop to guarantee the investor against losses that could be caused by financial difficulties of brokerage houses. While this would not affect the equity risk that is always present in stock-market investment, it will assure the investor that the stability of the securities industry itself does not become cause for concern.

To relieve the worries of many of our older citizens living on fixed incomes, I urge the Congress to pass my proposal to tie Social Security benefits to the cost of living.

This proposal—passed by the House, awaiting Senate action for the past month—will keep the burden of the fight against inflation from falling on those least able to afford it.

To stimulate an industry bearing the brunt of high interest rates, I urge enactment of the Emergency Home Finance Act of 1970. This would attract as much as 6 billion dollars into the housing market in the coming fiscal year. More than a third of a million families need this legislation for home financing now, and the resulting new construction of more than 200,000 houses will also help provide many new jobs.

This housing bill was passed unanimously by the Senate. It has been awaiting action for three months in the House. It is time for the Congress to act.

To help the small businessman who finds it difficult to get necessary credit, I have asked the Congress for greater authority for the Small Business Administration to stimulate banks and others to make loans to small businesses at lower interest rates.

I submitted this legislation to the Congress three months ago. It's time for the Congress to act.

To strengthen our railroad industry, I am asking for legislation that will enable the Department of Transportation to provide emergency assistance to railroads in financial difficulties. I am also urging the independent Interstate Commerce Commission to give prompt attention to the urgent financial problems of this industry.

And, finally, to curb inflationary pressures throughout our economy, I call upon the Congress to join me in holding down Government spending to avoid a large budget deficit. This requires a new restraint on spending programs and the passage of the revenue-producing measures that I have already made.

There is an old and cynical adage that says that, in an election year, the smart politician is one who votes for all bills to spend money and votes against all bills to raise taxes.

But in this election year of 1970, that old adage cannot apply. The

American people will see through any attempt by anyone to play politics with their cost of living. Whenever a member of Congress displays the imagination to introduce a bill that calls for more spending, let him display the courage to introduce a bill to raise the taxes to pay for that new program.

Long before the art of economics had a name it was called "political arithmetic." The American people expect their elected officials to do their political arithmetic honestly.

The actions I have taken today, together with the proposals I have made, are needed now to help us through this time of transition.

I believe this is the right program at the right time for the right purpose. There is no more important goal than to curb inflation without permitting severe disruption. This is an activist Administration, and should new developments call for new action in the future, I shall take the action needed to attain that goal.

Before I close today, I would like to give you a broader view of the significance of what is happening in the American economy.

We have more at stake here than a possible difference of one or two tenths of a percentage point in the price level in 1970. All of us have to make decisions now which will profoundly affect the survival of a free economic system throughout the world.

Industrial countries around the world all face the problems of inflation. By solving our problems here without throwing away our freedom, we shall set an example that will have great impact on the kind of economic systems others may choose.

Our free economic system has produced enormous benefits for the American people. The United States, with 10 per cent of the free world's people, produces 40 per cent of the free world's output. We did not gain that production power by shackling our free economic system.

The average American has the highest real disposable income in the world, and it is higher today than ever before in our history. We did not reach that height by turning over economic freedom to government.

In the next five years, and in real terms, the American consumer will be able to buy almost 20 per cent more than he does today. To reach that attainable goal, we need no artificial dependence on the production of the weapons of war. On the contrary, we will all share much more fully in a peacetime prosperity.

As I see it, prosperity is not a period of good times between periods of hard times—that's false prosperity, with people riding high but riding for a fall.

Nor is prosperity a time when the well-to-do become better off while everyone else stays the same or falls behind—that's partial prosperity. It only widens the gap between our people.

The true prosperity that I envision offers a new fairness in our national life.

We are working toward a system that will provide "job justice"— open and equal opportunity for every man and woman to build a good career.

We are working toward a system that replaces the old ups and downs with a new steadiness of economic growth within our capacity to produce efficiently.

We are working toward a system that will deliver a higher standard of living to a people living in peace.

That is the hope offered by a modern free-enterprise system—not managed by government and not ignored by government, but helped by a government that creates the climate for steady, healthy growth.

As we move forward into a peacetime economy, I am confident that we will achieve the only kind of prosperity that counts—the prosperity that lasts, the prosperity that can be shared by every American.

# New economic policy         richard m. nixon

I have addressed the nation a number of times over the past two years on the problems of ending a war. Because of the progress we have made toward achieving that goal, this Sunday evening is an appropriate time for us to turn our attention to the challenges of peace.

America today has the best opportunity in this century to achieve two of its greatest ideals: to bring about a full generation of peace, and to create a new prosperity without war.

This not only requires bold leadership ready to take bold action—it calls forth the greatness in a great people.

Prosperity without war requires action on three fronts: We must create more and better jobs. We must stop the rise in the cost of living. We must protect the dollar from the attacks of international money speculators.

We are going to take that action—not timidly, not half-heartedly and not in piecemeal fashion. We are going to move forward to the new prosperity without war as befits a great people—all together, and along a broad front.

The time has come for a new economic policy for the United States. Its targets are unemployment, inflation and international speculation. This is how we are going to attack them:

First, on the subject of jobs. We all know why we have an unemployment problem. Two million workers have been released from the armed forces and defense plants because of our success in winding down the war in Vietnam. Putting those people back to work is one of the challenges of peace, and we have begun to make progress. Our unemployment rate today is below the average of the four peacetime years of the 1960s. But we can—and must—do better than that. The time has come for American industry, which has produced more jobs at higher real wages than any other industrial system in history, to embark on a bold program of new investment in production for peace.

To give that system a powerful new stimulus, I shall ask the Congress, when it reconvenes after its summer recess, to consider as its first priority the enactment of the Job Development Act of 1971.

---

Address given by the President on August 15, 1971.

I will propose to provide the strongest short-term incentive in our history to invest in new machinery and equipment that will create new jobs for Americans: a 10 per cent job-development credit for one year, effective as of today, with a 5 per cent credit after Aug. 15, 1972. This tax credit for investment in new equipment will not only generate new jobs, it will raise productivity, and it will make our goods more competitive in the years ahead.

Second, I will propose to repeal the 7 per cent excise tax on automobiles, effective today. This will mean a reduction in price of about $200 per car. I shall insist that the American auto industry pass this tax reduction on to the nearly 8 million customers who are buying automobiles this year. Lower prices will mean that more people will be able to afford new cars, and every additional 100,000 cars sold means 25,000 new jobs.

Third, I propose to speed up the personal income tax exemptions scheduled for Jan. 1, 1973, to Jan. 1, 1972—so that taxpayers can deduct an extra $50 for each exemption one year earlier than planned. This increase in consumer spending power will provide a strong boost to the economy in general and to employment in particular.

The tax reductions I am recommending, together with the broad upturn of the economy which has taken place in the first half of this year, will move us strongly forward toward a goal this nation has not reached since 1956—15 years ago—prosperity with full employment in peacetime.

Looking to the future, I have directed the Secretary of the Treasury to recommend to the Congress in January new tax proposals for stimulating research and development of new industries and new technologies to help provide the 20 million new jobs that America needs for the young people who will be coming into the job market in the next decade.

To offset the loss of revenue from these tax cuts which directly stimulate new jobs, I have ordered today a 4.7-billion-dollar cut in federal spending.

Tax cuts to stimulate employment must be matched by spending cuts to restrain inflation. To check the rise in the cost of Government, I have ordered a postponement of pay raises and a 5 per cent cut in Government personnel.

I have ordered a 10 per cent cut in foreign economic aid.

In addition, since the Congress has already delayed action on two of the great initiatives of this Administration, I will ask Congress to amend my proposals to postpone the implementation of revenue sharing for three months and welfare reform for one year.

In this way, I am reordering our budget priorities to concentrate more on achieving full employment.

The second indispensable element of the new prosperity is to stop the rise in the cost of living.

One of the cruelest legacies of the artificial prosperity produced by war is inflation. Inflation robs every American. The 20 million who are retired and living on fixed incomes are particularly hard hit. Homemakers find it harder than ever to balance the family budget. And 80 million wage earners have been on a treadmill. In the four war years between 1965 and 1969, your wage increases were completely eaten up by price increases. Your paychecks were higher, but you were no better off.

We have made progress against the rise in the cost of living. From the high point of 6 per cent a year in 1969, the rise in consumer prices has been cut to 4 per cent in the first half of 1971. But just as is the case in our fight against unemployment, we can—and we must—do better than that. The time has come for decisive action—action that will break the vicious circle of spiraling prices and costs.

I am today ordering a freeze on all prices and wages throughout the United States for a period of 90 days. In addition, I call upon corporations to extend the wage-price freeze to all dividends.

I have today appointed a Cost of Living Council within the Government. I have directed this Council to work with leaders of labor and business to set up the proper mechanism for achieving continued price and wage stability after the 90-day freeze is over.

Let me emphasize two characteristics of this action: First, it is temporary. To put the strong, vigorous American economy into a permanent strait jacket would lock in unfairness. It would stifle the expansion of our free-enterprise system. And, second, while the wage-price freeze will be backed by Government sanctions, if necessary, it will not be accompanied by the establishment of a huge price-control bureaucracy. I am relying on the voluntary co-operation of all Americans—each one of you—workers, employers, consumers—to make this freeze work.

Working together, we will break the back of inflation—and we will do it without the mandatory wage and price controls that crush economic and personal freedom.

The third indispensable element in building the new prosperity is closely related to creating new jobs and halting inflation. We must protect the position of the American dollar as a pillar of monetary stability around the world.

In the past seven years, there has been an average of one international monetary crisis every year. Who gains from these crises? Not the workingman; not the investors; and not the real producers of wealth. The gainers are international money speculators. Because they thrive on crises, they help to create them.

In recent weeks, the speculators have been waging an all-out war on the American dollar. The strength of a nation's currency is based on the strength of that nation's economy—and the American economy is by far the strongest in the world. Accordingly, I have directed the Secretary of the Treasury to take the action necessary to defend the dollar against the speculators.

I have directed Secretary Connally to suspend temporarily the convertibility of the dollar into gold or other reserve assets, except in amounts and conditions determined to be in the interest of monetary stability and in the best interests of the United States.

Now, what is this action, which is very technical? What does it mean for you?

Let me lay to rest the bugaboo of what is called devaluation.

If you want to buy a foreign car or take a trip abroad, market conditions may cause your dollar to buy slightly less. But if you are among the overwhelming majority of Americans who buy American-made products in America, your dollar will be worth just as much tomorrow as it is today.

The effect of this action, in other words, will be to stabilize the dollar.

Now, this action will not win us any friends among the international money traders. But our primary concern is with the American workers, and with fair competition around the world.

To our friends abroad, including the many responsible members of the international banking community who are dedicated to stability and the flow of trade, I give this assurance: The United States has always been—and will continue to be—a forward-looking and trustworthy trading partner. In full co-operation with the International Monetary Fund and those who trade with us, we will press for the necessary reforms to set up an urgently needed new international monetary system. Stability and equal treatment is in everybody's best interest. I am determined that the American dollar must never again be a hostage in the hands of the international speculators.

I am taking one further step to protect the dollar, to improve our balance of payments, and to increase sales for Americans. As a temporary measure, I am today imposing an additional tax of 10 per cent on goods imported into the United States. This is a better solution for international trade than direct controls on the amount of imports.

This import tax is a temporary action. It isn't directed against any other country. It is an action to make certain that American products will not be at a disadvantage because of unfair exchange rates. When the unfair treatment is ended, the import tax will end as well.

As a result of these actions, the product of American labor will be more competitive, and the unfair edge that some of our foreign competition has had will be removed.  That is a major reason why our trade balance has eroded over the past 15 years.

At the end of World War II, the economies of the major industrial nations of Europe and Asia were shattered.  To help them get on their feet and to protect their freedom, the United States has provided over the past 25 years 143 billion dollars in foreign aid.  This was the right thing for us to do.

Today, largely with our help, they have regained their vitality.  They have become our strong competitors, and we welcome their success.

But now that other nations are economically strong, the time has come for them to bear their fair share of the burden of defending freedom around the world.  The time has come for exchange rates to be set straight and for the major nations to compete as equals.  There is no longer any need for the United States to compete with one hand tied behind her back.

The range of actions I have taken and proposed tonight—on the job front, on the inflation front, on the monetary front—is the most comprehensive new economic policy to be undertaken by this nation in four decades.

We are fortunate to live in a nation with an economic system capable of producing for its people the highest standard of living in the world —a system flexible enough to change its ways dramatically when circumstances call for change, and, most important, a system resourceful enough to produce prosperity with freedom and opportunity unmatched in the history of nations.

The purposes of the Government actions I have announced tonight are to lay the basis for renewed confidence, to make it possible for us to compete fairly with the rest of the world, to open the door to a new prosperity.

But Government, with all its powers, does not hold the key to the success of a people.  That key, my fellow Americans, is in your hands.

A nation, like a person, has to have a certain inner drive in order to succeed.  In economic affairs, that inner drive is called the competitive spirit.

Every action I have taken tonight is designed to nurture and stimulate that competitive spirit; to help us snap out of that self-doubt and self-disparagement that saps our energy and erodes our confidence in ourselves.

Whether this nation stays No. 1 in the world's economy or resigns itself to second, third or fourth place; whether we as a people have faith in ourselves, or lose that faith; whether we hold fast to the strength that makes peace and freedom possible in this world, or lose our grip—all that depends on you, on your competitive spirit, your sense of personal destiny, your pride in your country and in yourself.

We can be certain of this:  As the threat of war recedes, the challenge of peaceful competition in the world will greatly increase.

We welcome competition, because America is at her greatest when she is called on to compete.

As there always have been in our history, there will be voices urging us to shrink from that challenge to competition, to build a protective wall around ourselves, to crawl into a shell as the rest of the world moves ahead.

Two hundred years ago a man wrote in his diary these words: "Many thinking people believe America has seen its best days."  That was written in 1775, just before the American Revolution, at the dawn of the most exciting era in the history of man.

Today we hear the echoes of those voices, preaching a gospel of gloom and defeat, saying that same thing:  "We have seen our best days."

I say, let Americans reply:  "Our best days lie ahead."

As we move into a generation of peace, as we blaze the trail toward the new prosperity, I say to every American:  Let us raise our spirits. Let us raise our sights.  Let all of us contribute all we can to the great and good country that has contributed so much to the progress of mankind.

Let us invest in our nation's future.  And let us revitalize that faith in ourselves that built a great nation in the past, and will shape the world of the future.

# The executive order on wages, prices

### richard m. nixon

WHEREAS, in order to stabilize the economy, reduce inflation and minimize unemployment, it is necessary to stabilize prices, rents, wages and salaries; and

WHEREAS, the present balance-of-payments situation makes it especially urgent to stabilize prices, rents, wages and salaries in order to improve our competitive position in world trade and to protect the purchasing power of the dollar:

NOW, THEREFORE, by virtue of the authority vested in me by the Constitution and statutes of the United States, including the Economic Stabilization Act of 1970 (P.L. 91–379, 84 Stat. 799), as amended, it is hereby ordered as follows:

Section 1. (a) Prices, rents, wages and salaries shall be stabilized for a period of 90 days from the date hereof at levels not greater than the highest of those pertaining to a substantial volume of actual transactions by each individual, business, firm or other entity of any kind during the 30-day period ending Aug. 14, 1971, for like or similar commodities or services. If no transactions occurred in that period, the ceiling will be the highest price, rent, salary or wage in the nearest preceding 30-day period in which transactions did occur. No person shall charge, assess or receive, directly or indirectly, in any transaction prices or rents in any form higher than those permitted hereunder, and no person shall, directly or indirectly, pay or agree to pay in any transaction wages or salaries in any form, or to use any means to obtain payment of wages and salaries in any form, higher than those permitted hereunder, whether by retroactive increase or otherwise.

(b) Each person engaged in the business of selling or providing commodities or services shall maintain available for public inspection a record of the highest prices or rents charged for such or similar commodities or services during the 30-day period ending Aug. 14, 1971.

(c) The provisions of Sections 1 and 2 hereof shall not apply to the prices charged for raw agricultural products.

---

Official Executive Order given by the President on August 15, 1971.

Section 2.   (a) There is hereby established the Cost of Living Council, which shall act as an agency for the United States and which is hereinafter referred to as the Council.

(b) The Council shall be composed of the following members: the Secretary of the Treasury, the Secretary of Agriculture, the Secretary of Commerce, the Secretary of Labor, the Director of the Office of Management and Budget, the Chairman of the Council of Economic Advisers, the Director of the Office of Emergency Preparedness, and the Special Assistant to the President for Consumer Affairs.   The Secretary of the Treasury shall serve as chairman of the Council, and the Chairman of the Council of Economic Advisers shall serve as vice chairman.   The Chairman of the Board of Governors of the Federal Reserve System shall serve as adviser to the Council.   [The Secretary of Housing and Urban Development was added to the Council later.]

(c) Under the direction of the chairman of the Council, a special assistant to the President shall serve as executive director of the Council, and the executive director is authorized to appoint such personnel as may be necessary to assist the Council in the performance of its functions.

Section 3.   (a) Except as otherwise provided herein, there are hereby delegated to the Council all of the powers conferred on the President by the Economic Stabilization Act of 1970.

(b) The Council shall develop and recommend to the President additional policies, mechanisms and procedures to maintain economic growth without inflationary increases in prices, rents, wages and salaries after the expiration of the 90-day period specified in Section 1 of this Order.

(c) The Council shall consult with representatives of agriculture, industry, labor and the public concerning the development of policies, mechanisms and procedures to maintain economic growth without inflationary increases in prices, rents, wages and salaries.

(d) In all of its actions the Council will be guided by the need to maintain consistency of price and wage policies with fiscal, monetary, international and other economic policies of the United States.

(e) The Council shall inform the public, agriculture, industry and labor concerning the need for controlling inflation and shall encourage and promote voluntary action to that end.

Section 4.   (a) The Council, in carrying out the provisions of this Order, may (I) prescribe definitions for any terms used herein, (II) make exceptions or grant exemptions, (III) issue regulations and orders, and (IV) take such other actions as it determines to be necessary and appropriate to carry out the purposes of this Order.

(b) The Council may redelegate to any agency, instrumentality or official of the United States any authority under this Order, and may, in administering this Order, utilize the services of any other agencies, federal or State, as may be available and appropriate.

(c) On request of the Chairman of the Council, each executive department or agency is authorized and directed, consistent with law, to furnish the Council with available information which the Council may require in the performance of its functions.

(d) All executive departments and agencies shall furnish such necessary assistance as may be authorized by Section 214 of the Act of May 3, 1945. 59 Stat. 134 (31 U.S.C. 691).

Section 5. The Council may require the maintenance of appropriate records or other evidence which are necessary in carrying out the provisions of this Order, and may require any person to maintain and produce for examination such records or other evidence, in such form as it shall require, concerning prices, rents, wages and salaries and all related matters. The Council may make such exemptions from any requirement otherwise imposed as are consistent with the purposes of this Order. Any type of record or evidence required under regulations issued under this Order shall be retained for such period as the Council may prescribe.

Section 6. The expenses of the Council shall be paid from such funds of the Treasury Department as may be available therefore.

Section 7. (a) Whoever willfully violates this Order, or any order or regulation issued under authority of this Order, shall be fined not more than $5,000 for each such violation.

(b) The Council shall in its discretion request the Department of Justice to bring actions for injunctions authorized under Section 205 of the Economic Stabilization Act of 1970 whenever it appears to the Council that any person has engaged, is engaged, or is about to engage in any acts or practices constituting a violation of any regulation or order issued pursuant to this Order.


**QUESTIONS**

1. Compare the speech of President Nixon given in June 1970 with that given in August 1971. What happened during the year to change so importantly the President's mind about wage and price controls?

2. The President's message of August 1971 contained much more than wage, price, and rent controls. Take each of the proposals of this message and explain (a) just why it was included in the "package," and (b) to what extent it was successful in achieving the objective set for it.

3. Why are inflation and its effects so undesirable? When is an in-

flation rate serious?  Compare the inflation record of the United States with other countries of the world.  How do you explain the great differences among the various countries of the world?

4. Do you believe that price inflation from 1966 to 1971 could have been averted?  Explain precisely how.

5. Do anti-inflation remedies differ depending upon the basic causes of the inflation, or is the remedy much the same for all types of price inflation?

6. Has business been responsible for price inflation in the United States?  Has business helped to restrain price inflation?  Explain.

7. Examine and evaluate the good and bad impacts of the President's August 1971 economic policy statement, and subsequent actions, on business in general and for particular industries and businesses.

# Actions to assure continued economic progress

## the president's task force on economic growth, neil h. jacoby, chairman

The President's Task Force on Economic Growth, chaired by Neil H. Jacoby, summarizes its major recommendations in the following way.

Over the past eighty-five years the real output of the American economy has grown at an average rate of 3.3 percent a year, a very high rate in comparison with most other countries. Since 1965 productive capacity has been rising 4 percent a year. This remarkable economic growth brought unparalled and widely diffused material welfare to the American people. We enjoy higher standards of living and more freedom and mobility than any people in history.

Although this record is a source of satisfaction, the conjuncture of expanded production and consumption, of population increase and concentration, and of accelerating technology confronts the American people as they end the Sixties with aggravated social and environmental pressures that are, in part, unmeasured costs of economic growth. New public policies must be plotted and pursued during the Seventies, if our society is to cope successfully with those pressures and to maintain strong economic growth in the future.

The wellsprings of our economic growth are the basic beliefs and institutions of our society—individual freedom, private enterprise, competitive markets, profit incentives and rewards, and a government that has nurtured these institutions, encouraged saving, and invested heavily in education and the production of knowledge through research. These basic attitudes, incentives, institutions and policies must be preserved.

In the development of our economy, government was never simply the protector of a free enterprise system. It also managed the public domain, developed transportation, encouraged infant industries, established monetary institutions, instituted a social security system, and undertook a host of other functions required to meet the opportunities and problems of an urbanizing, industrializing society. We must now meet the emerging problems posed by the growing social costs of

*Policies for American Economic Progress in the Seventies* (Washington, D.C.: Government Printing Office, May 1970), pp. 1–5.

production and consumption with similar energy and resolution.  We have the opportunity to use technology to serve human needs.  We can influence population and its spatial distribution.  We can preserve the physical and social environment that will facilitate future economic growth. We can stimulate growth for greater human well-being.

The decade ahead holds a potential for continued economic growth of 4 percent or more a year.  To realize maximum gains in output, and even more important, to make the greatest improvement in the quality of American life, we believe that economic policy during the Seventies should have three major thrusts:

*First*, keep the U.S. economy expanding steadily along a path of full employment without inflation.

*Second*, increase efficiency in both the public and private sectors of the economy, by more extensive use of modern management practices and by making competition more effective in all markets.

*Third*, reallocate the nation's resources so as to protect and improve the physical and social environment, thereby enhancing well-being and facilitating future economic progress.

We propose the following actions in 1970 and in the years beyond.


## IMPROVING THE ENVIRONMENT TO FACILITATE ECONOMIC GROWTH AND PROGRESS

1. *A high-level Agency for Environmental Protection should be established, either within a Federal department or as a separate body,* to make studies of the environmental impacts of economic growth, and to propose measures for protecting the environment and for internalizing the external costs of production and consumption.

2. *Strict Federal, State and local standards should be enacted and enforced against actions that degrade the environment.*

3. *Federal programs for urban rehabilitation, urban mass transit, housing, recreational, educational and cultural facilities are necessary.*

4. The appropriate Federal agency should *develop indicators of social and economic well-being to guide long-term public policy; and the Department of Commerce should improve the national income accounts and GNP as measures of economic growth.*


## GUIDING POPULATION FOR MAXIMUM ECONOMIC WELL-BEING

1. *Congress and the President should establish a Joint National Commission on Population and charge it with studying the long run relation-*

*ships between rates of growth, levels and locations of U.S. population
and the economic and social well-being of people, and recommending
population goals and policies.*

2. *Congress and the Executive agencies should weigh the desirability
of population dispersion away from densely settled areas along with
other factors in administering Federal programs of procurement or in
locating facilities.*

## RAISING EFFICIENCY IN THE PUBLIC SECTOR BY BETTER ORGANIZATION AND MANAGEMENT

1. *The President, in collaboration with the Governors of the States,
should stimulate a movement to reorganize and strengthen local government.  As an initial step, the President should consider convening a
White House Conference on Governmental Reorganization in Metropolitan Areas.*

2. *The Bureau of the Budget should extend the Planning-Program-
ming-Budgeting System to all major categories of Federal expenditures
amenable to this type of analysis.*

3. *The Bureau of the Budget should, through its Office of Executive
Management, offer advice and technical assistance to State and local
governments on methods of improving public administration, and including the installation of PPB Systems where appropriate.*

4. *The Civil Service Commission should be instructed to study possible change in, or supplements to, the present standard salary system
which would provide incentive and reward to superior performance.*

5. *The Bureau of the Budget should arrange for the development of
measures of productivity in the performance of measurable governmental functions.*

## RAISING EFFICIENCY IN THE PRIVATE SECTOR BY EXTENDING COMPETITION AND BETTER ALLOCATION OF RESOURCES

1. Make fuller and more productive use of manpower:
    a. *The Federal Government should strengthen job training, re-
    training and worker relocation programs, and should assist
    more fully in the manpower adjustments arising from major
    technological changes.*
    b. *The Department of Labor should make available promptly on
    an inter-area basis detailed information about specific job va-
    cancies.*

   c. *Federal assistance should be given to new experiments in combining work with education, including work-study programs.*

   d. *The ceiling on the amount of earnings of persons eligible to receive full Social Security benefits should be raised* in order to make fuller use of the productive capabilities of persons aged 65 and over.

2. *The productivity of Federal research and development expenditures should be reviewed, with a view to enhancing their overall contribution to economic growth.*

3. *The President should appoint a Commission on Business Regulation with adequate authority, funds and time to study and to formulate proposals for simplification and consolidation of governmental regulations.*

4. *Congress and the Executive should review all public subsidies, consider alternatives, and phase out those subsidies not yielding values to society worth their costs.*

5. *Federal and state governments should review all price-fixing and price-maintaining legislation and phase out governmental interferences with prices where markets can be effectively competitive.*

6. *Appropriate governmental actions should be taken to assure freedom of entry into all occupations and professions, and to review the reasonableness of standards of entry and of their administration.*

7. *The Federal tax structure should be reformed to increase its equity and to strengthen fiscal stimulants to economic growth.*

8. *The President should take a new initiative toward mutual reduction of barriers to international trade, in an effort to reverse world protectionist trends.*

9. *Governmental restrictions upon private foreign investment should be removed in the near future, in the interests of faster growth of the U.S. and the world.*

## FISCAL AND MONETARY STRATEGY FOR SUSTAINED PROGRESS

After the current transition from inflation to reasonable price-level stability has been completed, high levels of demand and employment seem probable during most of the Seventies. Despite probable cuts in defense spending, Federal expenditures, and the revenues necessary to finance them, appear likely to be at relatively high levels. Steady noninflationary economic growth calls for the following basic policies:

1. *The basic fiscal rule should be to achieve a balance of total revenues and expenditures in the unified Federal budget under conditions of full employment, and to allow stabilizing surpluses or deficits to*

*develop automatically if aggregate demand moves above or below the full employment level.*

2. *The basic monetary rule should be to complement the operation of the automatic fiscal stabilizers, by appropriate and moderate adjustments in the rate of growth of the appropriate monetary variables.*

3. *If the combined impacts of the automatic budget stabilizers and of monetary measures are insufficient to maintain full employment or to prevent inflation, income tax payments should be changed to provide the additional stimulation or restraint required.*

4. *To assure prompt action in case of need, Congress should grant the President limited authority to raise or lower personal and corporate income tax payments by up to 10 percent at his discretion, for a maximum period of one year and subject to veto by Congress.*

## CONTINUING STUDIES OF ECONOMIC GROWTH

Because continuing inquiry into the issues and policies of economic growth and well-being are necessary, *the President should establish by Executive Order a Standing Committee on Economic Growth within the Executive Branch, under the chairmanship of a member of the Council of Economic Advisers, which Committee shall make an Annual Report to the President.*

Implementation of the recommendations made in this Report would make an important difference in the performance of the U.S. economy.

## QUESTIONS

1. If you were a member of the President's Task Force on Economic Growth, would you accept all these recommendations? Are there other suggestions you would advocate be included in the report?
2. What priority do you give economic growth as a major objective of national policy? To what extent are other objectives dependent upon strong economic growth? What national objectives, if pursued too vigorously, can serve to retard economic growth? How can a proper balance between growth and other national objectives be achieved?

# Business Pleas
# For and Against Free
# Trade

**15**

# The case for limiting steel imports        roger m. blough

**Roger M. Blough, Chairman of the Board of United States Steel Corporation, presents the following case for restricting foreign imports of steel.**

Periodically one can hear an announcer's voice on radio or television saying "7, 6, 5, 4, 3, 2, 1, 0." He may be counting down for the blast-off of a new adventure into space.

Currently, anyone can count down—with exactly the same numbers—and be measuring the decline of the U.S. trade balance from nearly $7 billion in 1964 to close to nothing at the present time.

The impact today may be mainly in terms of public concern about gold, and balance of payments. But the impact tomorrow may be more tangible in terms of employment, of deteriorating possibilities for growth of the economy—in short, in terms of whether we go forward or run the serious risk of depression. This is not a problem of steel alone, but steel is dramatically affected.

The seeds of the problems were sown some 35 years ago when, midway through the Depression, this nation apparently made a commitment in each of two inconsistent directions. One was to cast aside the Smoot-Hawley tariff and move toward freer trade—in the direction of laissez-faire economics so far as the world market was concerned.

At the same time, we began moving in the direction of an ever-wider departure from laissez-faire economics insofar as the internal economy is concerned, with ever more governmental involvement in attempting to mould our internal economy.

· · ·

Only now are we beginning to learn how inconsistent this was; that we can't have it both ways. Other nations found out long ago, and their governments have long been involved in shaping their foreign trade policy so it could be supportive of their domestic economy.

This decision of the Thirties was compounded by another in the Forties. After World War II, the economy of the United States was relatively intact as compared with those of Europe and Japan. Thus, for some years the U.S. economy appeared to be so strong that we thought we could afford loose fiscal and monetary policies together with other inflationary policies within the internal economy, on the one

Roger M. Blough, "The Case for Limiting Steel Imports," *Los Angeles Times*, December 20, 1968, Pt. II, p. 7. Reprinted by permission of Mr. Blough.

hand, and, on the other, the luxury of pursuing a foreign policy which evidenced little concern for what would support our domestic economy.

We now see, of course, that virtually every nation in the world follows both a foreign policy and a foreign trade policy designed to be essentially supportive of its domestic economy. In a world in which fundamental laws of economics have not been repealed, and in which nationalism is unfortunately neither dead nor declining, the United States is only now beginning to learn that it cannot alone be different.

. . .

Thirteen years ago, less than half of our import trade was in manufactured goods. Today more than two-thirds of it is in that category. It is here that it was once believed that the United States had a vaunted advantage in superior technology, an advantage easily sufficient to support a level of labor costs well above that of the rest of the world. But, as the years have rolled by, that technology has been spreading fast and world-wide. Unfortunately for us, however, our high levels of labor costs have not been spreading to other nations nearly as fast.

Thus, our imports of manufactured goods tripled in the last decade, while our exports barely doubled. Moreover, our share in world exports of manufactured goods declined from about 28% to only about 20%.

This might have been expected; because after all, over 75% of the costs throughout the economy as a whole are labor costs—not alone in the final manufacturing process, but in bringing the raw material into semi-manufactures and then into the manufactured product.

It is in this area of manufactured goods that we have our highest employment. And it is here that we must, therefore, have our greatest concern as to what is happening to our competitiveness in world trade.

Steel is but one example of what has been happening, but certainly a most shattering example. Annual imports of steel have risen from a little over a million tons to nearly 18 million tons in just over a decade. In August, imports were at an annual rate in excess of 24 million tons—greater than the production of the largest steelmaker in the United States.

As a Senate Finance Committee report pointed out, unless our domestic steelmakers' markets grow at somewhere near 2-½ million tons a year, they cannot continue to finance the modernization of their facilities which ought to occur. If they cannot participate fully in future market growth, they will have no adequate justification for a continuing high rate of investment in domestic steelmaking facilities.

Thus in a short time, this nation could arrive at a point where its domestic steelmaking facilities will no longer be adequate to meet the needs of an economy upon which only the requirements of even a limited war may have been forced.

No other major nation has looked at its domestic steel availability as casually as have we. Russia certainly does not. Every other nation of consequence considers its steel industry enough of a bastion of its economy that it makes certain that its trade policies are supportive of the industry. We cannot further delay reaching—and implementing—the same conclusion in this country.

I believe, in short, that the people of this nation must support and encourage their government reasonably to limit the influx of foreign steel.

Steel's problem is not that of comparative inefficiency. Domestic mills on the average are at least as efficient as those in any other nation. Our product quality is still the standard of the world.

The domestic steel industry's problem has not been lack of capital spending, which has run at a phenomenal rate throughout the sixties. But the lower cost of Japanese labor means the Japanese can put new capital equipment in place for no more than one-half to one-third of what it costs their American competitors.

Steel's problem is not lack of research. Domestic steel has the most forward-looking research in the world. Comparatively, it spends as great or greater a portion of its revenues on research as does the steel industry of any other nation.

Finally, the American steel industry's problem is not related to overpricing or profit maximization. The plain fact is that the industry remains near the bottom of most anyone's list when rating industries in terms of return on net worth. So it is clear that the $25 to $40 per ton difference between the American steel industry's prices in its domestic market and the prices of its foreign competitors in the same market could not be met across the board without plunging the industry into a serious loss position.

What, then, is the steel industry's problem, and what can be done about it?

For one thing, governmental policies with respect to the internal economy are highly relevant.

Part of the problem lies in the wide disparity of wage costs in the United States and those in other major steel-producing areas. The cost of an hour's work in Japan is only a quarter of that in the United States, and the gap has not been shrinking.

Over the decade from 1957 through 1966, Japanese steel hourly employment costs increased at a percentage rate two and one-quarter times the rate in the United States. But because that rate applied to a lower base, the actual spread in the costs of an hour's work widened by about 85 cents.

Unless we have a very significantly lower rate of wage inflation here, there will be no accommodation to our problems nor to the problem of other manufacturing industries in the foreseeable future.

Inflation is and remains primarily a result of governmental actions. Ultimately, any government's monetary and fiscal policies will set the stage in which there may or may not be serious wage rate inflation. It is difficult for a union to disengage itself from the general economic flow surrounding wage changes.

Thus, the policies of government regarding the internal economy are an important contributing factor to the increasing noncompetitiveness of American steel and other manufactured goods.

Even when there is a constructive change of policy, the ultimate benefits may be too long delayed to be helpful, particularly when help is needed as promptly as it is in the case of American steel.

. . .

The second major factor contributing to our problem lies in the way in which the policies of other governments contribute to the ability of their own steel industries to enjoy a relatively sheltered domestic market, while at the same time enjoying considerable assistance in selling into the world market—including the United States.

For example, if a ton of sheet metal were shipped from the United States to an automobile manufacturer in France, not only would it bear all of the tax burden of doing business in the United States, the freight to transport it to France, and some duty, but there would be added a tax equivalent to the value-added tax had the ton of steel been manufactured in France and sold there.

In turn, when the French steel manufacturer ships to Detroit, his domestic tax burden of about $30 a ton is remitted, and when the steel arrives in the United States, none of the tax burden attributable to an American steel manufacturer is levied. This is anything but free trade or fair competition.

There is a profusion of these barriers and subsidies; and there are competitive practices amongst foreign competitors which are frowned upon by our own antitrust laws.

Every one of us would prefer to declare himself generally in support of freer trade. But we cannot do so unknowingly; we must ask ourselves under what conditions world trade in steel is now practiced.

. . .

Our current problem will not go away by itself—most certainly not within a period of time which could be considered useful. Surely it is unrealistic to expect the current trend of inflation to be sufficiently reversed in time to do the job. And the elimination of nontariff barriers, of subsidies and of the practice of remission of value-added taxes cannot be expected to occur even within a time period equal to that of the long-drawn-out Kennedy Round remissions.

Likewise proceedings under our countervailing duty laws or under our dumping laws cannot be expected to do enough of the total job which needs to be done—certainly not in the short run.

The health of our domestic steel industry will not await the possibility that any or all of these circumstances may improve sufficiently within the foreseeable future to be useful. The domestic industry faces the fact—now—that almost none of the growth of its domestic market can be counted upon as available to it. It needs governmental action to limit the growth of imports beyond a reasonable level.

And it needs it now.

# The aerospace industry wants free trade

**daniel j. haughton**

Daniel J. Haughton, Chairman of the Board of Lockheed Aircraft Corporation, presents a plea for free trade as being in the best interests of the country and of the aerospace industry.

. . . a strong aerospace export program is vital to the nation's interest as well as the aerospace industry's and . . . such a program requires liberal trade policies for its fullest success.

This is the message from our industry point of view. And yet I don't think we need restrict ourselves to that. We are faced here with a national issue that goes deep into our history and out into our future. Do we go forward confidently to build our nation's future within the area of free international trade or do we retire in defeat within the walls of growing protectionism and leave international trade leadership to others?

Our answer—both as members of the aerospace industry and as responsible citizens—is that we must go forward.

In a quickly changing world, a good policy is one that brings the greatest benefits over the longest period of time to the most people. And in the field of international trade that policy is liberal trade relations.

The United States has maintained this policy in general over the last three decades and under both political parties. It has been a sound and rewarding policy. Under it free world exports have grown from $60 billion in 1948 to more than $200 billion today, and our nation as well as other nations have reaped the economic benefits. But our rewards have been more than just economic. Our trade has brought influence and prestige to our nation. It has helped us export not only our products and our technology but also our ideas and our ideals. It has helped us maintain friendly relations abroad and a position of leadership in the international community. It has, I think, been a force for peace at a time when peace has been threatened on every side.

Is it any wonder then that we in the industry are concerned by the growing protectionist sentiment both at home and abroad? It is easy to understand this sentiment and some of its causes—national tensions

Speech before the Aircraft Industries Association International Committee, Washington, D.C., March 25, 1969. Reprinted by permission of Mr. Haughton.

and distrust, private self interest, growing nationalism, concern over gold flow, and a score of other economic, social, and political problems.

It is easy to understand this sentiment. It is harder to resist it. But we must resist it, for the answers to our problems—all of them—are not to be found by turning away from them but by facing them squarely. And protectionism—whether by high tariff barriers or by the host of non-tariff barriers we now see springing up—is no answer at all. It pushes us toward more inflation, it reduces the benefits of competition, it increases cost to the consumer, and it dims our image abroad and strains our international relations at the very time that we are making an effort to improve them. With our government continuing to work diligently to establish better international relations on the diplomatic level, it makes little sense for us to tear them down in terms of trade.

Protectionism in the long run serves no important national interest. It may not even serve the selfish interests of those who seek it in their own behalf since protectionist measures have a way of backfiring.

But the arguments against protectionism are well known. What we are confronted with today is not arguments but a spate of non-tariff barriers—quotas, import deposits, administrative taxes, taxes on value added, and all the other devices that threaten to cancel out many of the gains made in the 1966 Kennedy Round. These non-tariff barriers are not peculiar to our own country, of course—and it may be in the complex environment in which we live that some of them may be justified or justifiable on a temporary basis. But in the mass they add up to a threat against the free trade policies toward which we and other nations have been striving for so long. They threaten to turn the clock back to an older era and reverse the long-term trend toward freer trade.

This trend toward protectionism is of particular concern to our industry, and its possible effect on us should be of concern to the nation. We are a prime target for reprisals against barriers raised by our own country, and those reprisals could hurt us and our nation alike.

I don't need to give you people a long review on our position in the economy or the importance of our export program. You are all aware that the aerospace industry is the largest manufacturing employer in the nation—1,400,000 people. And you know we are one of the country's principal manufacturing exporters. Our exports last year were just under $3 billion. Interestingly, this is about three times the nation's trade surplus in 1968.

We make a significant contribution on the plus side to our nation's balance of payments and have done so for many years. A recent National Industrial Conference Board study analyzed the rapid increase in U.S. imports in the past few years. Transportation imports rose twice as much as the next category, machinery. Yet, despite this, the U.S. continued to enjoy a trade surplus in transportation equipment, primarily because of the large exports of aircraft.

So we are concerned. We know we can continue to help our country's balance of trade in the future, and we want the chance to do so. We know those thousands of jobs involved in our exports are important and we'd like to retain them. And we know that anything that weakens our export base will weaken our technological strength. We don't want this to happen and we don't think the government does.

Fortunately, I am optimistic enough to think that it won't happen. I know the pressures for protectionism, but I also know the weight of the arguments against it. I am encouraged recently to find that some of our government and business leaders are speaking out on the side of more liberalized trade. Last month a joint Congressional committee heard from officials of both the Johnson and Nixon administrations. William M. Roth, well known to you people as U.S. special representative for trade negotiations, testified that the import quota campaign in Congress has not made an economic case for over-all protection. And Secretary Maurice H. Stans said that "in a period when we are fighting inflation, we should not invite price increases by erecting barriers to imports." Rudolph Peterson, president of Bank of America, recently expressed his belief that "long-term national self-interest is intimately intertwined with greater and freer trade and capital movement" and that we are moving toward "growth in regional common markets and trade associations."

These are encouraging words, but the battle is not yet won. Our message may be a simple one, but we must repeat it over and over, as clearly as we can, because the present year is crucial. It is the year in which our country will determine whether to press forward or go back.

I know that there is a temptation to go back. We are faced with more problems, more uncertainties, more confusion than we have had in a good many years. We have problems about our international role. We have fears about the international monetary system. We are concerned with the task of fighting inflation while at the same time maintaining full employment. The balance of payments problem seems to be always with us. And meanwhile we have social problems without end.

In this kind of environment it is perhaps easy to look for short-term simple solutions, to narrow our responsibilities, to fall back upon the immediate answer, to turn inward upon ourselves. It is easy to give up basic goals.

What we must guard against in these times is a failure of nerve.

Our country has always believed in competition. Today we must have the courage to compete—not only here at home but overseas.

Sure, it may be harder. Our foreign competitors are growing stronger and more skillful. They sometimes have advantages that we lack—from lower labor rates to government subsidy. Their technologies are advancing. Their attitudes are changing.

We can find all kinds of excuses for withdrawing from the competition or protecting ourselves against it. But I think we have to recognize these for what they are—simply excuses. If we are not courageous enough or innovative enough to meet this tougher kind of competition, then perhaps we don't deserve the claim to leadership that we have always made.

Personally, I think we *can* meet this new kind of competition in this new international environment. I know that other industries are doing so but I'd like to point to our own industry as an example because it's the one I know most about.

In the past the aerospace industry has had advantages that we don't today. We no longer enjoy the large technological lead that we had after World War II. European and other countries have rebuilt their technical strength—with our help, with aid from their own governments, and with their own skills—until today in many aerospace technical fields they equal us and in some they may be surpassing us. They are also rebuilding their managerial skills and their marketing skills. As a result, we find them worthy and difficult competitors in many areas.

And yet in spite of all this, we have kept our export program strong. I think a large part of our success is due to our ability to adapt to the changing environment and seek out new ways of marketing our products. The one that occurs to me as the best example is that we have found new ways to allow our foreign customers to participate— foreign subcontracting, cooperative ventures, licensing, the purchase of services from abroad, co-production, overseas investment, and others. The key to all this has been our ability to work out ways to share our design and production skills with our foreign customers in ways that serve their own national interests while serving ours.

And this kind of innovation need not only apply to technical or production matters—it should apply to the whole spectrum of foreign marketing. As you know, we are now making every effort to apply it to export financing—one of the problems your own committee has been wrestling with.

We still have our problems . . . but the fact is that we *have* been able to compete in international markets and compete successfully. And that competition has been good for us—as well as for our industry and our customers. Sometimes I'm tempted to think it's a little *too* good for our customers—particularly when I think about my own corporation's efforts right now to sell a certain commercial transport abroad. But I know basically it's a better airplane because of the competition we get from others, just as theirs are better airplanes because of the competition they get from us. And I think this is the way to go.

I think it's the way for all American industry to go. It's the way we've been going at home ever since our nation was founded, and it's the way we've been going abroad ever since we embarked on a free trade policy back in the 30s. If we admit the value of competition at home, we've got to face up to the value of competition abroad.

But we won't go this way by raising trade barriers and sitting quietly behind them. We can only do it by continuing on the path we have laid out—by working toward the reduction of barriers so that we can provide for true international competition. We can't solve our industry's or our nation's problems by restricting imports. We *can* help solve them by increasing exports. And I believe that American industry has courage enough and ingenuity enough to make the effort. We will make it under conditions of liberalized trade. We certainly won't make it under a return to protectionism—and this will be a tragedy for us all.

## QUESTIONS

1. Compare the positions of Blough and Haughton. Which position is the most persuasive? Explain. How do you explain the completely different positions these two men take toward trade protection?

2. If an industry is in trouble in the sense that it cannot compete at home and abroad and it is offered the choice of increased protection from foreign competition or help toward increasing its exports, what do you think it should choose, and why? Should the federal government give an industry such a choice?

3. Discuss the theoretical premises of free trade. Should all countries strive toward such a state?

4. What is responsible for current sentiment toward protectionism throughout the world? What is your forecast of the consequences of a continuation of such a trend?

# There are holes in the free trade argument

### richard n. farmer

In this article, Richard N. Farmer, Chairman of the Department of International Business Administration at Indiana University, argues that the long-accepted, idealized goal of free trade may not be as acceptable today as purists claim.

Economists have preached the virtues of free trade for a couple of centuries—and for just as long, certain groups have fought stubbornly, and with considerable success, for trade barriers and controls. Thus in 1970, the American textile industry has almost succeeded, after years of effort, in getting quotas applied to many categories of imports. Narrowly defeated was an even more restrictive trade policy; it would have included more than eighty other industries that desired quota protection.

Business and other groups are split on this issue, however. Some firms want more restrictions and are often joined by trade unions and local civic organizations, for example. They feel that they are damaged by freer trade and competition from abroad, and they have worked diligently for decades to get trade cut off. Their favorite modern weapon is the quota because it provides absolute protection; only so much of the despised foreign goods can enter the country. With only tariff protection, it is always possible that foreign prices will be so low that competition will develop even if the tariff is relatively high.

Other large firms and supporting groups have joined the academics and insist on freer trade. For a number of decades, this influence has been ascendant in American politics, and trade barriers have been relaxed steadily since 1934. But the trend may be shifting as dissenters move across to the protectionist side. This is particularly noticeable in the trade union movement. In recent years, a number of large unions once in favor of free trade have expressed their doubts about such policies.

The case for free trade is logically consistent and complete, and has never been overturned since it was formulated over a century ago. Even casual students of economics are usually exposed early to arguments presenting the basic comparative advantages, and it can be demonstrated conclusively that the effects of free trade are to expand total income, increase productivity, and generally create a more efficient economy.

Richard N. Farmer, "Tariffs, Quotas, and Class Structure," *Business Horizons*, XIII (December 1970), 29–34. Reprinted by permission.

The only two valid arguments accepted in favor of trade restrictions have little relevance in modern America, although they might apply elsewhere. The first covers infant industries and is hardly credible in a country that is noted for being first to develop new industries and hence has no early foreign competition. The second argument insists that defense items should be produced at home in order to avoid having to rely on unstable foreigners. This argument also seems much less relevant in an atomic age, where any major war may be over before the first shipment from abroad can be stopped. These arguments, along with many others of even less merit, are used, of course, in many quarters in the United States. And sometimes they work, insofar as Congress approves protectionist measures.

The problem posed here is why, after two-hundred years, a rational position that can demonstrably raise incomes and economic efficiency is still fiercely resisted. Present international trade barriers probably cost the United States well over $20 billion in income every year. Why does a presumably self-seeking, rational group of people deliberately throw away so much, particularly when money is desperately needed to finance so many social needs?

Certainly economists cannot be blamed. For centuries, this group has patiently conducted students through the subtle complexities of comparative advantage, given testimony to Congress in favor of free trade, and written group letters to Presidents protesting obviously irrational policies. Yet trade restrictions remain popular. Is it possible that we have been working at the wrong end of the political economy? We have stressed economics without deeply analyzing what goes into the politics of trade restrictions. The social attitudes and class positions of winners and losers in the trade war are key components of the political consideration, and the following analysis suggests why it may be so difficult to convince people of the soundness of a good economic argument. Economists have pointed out that the winners in a free trade situation normally far outnumber the losers, both in numbers and money, but the losers doggedly fight on. Relatively little has been said, however, about the kinds of people winners and losers are. What is needed to understand the problem is a taxonomy of both types.

## THE WINNERS

Winners in a free trade situation tend to be the high productivity firms, along with persons connected with them. Table 1 suggests a typical pattern. Such firms as those making electronic components and metal-working machinery have high value-added per employee, which is

TABLE 1    Selected Industry Productivity Changes, 1958–67

| Industry | Value-added per Employee | | Percent Change, 1958–67 |
|---|---|---|---|
| | 1958 | 1967 | |
| Men's and boys' furnishings | $4,140 | $5,930 | 143 |
| Women's and children's underwear | 5,360 | 7,310 | 136 |
| Children's outerwear | 4,700 | 6,500 | 138 |
| Fabricated textiles * | 5,660 | 8,040 | 142 |
| Electronic components | 7,240 | 11,400 | 157 |
| Electrical products * | 9,230 | 14,300 | 155 |
| Metalworking machinery | 8,600 | 14,900 | 174 |

SOURCE: *Statistical Abstract of the United States, 1969* (Washington: U.S. Gov't. Printing Office, 1969), pp. 717–21.
* Not elsewhere classified.

another way of suggesting that they have good comparative advantages. Firms with much lower value-added per person are more vulnerable to foreign competition, as the top part of the table suggests. Since their productivity is lower, they are not in a position to take proper steps when foreign competitors invade their markets.

When trade is restricted, the high productivity firms will suffer if foreign trade restrictions against them are increased as a retaliatory measure. One common result of such trade warfare is a transfer of labor from more or less productive activities. This in itself might not be a formidable problem if sectors of lower productivity show rapid productivity gains. But as suggested in Table 1, they tend to improve less rapidly over time than sectors with higher productivity.

Other winners in a free trade situation include all consumers, particularly if the effect of trade restriction is to raise prices of consumer goods, as in the present textile case. But an often overlooked point is that the biggest winners will be the biggest consumers—and in the United States, this tends to be the highest income groups. Therefore, the top half of the income distribution pyramid tends to gain somewhat more than the bottom half on this count. It may also be true that the more sophisticated consumers, who have more sophisticated tastes, also will gain from the availability of a product mix that includes foreign items. One does not normally count the psychic cost to sophisticates of having esoteric foreign items excluded by quota or high prices, but such costs may be very real.

Since income tends to be closely correlated with education, a curious result of free trade is to favor the more literate, more educated, and more sophisticated segment of the population. Such persons are more flexible, both occupationally and geographically; they tend to be more productive; and they can adjust to change somewhat better than less educated persons. They also tend to become managers and technicians in the more productive, higher value-added firms.

Local taxes tend to be somewhat regressive, so such persons, if the policy of free trade is adopted, add to their already larger incomes by paying less for various consumer goods. If incomes generally are higher because of free trade, it does not follow that everyone is better off. Indeed, much of the money income gain, and perhaps even more of the psychic income gain, may in fact be enjoyed by the upper middle class.

Thus the winners take on a profile which is seen as quite desirable in the modern intellectual mainstream. They are flexible and adaptable. They also are cosmopolitan and, in their professional and technical roles, the people who can build, manage, and maintain productive systems that grow more productive through time. They are, in short, nice people like us.

## THE LOSERS

The losers are the reciprocal of the above. They are the provincials, the less educated, those with lower incomes and limited flexibility. They tend to be less mobile, and, because they are not very productive, have lower incomes and are more sensitive to competitive pressures from abroad.

The losing firms also have somewhat unfavorable characteristics. They are the smaller firms, have low productivity, and resist new ideas. The owners and managers of such operations also are much more provincial than typical upper middle-class citizens, although in other respects (for example, income) they may be similar. One survey suggests that the major difference between smaller firms with lively export sales and those that ignore such possibilites is nothing more than the state of mind of the owners and managers. Cosmopolitan individuals tend to search out foreign markets, even in somewhat unlikely situations; similarly placed provincials rarely do so. Such persons may enjoy considerable local prestige, but they have none nationally, since being provincial is not sharing in the action these days. Their politics and attitudes tend to be hyperconservative; the cosmopolitan Republican supports Nixon or Rockefeller, but the provincial stands firm with Goldwater or Reagan.

The well-educated, upper income provincial may well benefit indirectly from world trade as a consumer, as described earlier, but such benefits are marginal compared to the considerable benefit of being left alone to run the small subsystem without threat from foreigners. For the provincial, the real payoff is in keeping the world the same, in isolating his small piece of it from dangerous change. This pattern does not always follow industry lines. Some extremely capable and change-oriented cosmopolitans are in the textile industry, for example; others can be found in various corners of industries considered backward by American standards. Such persons and firms are relatively easy to identify. One way is to find the exporters and importers. The owners and managers of a firm directly involved in foreign trade are likely to accept the cosmopolitan position of readiness to change rapidly. Table 2 is a list of conditions that one would expect to find in the creative, change-oriented firm. Conditions exactly the opposite probably exist in the firm seeking protection from competition, although no such study has yet been done. It is likely

TABLE 2   Characteristics of Change-Oriented Firm

1. A relatively small degree of formalization of relationships among the organizational positions (flexibility of structure may be a necessary quality of the truly creative organization).
2. Careful attention given to not overspecifying the human resources needed for a specific task.
3. A flexible power-authority-influence structure or network oriented primarily toward the task at hand.
4. Relatively large areas of discretion and healthy amounts of participation and autonomy for those who are expected to exhibit creativity.
5. Perhaps broadened spans of control to decrease the likelihood of management by direction and control. (This will probably mean flatter or at least non-pyramidal structures.)
6. Measurement of results and associated evaluation of personnel based on the longest time span compatible with economic survival.
7. A tendency to utilize actual results accomplished within this time span, rather than adherence to minutely prescribed procedures as the standard for evaluation and measurement.
8. A tendency to organizationally or, at least, conceptually separate the idea generation function from the idea evaluation function.
9. A tendency toward the maximum number of open communication channels interconnecting all those knowledgeable units relevant to a particular problem area.
10. A conscious attempt to institutionalize an organizational reward system, basically intrinsic in character, which appeals to the needs of the creative individual. (Suggestive mechanisms here might be considerable self-selection of task assignments, given some broadly defined constraints; increased freedom of work scheduling; increased autonomy concerning work methods; enhanced opportunities for professional growth and recognition; and, perhaps, differential extrinsic reward systems for professionals and nonprofessionals involving parallel promotional chains based on different but appropriate criteria.)
11. Of primary importance, but somewhat intangible, a managerial philosophy and attitudinal climate which projects the assumption that employees are generally capable, well-trained, and able to exert creative efforts in the pursuit of organizational goals.

SOURCE: Larry L. Cummings, "Organizational Climes for Creativity," *Journal of the Academy of Management*, VIII (September, 1965), pp. 220–27.

that the lower the creativity level, the more likely [that] a firm or industry will seek protection.

A final category of losers in a free trade situation might be called the "wheeler-dealers." This is particularly true in quota situations, where "pieces of paper" (formal, official quotas) have value. He who can get the piece of paper has a big income, however obtained. For example, American petroleum import quota legislation until recently admitted $2 foreign oil for competition with $3 local oil. The firm or individual who could get an official quota of 20,000 barrels was, in effect, being given about $20,000 in cash by his beneficent government. If a piece of duly sanctioned paper is worth $20,000, or $20 million, or even $20, we can expect the wheeler-dealers to obtain it. If one scans all the arguments for and against the quotas on textile imports, one is impressed by the lack of information or argument on this danger. Yet if quotas go into effect, one certain result will be big gains for wheeler-dealers. We can expect lively maneuvering for pieces of paper, with all the potential for corruption, confusion, and lobbying that this implies.

It is also surprising that governments have not long ago realized what kinds of random capital gains they pass out along with various restrictions, with some favored group getting an economic advantage under stated conditions. Yet such considerations are—and always have been—rarely considered in studying the implications of tariffs, quotas, and other trade controls.

Thus, the losers in a free trade situation emerge as the conservative, provincial set, persons unwilling to accept rapid change, quite localized in activities, and typically considerably less productive than the winners. The wheeler-dealers are in a class by themselves, since their politics appear to be to take advantage of whatever windfall comes their way.

Here we have a liberal-conservative split of a classic sort. Since millions of persons are in both camps, we constantly hear acrimonious debate about the trade problem, and national policy sways one way and then the other, depending on political currents, perceived foreign pressures and opportunities, and the nature of foreign competition and the balance of payments at any given time. At present, it would appear that the protectionists are becoming more potent politically, as shown by renewed interest in wide ranges of trade protectionist schemes actively being considered by Congress.

## DEALING WITH PROTECTIONISM

If we really believe in free trade, one world, and a rapidly rising standard of living, then protectionist sentiments are dangerous. They tend to make these goals more difficult to achieve.  Hence, what might be done to deal with these class and sociological elements in the protectionist make-up?

It would appear that traditional economic arguments only convince those who are already convinced or are already committed to the cosmopolitan, change-oriented way of life.  Such arguments certainly have their uses, but winning over large numbers of provincials is not one of them.  To do this, it would seem that careful consideration must be given to reaching those persons who see in foreign competition at any level something unsavory in both economic and social terms.  The future of freer trade may depend on how well such approaches can be made.

One useful first step is for the cosmopolitans to stop being so stupidly superior toward more provincial types.  One often senses the superciliousness of those who have achieved a certain academic point of view and damn the peasants for not getting the word.  Any so-called economist in the United States who seriously comes out for major trade restrictions would cease to become an economist, at least in the judgment of his professional peers.  Yet economists have not really considered the marketing of their ideas to people who happen to disagree, for what seem to them to be good reasons.  If they cannot sell a good idea in 150 years, something must be wrong with their marketing approach!

What appears to be wrong is that the problem is considered an intellectual exercise for the Establishment elites and insiders, whereas the persons buying are likely to be highly suspicious of this approach.  It may be possible to take a closer look at the losers, figure out just who they are and how they might respond to various approaches, and then sell the idea on this basis.  There is little evidence, however, that anyone has tried this in any significant way.

Related to this problem is the fact that losers often are highly visible (for example, the man who loses his job), whereas winners are diffused throughout society.  The 10 million who each save a few dollars a year buying shirts are swamped by the few thousand who collectively are out a million dollars or so.  In addition, the winners, often being in better economic circumstances, can often afford the loss, whereas the losers may be unable to do much about their loss.

We are really dealing with a marketing question, namely, how does one get at a group which is highly resistant to change?  Intellectual honesty may be fun, but it has not gotten the job done.  Perhaps using the methodologies of public relations and marketing are preferable, particularly if the stakes are high—as most thoughtful persons would argue.  It might also be useful to consider all sorts of institutional blockages within the United States and how to minimize them, if free traders are to win the argument. In the end, an irrational professional or firm entry restriction internally is about the same as a foreign restriction, and we have far too many of both kinds already. One simple and useful change could be the establishment of an employment information system on a national level, so that persons seeking work in one state could find out about opportunities in another. Experiments in technology and management information transfer among firms, even in the United States, have suggested how difficult such transfers are, yet these problems are parallel to those involving foreign trade. In the end, we have to figure out how to get at individuals and firms who continue to reject the logic of rational argument. But it is far from clear how this might be done.

Three major groups are involved in the free trade argument; each can be sociologically defined. The winners in a free trade situation tend to be flexible, change oriented, and cosmopolitan. The losers are inflexible, provincial, and static. The third group, by implication, are those in the middle, who may not have taken any position or who are swayed one way or another by current events.

Since these groups differ in terms of their outlook on the world, it would seem useful to consider gaining support for free trade by planning arguments which reach a reasonably well-defined group. The difficulty, of course, is that this group is hard to reach with conventional free trade arguments.

If one wished to isolate the United States from the world, it would be possible to turn the argument around and try to figure out how to convert change-oriented people to a more static outlook. Perhaps this is not as far-fetched as it may seem, since some ecologists seem to be calling for just this sort of change. Instead of perpetual change, rising incomes, and international orientation, it is argued that people should become more provincial, more static, and less change oriented. This sort of no-growth philosophy has not yet been extended to international trade, but it easily could be. In any case, consideration of the general social orientation of the target groups might be a useful place to begin a meaningful change process.

# Chapter 15 Question

1. Does the distinction between "winners" and "losers" in Farmer's article explain different approaches to free trade, as exemplified by the arguments of Blough and Haughton?

# Union Conflict with Management and Society

**16**

# Union-management conflict

## leon c. megginson and c. ray gullett

**Leon C. Megginson is Professor of Management at Louisiana State University, and C. Ray Gullett is Assistant Professor of Management at East Texas State University. They examine in the following article the underlying causes of union-management conflict and present a predictive model for the relationship.**

We may study intergroup behavior from a number of different approaches. First, we can select the relationships (e.g., the line-staff-relationships) that exist between and among the various major departments within a company. Second, the interactions among groupings at the level of informal intergroup relationships could be investigated to show that the force of the informal work group upon the behavior of an individual affects not only his behavior with respect to the other members of his group, but also his behavior toward members of other groups. Still a third approach to intergroup behavior description would be a look into the internal workings of a union in order to describe intergroup factionalism and power struggles. Fourth, the continuing power struggle between management and labor affords an excellent laboratory for studying cooperation, competition, and conflict.

The purpose of this article is to study the last mentioned phenomenon, that of union-management relationships. The approach followed is a behavioral one which attempts to discover some basic reasons why each side behaves as it does toward the other. The study attempts to deal with the reasons for the degree of conflict which exists between the two groups and how each side can generate intensified or decreased conflict in their relationship. A model is then constructed which can be used as a predictive tool for estimating union-management conflict levels. No ethical value judgments as to the desirability of either increasing or decreasing the level of conflict between the groups are offered.

Although we find many definitions of the word "conflict," Dubin's definition seems most appropriate for this study. He defines conflict as the "actual or threatened use of force in any continuing social relationship. Force is the attempt to override opposition by an act designed to produce injury to the other party." This definition is useful

Leon C. Megginson and C. Ray Gullett, "A Predictive Model of Union-Management Conflict," *Personnel Journal*, June 1970, pp. 495–503. Reprinted by permission.

because it stresses action, or the threatened use of action, to override the opponent's wishes in favor of one's own.

## SIMPLIFYING ASSUMPTIONS

It is well known that the more complicated a model of "real world" behavior becomes, the more closely it generally approaches reality. But we also know that the more complicated the model is, the harder it is to be understood itself and the less useful it is as a learning or predictive device. Therefore, we are taking an intermediary approach by making some simplifying assumptions which it is believed do not impair the effectiveness of the predictive model. These simplifying assumptions involve holding a number of variables in the labor-management relationship constant.

## OMISSIONS

We begin by ruling out both industrial giants and the very small firms as subjects for our study. Kerr pointed out that the unions—or perhaps management itself—chooses the giant firm with which to do battle over terms of a contract that will set precedents not only for a single industry, but often for other important segments of the national business community. The strategic place the large firm possesses for collective agreement pattern setting thus makes it more susceptible to industrial conflict with the unions with which it deals. Conversely, the very small firm is highly dependent on the patterns set by larger firms as it is in a relatively weak bargaining position, and usually can do little to resist the demands of a large and powerful union.

Secondly, we will assume that production patterns are not highly irregular, but follow a steady flow since a moderately stable production pattern throughout the year typifies most United States industry.

Also omitted from our list of variables is the problem of interunion rivalry. Given the fact that there are other unions attempting to sway the allegiance of the workers from the union in power, there will be a greater degree of conflict generated between management and the union. Kornhauser, Dubin, and Ross found that de facto stabilization of bargaining rights is conducive to more peaceful union-management relations, while interunion rivalry has pronounced unsettling effects. As long as most unions in the United States remain members of the AFL-CIO, and as long as this federation is able to accomplish the settlement of jurisdictional disputes and to establish no-raiding agreements between its members, it is believed that this variable can be safely ignored as an important conflictual influence.

Finally, it is assumed that the union and management representatives have had some experience in dealing with each other. Sloane and Witney point out that relationships between management and union leaders tend to be less conflictual as time passes. This assumption is believed to be valid because relatively experienced relationships typify most union-management associations in the United States.

## CONFLICTUAL "GIVENS"

In any theoretical framework there are germane factors which must be assumed to be present and accepted as fixed factors. These then become part of the fixed environment for the resulting analysis. There are several such given factors in our analysis.

The first basic "given" is that some degree of intergroup conflict is inherent in every union-management relationship. As Chamberlain points out, "What is involved here is a power struggle, a conflict of relationships which has gone on over the years, perhaps over the centuries." Indeed, it is fair to say that any relationship in which the authority of one individual or group over another is in question occasions some degree of conflict.

Although sweeping generalizations are dangerous, inasmuch as they necessarily are somewhat inaccurate in specific cases, an attempt is made in the following paragraphs to outline some of the factors which contribute to at least some minimum level of conflict between organizations.

### Differing Goals and Value Systems

One basic difference between the two groups lies in their goals and value systems and the methods used to reach those goals. We stress here the orientation of the groups toward the basic beliefs or values that they possess concerning the reasons why their organization exists, the objectives that they wish to attain in order to uphold these values, and the resultant techniques they employ in order to obtain these objectives.

Management tends to perceive of its task as the effective utilization of the material and human resources of the firm in order to produce a good or service for its customers and hopefully, a profit for the owners of the firm. Thus, the firm's industrial relations must contribute to, or at least not detract from, the over-all efficiency and productivity of the firm.  In the view of management, demands and actions of the union often are detrimental to this over-all efficiency.  In referring to this fact, Bakke states that "any manager, whatever his philosophy or degree of benevolence will 'get tough' when the productiveness and profitability of his own firm starts going down."

The union tends to view itself as attempting to regulate the decisions of management in those areas of activity which affect the working force.  Both legally and in terms of union interest there is no logical limit to the matters over which unions assume they might bargain with employers.

Thus, while management views its responsibilities for the long-term profitability and success of the enterprise as depending upon its freedom of action and maneuverability, union representatives see themselves as checks on this arbitrary and unilateral action necessary to maintain and increase the economic welfare of their members.

No implication is intended here that management is disinterested in the economic welfare of its employees.  But management is oriented toward a philosophy which states that flexibility and change are necessary to achieve maximum economic welfare for both the firm and its employees.  Further, management's responsibilities are to a number of groups, only one of which is comprised of its employees.

We have shown that differences in values, goals to be achieved, and the methods to achieve the goals exist between these two groups.  Conflict is thus likely to arise because both these organizations try to achieve the differing objectives through the same medium; namely the business, the firm, the corporation.  Or, in alternate phraseology, we may say that there is a competition between interested parties for the scarce resources of the firm.

### Quasi-Political Nature of the Union

A second reason why some degree of hostility is a necessary "given" in these intergroup relations is the nature of union organizations themselves and the way in which solidarity within them must be built and maintained.  Union organizations are not economic entities in the same sense as business organizations; instead they could better be described as a "movement." Although it can be argued with some effectiveness that unions today are not the evangelical organizations they were in the 1930's, the nature of unions is still basically the same: They are quasi-political organizations which must promote solidarity within their ranks in order to be effective.

But what does this need to build solidarity within the union's membership have to do with intergroup conflict?  Psychologists and sociologists have found through research—and union leaders would agree—that one important way to generate unanimity within the ranks of the union is to focus attention on the "unfair" and "unjust" behavior of some outside force—usually management—toward the members. For example, one research project found that heightened in-group solidarity and cooperativeness was observed at the very time when intergroup hostility was at its peak, that is, during the period when the groups asserted emphatically that they would not have anything more to do with each other.

If management is acting in ways considered unjust by its employees, union leaders will likely use those actions to generate zeal within the ranks of employees for the union and its demands. But it is also true that in order to achieve and maintain in-group solidarity, it may be necessary for union leadership to look for issues where perhaps no serious ones currently exist in the minds of the workers. It may be necessary to create a degree of worker dissatisfaction with current managerial actions.

While this quasi-political nature of unions and the need to promote in-group solidarity by common resistance against an out-group will vary with circumstance and with specific unions and managements, it must be accepted as a "given" in the union-management relationship.

### Status of the Group's Representatives

A closely related reason for some given level of conflict between the two groups involves the position of the representatives of each group. Since each side's representative faces a certain degree of pressure from those he represents, it is not in the representative's best interest to be too cooperative with the other side. Cooperation may be looked upon as the equivalent of capitulation which results in the representative losing both his status and his position with the group he represents.

The results of this in-group orientation are that completely cooperative associations are virtually impossible.

## VARIABLES INFLUENCING THE DEGREE OF UNION-MANAGEMENT CONFLICT

In addition to the basic assumptions made and the conflictual givens, there are variable factors which influence the union-management relationship.

The relationships that have existed in the past between the two organizations can strongly color the degree of cooperation and conflict that is present in an existing industrial relations situation. The often bloody and conflictual relationships of the 1930's left scars on participants from both sides which often faded only as the individuals who participated in them passed from the scene and were replaced by others who did not personally experience those conflicts.

An example of such conflict is the famous "Battle of the Overpass" in 1937 in which Walter Reuther and a group of unionists did battle with company guards at an overpass between buildings at the Ford Motor Company's River Rouge Plant. That bloody struggle, in which 16 union leaders (including 6 women) were badly beaten, eventually led to the unionization of Ford.

The significance of events such as these to present relationships can be expressed in terms of the attitudes they create in the minds of the other side and the tendency of these attitudes to remain fixed or at least change much more slowly than objective events do. One result of this tendency to relate to the past is that a management and union with a history of high conflict are more likely to remain hostile to one another even when some of the bases of this conflict no longer exist. It can also be concluded that conscious effort by either side to emphasize or de-emphasize past relationships which were conflictual can have strong effects upon the level of conflict between the groups.

### Perceived Legitimacy of Each Side for the Other

A significant factor which will contribute to the extent of intergroup hostility or cooperation that exists between management and labor is the degree to which each side views the other as "legitimate" as to its ends and means. This legitimacy involves recognition of the organization by those with whom it deals. It is based upon not only the acceptance of its point of view but of its right to a point of view, as well as its privilege of functioning and of its methods of operation.

If the company is determined to deal with the union only to the extent imposed by law and by the power of the union itself, the degree of hostility between the two groups can be predicted as great. Management may view its dealings with the union as only a temporary phenomenon and, therefore, do everything possible to destroy the union itself. It inevitably follows that the sentiments and action of either party along these lines will generate combative reactions in the other which will result in increased intergroup hostility and anxiety. Walton and McKersie state that management and labor's dislike "for each other frequently assumes irrational proportions. Because of the prospect of irrational and extreme behavior, the relationship is marked by considerable anxiety."

The relationship between the Kohler Company and the United Auto

Workers Union exemplifies this truth, for although the firm is now unionized, apparently neither considers the position of the other as "legitimate," so the relationship would be classified as conflictual.

Management is often not alone in viewing the interests of the opposing group as less than legitimate, for some union leaders are persuaded that the economic and class position of management is in conflict with the best interests of the working man.

It should be remembered that there is not a dichotomy existing in the perceived legitimacy of each side toward the other.  Acknowledgment of the other's legitimacy might best be depicted as a continuum with many possible shadings of relationships.  It is also appropriate to note that these relationships can, and probably do, change over time and can certainly move in either direction.

### Personality Factors of Key Leaders

Key leaders on both sides, including those who influence and take part in the collective bargaining process and those who administer the agreement between bargaining sessions, have an important effect upon the relationship that their groups have with one another.  The fact that personality plays a role in the determination of intergroup relationships may be demonstrated by referring to labor patterns adopted by management through the impact of a single individual.  The bargaining tactics of General Electric have been designated "Boulwarism" because of the strong influence of Lemuel R. Boulware.  From labor's side, John L. Lewis of the United Mineworkers is perhaps a good example of a strong personality's effect upon the union-management relationship.  Kuhn predicted that where there is a clash of personalities between those representing each side, "Personal relations are apt to involve bickering and repeated aspersions about motives of sincerity."

If personality factors of the leadership have a strong effect upon group conflict or cooperation, what type of personality attributes encourage trust and friendliness and what sort of personality inhibits this relationship?  Walton and McKersie concluded that a person who rates high on authoritarianism, i.e., an individual characterized by conservatism, emotional coldness, power seeking, and hostility toward out-groups, is relatively more likely to initiate a low-trust competitive pattern in labor management relations.

The amount of self-esteem of key persons in a labor-management system may influence their responses to challenges in the situation. For example, Titus and Hollander found that ego involving problems tend to produce rigidity in problem solving for those with an authoritarian personality.  Thus, an individual whose personality can be described as authoritarian is more likely to perceive the actions of representatives of the other group as threats and to view their actions as power moves.

In a further attempt to verify the hypothesis that personality factors do influence intergroup behavior, research evidence has indicated that a change of leadership in one of the two groups has often resulted in improved relationships. Thus, either side might consciously attempt to influence its relationships with the other group by placing in positions of frequent contact with the other side individuals who tend to generate cooperative *or* conflictual relationships.

### Emphasis on Conflictual or Cooperative Aspects of Problems

It was shown earlier that one cause of inevitable conflict between the two groups being discussed is each side's pursuit of opposing goals within the framework of the same organization. Thus, the relationship between the two parties tends to be a contest—in some degree—for the scarce resources of the organization.

But many issues contain at least the potential for some degree of mutual accommodation and goal achievement, and the approach of the parties to each other and to the common problems between them can determine the degree to which the issue becomes one of fixed sum relationships, or the gain of one at the expense of the other. While the question of how economic benefits will be distributed between the parties is one of inherent conflict, many questions which might be defined as power oriented problems are capable of mutually satisfying arrangements.

The approach of the parties to their common problems can, therefore, be divided into two extremes along a spectrum of approaches. The two ends of the continuum might be termed (1) a power struggle orientation and (2) a problem solving orientation. In the power struggle approach, the parties see themselves as battling for the upper hand in any dispute and any gains made by the other party as losses incurred by themselves. Those questions which involve changes in existing authority and power involve the greatest potential for cooperation or conflict. Those questions, described as "management prerogatives" and "union rights," could best be described as the degree of freedom to act independently of the other party. For the union, rights and authority involve the extent to which the union has a voice in the way management runs the business. While neither side can completely relinquish its views concerning questions of this sort, for there is often a redistribution of power from the settlement of issues in even the most accommodative relationship, the important consideration is the degree to which both sides emphasize the power portion of each issue that comes up.

The problem solving approach, while not ignoring the fact that power redistribution may occur from the decisions made by the parties, does not place primary emphasis on this aspect of the issues at hand. Under this approach the parties attempt to find solutions that will not involve loss for one side [to] the other, or at least look for solutions that will be of minimum sacrifice to the other. Whether or not mutually accommodative solutions are reached is perhaps not as important as the *desire and willingness* of both sides to reach them. In an atmosphere of mutual accommodation, the power aspects of the problem are de-emphasized. As parties move away from the power orientation end of the spectrum, they are likely to find a number of new problems which may hold mutually accommodative potential. We might assume, then, as some issues are found which move the parties away from the power orientation and increase the degree of mutual accommodation, other issues would be perceived by the parties as holding mutually satisfying potential.

## Superordinate Goals

In his studies of intergroup behavior, Sherif found the most effective measure for reducing intergroup friction was the introduction of a series of superordinate goals. These have "high appeal value for both groups, which cannot be ignored by the groups in question, but whose attainment is beyond the resources and efforts of any one group alone." Finding areas of cooperative endeavor between management and the union is thus believed to be a means of reducing hostility and frustration.

What are some of the problem areas that may contain potential for union-management cooperation? Although no listing of such areas could be either complete or applicable to all relationships, a few examples of specific cooperative endeavors would be helpful in understanding the phenomena.

Historically, the use of profit sharing as a means for stimulating employees to produce more efficiently has been opposed by unions, but in recent years union acceptance has become more prevalent. An indication of this shift is shown by the fact that "The coverage extends to over two million persons—12% of plant and 22% of office employees—in medium sized and large establishments within all metropolitan areas. . . . In terms of worker coverage, it has doubled in importance over the past decade." The success of the Kaiser Steel–United Steelworkers' sharing plan is an example of a reasonably successful plan for increasing cooperative action of both management and labor. It has resulted in such gains as cost savings, stable company-union relations, and a decrease in incentive grievances.

A second example of cooperative action is the steel industry in which a human-relations committee consisting of both labor and management members has been established. It functions during the life of the contract by studying problems of technological change, revisions or eliminations of incentive methods of pay, changes in seniority districts, and stabilization of employment which cannot readily be confronted and resolved in the normal negotiation period of sixty days.

Bakke has suggested these and other possible areas for mutual accommodation such as:

> cost and waste reduction, safety promotion, technological improvement, automation, training programs, the improvement of standards and administration of unemployment insurance, workmen's compensation, health insurance. . . .

## EXTERNAL FACTORS AFFECTING CONFLICTUAL LEVEL

The labor-management relationship cannot be considered in isolation. It is affected by the ecology in which it occurs. Although the total cultural *milieu* has an impingement upon the relative position in the power struggle of the two parties, only the most cogent ones will be discussed.

It is relevant in a study of this nature to consider the effects of government activity upon the intergroup relationship. And with a trend toward more governmental control of union-management activities, an attempt should be made to predict the future effects of this trend upon conflict and cooperation between the two parties.

What has been the effect of increasing governmental influence upon the degree of conflict and cooperation between the parties? Although both sides have bitterly contested legislation which would hamper their freedom of action, once the legislation was enacted and upheld in the courts, it removed from controversy issues which formerly resulted in possible dispute. In other words, since neither party could influence the outcome of the issue in a significant way by putting pressure on its opponent, no longer was there conflict over the issue. Conversely, the return of an issue to, or the maintenance of an issue in, the hands of the interacting parties tends to allow at least greater possibility for conflict.

While we are not necessarily advocating increased government control over industrial relations, for this is an ethical value judgment, the very fact that governmental action is somewhat effective in reducing labor-management conflict seems to be influencing public opinion in the direction of additional demands for governmental action with regard to union-management relationships. This action involves not only legislation, but also the "moral suasion" of the government.

In summing up, it might be said that (1) governmental activity in the industrial relations field tends to decrease conflict between the parties, and (2) that the success of this activity has generated increasing public pressure for more governmental action.

The likelihood that in the advent of a strike, the firm's customers will take their business to a competitor and not return when the strike is ended will have a strong impact on the extent to which management and the union can tolerate a strike.  If it is anticipated that customers not served during a strike will take their trade elsewhere permanently, the cost of strikes will be greatly enhanced and there is more pressure on the parties to maintain peace.

## CONFLICTUAL MODEL

This study has attempted to identify and isolate selected variables which influence the degree of union-management conflict.  Also, an effort has been made to develop a model which could be used to predict the extent of conflict under modifying assumptions and given factors. Figure 1 is a graphical summation of the significant forces assumed to

FIGURE 1   Conflict Model

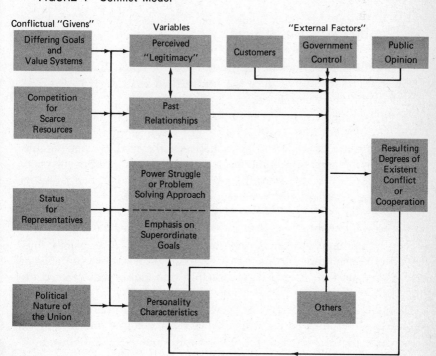

affect the level of conflict between union and management which have been discussed in this paper.

## INTERDEPENDENCE OF CONFLICTUAL VARIABLES

The union-management relationship is assumed to be a system in which each of the factors is interrelated and interacting. Thus, the inclusion of two-directional arrows between the conflictual variables is intended as a means of showing the interrelatedness of, and interaction between, each variable. For example, a change in the perceived legitimacy of one side by the other might affect the parties' approach to problem solving and their emphasis on cooperative or conflictual relationships that have existed in the past. The change might also call for placing in positions of frequent contact with the other side those individuals who tend to generate a greater or lesser amount of conflict with their opposite number. Similar interdependencies can be imagined by manipulating any one of the variables.

The model also depicts the resulting level of conflict as "feeding back" upon the conflictual variables and further influencing them toward the generation of a greater or lesser degree of conflict between the two groups in future relationships.

## IMPLICATIONS FOR THE FUTURE

What are the implications of the present state of union-management relationships today? What does the future hold with regard to the degree of conflict between them?

Before commenting on the situation today, or making an attempt to discern trends for the future, we should again emphasize our basic point that some degree of conflict between the parties is inevitable, with at least some minimum level of controversy present in every union-management relationship. Also, on the whole, the trend in labor-management relationships has moved during the last generation away from the conflictual end of the spectrum toward the more accommodative relationship.

But the union-management relationship is not, as was briefly indicated in the beginning of this article, one of enthusiastic acceptance of the other side, but instead a relationship that Bakke has termed antagonistic cooperation.

The state of the relationship between relatively mature union and management organizations seems to have stabilized into one of realistic acceptance of the other party, but certainly one of less than wholehearted cooperation.  We believe that this is perhaps the most realistic relationship for the association between most unions and managements now and in the future.  We are also aware that the manipulation of the variables which we have discussed, either consciously or unconsciously, by the parties in a specific relationship can determine the conflictual level between them.

The authors have thus attempted to develop a roadmap, broad in stroke though it may be, of the "territory" of union-management conflict: its causes and its cures.  As pragmatists we must agree that either side in the relationship may find it quite advantageous to its aims to either raise or lower the conflictual level of the relationship.  The criteria for both sides will no doubt be "what will work best" for the achievement of organization ends.

We do feel that increased awareness by both sides of what variables are involved and what a change in a variable will do to the existing relationship in terms of conflict should aid in the effectiveness of both sides in the pursuit of their particular goals.

## QUESTIONS

1. Do you agree with the authors as to the underlying reasons for union-management conflict?
2. Is union-management conflict inevitable?  What forces do you consider important in reducing conflict?
3. Describe areas in which the potential is high for union-management cooperation?
4. Do you agree with the authors that their model has predictive powers?  Explain your position.

# Consumers, Business, and Government

**17**

# Consumerism
# and marketing

# max e. brunk

Max E. Brunk, Professor of Marketing, Cornell University, rejects the idea of the helpless consumer and examines some of the nonconsumer forces behind consumerism and their implications to business in what he calls the "meddlesome Seventies."

Consumerism is a movement of activists who champion issues which appear to be beneficial to consumers. This definition is blunt and to the point. It will not make the consumerist happy for it exposes the spurious inference that there is, outside the marketplace, a bona fide movement of consumers who join in common cause on their own behalf. Nevertheless, in order to understand the growth, strength and power of consumerism one must realize that it is not a movement of consumers themselves. The term implies protection of the consumer but the flood of proposals for ways and means of protecting the consumer are not generally traceable to those seeking protection for themselves. To the contrary the specific issues of consumerism are initiated by those who, for assorted reasons, seek to protect others from harm. It is this third party involvement in a buyer-seller relationship that gives consumerism its uniqueness. The consumer activist, regardless of motive, is indeed a crusader.

Time will not permit an exploration of all the motives of the consumerist. They obviously range from selfish to unselfish, from dishonest to honest, from ignorant to the well-informed. Regardless of motive the consumer activist contends that consumers should be protected from physical and economic harm, that consumers should be informed and educated in product knowledge, that consumers should have a choice in the marketplace and finally that consumers should have proper legal redress for wrongs. These aims are similar to the four consumer rights identified by President Kennedy in his 1962 address on consumer interests . . . the right to safety, the right to be informed, the right to choose and the right to be heard. On the surface one can scarcely argue with such virtuous aims until one realizes that under consumerism they are subjected to third party interpretation and in this sense may or may not be in the consumer interest.

In a normal market relationship the buyer's right to accept or reject in the marketplace imparts a very forceful economic meaning to these

Talk Before the National Broiler Council in Atlanta, Georgia, October 7, 1970. Reprinted by permission of the author.

aims consistent with each individual's particular set of values. But competitive enterprise is rejected by the consumerist who identifies protection in terms of third party values. And because such values can always be made to appear rational they are condoned and often vigorously supported by the general public. As a result an endless myriad of laws, regulations and coercions are rapidly displacing the free decision of the individual in the marketplace and the right of the consumer to choose increasingly becomes a mockery.

Without much doubt I reveal my personal convictions on consumerism. I think most of all I resent the hypocrisy of the politics behind consumerism . . . the illusion that someone is doing something for me when in fact they are only doing something, at my expense, to serve their own selfish political interests. I hear business leaders today claiming that consumerism is anti-business. They have fallen victims to the hypocrisy of consumerism. They are mistaken. Consumerism is aimed at the consumer. Business can adjust and endure under consumerism much better than consumers. To business, consumerism merely closes the doors to certain opportunities, redirects business effort or alters the competitive advantage one business might have over another. But look what it does to the consumer who pays the cost and loses the benefits that a prohibited product or service could have provided.

I reject the contention that the consumer is ignorant, stupid or uninformed merely because her actions are not consistent with either my beliefs or the beliefs of any professional consumerist. In my opinion consumers with dollars in their pockets are not by any stretch of the imagination weak. To the contrary they are the most merciless, meanest, toughest market disciplinarians I know. I reject the thesis that there is any one universal value in marketing that can be made applicable and acceptable to all 200 million American consumers. Any businessman trying to capture the favor of the consumer knows this. They know that the value and needs of different consumers change with almost every purchasing decision. Surely we need to distinguish between the proper role of government in protecting consumers from deceptive practices and the inappropriate role of serving as intermediary between buyers and sellers in making value judgments.

In our zeal to protect the "innocent" consumer we need recognize that each protective step puts an added limit on our productive capacity as a nation. It may be argued that a wealthy nation can afford such luxury and, while this is true, we need also to take into account the price we are paying for consumerism.

Risk is inherent in every consumer purchase . . . in every consumer act. The efforts of man to eliminate risk in the marketplace contain much political appeal but are nonetheless futile because the reduction of one kind of risk must always be accompanied by a compensating increase in another kind of risk. The cost of protection is deprivation. The restricted use of D.D.T. not only keeps people from being harmed but also increases their exposure to malaria. The proper balance between these two risks is a value judgment for society to determine. We can, if we desire, achieve a high degree of auto safety by reducing speed but society rejects the sacrifice and instead with the safety belt accepts a lower safety level requiring less sacrifice. Some of the most protected members of our society are the inmates of our prisons. The distinguishing characteristic of these unfortunates is that they know the personal cost of their protection by having an acute awareness of their deprivations. But the cost of consumer protection is not so apparent. We have no way of putting a value on the sacrifice in foregone products and services that a free market could provide. We would not have the violence on our campuses or streets today if the disruptors bore greater risks of being penalized. The increased violence we tolerate is the price we pay for reducing the risk of penalizing the innocent. The jurist who said that it is better to let a hundred guilty persons go free than convict an innocent man either did not understand the nature of risk or had little respect for social order. In 1747 Voltaire wrote "It is better to risk saving a guilty person than to condemn an innocent one." Later Blackstone wrote "It is better that ten guilty persons escape than one innocent suffer." Now, once again, our odds are up and I'm beginning to wonder what par really is for the innocent man.

So far I have identified the consumerist only as a kind of self-appointed, omnipotent guardian of the consumer. Who is the consumerist? Where do his ideas come from? What gives him motive? To some degree I think we are all consumerists at some time or another. We all have ideas about how other people should behave or be made to behave. When we get worked up about some issue we may even become activists and try to force our opinions on others. However, the most potent and dangerous consumerists are found in the ranks of elected public officials, career public workers, authors and writers, college professors, school teachers and preachers . . . people who have time on their hands to worry about others . . . people whose status depends on publicity and popularity. It is interesting to observe that the consumerist sometimes has as much difficulty convincing the consumer of her need for protection as in convincing a regulatory body to do something about it. But in final analysis the consumerist with the real punch is the elected official who champions laws, the appointed official who establishes regulations, or the self-appointed crusader who needs only to release a report or make a speech to hit the headlines. I doubt that my Congressman is responsible for the eight sets of seat belts that came in my last car but I got them and I paid for them. While some Congressmen deem it expedient to play on the political opportunities of consumerism we can be thankful that most of our public representatives, perhaps much better than the general public, understand the shams of consumerism. In a very real sense these responsible representatives often protect the consumer from the consumerist.

So far I have talked in broad generalities. Perhaps a specific illustration can do more to expose consumerism in its true light. This is dangerous because there are supporters to be found behind almost any consumer issue. I know I could get some support for banning alcoholic drinks from the market and if I tried hard enough I might even find some support for banning milk. I have heard it said that if strawberries were a manufactured product they would be restricted from the market today because so many people are allergic to them!

Anyway my little story has to do with unit pricing. Some consumerist got the bright idea a few years ago that if all products in the retail store were marked as to price in equivalent units of pounds, quarts, square feet and the like then the consumer could better identify the best buy. There was an implied assumption that the variety of package sizes on the market were a calculated attempt to deceive the consumer.

Gradually the idea began to catch on and more and more people began to accept and champion it. I know of no strong bona fide consumer support for the idea but I do know of a lot of passionate pleas by consumerists who thought the idea had merit especially for people on a tight budget. Finally the proposal gathered enough steam to be ordered in effect by the Department of Consumer Affairs in New York City. But before it could be invoked the courts ruled that the Department had no authority to require conformance. The matter currently rests there while steps are being taken to establish the needed authority. [Ed.: New York City now has unit pricing in the stores.]

But as in any fight charges and countercharges flew around rather wildly. The merchants claimed that the costs of so marking products would be prohibitively expensive . . . that the net increase in cost would have to be borne by the consumer. The consumerists claimed that such marking would enable some consumers, and particularly those who needed it most, to save up to 10 percent on their grocery bill. But no one really had any facts though the idea sounded plausible and workable. This is the typical way consumerist issues arise and generate support, not among consumers, but rather among those who would like to do something for the consumer. It also reveals the typical negative reaction of the business community which serves only to add the fire of certainty to the consumerist's eyes.

Fortunately this is one idea that could be tested with a reasonable degree of preciseness and one of my colleagues at Cornell, Professor

Daniel Padberg, undertook to do just that with a midwestern chain. The most interesting of his conclusions is that both the costs and benefits were grossly overstated. The costs in the smallest stores ran to over 4 percent of the sales value but in large supermarkets they amounted to less than a tenth of one percent of sales. But a check of product movement indicated no significant shift in purchases by the consumer. In two broad food categories the consumer actually traded up to the higher cost per unit item, in the cereal category she traded down and there was no change in the others. Surveys of consumers shopping these particular stores revealed that awareness of the availability of the information was greatest among the high income, well-educated consumers. Despite these findings, the only real facts on the issue available, it is my prediction that the consumerist will continue to champion unit pricing, will continue to talk about how it will benefit the poor and eventually succeed in getting widespread regulations making unit pricing mandatory.

The issue of unit pricing did not originate from any factual base and accordingly facts are not likely to alter the decisions of those who champion its cause. It makes no difference that the theory of unit pricing is based on a false and strictly materialistic premise. It makes no difference that it gives the large merchant a competitive advantage over the small. It makes no difference that the wealthy take greater advantage of the information than the poor. Even if the benefits are not very great it may be argued that the costs are insignificant. At least the consumer doesn't need a computer when she shops and she gained a notch in her right to be informed. But is the cost really insignificant if we add this to the hundreds of other laws and regulations that have been so forced on the consumer within the last several years? I believe this case illustrates practically all the generalities I described in the first part of my talk. Now it is time to turn to the subject of how the business community—how the marketer—can live in the era of consumerism . . . the era of the meddlesome Seventies.

It is clear that the marketer now needs to keep an eye on both the consumer and the consumerist. The activities of the consumerist [are] causing the consumer to increasingly rationalize her actions in the marketplace and this verbal justification is in turn affecting her behavior. Shrewd marketers in the past have always responded more to the actions of the consumer than to her talk. The literature of market research is full of examples in which the consumer said one thing but did another. This is nothing more than the inability of one to always sound rational in explaining actions. In fact none of us like the thought of being unable to explain our actions in some logical way to a second party. All I am saying is that consumerism is stirring up a self-consciousness in consumers and that marketers in the future will need to give greater heed to materialistic values that can be easily rationalized by the consumer.

On the other side of this coin is the risk that marketers will overreact to what they hear from consumerists. To some degree I think we are going through this stage today. I know of at least one major chain which attempts to appeal to the consumer by quickly adopting almost every consumerist idea that comes along. Sometimes it pays. Sometimes it doesn't. The point to keep in mind in trying to separate the good from the bad is that most of the talk comes from consumerists while the real action comes from consumers.

In considering the impact of consumerism on marketing, any industry should recognize that consumerism breeds on suspicion of the motives of business. Something has to be wrong, someone has to be unhappy for consumerism to exist. The consumerist sees different sized packages on the market not as an attempt to meet the differing requirements of people but rather as a deliberate effort to confuse the consumer. In the consumerist's mind fractional ounce contents have nothing to do with efficiency or cost savings but [are] used to make comparative pricing difficult. Codes are put on packages to hide vital information from the consumer. Colors and printing are used to deceive. Packaging is used to cover faulty merchandise and advertising is designed to make people act impulsively against their better judgment. The list is endless, and it always will be, for this is the nature of consumerism. However, I believe this observation tells us that the more business conducts its affairs in the open—lives in a goldfish bowl so to speak—the less it will be subject to the whims of the consumerist.

Permit me to give a simple example. As you know the red meat industry code dates many of its prepared meats with a four digit number. The first and last digit added are the month, the two center digits the day of the month. The packer uses this information for the identification of a given lot if for some unforeseen reason he must make a withdrawal from the market. But that is not the point. The cryptic code causes the consumerist to think that something is being hidden from them. Writers take delight in letting people in on how to read the "secret" code. Once the code is translated the fact that it has little meaning to the consumer is inconsequential. Why does the business community bait the consumerist like this? Wouldn't it be much better to use a simple lot number or perhaps even better to print an open date on the package? There has been so much publicity on this in recent months that the consumer is beginning to wonder about all those funny numbers stamped on all canned goods. After all the consumer is buying and eating the stuff. Isn't she entitled to know?

This little example may sound trivial to you but I assure you it is not so considered by the industries involved. It's not at all unlike the truth-in-lending law. How many consumers do you think wanted this law for their own protection? How many thought it might be a good idea for someone else? How much more do you now know about interest rates and carrying charges than before the law was passed? How many dollars has it saved the consumer? Regardless of how you choose to answer, the truth-in-lending law is now safely tucked away on the books where it can be forgotten. The few mills of marketing margin that it will permanently cost may even be worth the silencing of the consumerist on this issue. I only regret that it has freed the consumerist to dream up some other issue that might hurt me more.

Consumerism is made up of little issues each affecting . . . relatively few consumers or businesses. It thrives on the importance of being unimportant. It enlists the passive support of the majority against the vigorous opposition of the few and in this way it grows on our economy like a cancer. You people in the broiler industry are not particularly concerned about truth-in-lending, code dating, auto or mine safety. In fact not being involved they may sound like pretty good ideas to you. But I rather expect you may see some problems and exorbitant costs in such things as Federal inspection that are not apparent to the auto dealer down the street.

On the surface one might expect the specific issues of consumerism to serve as a congealing force uniting an industry in defense behind a common cause. But we forget that industries such as yours are made up of competitors and that most consumer issues do something to alter competitive advantage. Any new law or regulation that costs your competitors more than it costs you or that weakens your competitors product franchise more than yours might not on the surface look so bad to you. Recognizing the way the market works you know that it is not so much your absolute costs as your relative costs that determine your profit position and being in relatively favorable position you may even feel tempted to oppose the majority point of view of your fellow industry members. Of course the fallacy of this thinking which tends to destroy the cohesiveness of an industry is that competitive advantage created from such issues are very short lived. If your competitive advantage lies in some distribution network, package design, freezing process or the like you only succeed in forcing your competition into following your pattern of doing business. And you are right back where you started unless in the meantime your competitors have found a better way of doing it.

Viable members of any trade organization never lose sight of the fact that competitive position within an industry must always be subservient to the competitive position among different industries. In fact the strength of any trade organization largely depends on its members' willingness to compromise on issues affecting the industry. No good member of a trade association always gets his way. I have digressed into this little sermon because consumerism can and often does threaten the cohesiveness of an industry.

There is one other timely concern of the marketer and that has to do with current efforts to center the issues of consumerism in one governmental agency, office, bureau or department. Provision for such an office came out of Senate Committee hearings this past week and the House has already acted on a somewhat different version of the same measure. Mr. Nader in particular has been outspoken for the creation of a Department of Consumer Affairs calling this the most important consumer legislation ever.

At the present time the organization of government permits consumer interests to be served in a wide variety of ways. One study several years ago revealed that no less than 33 Federal departments are engaged in various phases of consumer protection. These agencies were involved in 118 different consumer protective activities requiring the services of 65,000 full-time employees. In addition there were 178 other programs indirectly related to the consumer interest. And this is but a small part of the activity that goes on in Washington and at the state and local level where we also have extensive policing of a wide variety of marketing processes from weights and measures to sanitation and trade practices. This all adds up to a highly protected consuming public and it raises a number of questions. Would the consumer interest better be served by concentrating these activities in a singular agency? Can such an agency serve as an effective spokesman for the consumer in the promulgation of new laws and regulations? What interest groups would be most influential with such an agency? To what degree should such an agency act as intermediary between buyers and sellers?

In the past government has established consumer protection laws and regulations in response to needs as they arise. The administration of these activities has been delegated to agencies and departments accustomed to working with the special businesses involved, be it agriculture, finance, commerce, drugs, labor, housing or what not. The proposal for a central consumer agency shifts the audience center from supplier to buyer and by this process cuts across our total economy. Because almost every issue of consumer protection is related to the operational idiosyncracies of the supplier involved, such an agency would encounter both conflict and duplication of effort with every other department of government. It may be that this is typical of government but I don't think it is good government.

How effective a spokesman for the consumer such an agency might be is demonstrated by the past activities of the President's Special Assistant for Consumer Affairs. During its eight-year gestation period much effort has been made to gain consumer, business, and labor support for the program. Many talks have been given, press conferences held, and consumer meetings scheduled. Although the office of Special Assistant has carried White House identity and has been served by three different, highly respected and competent ladies, the general public has never really taken the office very seriously. It should be apparent to the most ardent supporter of the program that bona fide consumer interest has failed to develop.

Apparently the consumer already knows that any remedial action he deems necessary is most directly accomplished as a result of his actions in the marketplace. He also knows that the marketplace respects his actions either when he is in the minority or with the majority. He does not expect to impose his consumption values on his neighbor anymore than he expects his neighbor's values to be imposed on him.

Regardless of any new agency that might be created to represent the consumer and regardless of the growth of consumerism, the only true reading of the consumer is to be obtained by observing her actions in the marketplace. There can be no true spokesman for the consumer other than the actions of the consumer herself. Try as she might she will rationalize her actions but she cannot explain them in full. That is why she cannot tell you what new or modified goods and services would better serve her needs. In marketing research I have spent the better part of my life ringing consumer doorbells in a futile effort to get them to tell me how some product or market service can be improved or what new products or services they want, only to find that in response they failed either to visualize their alternatives or identify the true values to which they in final analysis respond. The consumer, in her mute but effective way, can only bring all her value considerations to bear in response to what is offered her. She has her own built-in protective device. If you displease her . . . if you do not offer her the best alternative . . . if indeed you deceive her in terms of her own values, she simply and quickly votes "no" in the marketplace. That is the miracle of the free market . . . the miracle the consumerist refuses to recognize.

## QUESTIONS

1. Who and what is behind "consumerism"?
2. Do you accept Brunk's assertion that consumerism is more likely to affect the consumer adversely than the marketer? Why does he say this?
3. Brunk rejects the idea of one federal agency to handle consumer affairs. Are his reasons acceptable to you?
4. What are your feelings about the general tenor of this article?

# The corporate deaf ear     e. b. weiss

**E. B. Weiss is Vice-President and Director of Special Merchandising Service at Doyle Dane Bernbach Inc.** In the following article he is highly critical of business for not paying more attention to consumer complaints, and he forecasts that if business does not pay more heed, a number of actions will be taken by government to protect consumers.

Communication channels between large corporations producing consumer lines, as well as large retailers, and the individual consumer (where, in fact, channels exist at all) tend to be one-way input systems —woefully clogged.  Moreover, this one-way communication system between the individual member of society and the corporative society (to call it a "system" is abominable semantics!) is a half-way communication channel within the corporation itself; it reaches only halfway up the various executive levels.  Now computer technology threatens to complete the isolation of corporations from the individual consumer, especially at middle executive levels.  The first signs are clearly evident in giant retail corporations, despite the fact that the retailer is closest to the consumer.  The continued stultification of the public relations function (the usual end of the tenuous communication link between corporation and consumer) adds the final destructive touch to the already marginal corporative hearing capabilities.

It is ironic that, in this age of amazing technological communication innovation, corporate deafness with respect to the individual customer is in the process of becoming total.  (Have you ever tried to complain about a "lemon" to one of Detroit's Big Three, or sweated through an adjustment with a major department store?)  It is equally ironic that, in this age of awakened corporate social responsibility, our corporations tend to listen less to individual society members than ever before; yet listening to the individual in our society and reacting promptly, intelligently, and even sympathetically constitute a major corporate social responsibility, particularly in a sophisticated society.

Surely it is as obvious as it is inevitable that individuals, when frustrated, will in due time form into groups (as labor did decades ago) and even stage demonstrations (as the food industry discovered two years ago).  And surely it is equally obvious that the frustrated individual will turn to government, where hearing capabilities are ex-

---

E. B. Weiss, "The Corporate Deaf Ear," *Business Horizons*, XI (December 1968), 5–15. Copyright, 1968 by the Foundation for the School of Business, at Indiana University.  Reprinted by permission.

traordinarily acute. I do not refer to communications from the public involving fraud; our large corporations have pretty well stamped out the fraudulent. I refer to those communications from the public representing the "gray area"—situations embracing product, service, and so on that do not violate the law, but which properly raise the hackles of more knowledgeable consumers (whose numbers are clearly multiplying). Consumer legislation does not concern itself with fraud; its objective is to whiten these gray areas of business practice, which an enlightened public finds increasingly irritating.

Top corporate management is now deeply concerned about the corporation as a citizen. Yet my careful reading of thirty-one recent speeches by top management executives on various aspects of the new dimensions of corporate social responsibility fails to unearth a single word on the imperative corporate responsibility for improving communication with the individual consumer. I am not concerned at the moment with corporate *mass* communication with the public on matters of social significance, although both advertising and public relations tend to be painfully amateurish in this area. (Most "image" campaigns are merely self-righteous egotistical exhibitions.) My concern is with the individual who, for any of a variety of reasons (civic, social, critical, or suggestive), decides to communicate with a large corporation by letter, phone, or personal visit. Here, I maintain, corporate management has laid up a solid wall of indifference and even calculated obstruction. All this in an age in which our society is just beginning to reemphasize the supreme importance of the individual.

This was bad enough when the retailer listened willingly to the shopper, but now our giant retailers turn an equally deaf ear to the customer as our giant manufacturers do. Business does listen to the lunatic fringe of our society; a few crank letters, for example, have led to the cancellation of more than one television sponsorship. But business does not listen to the intelligent individual members of our society!

The business community now accepts, with some resignation and less cooperation, the inevitability of consumer legislation, as well as the probability that more is on the way for years to come. But it seems not even dimly aware of the relationship between consumer legislation and corporate deafness where the individual is concerned. As a result, government is clearly in the process of becoming the confidant of the shopping public, which is unquestionably developing the habit of addressing its individual complaints and inquiries concerning products and services to Washington (as well as to state offices and even to local administrators). Politicians are offering individuals what amounts to a wailing wall. Politicians monitor individual grievances, and then act —with consumer legislation, additional regulation, and so on. This does not bode well for the future of the free enterprise system even in its present form (which may or may not be a calamity depending on one's viewpoint).

It is shocking to realize that not one piece of consumer legislation has been initiated by business management. On the contrary, every one of the recently-passed consumer laws was fought—usually bitterly —by business (truth-in-packaging was fought for five years, truth-in-lending for six). Yet, if top corporate management had not been so thoroughly shielded from those individual consumers who tried futilely to communicate, consumer cooperation rather than confrontation would have been the rule rather than the extremely rare exception.

Early this year, W. E. Sturges, vice-president, S. S. Kresge Co., said: "I predict enormous success for those manufacturers and retailers who find new ways to give the American woman the security in her purchases that she must and will have. The American consumer will become more demanding and more impatient with those manufacturers and merchants who leave her with problems after she gets the merchandise home." Yet there may not be a half-dozen corporations that have laid down a truly modern socially responsible policy of open-channel communication with individual members of our society. Kresge is *not* among the half-dozen!

William M. Batten, chairman of the board, J. C. Penney Co., Inc., addressing himself to this point before the National Retail Merchants Association's annual convention about a year ago, pointedly remarked:

> Meeting competition has long been the primary yardstick which we have used for measuring our performance. But today, *how* we meet competition is under the careful scrutiny of many people in positions of power and of opinion-molding influence. And the results of their scrutiny have broad implications for our operations. . . .
>
> In those cases where changes are simply not possible—because of expense, the nature of the product, or the limitations of current technology—can we say that we have no obligation? Don't we then have a duty to inform the consumer as to *why* things are as they are *instead of simply shrugging off her complaints?*

## THE SOPHISTICATED CONSUMER

The attitudes of consumers toward business as a social institution become less favorable as public income and education levels rise. Thus the issue is crystal clear: an affluent society of sophisticated consumers—this is the fundamental characteristic of tomorrow's markets —is just beginning to demand new standards from business. Those standards will include respect for the individual consumer. Today's affluent sophisticates control the major share of the nation's disposable dollar; they are marketing's choicest customers. Ultimately, they will represent the major share of the population in numbers; higher education for everyone and social progress make this a certainty. They are exceedingly articulate; they are our political influentials. When government listens to them, it listens at the highest levels, including the Presidency. When corporations listen, even to the typical minimum degree, the listening usually is done by the public relations department. But, as I will analyze in greater detail, public relations does not represent the public, is not responsive to the public, tends to be unaware of or even antagonistic toward the great new social trends, and treats the individual consumer with more cynicism and cold-bloodedness than was ever true of the banker in the days when bankers personified these characteristics.

As a consequence of the growth in affluence and sophistication, we are witnessing the first stages of a revolt of rising expectancy (a phrase that Churchill would have doted on). Customers today expect products to perform satisfactorily, to provide dependable functional performance, and to be safe. This threshold of acceptable performance is steadily advancing. It is precisely this widening revolt of rising expectancy, this steadily rising threshold of acceptable performance, that is the key to the seller's new legal as well as moral liabilities (increasingly, it will be the seller who must beware). The individual consumer will expect—and demand—to be heard by our large corporations and will insist that this is a corporate moral, ethical, and social responsibility.

President George Koch of Grocery Manufacturers of America (which fought truth-in-packaging for five years) acknowledged recently that: "The rise in consumer activities is the end result of a changing, modern era in which the product manufacturer, distributor—and even the retailer—have become *remote to the consumer.*

"She can't take her complaint to her friend at the corner store because he's no longer there. *We must assume more responsibility for communicating with consumers in order to keep ourselves informed of their needs. . . ."*

But, to date, the food industry's dialogs with the public have been puny gestures, and the individual is no better heard in the food industry today despite these noble sentiments. The industry has not yet put its *ear* where its mouth is! The strong response to the messages in the "You have a friend at Chase-Manhattan" campaign and in the early days to A&P's "We care" theme was the tip-off. Here was ample evidence that the public wanted someone who cared in its business contacts. Yet I doubt that the individual depositor finds any more friends at Chase-Manhattan than at any other major bank. I am positive that, in the individual stores of A&P, it was the rare employee who cared.  And I doubt that depositors will get a warm reception if they accept Irving Trust's invitation to "Call us Irving."

But, whether or not my cynicism is justified (I insist that corporation image campaigns based on largely fanciful images carry the seeds of their own futility), the point is that creative advertising men recognized the public's vast desire for friendliness, for caring, for first-name contacts in its relationshp with business.  Unfortunately, business management lags far behind the professional image creators in actually bringing the image into real life.

I have stated that this breakdown in individual communication between corporations and the public has been accelerated by the computer.  This is almost frightening because the sophisticated uses of the computer in functions that relate to the public are still in the adolescent stage.  Quite recently, Gulf Oil admitted its "cold-hearted" computers "couldn't care less" about dissatisfied customers.  In a mailer, Gulf tells credit card users that, henceforth, customers' complaints will be answered by "a real, live person who wants you to be satisfied; letters are to be addressed to Jim Insell, 'our listening specialist.'"  I rather doubt that Jim Insell will ever duplicate the early performance of General Mills' Betty Crocker.  My observations of these programs, presumably planned to reopen a corporate listening post with consumers as individuals, are that: they are merely public relations gestures; they are underbudgeted and understaffed; they become thoroughly automated; and the communications with the public are largely form communications.

The consumer seldom has reason to conclude that anything has really been accomplished; how could this be otherwise when management is not even dimly aware of what transpires in this department and when the department's directives are extremely limited in scope and make no provision for elasticity of policy and practice?

It seems to me inevitable that this yawning chasm between corporation and individual consumer will lead to these portentous developments:

> New legislation will give government the authority to arrive at legally enforceable decisions regarding individual consumer inquiries and complaints, thus completing the isolation of our corporations from the individual public.
> This legislation will provide for a new type of federal and, possibly, state court, a court that will pass judgment on consumer complaints covering a product's performance and service (as differentiated from fraud).
> Additional legislation will provide for still stricter standards covering product performance, safety, defects, and so on.
> New legislation will give additional powers to the Federal Trade Commission as well as to the Department of Commerce—powers

to act as the consumer's "friend in court" in the gray areas of marketing to which I refer.

The consumer will ultimately be represented by a Cabinet officer, and Betty Furness' department will eventually become huge.

Legal liability of the seller (especially the manufacturer) will be broadened, a trend already evident in recent court decisions.

These developments are not merely probable; each and every one is inevitable. This conclusion seems inescapable when one bears in mind the business community's miserable record of constructive self-regulation in the public interest. I take the position that the total area of free enterprise has been narrowed down more by business' abuse of free enterprise than by government initiative. Business has abdicated to the politician industry's privilege, as well as responsibility, to establish and maintain open and responsive communication channels with the individual consumer. That abdication began before computer technology had begun to leave its mark on our society, even before corporate giantism began to dwarf the individual consumer. Politicians astutely measured the scope of the privilege and happily accepted the responsibility.

## A PROGRAM FOR BUSINESS

If business hopes to launch a program that could dampen the political drive for the preceding six developments, it must start with a clear understanding of the pressures within our society that make these sociopolitical and socioeconomic concepts probabilities. First and foremost, business must revise its traditional concepts of free enterprise, of its relations with and obligations to society. If businessmen insist that free enterprise permits them to be indifferent to those qualities on which people put high value, then the public will quite naturally conclude that free enterprise has too much freedom. Accepting, and acting out new dimensions of social responsibility is the essence of the new order of our business society. Business must now become *socially* oriented as well as *profit* oriented (the two concepts, it is now being understood, are not necessarily antithetical). And since it is human to want contact with humans—in a humane way— an increasingly sophisticated society will demand a more personal relationship between seller and buyer, even in a computerized age. This does not imply a return to the days of the country general store, but there is no reason to assume that the public will continue to tolerate a corporate environment in which the individual is treated as an unwelcome intruder.

It is a sad commentary on the widening gap between buyer and seller that Ralph Nader is considering opening a law firm that would represent the public interest in Washington with legal services fully equal to those that business interests are already receiving from leading law firms. Would such a law service be required if the public did not feel totally frustrated in its attempts to communicate with our leading corporations?

Politicians cling to the conviction that it is essential, when campaigning, to "press skin." How many management executives (including even top executives in retailing) ever press skin with shoppers? Is it not a fact that top management's knowledge of the shopper comes from neatly tabulated research reports—research reports that dissect the shopper in the mass rather than individually (and which have been known to be as neatly censored by lower-rank executives as they are neatly tabulated)?

The old-time merchants spent their time on the store floor meeting shoppers. To present-day management executives, the shopper is a numeral on a chart; few manufacturing executives at the management level spend even one day a year in retail stores talking to shoppers; the same goes for retail executives. How many management executives have *ever* had placed on their desks, for just one week, *all* the mail from the public—unedited, and uncensored? Congressmen examine their mail from their constituents carefully, but the management executive who sees even a single uncensored letter from the public is a rarity.

This state of affairs is made still worse by the computer, which "embezzles" the little that remains of the civilized structure of business. This is especially true of mass retailing, where the abuse of the computer is leading many large retailers into precisely the frosty, dehumanized stance that typified banks and bankers years ago. (It is an ironic fact that the computer is pressuring banks toward a somewhat *more intimate* customer relationship, while being permitted to pressure retailing into a remote, detached, uninterested relationship toward its customers.) Actually, this began years ago, long before mass retailers had begun computer installations. It began on the retail floor with salespeople. Then it moved one or two rungs up the retail executive ladder. It became more difficult for a customer to talk to a buyer, or even to an assistant buyer. Today, if a customer does manage to wangle an interview with a buyer, the buyer is inclined to prove to the customer that the salesperson takes second place in the art of frustrating, aggravating, and even insulting the customer.

Now the same attitudes have moved up into still higher retail executive echelons. Indeed, at these executive levels the individual shopper encounters—believe it or not—a total nonresponse. A few months ago, *The New York Times* carried a report on this subject which included the following:

Department stores, one of the principal offenders in nonresponse, put the blame on computers.  Undoubtedly, the complexities of automation have caused problems for many businesses, including many that never should have indulged in the luxury of depersonalizing their establishments.  But the letters of complaint are not addressed to computers; *perhaps, if they were, they would be answered!*  The letters are addressed to persons who are paid to do certain tasks, one of which involves the long lost art of soothing dissatisfied customers.  But they do not answer these letters, and their secretaries only answer their phones.

The salesclerks' situation will continue to deteriorate; the labor market leaves little hope.  More retail executives, at more levels, will become more intolerant of any "interruptions" by customers; unsophisticated computer usage makes this inevitable.  But I am positive that even new generations, who have been brought up in an era in which the shopper is always wrong, will not indefinitely accept this state of affairs with docility.  The younger generations in particular will rebel; they are not so easily pushed around.  As a consequence, mass retailing will find itself increasingly regulated in the public interest.  It will be richly deserved!

In the United States in 1960 there were less than 41 million high school graduates, and less than 8 million college graduates.  In 1985, each of these impressive figures will have more than doubled—90 million high school and 20 million college graduates.  I doubt they will buy goods for long if they are offered,in a condescending fashion.  I am sure they will not accept ideas or relationships presented in a context of the lowest common denominator.  And I am equally positive they will turn to government if industry persists in turning off its hearing aid when they try to communicate as individuals.  Management had better beware of our "demonstration-oriented" society; the public has become knowledgeable in planning and executing political and social demonstrations.  It has the know-how to mount, almost overnight, a vigorous confrontation with industry.  We may not have a renewal of the food demonstrations, but we are almost sure to have a succession of demonstrations, in one form or another, if the public concludes that business has no genuine interest in listening.

Recently, the Washington bureau of *Advertising Age* reported: "We have already pointed out editorially how the food industry bungled truth in packaging.  There was diligent reform by many individual companies, *but no concerted industry effort to create machinery to deal with customer complaints.*"  That is still true of practically all industry.  Over the past five years, product lines in most food categories have broadened at an extraordinary rate, which has posed a shopping problem.  Some consumers no doubt complained to the major food processors, but did their complaints ever reach top management—unedited?  One study disclosed that a typical food supermarket offered fourteen different packages of white rice; not one was in a 1-pound package.  The same was true of the six packages of salt, which ran a confusing range from 4/10 oz. to 5 pounds.  Imitation maple syrup (seven choices) was available in miscellaneous ounces, pints and ounces, and pounds and ounces.  Toilet tissue was packed in rolls of 650, 800, and 1,000 sheets, some single-ply, some double-ply.  Of the ten cans of tuna, none was 1 pound or even ½ pound.  Now the food industry, prodded by the government and using government machinery, is moving to lessen this shopping confusion.  But this action followed truth-in-packaging; if industry had listened earlier, it would have escaped governmental hands.

## WHAT ABOUT PUBLIC RELATIONS?

No industry has ever undertaken a public relations program until it lost a measure of its freedom.  Then it expects the identical policies that led to the public confrontation to become accepted by the public through the magic of public relations!  Management must outgrow the belief that a socially acceptable public image can be created by public relations.  That may have been feasible occasionally when the public was naive; it will rarely be possible as the public becomes more sophisticated.

I referred earlier to the destructive role that public relations plays in this situation.  It is my deep conviction that the public relations fraternity has lost contact with the public.  And the combination of top management divorced from the public and of public relations misguided is at the root of the current difficulty.

Gibson McCabe, president of *Newsweek,* talking on this point before a meeting of the Detroit chapter of the Public Relations Society of America, said:

I think that business leaders—along with scholars, politicians, and educators—are more and more coming to see the need for the private sector of our economy to move more actively toward getting at the roots of social discontent.  And, as they do so, they should rightly be able to look to their public counselors for help in establishing goals and putting sound programs into action.

But, except in isolated instances, it seems to me that *this is precisely where public relations is at its weakest*—or, at least, has made its poorest showing to date.

In preparation for my meeting with you today, I made an informal survey of *Newsweek's* top 30 editors.  Probably best expressing the general tone of our editors' comments was this statement from a man who has had occasion to deal more regularly with PR people than some of the others: "Most PR men are okay and helpful on routine matters," he said, "but very few come through in the clinch, when it really counts. Whenever a company is involved in a tense situation, we find the PR man to be of little help, and often more of a hindrance. In short, when the heat's on, don't depend on PR."

All of which brings me to a critical point I want to make—solemnly, emphatically, and, I hope, persuasively: the public relations practitioner today has got to get himself actively and creatively involved in a world of social change. And if the reactions of our editors are an accurate barometer, *it would seem that few of you, to date, are doing so*. It is one thing to be able to report third-quarter financial results, but *quite another to inspire change on a social front*.

How can the public relations industry possibly place management in the mainstream of our new society when public relations itself is still unaware of the existence of a new social order? If public relations strategic planning had anticipated the new mores of our society and had insisted that its strategic concepts be made into company policy and practice, surely truth-in-packaging, truth-in-credit, auto tire standards, safety standards for autos, the drug industry's problems, and, in fact, the entire protect-the-consumer movement would not be staring industry in the face today. Too often, public relations counsel has actually tended to isolate our corporations from the vast changes in our society and from people. Yet, as I mentioned earlier, it is in the public relations department that individual communications from the public tend to wind up.

The public relations programs of our major corporations tend to be:

Inward-looking rather than outward-looking—the factory image rather than the consumer image

Rather naive and therefore outdated regarding basic assumptions concerning our modern, sophisticated society, and inclined to be unaware of, or unwilling to accept society's mounting demands for broader socially-oriented programs by business

Reflective of the attitudes of the old guard of business—the U.S. Chamber of Commerce and the National Association of Manufacturers—rather than reflections of the new attitudes of our public

Still premised on the outworn assumption that a few thousand influentials mold the thinking of our people (actually, we have millions of influentials today, and the total continues to grow)

Lacking in original strategy, failing to guide clients toward creative interpretation and implementation of required new functions.

I have already made clear my conclusion that consumer legislation is directly traceable to the deaf ear industry turns to the individual consumer. With respect to consumerism, I hold these to be incontrovertible truths: consumerism represents *a long-term and powerful* trend, and consumerism will cover most phases of the total marketing function and even now is changing the more modern manifestations of caveat emptor into legislatively compulsory caveat vendor.

Yet, how many top management executives in the major and traffic appliance industry, the entertainment products industry, are really adequately informed about the rising public clamor concerning servicing? Surely it can only be lack of knowledge at the top level that can account for the permissive drift into inevitable truth-in-servicing consumer legislation. (Pressures are mounting even at state and city levels for bills licensing servicemen.)

Last year, the state of New York asked CBS to conduct a survey of the television repair industry. In twenty homes, the third video IF amplifier tube was made inoperative by opening the filament—equivalent to any of the other tubes burning out. Of the twenty servicemen called to repair the sets, seventeen were reported to be dishonest. Including a charge for service and labor, the fee should not have exceeded $8.93. Three servicemen said the tuner needed repair, and the fees ranged from $31.45 to $37.20. One other said the automatic gain control needed service and charged $34.23. In five cases, tubes were needlessly repaired, and the fees ran anywhere from $11.71 to $20.10. The cheating on the service repairs ranged from $4.00 to $30.00, assuming $8.00 as the correct charge.

*U.S. News & World Report* carried a round-up article on this subject that started this way:

> An affluent America, to the dismay of many citizens, is finding it difficult to keep repaired the gadgets, equipment and conveniences that are supposed to make living simpler in this country today. . . .
>
> Families everywhere complain that it takes days—even weeks— to get a serviceman to come to their homes; that the work is often sloppy; that the growing practice of charging a minimum fee for a service call is making simple jobs too costly.
>
> Actual examples, reported by staff members of *U.S. News & World Report* from across the country, reveal *a rising tide of anger and frustration.*
>
> How many management executives are really aware of this rising tide of frustration and anger?

Senate Commerce Committee Chairman Warren Magnuson is cosponsor of three pertinent bills on which his committee will hold public hearings: guarantee disclosure and product servicing act to require pinpoint disclosure of the extent of a warranty and its conditions (this bill also would create an advisory council on guarantees, warranties, and servicing to study and report to Congress on the situation); a new-car vehicle guarantee act; and household appliance guarantee act. Both the car and appliances guarantee bills would authorize the Secre-

tary of Commerce, after consultation with the Federal Trade Commission, to set standards for warranties, create an arbitration procedure for settling complaints, allow the Secretary to set standards regulating the manufacturer-dealer relationship in warranties, make clear
that ultimate responsibility under a warranty agreement rested with
the manufacturer, and assure that dealers are compensated adequately
for warranty work.

The proposed advisory council would study and investigate adequacy
of performance under guarantees, and the methods of resolving disputes on adequacy of such performance and the extent of difficulty in
securing competent servicing of mechanical and electrical products
under warranties and guarantees as well as under customary service
agreements. It would also study difficulties encountered in obtaining
relief for inadequate performance under guarantees and customary
service agreements.

Relate the preceding legislative program to the six predictions listed
on pp. 474–475, and form your own conclusions regarding the validity of
those forecasts. It is hardly necessary to draw a final conclusion; the
conclusion draws itself. A more knowledgeable, as well as a more
affluent, consumer clearly wants someone with whom to communicate
concerning purchases. Those communications may include compli-
ments as well as complaints, constructive suggestions as well as adjustments. If business continues to narrow down the already narrow
communications channels available for this purpose—and if those communication channels terminate in public relations—then the consumer
will turn in still larger numbers to government where communication
channels are multiplying and where even top-ranking officials lend an
attentive and sympathetic ear.

That can only mean still less freedom for free enterprise. If this is
the cause, the end result will be richly deserved. It is the height of
irony that at the moment corporations are beginning to act out their
new responsibilities as involved members of our society, they are
simultaneously turning a deaf ear to the individual members of society.
How is it possible to be socially conscious while ignoring the individual?

## QUESTIONS

1. Contrast the emphasis of Brunk and Weiss on (a) the causes of
   consumerism, (b) the impact of consumerism on business, and
   (c) the reaction of business to consumerism.
2. Is Weiss too harsh on business? For instance, he upbraids business for not initiating consumer legislation. When and under

what circumstances do you think it is incumbent on business to initiate legislation to protect consumers? Should business be expected to look out for consumer interests without legal measures of force?

3. Have corporations generally been deaf to consumer cries? Explain your evidence and your position.

4. In how much agreement are you with Weiss' forecasts concerning consumer legislation and protective agencies?

# An ironic sidelight on cyclamates

## frederick andrews

Frederick Andrews, in this article from *The Wall Street Journal*, shows how legislation designed to protect the consumer can take some strange twists.

Thanks to Congressman Charles A. Vanik, the Laotian refugees will be spared the threat of Slender laced with cyclamates.

The Ohio Democrat hit the ceiling a few weeks ago when he learned that the Agency for International Development was paying to ship 60,000 cases of the diet beverage to the hapless refugees. Cyclamates are no longer allowed in the American version of Slender, and Carnation Co., Los Angeles, contributed its surplus supplies of the previous cyclamate version for shipment to Laos.

The shipment was "insulting to the people of Laos," Mr. Vanik declared, "a gift of something that should be thrown away." He says Carnation's gesture was "cheap and cruel," a move to reap "a sweet tax break" by dumping its tainted product abroad. It is "absolutely absurd," Mr. Vanik snorted, "to send a low-calorie diet food to a starving people."

. . .

Not everyone thinks it's so absurd. "Because of what Mr. Vanik has done, thousands of people will be deprived of nutritious food," Norval Hadley, an official of World Vision Relief Organization (Monrovia, Calif.), says bitterly. His group had counted on the Slender to help feed as many as 200,000 Laotian refugees, said to be in desperate need of food. Mr. Hadley vows the Slender would have helped them, and the minute traces of cyclamates done no possible harm.

A Carnation Co. spokesman says simply that the Slender was "a nutritious product" with "an extremely low level of cyclamates." The effect of cyclamates is "still controversial," he says.

But AID doesn't buck Congressmen, and Mr. Vanik's remarks doomed the Slender project. The 60,000 cases—coming to 632 tons— had already sailed from San Francisco for Bangkok (at a cost of $42,000 to the taxpayers), but they won't be given to refugees. Two other scheduled shipments Mr. Vanik didn't know about—one of 750 tons from Houston and another of 600 tons from Baltimore—have been scratched. And 100 tons already in Laos won't be distributed, either.

And that's too bad, Mr. Hadley contends. World Vision Relief has

Frederick Andrews, "An Ironic Sidelight on Cyclamates," *The Wall Street Journal*, August 7, 1970, p. 6. Reprinted with permission of *The Wall Street Journal*.

used Slender and similar diet concoctions for years, he says. All are low in calories but rich in essential proteins. "There's no question Slender is a very good food," he asserts. "'We have every confidence it would have saved lives."

According to Mr. Hadley, his group investigated the possible health hazard "very thoroughly" before deciding to proceed. It also obtained approval from health authorities in Vietnam and Laos. The relief official says Carnation Co. assured World Vision that a 110-pound refugee would have to consume 280 cases of Slender a day to reach a harmful cyclamate level.

But some people consider it "reprehensible" for the relief agency to distribute food with cyclamates, which have caused cancer in laboratory rats, studies show. It's "implied racism," says Dr. George Joseph Roth, the San Francisco physician who first brought the Slender shipment to light. "If it's no good for us, it's no good for them."

Dr. Roth, a strong war critic, dismisses Carnation's figures as useless in showing how much—or how little—of the substance could harm a human being. He doesn't say the Slender would have hurt the Laotians —simply that the effect of cyclamates of people isn't known.

Mr. Vanik doesn't claim the Slender would have hurt the Laotians, either. According to Mark Talisman, one of his aides, "The Food and Drug Administration banned the stuff, and you have to go by that."

The FDA hasn't made public any data that diet foods with cyclamates hurt anyone. The FDA moved against cyclamates late last year after tests showed that large doses of the chemical produced bladder tumors in rats. Under the law, the FDA can't approve a food additive that causes cancer in animals, even though specific proof of a hazard to humans may be lacking.

"There's more convincing evidence that cigarets cause cancer than that cyclamates do," one Senate source says. "It's apparent the Slender wouldn't have harmed anyone. But AID couldn't risk being attacked for giving a cancer-producing substance to Asian refugees." Another Senate source agrees: "Peking and Hanoi would have had a field day."

The politically-attuned Congressional people think AID and World Vision should have known better. World Vision's Mr. Hadley, by contrast, feels that AID (and Carnation Co.) couldn't have been nicer. He blames Mr. Vanik, along with Sen. Alan Cranston (D.-Calif.) and San Francisco's ETV Channel KQED, for giving the affair a public airing.

· · ·

AID would wash its hands of the whole affair. It protests it was dragged in only at the urging of Oregon's Sen. Mark Hatfield, who learned last spring the Laotians were in dire straits as a result of the heavier fighting in Laos. World Vision Relief had the Slender on hand, but no cash to ship it.   Sen. Hatfield publicly urged AID to find the money.   (The agency spends up to $7 million a year to ship such relief goods for private agencies.)

"We were under a great deal of pressure to get these nutrients to these refugees," says R. Samuel Dillon, a Congressional liaison official with AID.   He says that when cyclamates first came under fire, AID made "an informal study" of whether to halt their use in relief.   AID did nothing then, but since the flap over Slender, the agency has announced it will pay no more freight for cyclamates.

Mr. Dillion also says World Vision believed it had informal FDA approval of its project.   If it did, FDA didn't speak up.

Dr. Roth, the anti-war physician, says he tumbled to the Slender shipment when a longshoreman patient mentioned it.   The doctor had the man return to the docks, rifle a carton, and take photographs.   Dr. Roth then called the San Francisco Chronicle, which wasn't interested, and Channel KQED, which eventually included the report in its popular "Newsroom" program.

Dr. Roth says that when he inquired at Carnation, the company was evasive.   "It was perfectly apparent they were about to dump the stuff."

Wes Michaelson, an aide to Sen. Hatfield, says Dr. Roth confided he had acted, among other reasons, to embarrass the Administration.   In an interview, Dr. Roth was openly scornful of AID and World Vision, but he denied he had acted to put the Administration in a bad light. "Our feeling was multiple," he says.

Congressman Vanik was shooting from the hip in the June 22 speech that caused all the stir.   Mr. Hadley and a spokesman for Carnation says the Congressman didn't bother to inquire with them before making his charges.   When Mr. Vanik asserted that Carnation's gift "could provide the basis for a multimillion dollar tax write-off," he didn't say for sure.   "We're in the dark" about the tax aspects, one of his aides said later.

It appears the Congressman overshot his target. Carnation Co. was eligible for a nice tax break, but not likely of the multimillion dollar variety.   By giving the Slender to charity, Carnation could deduct its wholesale value.   If the company had dumped the concoction in the Pacific, however, it could still deduct its cost.   (Carnation gave the Slender away last year—after the cyclamate scare but just in time to benefit from this provision of tax law.   The provision was changed, effective this year.)

. . .

Carnation Co. won't say how it treated the deduction.   Its tax returns are confidential, it says.   An estimated 200,000 cases of Slender were involved, which wholesale for about $5.50 each.   That makes about

$1.1 million in wholesale value, but Carnation won't disclose its mark-up, the difference between wholesale value and cost.

According to Carnation's annual report, however, last year it enjoyed an average gross profit of about 26%. On this basis, Carnation apparently reaped a $150,000 tax saving through its Slender philanthropy.

Carnation's annual report also discloses that the company incurred a total loss of $3.8 million in the cyclamate episode, offset by a $2.0 million tax saving. That figure includes much more than the Slender destined to Laos, of course.

As the Indochina war goes, the fuss over Slender was a minor-league flap. The shipments were spiked, and it's hard to see how things could have come out differently. But the entire episode seems a bit shabby, and almost no one comes off very well. The Slender has been destroyed, or soon will be, but the relief agency has found no substitute. The Laotians are being victimized not only by the shooting conflict, but by our propaganda war.

"All this mess, and in the meantime, what's happening to the people over there? They're the real losers in this," declares Mr. Michaelson, Sen. Hatfield's aide. "We're just advocating that we feed the people. Apparently our Government doesn't have the resources to do that."

### QUESTIONS

1. Whose side of the argument would you choose to defend in this case, Congressman Vanik's or Mr. Hadley's?

2. Consider the fact that no food is absolutely safe to man; all foods contain some toxic or other deleterious matter. For instance, broccoli, Brussels sprouts, cabbage, kale, turnips, and other foods have small amounts of a substance that can interfere with the iodine balance in the thyroid gland. The thyroid gland needs iodine to make thyroxin, a substance used by the body to make energy from foodstuffs. Even the potato contains minute quantities of solanine, from a family of poisonous materials that, in large amounts, interferes with the normal activity of the nervous system. Alcohol, of course, is not only an intoxicant but also contains poisonous matter. Now, where should the line be drawn as to what can and cannot be sold? How should such decisions be made? Who should make them?

# Economic aspects of consumer product safety

### j. fred weston

**J. Fred Weston, Professor of Finance and Business Economics, Graduate School of Management, University of California Los Angeles, discusses in the following paper the trade-offs that influence both consumers and producers in choosing degrees of product safety. He also asks how the market mechanism operates in producing given levels of product safety and how it can better function. He also examines government's role in this area.**

My assignment was to analyze the implications of economic factors in product safety. One important function of economic theory is to explain and understand the characteristics of the world important for both public and business policy. It is therefore useful to examine the facts as a basis for testing some economic principles.

In our efforts to unearth the facts, my associates and I have been unable to compile much needed relevant information for testing the central issues. We found that some 2 million people per year die from disease and accidents. Deaths from accidents now total over 115 thousand per year. Some 45 million people are injured per year. The "certain" costs of accidental injuries [were] estimated at $13.6 billion for 1968. We have a tabulation by type of injury and place of occurrence, with over 40% of accidents occurring in the home.

But at this writing, I have been unable to obtain data on accident rates over time by type of consumer product. Nor is information available analyzing sources and causes of these accidents, other than those for motor vehicles. Here the facts are startling. According to the National Safety Council, 93.7% of auto accidents occurring in 1967 involved improper driving—excessive speed, a wrong turn, a turn into the wrong lane, going over the middle line in the wrong direction, following too closely, etc. Drinking of alcohol is a factor in at least half of all fatal motor accidents, and the estimate is that it is 70% for the state of California. Safety belts are now available to ⅔ of all passenger car occupants. These are used on the average 40% of the time; the net usage figure or percent of all exposure hours during which belts are used is about 25%. The National Safety Council estimates that if all passenger car occupants used belts at all times, such use would save 8,000 to 10,000 lives annually.

These data suggest that the user may be a major factor in accidents

J. Fred Weston, "Economic Aspects of Consumer Product Safety," Presentation to the National Commission on Product Safety Hearings, Washington, D.C., March 4, 1970.

and may be the most productive object of efforts to increase safety. On the other hand, since the average level of improper use may be very high, perhaps products should be produced to achieve a degree of safety at a low average level of care and responsibility on the users' part.

Another set of data suggests some relations between product safety and economic principles. An engineering study [by Chauncey Starr] of risks and benefits in connection with product use and consumer activity suggests the existence of stability in society's preference functions expressed through the market system. Since this study has some important implications, it will be briefly summarized. I will describe the units of analysis, indicate the nature of the results, the conclusions that were drawn, and then set forth the implications that an economist would draw for consumer choice in an enterprise system.

The article in *Science* [see Figure 1 below] magazine developed data comparing relations between risk and benefit to consumers. Risk was defined as the fatalities per person hour of exposure. Benefit is measured in two different ways, depending upon whether the activities are voluntary like hunting, skiing, or private flying, or involuntary like the use of electric power, natural disasters, lightning, and earthquakes. The use of motor vehicles was put into an involuntary activity because it is difficult to imagine conducting the affairs of our modern life without them.

FIGURE 1    Risk (R) plotted relative to benefit (B) for various kinds of voluntary and involuntary exposure.

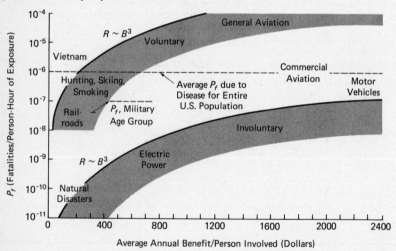

SOURCE: Chauncey Starr, "Social Benefit Versus Technological Risk," *Science*, 165 (September 1969), 1234–1235.

For voluntary activities, benefit is measured by the amount of money spent on the activity by the average involved individual. These measurements are all per annum for a recent year. Involuntary activities are measured by attempting to estimate the contribution of the activity to the individual's annual income or the equivalent.

Let me illustrate these concepts by reference to motor vehicles, where the subject matter is generally known. Risk is measured by the total number of fatalities per year, divided by the number of vehicles registered, times the average person per car, times the average hours of usage per year. The fatalities per year have been running 50,000. There are a little over 80 million vehicles registered in the United States. It is estimated that on the average 1½ persons have the use of 1 car. On the average, a car is used 400 hours per year. Carrying out the appropriate multiplications and divisions, we find that the risk of using a motor vehicle is 1 fatality for every 1 million person-hours of exposure.

Benefit is measured by the sum of the money spent on automobiles —initial purchases, maintenance expenses, insurance, gas, plus the value of time savings per person. The article estimates that the use of an automobile enables a person to save one working hour per day and that this time is worth $5 an hour.

One of the critical measures set forth in this article is a psychological standard against which risk acceptance is measured. It is the risk of death by disease. This is calculated as follows. The deaths in a year from disease and accidents are approximately 2 million people. The total number of hours per year is approximately 10,000. The numerator is the deaths in a year, or 2 times $10^6$. The denominator is our total population (200 million persons) times the number of hours, giving 2 times $10^{12}$, the total person-hours. Performing the indicated calculations, it turns out to be 1 over $10^6$ or 1 in a million hours of exposure. These and other results are summarized in the two figures presented.

The bottom line [in Figure 1] is the curve for involuntary activities. The upper line is voluntary activities, riding the railroad, hunting, skiing, smoking, private aviation. For both curves, risks are a function of benefit. For both curves, differing by a constant, for any unit increase in risk, the incremental benefit must be tripled. The line for voluntary risks is about a 1000 multiple of the line for involuntary risks.

Figure 2 exhibits the interesting results of the relationship between population participation rate and risk rate. The data suggest that as the participation rate rose, the accident risk rate of automobiles declined until it approximated the disease risk rate.

From the data, the study drew four conclusions. One, that there is a surprising stability of relations which may reflect consumers free

choice under a competitive economic system. Second, for a unit increase in risk, benefits must increase by a third power. Three, the
public is willing to accept voluntary risks roughly 1000 times greater
than involuntary risks. Fourth, the statistical risk of death from disease appears to be a psychological yardstick for establishing the level
of acceptability of other risks toward which an industry like the automobile tends over time. This immediately raises the issue of whether

FIGURE 2   Risk and participation trends for motor vehicles

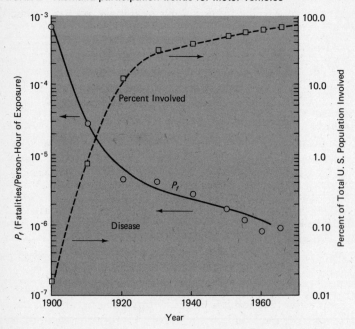

SOURCE: Chauncey Starr, "Social Benefit Versus Technological Risk," *Science*, 165 (September 1969), 1234–1235.

the government or society should substitute its judgment over the
judgment of individuals as to what level of risks they expect an industry appropriately to achieve.

This engineering study of risks and benefits has implications for the
theory of competitive economic behavior. This relates to a basic question posed by [the] Commission on Product Safety. "Does the presence of monopoly destroy consumer freedom of choice?" This issue
arises particularly in connection with oligopoly industries. While
there is wide disagreement in the oligopoly literature there tends to be
a polarization in the direction of suggesting that for homogeneous
products there may be a tendency toward a monopoly solution of the
oligopoly industry. In heterogeneous oligopoly on the other hand,

there is wider agreement that there is competition in product differences in quality. Therefore, the competitive solution is approximated. It is increasingly difficult to find examples of homogeneous oligopoly. The traditional areas were nondurables and producer materials. But there is increased heterogeneity in new product characteristics expressed in the form of diet foods, speciality steels, etc.

The physical accident possibility is greatest with durable goods. In the list of products that this Commission was charged to investigate, all are in fact consumer durable goods. Heterogeneous products characterize these industries, and their behavior is competitive behavior.

With this background of fundamental premises, a number of additional questions raised in connection with product safety can now be analyzed. One fundamental question raised by the Commission is whether advertising stresses style and periodic redesign (designed-in obsolescence) rather than safety and durability in order to distort rational consumer choice. On the premise of effectively or workably competitive economic conditions in the relevant industries, these competing firms seek to maximize the response of consumers to their efforts. When a firm can gain customers by appeal to increased degrees of safety and durability, the firm will do so and increase its market share and returns. Arjay Miller in his *New York Times Book Review* article on business responsibility described the efforts by the Ford Motor Company to sell safety in their 1956 advertising campaign. The response was not commensurate with efforts in alternative uses, so the priority of emphasis in their advertising was altered.

A firm would always sell the degree of safety consumers will buy. If consumers do not respond, we have a national policy decision. Should national policy impose safety standards that the consumer would not otherwise buy? This in turn poses another question. If the consumer is required to buy a safety item and then does not use it, should government enforce its use? This raises the broader question of consumer choice to which we may next turn.

There are two divergent points of view on the role of advertising. One view holds that the consumer is completely controlled by the vast amount of advertising by the large corporation. Thus, it is argued that consumer freedom of choice has been eliminated.

On the other hand, major dramatic and persuasive examples can be provided of the failure of advertising to dominate the customer. A long list of attempted new product innovations could also be developed to demonstrate that the consumer does not buy in proportion to advertising efforts alone.

The Commission has asked whether business firms stress salable products rather than safer products. But again, how could a producer survive if he did not produce salable products? Do higher production costs deter making safer products? This is no problem. Higher production costs of safer products are no deterrent to making safer products if the higher costs fall within the trade-offs by which the consumer himself makes his purchases. The costs are not excessive if the consumer will buy the product.

Another question along this line that the Commission raises is whether companies have a vested interest in capital investment in tooling, planning, and model design. It is a basic principle that companies cannot protect obsolete investments. If consumers would respond, a new firm or an existing firm would make the changes and the others would have to go along to protect their market share position. This argument is frequently made unanalytically and it is never supported by evidence.

A fourth question that the Commission has raised is whether producers are insulated from the social costs of unsafe products by inadequate private and public sanctions or by the protection of product liability insurance. "Why should a company worry if it sells a bad product if its product liability insurance will protect it?" This is a question that the Commission is raising.

It is logical to start with the latter point. Since product liability insurance will require rates set in relation to the costs incurred by the insurance company and paid, if the rates paid are relatively small, this suggests that the defect rate is very low. If it were high, the consequent suits would involve large charges for the insurance companies and the insurance rates would have to reflect them. Hence if product liability rates are not a deterrent, the probability is very high that both valid and invalid claims represent a low rate.

There are some problems in this area, however. One is that consumers may employ a product in a use for which it was not intended. There are price lines. For example, you can buy a power tool for $20 or for $500. The power tool for $20 is not expected to be able to work eight hours continuously. It does not have such capability built into it. The instructions say so. On the other hand, a power tool that you pay $500 for, you could use over longer sustained periods of time. If a consumer buys a $20 power tool and attempts to use it for five continuous hours, he is going to burn it out; he may even cause an electrical short and injure himself in the process. Whose responsibility is it?

Another problem is that local government units set forth specifications for a wide range of products that they buy. School districts set so many special product specifications which create so much diversity that the manufacturer, in meeting these very specific requirements, does not get enough of a production run to get adequate experience to really achieve the safety that he would like to achieve. Here is an area in which manufacturers have sought to try to get the local school districts to standardize on something or to have the national government set standards in order to improve safety. But the difficulty of changing attitudes of local school districts where you have literally thousands of buyers has been found to be very difficult.

The foregoing has discussed the role of advertising and the role of consumer choice. In summary, one view holds that business has effectively related to express consumer demands for trade-offs between price, aesthetics, degree of safety, and other dimensions of performance. An alternative view is that while these principles that business has applied are sound, business misjudged a change in the environment and attitudes that has taken place. This view argues that a fundamental shift in the profile of consumer utilities has occurred as a consequence of the six prime-moving factors described above.

In this connection, a variation of view number one is that one firm cannot push ahead in changing the trade-offs beyond what consumers desire or will buy. But here again, the evidence would appear to be that the fundamental shift in the profile of consumer utilities and priorities has been such that the consumer will insist on the government's providing for him what he may be unwilling to buy on an individual basis. This in turn implies that there will be an increased need and demand for government standards and regulations in the area of product quality, product information, and product safety.

But business has an important role to perform here. As responsible corporate citizens, and indeed related to their long-run survival and role in a society with changing value systems, and therefore consistent with long-run profit viability, business has a responsibility for leadership. An increasing portion of the advertising budgets of business firms must provide information. Providing information can be an exciting process; it need not be dull. Providing information will have a cumulative impact on the value of providing additional information.

Consumer attitudes have shifted and the profiles of consumer utilities have changed substantially. This would imply a need for shifting the proportions of advertising between information and psychological impact. I have seen no systematic analysis of trends in advertising content to provide evidence that business has either lagged in this regard or has optimized.

This brings us to a basic question, "Why do not our competitive markets do the job as they were supposed to do?" A more basic question is *whether* the competitive markets have done the job they were supposed to do. What are the relevant criteria and evidence? A number of trends have occurred. Number one, I think, is lack of basic knowledge in some instances. We did not know the effects of products when they were first introduced. Also there are cumulative effects over time. While smoking may have been a delightful thing in the time of Sir Walter Raleigh, when he first brought tobacco back to England, the cumulative effects over time appear to be less favorable.

I have argued that economic principles suggest that competitive markets can go a long way toward providing the trade-offs consistent with consumer preferences. On the other hand, it must be acknowledged that competitive markets are not necessarily perfect markets. The classical economic models were built around relatively simple products—wheat, corn, etc. While theories of monopolistic competition developed in the early 1930's and provided some modification in the shapes of demand functions, the inference of relative simplicity in products continued.

One of the six major trend factors discussed earlier in this paper was our rapidly advancing technology. A proliferation of more complex products has occurred. The increased complexity of products needs to be supported by a more effective and more powerful information transmission mechanism. The theory of perfect competition abstracts from the need of an information mechanism of this type. We need increased market information support.

But the greater need for market information also runs into stubborn realities. Much information proffered to consumers is not read or utilized. This problem is similar to the third competitive market imperfection. Experience suggests that only a small segment of the buying public responds to efforts by business firms to sell safety. Therefore if one or a few firms sought to shift the relative emphasis from efforts and responses based on optimization analysis to a different set of trade-offs, [their] market position would suffer and [their] survival would be threatened. The paradox is compounded in that the publication of exposés of the lack of safety features that the consumers have been unwilling to buy has aroused a great response and indignation on the part of consumers.

This suggests that some aspects of product safety are public goods, not private goods which a competitive market mechanism will provide. The consumer increasingly will demand that the government require in safety standards what the consumer himself would not buy in his individual freedom of choice. The paradox is further compounded in that after consumers have supported government standards to include devices such as safety belts, the data quoted indicate that the usage factor to date is 25%. It appears that there are also imperfections in the theory and process of providing public goods. Do we need to go further and provide enforcement of the use of standards that have been established by government?

A fourth imperfection of the competitive market relates to interdependencies and externalities. Consumers have free choice and they have unequal tastes for safety as well as other characteristics of product performance. But what one consumer does may affect others. If some consumers wear flammable clothes, an accidental spark which causes a conflagration will affect others. A household item which causes a fire in a multiple unit dwelling will affect a number of persons.

In addition, the composition problem arises. The use of a product by a few persons has different consequences when used by many in a crowded urban environment. The externalities problem with increased population and usage density appears to grow cumulatively and exponentially. Consumers do not voluntarily pay for externalities imposed on others. Individual producers are unable to reduce externalities if consumers will not buy the devices which limit or avoid the externalities. Hence interdependencies and externalities create additional types of public goods.

One of the major trends I described was the increased interdependence of people and the increased extent to which society bears the costs and consequences of individual decisions. To that extent such decisions are no longer individual decisions, but social decisions. Appropriate public policy depends on analysis of the social costs of individual decisions to determine whether, and what, government standards are called for.

The competitive market mechanism may have four imperfections which impede achieving social goals of product safety. These are (1) lack of knowledge, (2) an imperfect market information mechanism, (3) inability or unwillingness of consumers to buy safety in their individual market decisions, and (4) inability of the competitive market mechanism to eliminate, control, or to allocate on market principles the costs of interdependencies and externalities. This leads to the final question posed by this Commission.

The final section of this paper deals with the very fundamental question, "How can the American economic system produce safer consumer products?" Let me begin with a summary of some fundamental premises which I stated at the beginning of this presentation as a basis for evaluating alternative points of view. Of these fundamentals, I would regard as of overriding importance six major trends in our society that have altered in an important way the consumer and society's trade-offs between product characteristics including performance and safety in relation to the prices paid for those products and considerations of style and aesthetics. (1) The increase in population density makes the impact of the nature of products greater. (2) Technological change results in more complex products with a wider range of effects. (3) The increased affluence in our society gives rise to a greater variety of products, many of which throw a greater proportion of their cost onto society as a whole. Related to this is that we can afford a better quality of life and we are less patient with delays in achieving it.  (4) There is a greater social investment by society in people, and a greater interdependence reflected in society's bearing a greater cost of the consequences of poor quality or dangerous products.  (5) A major change has resulted from the fact that externalities in the form of smog, pollution, etc., have grown cumulatively at an exponential rate.  As a consequence, the quality of life problem takes on dimensions that did not exist in previous decades.  (6) Related to the above, particularly with rising affluence and less concern for subsistence in our society, attitudes and value standards have changed. Our aspiration level for the quality of life has grown, also probably exponentially.  We are in a period of transition with respect to goals and objectives for society.  As a consequence, consensus is clearly not as broad as it was presumed to be in earlier decades, and hence our goals and objectives are less clear.  Consequently, if the fundamental criterion has been to balance goals and objectives to costs and consumer preferences, the trade-offs undoubtedly have changed.

As a consequence, it is highly probable that the kind of stability in risks and benefits suggested by the empirical studies referred to in the earlier part of this paper may no longer provide valid guidance for either business or government policy.  If the psychological floor for the risks of products produced by business has appeared in the past to be 1 fatality per 1 million person hours of exposure, the shift in attitudes referred to has undoubtedly substantially lowered this psychological floor.

Two additional premises may be noted:  (1) The operation of an enterprise system can go a long way toward achieving the appropriate trade-offs between consumer preferences, costs, efficiency, and society's value standards.  (2) There are imperfections in the market process that prevent automatic assurance of effective trade-offs.

Within this framework of premises, is it possible to formulate an appropriate program for producing safer and other dimensions of more desirable performance of consumer products?  From the foregoing analysis of the imperfections in the competitive market processes, it is predictable that additional government standards will be enacted.  But additional study of the kinds of government programs is needed.  We must return to a consideration of fundamentals.  Have we specified our goals and objectives?  What are the facts on performance?  How far has performance in fact fallen short of our goals?  Can we have intelligent legislation that will on balance help the consumer and society without analysis of the relevant trade-offs?  Under what conditions should we seek to alter our collective objectives?  Should the degree of likelihood of consumer actual usage of items influence the selection and adoption of standards?  Should we collectively impose sanctions for nonusage and use other methods as well to achieve enforcement of usage? Would consumer attitudes toward enactment of government standards change if public policy provided for enforcement?

Since 1966 we have had a substantial beginning of experience on these matters. It would be useful to collect information on our experience to date to provide guidance for the future. What would an objective assessment show of the relative values of the protective and life-saving safety characteristics built into products by manufacturers prior to 1966 compared to the post-1966 period during which "the total number of consumer protection programs inaugurated in the major enactments jumped from around 250 to over 400." We need to collect and analyze these data to provide an objective basis for future business and governmental policy.

In the absence of the needed factual basis for policy, some generalizations and additional questions can be indicated. One is that whatever the present relation between product safety performance, our goals, and sound policy based on analysis of trade-offs, the achievement of increases in product safety will require the joint efforts of business, consumers, and government.

With the greater complexity of products, industry has a responsibility to provide increasingly greater information to the user. The technology of providing information has greatly improved. Information can be provided not only through written user or owner manuals, but supplemented by summaries, diagrams, comic books, etc. Have these and the potentials of TV for informing consumers to a greater extent than using psychological appeals been sufficiently utilized by business?

If the profile of consumer utilities has in fact shifted, business analysis of the trade-offs will yield changed results. Finally, business must effectively participate in the standards that increasingly will be set for product quality by the government. If business is unable to participate effectively in the establishment of such standards, it will lose an opportunity to contribute to efficient and really effective standards from the standpoint of the consumer.

What is the role of the consumer? As consumers, we should begin to make more consistent decisions. We want the attributes of an affluent society and we try to ignore the consequences. This implies changing our behavior. We want to drive our car alone to work, we do not want to use public transportation because it is less convenient and less comfortable, and then we complain about smog.

Another aspect of consumer inconsistency relates to usage. After support of government requirements to add requirements to products, the consumer should make use of the items.  We should accumulate experience on items added to determine the relative values of a rational analysis of alternatives.

The user bears a major responsibility for the performance of products.  While the producer of products should assume a relatively low average quality of usage, overall performance would be improved by raising the quality of user handling.  Clearly, major educational efforts directed toward the consumer would yield increasing returns.

I next turn to the role of government.  It is clear that a fundamental here is that consumers are going to increasingly ask government to do through law what consumers would not individually do through the competitive marketplace.  Does the government need to follow through consistently in terms of the implications of consumer preferences?  The government has required, for example, that safety belts now be installed on all automobiles.  But statistics of the National Safety Council indicate that safety belt usage per exposure runs about 25% and that 10,000 to 12,000 lives could be saved annually if safety belt usage approached 100%.  Given the tremendous social and monetary costs of 10,000 to 12,000 lives per annum, is it appropriate that the government include in such standards the requirement that they will be effectively used?

The imperfections of the competitive marketplace have resulted in increasing the total number of consumer programs to over 400 in recent years.  It is predictable that additional enactments will take place.  The large number of consumer protection programs makes it increasingly imperative that these programs have the results intended.  To achieve this end of efficient protection of consumers, three fundamental principles should be taken into account.

One is awareness of the trade-offs between performance, safety, price, and other variables.  In the extreme, products there were 100% safe would have to be sold at prices that few people could afford.  Standards that increase costs will deprive some consumers of their use.  The trade-offs should at least be considered.

Second, government should set standards to meet performance objectives, such as the percentage of accidents rate by the normally negligent user or other more specific performance standards, but not to freeze standards into a design requirement.  To freeze into products specific design requirements would impose very substantial costs on the consumer—unnecessary substantial costs.

Third, the time factor should be taken into account.  One of the generalizations in connection with the stock market is that in a bull market the market always goes too high, it overshoots where it should go based on fundamental economic and financial considerations, because of overoptimism.  The reverse occurs in a bear market, due to over-pessimism. This is a truism in connection with the stock market. I think that there is a similar fundamental truth in connection with consumerism and product safety. For a long time, consumers and the public were lethargic. We were in a bear market on consumer safety. We are now in a bull market in consumer safety. We have over dramatized it and we are going to overshoot.

But the time dimension is important. We should consider the trade-off of time versus cost, analyzing the present value of costs versus the benefits over time. Manufacturers, given appropriate time, can redesign to meet standards of performance, designed into the product over time. But requiring immediate changes may result in emergency "hang-on" devices which will militate against longer-run, effective solutions and thus be opposed to consumers' long-run interests.

## BRIEF SUMMARY

In summary, the competitive market mechanisms do not provide automatically for optimal product safety. With products of increasing complexity, the assumption of complete knowledge and its costless transmission does not obtain. In addition, consumers may not buy individually what they prefer collectively or what a social cost-benefit analysis would justify. Further, with increased population density and affluence, both interdependence and externalities have increased substantially.

To supplement the market mechanism in reaching our goals for product performance, the joint efforts of business, consumers, and government will be required. Business must meet increased requirements for achieving an effective market information mechanism. There must be a basis for confidence in the effective contributions of business to the formulation of standards.

Consumers must increase the consistency of their decisions and behavior. With increased interdependencies in our urban society, safety and health measures enacted by government will by necessity limit individual freedom of choice and freedom of behavior. Consumer usage of products is probably the greatest single factor influencing the safety performance record of products. Continued expansion of educational programs would yield high returns.

Additional government safety standards will be enacted over a wider range of products. Some fundamental principles should be recognized in these government enactments. One is that products cannot be 100% safe without cost increases that would deprive many of their use. Two is the need to recognize trade-offs between safety and other criteria important to consumers. Three, the government should set standards to meet performance objectives and to avoid freezing design requirements. Fourth, the time factor should be taken into account. The consumer is benefitted in terms of costs and product effectiveness if improvements are designed into products rather than forced on so swiftly that the additions cannot be incorporated into basic product design.

The need for clarification of goals, for measurement of performance vs. goals in product usage, for the analysis of effective balancing of the relevant factors for contributions to consumer and societal welfare continues. Much additional data are needed. Many questions remain unanswered. But some basic generalizations can provide some direction to policy actions taken.

In the absence of the needed factual basis for policy, some generalizations and additional questions can be indicated. One is that whatever the present relation between product safety, performance, our goals, and sound policy based on analysis of trade-offs, the achievement of increases in product safety will require the joint efforts of business, consumers, and government.

## QUESTIONS

1. Weston asserts that a business firm will always sell the degree of safety consumers will buy. If consumers will not buy safety devices on automobiles, should the government force them to do so?
2. Do Starr's risk and benefit calculations provide any clues as to what public policy might be in the product safety area?
3. You are the manufacturer of rotary power lawn mowers and are face-to-face with the issue of how much safety should be built into your machines. What safety features do you think should have priority? What factors would you consider to be most important in coming to a decision?
4. How do imperfections in the market mechanism bear on the product safety issue? Do you recommend that anything be done about these imperfections?
5. What roles in product safety do you recommend for (a) consumers, (b) government, and (c) private manufacturers?